The
BOOKER T. WASHINGTON
Papers

The
BOOKER T. WASHINGTON
Papers

VOLUME 13
1914–15

Louis R. Harlan
and
Raymond W. Smock
EDITORS

Susan Valenza
and
Sadie M. Harlan
ASSISTANT EDITORS

University of Illinois Press
URBANA AND CHICAGO

The BOOKER T. WASHINGTON *Papers*
is supported by
The National Endowment for the Humanities
The National Historical Publications and Records Commission
The University of Maryland

Library of Congress Cataloging in Publication Data

Washington, Booker T.   1856–1915.
   The Booker T. Washington papers.

   Vol. 13   edited by L. R. Harlan and R. W. Smock.
   Susan Valenza and Sadie M. Harlan, assistant editors.
   Includes bibliographies and indexes.
   CONTENTS: v. 1. The autobiographical writings.
—v. 2. 1860–89.–[etc.]—v. 13. 1914–15.
   1. Washington, Booker T., 1856–1915.
   2. Afro-Americans—History—1863–1877—Sources.
   3. Afro-Americans—History—1877–1964—Sources.
   4. Afro-Americans—Correspondence.   I.   Harlan,
Louis R.   II.   Smock, Raymond W.
   E185.97.W274   305.8'96073'0924   75–186345
   ISBN 0–252–01125–2 (v. 13)
   ISBN 0–252–01152–X (Set)

To Elizabeth G. Dulany

CONTENTS

vii

CONTENTS

CONTENTS

CONTENTS

CONTENTS

CONTENTS

INTRODUCTION

WITH THIS VOLUME the editors complete a labor of fifteen years to trace Booker T. Washington's passage through life. Washington's end sharply contrasted with his humble beginning on the dirt floor of a backwoods Virginia slave cabin. When he died in 1915, he received a hero's funeral, with obituary editorials from the press of the whole nation and letters of condolence from the high and mighty. They proclaimed him the black leader best attuned to the needs and demands of his age. Unfortunately for his historical reputation, however, the age to which he was so finely attuned, the decades of his power over the black community, was a time of proscription, hardship, and discouragement for black people. Furthermore, even while he lived, the changing times were rendering his outlook and his methods obsolete. The Wilson administration's control of national politics not only ended the political influence of the Tuskegee Machine but began policies of racial extremism that caused the rapid growth of the National Association for the Advancement of Colored People and its civil rights approach. The Great Migration that began in 1915, the year of Washington's death, swelled the black population of the cities and the North, where Washington's hold had always been tenuous.

Washington made what adjustments he could to the new age that was dawning. The new urban-industrial society, with its emphasis on technology and large-scale organization, rendered the artisan skills taught at Tuskegee somewhat anachronistic, though it should not be forgotten that the majority of blacks continued for decades to remain in the South and on the land. The National Negro Business League's promotion of small-scale black entrepreneurship, on the other hand, benefited from a trend toward racial solidarity and segregated businesses serving the needs of black customers in the growing urban ghettos. In his encouragement of the founding of the National Urban League, which shared many of his values but also some of those of the NAACP leadership, Washington made his adjustment to the urban age. He became an Urban League board member in 1914. Essentially, however, he remained a rural-based leader out of harmony or sympathy with urban life. The more he stayed the same, nonetheless, the more he changed in minor ways. Either because of the challenge of the NAACP or because of a sense of his impending death, he began to speak more forthrightly in his last years, both privately to white philanthropists and well-wishers and publicly in magazine articles and speeches, against violations of human rights such as residential segregation, lynching, and public school discrimination.

Residential segregation ordinances swept rapidly through the southern cities in 1914–15, and Washington finally took a straightforward public stand against them in an article that appeared posthumously in *The New Republic.* On another civil rights issue, that of the Jim Crow railroad cars, Washington employed a more characteristically moderate method. In 1914 he planned and orchestrated throughout the South what he called Railroad Days, a two-day campaign of black community leaders to urge railroad officials to provide equal accommodations both on the trains and in the depots. He also continued his annual letter on lynching, declaring it an unjustifiable crime whatever the provocation. He gave unequivocal support, after many years of hedging, to woman suffrage. When *The Birth of a Nation,* the first great motion picture, opened in Boston in 1915, Washington joined with his militant black critics in condemning the pejorative stereotypes of blacks in the film and urging that it be banned. After the ban failed in Boston, Washington supported similar unsuccessful efforts in other cities, though he had some misgivings about the publicity that black protests and picketing gave the film. Emmett Scott took the lead in promoting the idea of a black film that would counteract the negative racial imagery of *The Birth of a Nation.*

However much Washington responded ideologically to the challenge of the NAACP, his quarrel with its leaders did not abate. When Oswald Garrison Villard as an NAACP officer undertook to organize the Association of Negro Rural and Industrial Schools at a meeting in the NAACP headquarters, Washington took heated issue with Villard and discouraged his followers from attending. He considered the new organization an unwarranted invasion of his own bailiwick. He also declared it premature, since Thomas Jesse Jones was simultaneously undertaking a survey and evaluation of black higher and industrial schools under the auspices of the Phelps-Stokes Fund. Villard, who had less reason than Washington to trust the motives of the philanthropists, persisted in his educational organization plans.

Washington found a more congenial cause in the Urban League, for which he gave a series of addresses in Harlem. He also showed favor to the Negro Organization Society of Virginia, a moderate coalition of black community leaders that Robert R. Moton founded in 1914 as a southern, rural counterpart to the National Urban League. Moton hoped that after successful operation in Virginia the Negro Organization Society would spread to other states. In November 1915 Washington reluctantly canceled what would have been his last public address, before the society's statewide meeting in Richmond.

Washington had no part in the politics of the Wilson era. Only one of his political lieutenants survived in federal office, Robert H. Terrell as a federal judge in the District of Columbia. Washington considered Terrell's renomination by President Wilson and his confirmation by a Democratic Senate as a vindication of his political leadership and efforts to improve the quality of the black civil service. In the only other significant contact with the Wilson administration in this period, Washington persuaded the President and the Postmaster General to allow Tuskegee Institute to continue its separate post office.

Julius Rosenwald played a large role in Washington's relationship to philanthropy. Early in 1914 Washington sent Rosenwald photographs of the first completed Rosenwald-funded black rural school buildings. He also encouraged Rosenwald's substantial aid to the construction of black YMCA buildings. He tried to persuade George Eastman, who had long contributed to Tuskegee, to co-sponsor Rosenwald's school-construction program. Only a few months before his death, Washington secured a letter of introduction to Henry Ford that he never had an opportunity to use. He also enlisted the federal government in larger aid to black schools. Working through Secretary of Agriculture David F. Houston, who had formerly been a member of the Southern Education Board, and through Thomas Jesse Jones, Washington tried to ensure that blacks would receive a proportionate share of federal funds for agricultural education through the Smith-Lever Act of 1914.

Washington gave encouragement, as he had for years, to the forces of southern white liberalism and moderation. He addressed the Southern Sociological Congress and also spoke at the National Conference of Charities and Corrections when it met in Memphis in 1914. He continued also, however, to cultivate the more conservative whites, even offering to contribute to the erection of a Confederate monument in Opelika, near Tuskegee. In the spring of 1915 he toured Louisiana, speaking in behalf of racial goodwill and the economic and educational advancement of blacks.

Black agriculture and business suffered along with the white South in the economic crisis of 1914, brought about by the outbreak of World War I and the virtual cessation of overseas trade. Particularly hard hit were cotton farmers and the black banks that Washington and the National Negro Business League had sponsored and encouraged. Washington was helpless to stem the tide of bankruptcy. Among the black self-improvement schemes that Washington originated in this period was Baldwin Farms. Named for William H. Baldwin, Jr., the late president of the Tuskegee trustees and Washington's close adviser, Baldwin Farms was a community settlement of small farmers, Tuskegee graduates who paid for their tracts over long periods at low interest.

Washington took a pacifist view of the European war, as befitted a vice-president of the American Peace Society. He found it necessary to cancel a planned speaking tour of Europe. In January 1915 he carried out a brief, successful lobbying movement against the African Exclusion Bill, a measure that would have barred the immigration of persons of African origin, including those in the West Indies. During his last years back-to-Africa movements flourished, perhaps stimulated by the harsh racial climate of the Wilson era. Washington kept a close eye on the emigrationist plans of Chief Alfred C. Sam, and sought through agents to discourage American black participation in Sam's exodus. On the other hand, Washington gave rather absentminded encouragement to Marcus M. Garvey, founder of the Universal Negro Improvement Association, probably because he failed to notice the Jamaican's ultra-nationalism and assumed that the UNIA was similar to his own National Negro Business League.

Tuskegee Institute continued to prosper. Washington accepted a gift of five scholarships from Madame C. J. Walker but rejected her repeated request to include cosmetics and beautician training in the Tuskegee curriculum. When George Washington Carver threatened to resign over the issue of summer employment, as he had done in 1913, Washington, as often before, made an exception and compromised with his prize faculty member. He also persuaded Emmett Scott to stay at Tuskegee rather than accept the presidency of Clark University. The worst fire in the history of the institution destroyed the mule barn, but the school was able to survive this calamity without losing stride.

The passage of time brought other changes to Washington's family life. He and Margaret Washington welcomed Edith Meriwether into the family as E. Davidson Washington's wife, and Washington helped the couple establish themselves in Tuskegee, after Dave had studied in a secretarial school. In the spring of 1915, after a year of worsening health, Washington's sister Amanda Johnston died in Malden, West Virginia.

There were many signs of Washington's declining health. In the summer of 1914 his exhaustion caused him to take a week's vacation fishing and resting at Coden, on the shores of Mobile Bay. He ignored, however, the advice of Seth Low, chairman of the Tuskegee board of trustees, and of many others that he was working too hard. He continued for another year with little if any letup, but concerned observers could see that he was near collapse. He took another short rest at Coden in the fall of 1915, but it was not enough to restore his vigor. When he returned to campus the faculty pointedly gave him a chair and a shotgun as symbols of the leisure activities he should pursue, and members of his family urged him to slow down. He did make plans to visit the Mayo brothers' clinic in Minnesota as soon as he could fit it into his schedule, but he never reached there.

After giving two addresses, one at Yale University and the other at a black church on the same evening, Washington took the boat to New York City and arrived in an exhausted condition. He entered St. Luke's Hospital there, and continued from his hospital bed to try to direct affairs at Tuskegee down to the smallest detail. Washington apparently suffered from arteriosclerosis, physical exhaustion, and kidney failure. A preliminary diagnosis of syphilis by one staff physician was withdrawn after angry protests from Washington's personal physician, George Cleveland Hall of Chicago. When the attendant physicians despaired of Washington's recovery, he asked to be taken back to

Tuskegee to die. A few hours after the return home by train, he died on the morning of November 14, 1915. He was buried in the little graveyard on the campus he had built, beside his first two wives. His death marked the end of an era in Afro-American history.

In this last volume of the series, we want to express our great appreciation and heartfelt thanks to Elizabeth Dulany, managing editor of the University of Illinois Press. She has been the copyeditor for the entire series, and the volumes have benefited greatly from her meticulous and thoughtful reading of each volume. Though her duties and responsibilities at the press have grown since our work began fifteen years ago, she has been dedicated to the series and has seen it through to the end. Our volumes could not have been in finer hands.

The editors thank the National Endowment for the Humanities, the National Historical Publications and Records Commission, and the University of Maryland for their generous support of this project.

ERRATUM

VOLUME 9, p. 627, note 1, line 14, the word "history" should read "natural history."

SYMBOLS AND ABBREVIATIONS

Standard abbreviations for dates, months, and states are used by the editors only in footnotes and endnotes; textual abbreviations are reproduced as found.

1. A — autograph; written in author's hand
   H — handwritten by other than signator
   P — printed
   T — typed
2. C — postcard
   D — document
   E — endorsement
   L — letter
   M — manuscript
   W — wire (telegram)
3. c — carbon
   d — draft
   f — fragment
   p — letterpress
   t — transcript or copy made at much later date
4. I — initialed by author
   r — representation; signed or initialed in author's name
   S — signed by author

Among the more common endnote abbreviations are: ALS — autograph letter, signed by author; TLpI — typed letter, letterpress copy, initialed by author.

REPOSITORY SYMBOLS

Symbols used for repositories are the standard ones used in *Symbols of American Libraries Used in the National Union Catalog of the Library of Congress,* 10th ed. (Washington, D.C., 1969).

A-Ar   Alabama Department of Archives and History, Montgomery, Ala.

ATT   Tuskegee Institute, Tuskegee, Ala.

CtY   Yale University, New Haven, Conn.

DLC   Library of Congress, Washington, D.C.

DNA   National Archives, Washington, D.C.

ICU   University of Chicago, Chicago, Ill.

MH   Harvard University, Cambridge, Mass.

NN   New York Public Library, NYC

NNC   Columbia University, NYC

NcD   Duke University, Durham, N.C.

ViHaI   Hampton Institute Archives, Hampton, Va.

OTHER ABBREVIATIONS

BTW   Booker T. Washington

Con.   Container

NNBL   National Negro Business League

RG   Record Group

Documents 1914–15

To Charles William Anderson

[Tuskegee, Ala.] April 2nd, 1914

Dear Mr. Anderson: I congratulate you upon the fine approval registered at Washington by the Revenue Agent, Mr. Worthington after his examination of your office.

I am very much pleased indeed to make note of his fine expressions. With best wishes, I am Yours very truly,

Booker T. Washington

P.S.: I have been able recently to get into a little working touch with President Wilson, and if at any time, you think I can be of any special service to you, please do not hesitate to let me know. I think it also wise for you to keep in close and definite touch with Mr. George Foster Peabody. If I were you, I would write him a letter once in a while, and give him definite facts as to what you have done and are doing.

B. T. W.

TLpS Con. 68 BTW Papers DLC.

To Gifford Pinchot

[Tuskegee, Ala.] April 3, 1914

My dear Mr. Pinchot: I have kept your letter on my desk several days without answering in order that I might consider the best way of helping to accomplish the results you desire:

In the first place, let me say that I am heartily in favor of your candidacy. Nothing, I think, would be more inspiring and helpful to the nation than to have a man like yourself in the Senate.

Now, as to the best method of helping you. I do not believe it would help but rather hinder if I were to come out publicly in your favor, that is, I think the politicians in your state would use the fact of outside interference to drive votes from you rather than to bring them to you; in a word, what I would suggest is something like this: for you to get hold of one of the strongest and most reliable colored men in Pennsylvania and gradually work with and through him.

3

If you think well of this plan, Mr. Charles H. Brooks,[1] is, in my opinion, the man for such a purpose. He is rather a diamond in the rough; he looks rather rough and talks rather rough, but I have had dealings with him in connection with our Business League for a number of years and have always found him able to accomplish results — that is, what he goes after; besides he knows every part of the state and knows the standing of the colored people. I do not know just how he has aligned himself in recent years on the political issues, but I do know there is a good deal of unrest among the colored people in Pennsylvania because they feel that Mr. Boies Penrose has deceived them. I rather feel that Mr. Brooks would be inclined to do anything that I would suggest to him. If you think well of the general plan and then desire me to write him, I should be glad to do so. Yours very truly,

Booker T. Washington

Mr. Charles H. Brooks's address is — 1440 Lombard St., Philadelphia.

B. T. W.

TLpS Con. 516 BTW Papers DLC.

[1] Charles H. Brooks was secretary of the Reliable Mutual Aid and Improvement Society in Philadelphia.

To E. H. Gamlin

[Tuskegee, Ala.] April 4, 1914

Mr. Gamlin: Hereafter, it will be against the policy of the school for any store doing business in Greenwood to sell any of our students tobacco, cigars or cigarettes.

Booker T. Washington

TLpS Con. 652 BTW Papers DLC.

To Robert Russa Moton

[Tuskegee, Ala.] April 4th, 1914

My dear Major Moton: I think I owe you both a letter and an apology.

I wonder if you have seen my article on education in the South published in a recent number of "The Outlook."[1] Under separate cover I am sending you a marked copy of the article.

As you perhaps know, I have been doing some work in Southern California which has kept me away from my desk the greater part of March. I know what Mr. Scott has said to you in answer to your kind letter of March 11th. I do not grow at all sour or bitter because some good friends of ours, including Mr. Villard, do not always agree with me or understand me. I am simply trying to do the very best I can and do not proceed in any important direction without getting the very best advice I can from as many sources as I can. I hope people will not grow impatient with me if I do not yield to the temptation of becoming over-excited and "fly off the handle" every time something occurs that is meant to hinder or disturb the progress of our race. All such matters pain me just as deeply as they do any individual in this country, but I have reached the conclusion that we have got to depend upon broad education for all the people for the final doing away of these injustices.

It is far better for me to devote the greater part of my energies to doing that which, in my opinion, will broaden all the people and strengthen them in the direction of doing justice than to fritter away too much time and strength in trying to remedy temporary and often local conditions. In the last analysis, I must be governed by my own judgment, though that judgment may be very faulty. Of course I fully realize that on many points if I speak I shall be criticised adversely, and if I keep quiet the same will be true.

For example, during the last four or five months I have been through practically every Southern state, and I have yet to find any persons, white or black, who take Mr. Clarence Poe's suggestion to segregate the race on the farm seriously. It is generally understood by people who have given the matter any attention at all that Mr. Poe is simply emphasizing this idea for the purpose of advertising his paper. The whole idea is so utterly impracticable and preposterous that I cannot see how people can grow excited over it. Of course, however, the more excited they do grow the more Mr. Poe will like it because the greater amount of advertising will come to his paper. For one, I am simply refusing to fall into the trap of advertising his farm paper. Let me repeat, that I have never heard a single white man, aside from Mr. Poe, in any of the Southern states mention the matter of segregation in the farming districts.

For a number of months Mr. Poe carried an advertisement in his paper, offering a generous sum to people who would write letters on the subject of segregation. Notwithstanding this flattering offer, he could find very few people who would even write on the subject.

Until I can be convinced that there is a serious intention or effort in the direction of farm segregation, I must refuse to take the matter seriously. When I see you I hope to talk [the] matter over more in detail.

I wish very much you might come to our Commencement. It occurs the last Thursday in May.

I had a great trip through Southern California. I was there nearly three weeks and was speaking most of the time to colored and white people, and made a great many new friends for the cause of Negro education. Yours very truly,

Booker T. Washington

TLpS Con. 511 BTW Papers DLC.

¹ See An Article in *Outlook,* Mar. 14, 1914, above, 12:475–81.

From Robert Russa Moton

Hampton, Virginia   April 8, 1914

My dear Dr. Washington: Your letter of the 4th is just received. I knew you were on the Pacific Coast and had watched with interest and read with interest your speeches and accounts of the very cordial reception which you received.

I think you are absolutely right regarding the attitude of Mr. Villard and the National Association. So far as I am personally concerned, and I voice the sentiment of ninety-five percent if not ninety-nine percent of the thoughtful Negroes of this country and white people as well when I say, we have absolute faith in your judgment and in your methods of work. As I said to Mr. Villard, I am absolutely on your side, not leaning towards your side, and have always been there. I have sincerely and honestly tried to help Mr. Villard and those associated with him to do better what they are trying to do. It does seem that there are possibilities in that organization, but as it is constituted at present I don't think we can accomplish anything for them or with them and I have told Mr. Villard so.

I am just writing to-day saying I will preside at the meeting in New York on the 19th where you are to speak, and I think we might as well strike right out from the shoulder on what we are trying to do to help the Negro.

I have been asked to speak in Memphis at the Sociological Congress May 9th on the subject, "The Common Industrial Life." Other speakers will take up the following subjects: "The Common Cause of Justice," "The Common Interest of Health" and "The Common Basis of Religion." The general topic for discussion that evening will be "Inter-Racial Interests." I wrote Prof. Work asking him for any suggestions he might give me regarding my address. I have not heard from Mr. Work, but I suppose he is out of town. I would be glad of any advice or suggestions you may give me.

I am also on the program to speak at Atlanta at the Negro Christian Students' Convention on what colored people are doing towards co-operation with white people in the South. My speech is "Signs of Growing Co-operation," so I would be glad to have you or Mr. Scott give me suggestions on that. I am anxious that both of these addresses be as helpful as possible.

Mr. Carnegie has been at the Chamberlin Hotel since Saturday and has lunched every day since he has been here. I have seen more of him than I have seen before. He has spoken beautifully of you privately many times and in his address to the school yesterday he spoke again very enthusiastically of you and what you meant to this Nation. I spoke also and was glad to say some things regarding you which Mr. Carnegie did not say, all of which was received with applause, of course. I just have a note from him this morning from the Chamberlin Hotel — not a check though — but it is nice to have Mrs. Carnegie, Mr. Carnegie and his daughter see so much of Hampton in detail and

7

its work and to be so enthusiastic over it. It means a great deal to the whole cause. Sincerely yours,

R. R. Moton

P.S. I had seen your article in the Outlook and it is very good indeed.

TLS   Con. 511   BTW Papers   DLC.

To Robert Russa Moton

[Tuskegee, Ala.] April 9th, 1914

Dear Major Moton: I think I have done about all I can do in this matter at long distance. I am wondering if somebody in Virginia could not go directly to the president of the Norfolk & Western Railroad and go further in this matter. It is evident that the report of the committee is not very sincere. They evade the question as to making proper provisions, for example, for colored people eating. If somebody would have a personal conference with the president, it might be interesting to ask him how persons could have coffee, tea or milk wrapped up.

I do not care for my name to be further used in the matter without my knowledge or permission, but I should very much hope that the Business League or some other organization in Virginia might pursue this matter further. It is a good chance while we have got their interest aroused to get something good out of it. Yours very truly,

Booker T. Washington

TLpS   Con. 255   BTW Papers   DLC.

From Fred I. Hammonds[1]

Chanute, Kan., April 13, '14

Kind Sir and Bro': Being a humble Minister of the Gospel, I am interested in the present as well as the future blessedness of the human race and most especially my own race of people. So I am striving thro' study and prayer to assertain what is best for us as a "flagless" race, in this great chaotic condition of politics, so that I may best teach and lead my people.

So after some study and reflection, I am about to conclude, that the only salvation, in a political and industrial and civil and social way, for our race (called Negro) and all the laboring class, is the adoption of the doctrine of Socialism, as taught in the Bible and in economics. Therefore as you are one of the great leaders and educators of the race, I would like to have your candid opinion about "The Negro Race," working out its future political, civil and industrial destiny in the ranks and files of The Socialist Party?

Now, Bro' Washington, the reason I am writing you, as I shall write other leaders of The Race, is, that I believe the intire leadership of this Race, should and must, be brought to see the general race need and the[n] agree upon the best possible remedy, then united let us work together for good.

May I hear from you?

I await your reply. Yours for success,

Rev. F. I. Hammonds

ALS   Con. 521   BTW Papers   DLC.

[1] Fred I. Hammonds was pastor of the New Hope Baptist Church in Chanute, Kan.

To Fred I. Hammonds

[Tuskegee, Ala.] April 21, 1914

My dear Mr. Hammonds: I am greatly obliged to you for your interesting letter and for the suggestions that it contains. I think a good many of our people, those who are laborers or who are working in the trades, are likely to join the socialist party and I think that they should do so if they are so inclined. I think our people ought to get into all the organizations and unite their efforts with all persons who are seeking to improve social conditions. I do not believe the majority of the Negroes will go into the socialist party, however, because the majority of them are farmers and the socialistic program has no place for the individual landowner in it. The majority of our farming population are now struggling to get possession of land and are succeeding. Very truly yours,

Booker T. Washington

TLpSr Con. 521 BTW Papers DLC. Signed in E. J. Scott's hand.

Margaret James Murray Washington
to Edith Eugenia Meriwether[1]

Tuskegee Institute, Alabama April, 21st, 1914

My very dear Edith: I am so glad to get your letter. I want you and Dave to do what you think is best, whether it is Sept., or Dec. Dave seems to have it in his mind that he can persuade you for Sept., but I will have to leave this with you and him; both his father and myself will be so happy when the "knot is tied," and you will belong as much to us as you will to Dave.

I have thought that perhaps for the first year you would not be so lonely, and would be so much happier if you did some kind of school work, of course I am going to leave this to you and Dave. I am an old fashioned school teacher and have taught so long that I feel unhappy if I am not teaching, and I feel that all young people are the same.

Please be frank with me and whatever you want to say, say it; make any suggestions that you would like to make or that your mother would like to make, and I will carry them out the best I can. Yours lovingly,

Mrs Washington

TLS BTW Papers ATT.

[1] Edith Eugenia Meriwether, daughter of Sarah N. and James H. Meriwether of Washington, D.C., married BTW's son, E. Davidson Washington, in 1914. Edith Meriwether was a graduate of the M Street High School and Normal School No. 2 in Washington, D.C. She taught school in Durham, N.C., and Atlantic City, N.J., before her marriage to Washington. After E. Davidson Washington's death, she married Walter T. Shehee, of the Tuskegee faculty.

To M. Gatewood Milligan, Jr.[1]

Tuskegee Institute, Alabama   April 27, 1914

Dear Sir: In reply to your letter of April 17[2] let me say that I do not advocate the inter-marriage of the races nor do I know of any colored man who does. I noticed recently in an article in the Survey that Dr. W. E. B. DuBois, of the National Association for the Protection of Colored People, declared that Negroes and white persons should have the right to marry if they wanted to. But I am sure that he would never think of urging interracial marriage. He knows as does every one else who has had experience in these matters that, where such marriages have occurred the parties have generally met with ostracism from both races.

As you know we are a mixed race in this country. Whenever the black man intermingles his blood with that of any other race the result is always a Negro, never a whiteman, Indian or any other sort of man.

Still it is a mistake which students of home missions should not make, to assume that Negroes have no racial self-respect. I am very truly,

[Booker T. Washington]

TLd Con. 521 BTW Papers DLC.

[1] M. Gatewood Milligan, Jr., was a Presbyterian minister residing in Victor, Colo.

[2] As a study question for "special home mission work as related to freedmen," Milligan asked: "Does Booker T. Washington advocate inter-marriage between whites and blacks?" (Con. 521, BTW Papers, DLC.)

From Emmett Jay Scott

Tuskegee Institute, Alabama   April 27, 1914

Dear Mr. Washington: Mr. Fearing has just sent me a memorandum, covering your movements in the immediate future and for the summer. I very much hope you have fully considered what this arduous program will mean to you physically. It seems an almost impossible one.

I know, of course, that you are seldom disposed to consider yourself in such matters, but taking into account the hard year you have already had, and the hard work immediately ahead of you until the close of the school, it seems to me you ought to very carefully decide whether or not you want to go into such a hard campaign as has been outlined for you. Yours truly,

Emmett J. Scott

TLS Con. 644 BTW Papers DLC.

To Emmett Jay Scott

Milwaukee, April 30th, 1914

Have your letter regarding summer itinerary; agree with you it should not be made too strenuous. Advise Fearing by telegram to keep in mind my request not to make definite too many dates, but leave some dates to be fixed later. My impression is that he has arranged enough meet-ing[s] to cover summer and might return to Tuskegee soon. Impress upon him want plenty of time at Tuskegee during Summer School and Mosaic Meeting. Shall be in New York next Sunday. Might tell him see me in New York Sunday or Monday. Meetings in this state have done well.

Booker T. Washington

TWSr Copy Con. 842 BTW Papers DLC.

To Byrd Prillerman

[New York City] May 4, 1914

Find out facts telegraph me Biltmore Hotel, New York how my sister is and what she needs if anything.[1]

Booker T. Washington

TWcSr Con. 517 BTW Papers DLC.

[1] Prillerman telegraphed in reply: "Mrs Johnson somewhat better needs money." (May 4, 1914, Con. 517, BTW Papers, DLC.)

From Whitefield McKinlay

Washington, D.C. May 4th, 1914

Dear Dr. Washington: Has it ever occurred to you that with the re-appointment of Judge Terrell strengthened by his confirmation that you have secured the strongest vindication of your views and teachings, and it is the greatest moral victory the race has won since Emancipation.

When it is remembered that his reappointment was brought about by the most substantial element of the Bar Association of the District of Columbia, two thirds of whom are democrats of Southern origin, and was opposed by the most virulent Negro hating Southerner that ever sat in the Senate since the Civil War, who ordinarily would have been cowed by Vardaman. The mere fact that Terrell has made good, and so conspicuously superior to his associates on the bench, public opinion practically demanded his reappointment.

I flatter myself that I did not make any mistake when I suggested Terrell to you in the beginning, as I knew that above all things, that knowing this community thoroughly he would exhibit tact, make friends for us and make it possible for others to succeed him.

A few days ago I had occasion to call on one of these lawyers and during the interview I thanked him for his support of Terrell, and he boldly stated that he considered his character and ability justified him in his support that he gave. Now this man is a Virginian, a democrat and an intimate friend of Carl Schurtz's son and O. G. Villard. He further stated that he was one of your staunch admirers. I told him that when you passed through the City and had the spare time I wanted him to meet you. He is a man of means and his name is Paul E. Johnson, whose office is in the Woodward Building of this City. It is quite possible that we may get a contribution from him for your school. Very truly,

W McKinlay

TLS Con. 71 BTW Papers DLC.

From Madame C. J. Walker

Indianapolis, Indiana 5/5/14

My Dear Dr Washington: Your letter of recent date received, and contents noted. In reply to same will say that it was thoroughly explained to me that there were two kinds of scholarships of which I choose the one to help the students.

I thought by giving scholarships to the Tuskegee students I was not only helping the student but the school as well. If these scholarships do not help the school I have missed my mark.

Of course I understood that the additional $50.00 was for the general running expenses of the school.

While I am deeply interested in Tuskegee and would love to help you in that way, yet I do not feel able to assume the entire responsibility of five students at this time. I thought that if they were there in school without any help that the $50.00 per year each would help them to attend the day school.

While it is true I have a large business, yet with the increase in business comes the increase in expenses.

I am unlike your white friends who have waited until they were rich and then help, but have in proportion to my success I have reached out and am helping others, which may have been a mistake perhaps because I have been mistaken for a rich woman, which has caused scores of demands for help. Many of whom are so pathetic that it has been impossible for me to turn them down.

Sometime ago I made a proposition to you in regards to adopting my work as a part of the curriculum in your school. I think I have demonstrated the fact to you that my business is a legitimate one as well as a lucrative one. Should you see your way clear to reconsider and establish this work in your school, if successful it would mean Thousands of dollars to both Tuskegee and myself. You would not only help me, but would help thousands of others who are needy and deserving. Then I could not only give hundreds of dollars to Tuskegee but Thousands of dollars. If you can not see your way clear to adopt the work I do hope you will be willing to give me your indorsement in a public way.

Trusting you are well and wishing you unbounded success in your work, I am, Sincerely yours,

Mme C. J. Walker

TLS   Con. 774   BTW Papers   DLC.

To Melvin Jack Chisum[1]

[Tuskegee, Ala., *ca.* May 8, 1914]

Dear Mr. Chisum: I have sent to the colored newspapers of the country lately in two sections letters from railroad officials in answer to letters which I had written to these railroad officials regarding the poor and unequal accommodations furnished colored people in many parts of the country. The interest of the railroad people has been aroused in many ways, and they are beginning now to see that it is worth while to treat 10,000,000 people with consideration.

Now, let us follow up this whole matter by setting aside Sunday, June 7th and Monday June 8th, to be known as Railroad Days. On one of these days, or on some other day near these dates, I want to suggest with all the emphasis I can, that various groups of our people, through churches, secret societies, business leagues, woman's clubs, and other agencies organize themselves in a way to go directly to the railroad authorities and put before them the difficulties under which we labor in cases where there is in existence unjust treatment. I would suggest that the committees that go to these railroad officials should not be large; two or three good, sensible people will accomplish more in making themselves felt than a dozen or two.

I do not attempt to advise in detail how to bring about better conditions; that can best be left to the people in each community and each state; they know what the conditions are and know what remedies ought to be brought about, but I would urge in appointing these committees that the following subjects be given attention;

In their contact with the railroad officials the committees should call their attention to these points wherever local conditions make it necessary.

1st — Proper accommodations in restaurants controlled by the railroads.

15

2nd — Proper accommodations in the way of sitting rooms in the depots controlled by the railroads.

3rd — Proper and just accommodations on street cars, steamboats and railroad trains.

I want to repeat, that in my opinion if this matter is taken up vigorously and the principal railroad officials approached and talked to directly and frankly a change will soon take place in every part of the country where conditions of public travel are not now what they should be. If the committees are appointed on Saturday and Sunday the railroad officials could be approached on Monday, but the matter of the exact time is, of course, not important; only we should keep in mind the idea of letting this movement be brought to a head in one day, or in one single week, so that the railroad officials may be impressed with the bigness of the occasion and the opportunity which is before them to increase their revenue by doing justice to nine or ten million of their patrons.

I wish especially to urge upon ministers and other leaders to give notice of Railroad Day several times during the next few weeks in their pulpits. I am equally anxious that the colored newspapers should call attention to this day from time to time. It is a matter of the greatest importance and I believe that hard work and concentrated effort will help to change present conditions very noticeably. Yours very truly,

Booker T. Washington

Baltimore *Colored Man,* May 9, 1914, 1.

[1] At this time, Melvin J. Chisum was editor of the Baltimore *Colored Man.*

An Address before
the Southern Sociological Congress

Memphis, Tennessee   May 8, 1914

THE SOUTHERN SOCIOLOGICAL CONGRESS AS A
FACTOR FOR SOCIAL WELFARE

On Behalf of the members of my race who are here and on behalf also of those who are not here, I wish to express the deep gratitude which we feel toward Mrs. Anna Russell Cole,[1] the founder of this organization, for her generosity and foresight in making such a meeting as this possible.

I wish also to make known our gratitude to Governor Mann,[2] Dr. McCulloch, and other leaders who are devoting themselves with such unflagging enthusiasm to the task of making this great organization practically useful to both races in the South.

In the brief space that has been allotted to me on this program, I want to speak of some special ways in which it seems to me this Congress can promote the welfare of the people of the South.

First of all, it can serve as a medium for direct and candid expression of opinion on the part of the members of both races in regard to matters of common interest. No one living in the South, or out of the South, should expect everything to be done in a day. When we consider all that the South has been called upon to do and to bear in connection with the readjustment of its economic and social program, the wonder is that so much has been accomplished within so brief a space of time. What we want to be sure of is that progress in the right direction is constant and steady. One direction in which meetings of this kind can help is in bringing about a better understanding between the races. In spite of difficulties that grow out of the situation in the South, the races have many fundamental interests in common and there is much that should be done for the welfare of each race which can only be done with the hearty cooperation of both.

How can the negro in the South do his part, through this organization, to bring about better conditions? The leaders of our people, for example, can do much to spread the influence of this meeting to all parts of the South. They can let the masses of the people know that there is an organization made up of Southern white people who are interested in their welfare, to whom they can speak frankly about their desires and their needs. The influence of this meeting spread abroad among the masses of the colored people will lead them to feel that the South is their home, and that they have a share, no matter how humble, in all its weal and woe, in everything that concerns its welfare.

We should learn from this meeting, all of us, to manifest as much pride in whatever concerns our own community, our own city, or our own State as the white people do. We should feel as much humiliation on account of anything that hurts the reputation of the community in which we live as is true of the white race.

In the past, I fear that the white people and the black people have talked too much about each other and not enough to each other. We can use this Congress as a means of appealing directly to the white people. There are certain things we want them to do. The simplest and most practical way is to go frankly to the white people of the South and ask for what we want.

In every county of the South the colored people should get hold of the city, county, and State officials and make it possible for them to see the better life of our race. It is most important that we get hold of the Governor, sheriffs, judges, and other officials and bring them into direct contact with the needs and conditions of our people. Our leaders can use this organization for making it easier for the liberal-minded white people who are desirous of helping us to come into contact with us in a manner that will not embarrass them.

We have friends among the Southern white people. You will hardly find a colored man in the South, no matter how humble, and no matter, I was going to say, how worthless, who has not some white friend to whom he is accustomed to go when he is in trouble. It is these friendships between individual white people and individual black people which form the basis for cooperation between the races.

We can use this organization to create a sentiment among our people throughout the South which will serve to stop so much crime. In spite of all that may be said in palliation, there is too much crime committed by our people in all parts of the country. We should let the world understand that we are not going to hide crime simply because it is committed by black people.

We can use this Congress, too, in a way to impress upon the white people throughout the South that education does not unfit us for the common labors and duties of life; but in proportion as we get education we will be more useful in field and shop, in kitchen and laundry, as teachers, and in every walk of life.

We can use this Congress to let the world understand that in proportion as the negro is educated he does not wish to intermingle with the white people in a purely social way; but in proportion as the negro gets intelligence he finds happiness and satisfaction in social intercourse with members of his own race.

We can use this Congress to impress the world with the idea that we are proud of being negroes, and this pride should increase in proportion as the negro goes forward in all the useful lines of our civilization.

How can the white man use this Congress in promoting better conditions between the races in the South?

First, it can be used, as I have suggested, as a medium through which white people may get acquainted with the most useful and best type of black people in every community. The average white man, I sometimes fear, knows more about the criminal negro than he does about the law-abiding, self-respecting, and successful negro.

The white people can use this Congress to help advertise the better side rather than the worse side of negro life throughout the South. Too much space, I often fear, is given in newspapers to reports covering negro crime and not enough to reports covering the useful living and strivings of our race.

This Congress can be used to put in motion a public sentiment throughout the South that will insist that in the courts the negro may be sure of equal justice. The average black man has a notion that the court is a place of punishment rather than a place of protection. The total amount of time the best white people of the South lose every year in dealing with petty negro crime through the courts, if it were reckoned up, would represent a sum so large as to be startling. This Congress, directly and indirectly, can do much to stop the practice of arresting so many of our people for petty and trivial offenses, all of which impose a tremendous burden upon black people and white people in every community throughout the South.

This Congress can be used as a means of letting the people throughout the country know that the educated negro seldom commits crime, and in proportion as we get more education and better education the cost of punishing criminals will disappear.

This Congress can be used in creating a sentiment in every county in favor of better schools for negro children. It is often said that education for the negro has been a failure. We cannot say that a policy has failed until it has been actually tried. Education for the negro, especially in the rural districts, has not been tried in any effective way or upon a comprehensive scale. I say this although I am fully aware that in many counties it is poverty which retards white education as well as negro education.

The negro is going to get some kind of education at the hands of somebody, somewhere and at some time; and I believe the time has come when the white officials in every county should become the leaders and guides in the matter of giving to every negro child an opportunity to get a common school education. The Sociological Congress can do much to encourage the colored people in what they are doing to educate themselves, and to guide and foster every effort that is being made, from whatever direction, to improve the colored people and make them valuable and useful citizens of the communities in which they live.

As no color line is drawn in the courts in the matter of punishing crime, neither should any color line be drawn in the opportunity to get education in the public schools. The schools can always be supported out of the return that they bring to the State in the form of more efficient labor and better social order. The more money spent in educating the negro child, the less the State will have to pay for punishing crime. It should be the aim of this organization, in connection with those who are directing the schools, to prove to the South that education is one of the best investments that any country can make.

The white leaders in attendance on this Congress can use their influence in seeing to it that the negro gets fairer and more just treatment on the railroads throughout the South. In this connection I cannot forbear to commend to other portions of the South what has been done in the city of Memphis at the Union Station in providing adequate, comfortable, and even attractive accommodations for colored passengers. The time has come, too, when the strong white leaders of the South should no longer permit the negro to be used as a political "scarecrow." Too many selfish politicians have used the negro as a political "bogey man" in a way to deceive white people, and even to discourage some of the best black people in their communities. The negro is not seeking either social equality or political domination over the white man in any section of the South.

I want to see both races advance in the South. I have no racial prejudice. I want to see the negro lifted up for his own sake, but just as emphatically do I want to see the negro lifted up for the sake of the white man. I was born a slave here in the South. I love the South, and no white man can excel me in my devotion to the South. But I am aware of the fact that so long as the white man is surrounded by a race that is in a large measure ignorant, weak, and in poverty, so long will the white man be tempted to injure himself by unjust treatment of the weaker race by which he is surrounded. So long as there are hordes of ignorant colored women in any community, so long will they prove a temptation for some of the best white men of the South to degrade themselves.

There are millions of black people throughout the world. Everywhere, especially in Europe, people are looking to us here in the South, black and white, to show to the world how it is possible for two races, different in color, to live together on the same soil, under the same laws, and each race work out its salvation in justice to the other.

I do not wish to be misunderstood. Tremendous progress in all these directions has been made within the last fifty years. I speak as I do with frankness, and yet with love, because I want to see still greater progress brought about.

The negro here in the South, supported and encouraged as he is by the best element of the white people, has made progress in getting property, education, and a high Christian character that is not approached by any similar group of black people in Christendom. We must go on, patiently but courageously, year by year, devoting our best energies to the great big things, the fundamental things that underlie the progress and civilization of white people and black people throughout the South.

And this Southern Sociological Congress, in my opinion, as one of the great mediums in God's providence, has been brought into existence for this purpose.

James Edward McCulloch, ed., *Battling for Social Betterment: Southern Sociological Congress, Memphis, Tennessee, May 6–10, 1914* ([Nashville?]: Southern Sociological Congress, 1914), 154–59.

[1] Anna Virginia Russell Cole (1846–1926), the wife of a railroad official in Nashville, gave $7,500 a year to the Southern Sociological Congress. She also made several gifts to Vanderbilt University.

[2] William Hodges Mann (1843–1927), governor of Virginia from 1910 to 1914, was also the author of a Virginia prohibition act and an act promoting public high schools.

To Emmett Jay Scott

Boston   May 10, 1914

Dear Mr. Scott: As far as you and Mr. Fisher can find the time I hope you will send out from now on short pithy paragraphs to the colored papers on R.R. Day.

Impress on the people the importance [of] *going to see* the R.R. officials, not merely talking among themselves. Yours Sincerely,

Booker T. Washington

ALS Con. 634 BTW Papers DLC.

To Alexander Robert Stewart

Memphis, Tenn. May 14, 1[9]14

Dear Mr. Stewart: I hope you will take up with Mr. Gerard at Huntington, the matter of seeing that the new house at Huntington is rented and kept rented. I do not want to lose the income on that house. I have signed the papers and sent them to Mr. Baylis. Yours very truly,

[Booker T. Washington]

TLc Con. 644 BTW Papers DLC.

Extracts from an Address
before the National Conference
of Charities and Corrections

Memphis, Tenn. May 14, 1914

THE RURAL NEGRO IN THE SOUTH

Of the nearly 9,000,000 Negroes in the South, about 7,000,000, or 80 per cent, live in the rural districts. Of these 7,000,000 black people it is safe to say that more than 2,200,000 are actually working on farms as hired hands, or as independent farmers or croppers, as renters, or as independent owners. Included in this number are a great many girls and women, for it must be kept in mind that especially in the cotton-growing states it is a common thing for girls and women to work in the fields.

Despite all theory and academic discussion as to the value of the Negro in the economic life of the South, it is true in the cotton-growing

22

states that a large part of the banking business has for its basis the Negro and the mule. If a planter wants to borrow money, the decision of the bank will hinge largely on the question of the number of reliable Negro tenants he can control.

Here, then, is a tremendous amount of labor, and in it there are tremendous possibilities. These more than 2,200,000 people are not likely to leave the Southern states. Where they remain in large numbers no other class of laborers is likely to come in large number, and I also find that the majority of Southern white landowners do not want any other.

To put the matter in another form, forty per cent of the tillable land in the Southern states is in the hands of colored people in one form or another. The large number of colored laborers and the vast territory that they occupy make up a serious but interesting question for the South and for the whole country. In my opinion, in this mass of Negro labor is an undiscovered gold mine. How to improve the efficiency of these 2,000,000 black farmers is one of the problems that now confronts the South.

As I have just said, the prosperity of the South is bound up with the improvement that the Negro makes as a farmer. Just in proportion as the Negro becomes efficient, reliable and dependable will the prosperity of the South be increased; for we must keep in mind that 100,000,000 out of the 150,000,000 acres of improved land in the South is cultivated by Negro labor; that of every eleven bales of cotton raised in the South, seven are produced by Negro labor. One-tenth of all the farm property in the South is in the hands of Negroes. If the efficiency of the Negro in the South is increased, say 25 per cent — that is, if his farming is improved so that the average number of bales of cotton raised by Negroes will be increased one-fourth; that the amount of corn that he raises will be doubled and the bushels of sweet potatoes and other crops be proportionately increased, the agricultural wealth of the South will be increased by 25 per cent, that is, over $2,000,000,000 would be added annually to the agricultural wealth of the South. These are some of the possibilities of the Negro farmer.

That the Negro has great potential possibilities as a farmer is indicated by the progress that he has made along this line in the past fifty years. In 1863 there were in all the United States only a few farms controlled by Negroes. They now operate in the South 890,140 farms which are 217,800 more than there were in this section in 1863. Negro farm laborers and Negro farmers in the South now cultivate approximately 100,000,000 acres of land, of which 42,500,000 acres are under the control of Negro farmers. The increase of Negro farm owners in the South in the past fifty years compares favorably with the increase of white farm owners.

· · · ·

The Negroes of this country now own 20,000,000 acres of land or 31,000 square miles. If all the land they own was placed in one body, its area would be greater than that of the state of South Carolina.

It was during the past ten years that the Negro has made his greatest progress in agriculture. In that time, the value of the domestic animals which they owned increased from $85,216,337 to $177,273,000, or 107 per cent; poultry from $3,788,792 to $5,113,756, or 35 per cent; implements and machinery from $18,586,225 to $36,861,418, or 98 per cent; land and buildings from $69,636,420 to $273,501,665, or 293 per cent. From 1900 to 1910 the total value of farm property owned by the colored farmers of the South increased from $177,404,688 to $492,898,218, or 177 per cent.

The drift of Negro population in the South is countryward. Contrary to the general opinion the movement of Negro population in the South is toward the country. Prof. E. C. Branson, President of the State Normal School at Athens, Georgia, in an address before the Southern Sociological Congress at Atlanta, Georgia, on "The Negro working out his own salvation," called special attention to this fact. He pointed out that during the past census period the Negro population in general increased barely 10 per cent. On the other hand, Negro farm population increased more than 20 per cent.

· · · ·

I can best tell how not to succeed with Negro labor by using some illustrations that have come under my observation. Some years ago, when I was in Mississippi, a planter asked me to visit his farm. I found he had a large number of colored tenants, but I was surprised at the small acreage assigned to each family. In one case I happen to remember a family that had three or four strong persons at work every day, that was allowed to rent only about ten acres of land. When I asked the owner of the plantation why he did not let this family have more land he replied that the soil was so productive that if he allowed them to rent more they would soon be making such a profit that they would be able to buy land of their own and he would lose them as renters.

This is one way to make the Negro inefficient as a laborer — attempting to discourage him instead of encouraging him.

.   .   .   .

Another illustration: In one of the cotton raising counties of Alabama a colored tenant brought six bales of cotton and delivered them to the merchant from whom he had been renting and who has been furnishing him "advances." The colored farmer had kept pretty good account of his purchases and of the rent due. When he entered the store he told the merchant he thought he had made enough cotton to settle all he owed. After looking over his books the merchant agreed with him that the six bales would "bring him out clear." But before the colored man left the store the merchant learned that he had not brought in all the cotton he had grown, having two more bales at home. Immediately the storekeeper called the farmer aside and told him that he was sorry he had made a mistake in the accounts, and in going over his books again he found enough omitted charges to exactly cover the two bales the Negro tenant had left at home. Of course this Negro tenant was not long in putting an account of how he had been treated on the "grapevine telegraph," and soon every Negro in the neighborhood knew about it.

Through such practices, in not a few sections of the South, Negro tenants have been thoroughly convinced that no matter how much they economize or how hard they may work they are going to come out in debt at the end of the year, and they have become so discouraged and hopeless that they try to do only enough work to "make a showing" in order to get their "advances." If they work little they get nothing at the end of the year, they say, and if they work hard they get the same, nothing.

.   .   .   .

Having called attention to the negative side, let me now tell how a number of Southern white men who are large planters are succeeding with Negro labor. I am confining these examples almost wholly to Alabama, for these in most cases are personally known to me.

First, I mention G. W. McLeod,[1] who owns a large tract of land in Macon County, Alabama. He is a good example of the white planter who treats his tenants well. Mr. McLeod believes in having a good school in the community, so he gave an acre of ground upon which the school house was built, and $100 in addition to help put up the $700 schoolhouse. He deeded the land to a set of colored trustees. Mr.

McLeod also offers annual prizes to the best kept stock, best kept farm, best kept house, best cared for children, best attendance at Sunday school and church. The man or woman guilty of taking intoxicating liquors or engaging in family quarrels is not eligible to prizes and must go at the end of the year.

. . . .

From direct investigation I find that many valuable colored laborers leave the farm for the reason that they seldom see or handle cash. The Negro laborer likes to put his hands on real money as often as possible. In the city, while he is not so well off in the long run, as I have said, he is usually paid off in cash every Saturday night. In the country he seldom gets cash oftener than once a month or once a year.

Not a few of the best colored laborers leave the farms because of the poor houses furnished by the owners. The miserable condition of some of the one-room cabins is almost beyond description. In the towns and cities, while he may have a harder time in other respects, he can find a reasonably comfortable house with two or three rooms.

No matter how ignorant or worthless a colored man may be, he wants his children to have education. A very large and valuable element of colored labor leaves the farm because education cannot be secured in many cases. In a large section of the farming district of the South, the Negro finds public schools provided for him which run only from two to five months in the year. In many cases children have to walk miles to reach these schools. The schoolhouses are poor, in most cases beyond description. The teacher receives perhaps not more than $18 or $25 a month, and of course poor pay means a poor [teacher.][2]

. . . .

But conditions are changing for the better in all parts of the South. White people are manifesting more interest each year in the training of colored people, and, what is equally important, colored people are beginning to learn to use their education in sensible ways: they are learning that it is no disgrace for an educated person to work on the farm. As white people see this they are going to be willing to spend money on the Negro for farm training.

TM Con. 838 BTW Papers DLC.

[1] J. W. McLeod. See references above, 11:455 and elsewhere.
[2] Line and page end with the word "poor."

From Joel Elias Spingarn

New York   May 18, 1914

My dear Dr. Washington: On my return from Memphis[1] a day or two ago I found your letter of the 13th, asking for help to close your school year without debt, awaiting me, and I take pleasure in enclosing a small sum to be used for this purpose.[2] I take all the more pleasure in sending you the enclosure because certain speeches of mine have been misrepresented by the press, white and colored, in such a way as to suggest that I was wholly unappreciative of the magnificent work that has been actually accomplished at Tuskegee. If at any time when you are in the North you could find it convenient to have a little talk with me, I should welcome the opportunity of discussing these and other matters with you. Very truly yours,

J. E. Spingarn

TLS   Con. 773   BTW Papers   DLC.

[1] Spingarn and BTW both attended the Southern Sociological Congress at Memphis.

[2] The letter was docketed with the note "$25.00."

From Oswald Garrison Villard

New York   May 21, 1914

Dear Dr. Washington: I am very sorry indeed to see a recent letter[1] of yours to Mr. Willcox rather throwing cold water on the project of the Association of Negro Rural and Industrial Schools, of which Mr. Holtzclaw is the President. In your letter you only touch on the question of Dr. Jones' investigation. Of course, we have known all about that for some time past, but that does not affect the great essential need of these smaller schools. I have been after the General Education Board for a couple of years past to get them to do something to coordinate these rural schools, to weed out the unworthy, to insist upon standards of instruction and model curricula and proper accounting. As they did not act it seemed a most admirable idea that this should be undertaken by such men as Mr. Holtzclaw, Mr. Hunt, Mr. Hill and others, for

27

themselves. Particularly is cooperation of this kind necessary in the matter of money raising. You have personally had difficulty enough with Tuskegee, but Tuskegee and Hampton are in an easy position as contrasted with some of these small schools, and conditions are steadily getting worse. To put this on a scientific basis is of the utmost importance to the cause of negro education, it seems to me, just as it is vital that a fixed standard of accounts should be insisted upon. I feel sure that if you could know about this work and understand its purpose and had been present at its session and seen the spirit these men displayed, you would not be throwing cold water upon the enterprise. Sincerely yours,

Oswald Garrison Villard

TLS Con. 525 BTW Papers DLC.

¹ BTW wrote to William G. Willcox on Apr. 13, 1914, that he thought the Association of Negro Industrial and Secondary Schools a waste of time and money, since Thomas Jesse Jones was already in the process of surveying the black schools under the sponsorship of the Phelps-Stokes Fund. BTW favored, after the completion of the survey, the creation of an impartial organization that would inform the public about the character and scope of work of all the southern black schools. (Con. 97, BTW Papers, DLC.)

From Leslie Pinckney Hill

Cheyney, Pa. May 21st, 1914

Dear Dr. Washington: I understand that you have written to Mr. Willcox, relative to our Association of Negro Industrial and Secondary Schools, and that you stated that you think it will be a waste of time and money for anyone to attempt the work which we have outlined before Dr. Thomas Jesse Jones has completed the survey which he is now conducting for the Department of Education. You have also suggested that this survey may be the basis of some organization that will inform the public definitely concerning the character and scope of every school in the South, and that such an organization should be headed by disinterested people who know the South and its needs by first-hand investigation.

As Secretary-Treasurer of the Association, I ought to say that we all value the work which Dr. Jones and other experts are doing. We propose not to duplicate that work, but to supplement it. While these investigators are gradually accumulating data that ought to be of unquestioned worth, we are committed to making known to the public concrete needs which we all keenly feel, and which nobody can doubt.

Those needs are (1) a wider public interest in education for our people throughout the country; (2) money, and a more efficient method of securing and insuring it; (3) better standards of work, academic and industrial, both in quality and content; (4) a better trained teaching force; (5) instead of our struggling along, as we are now, each school doing its best or its worst in isolation, a general and effective co-operation. Many others I need not name.

Are any of these needs dubious, and are we mistaken in the warm conviction that we should immediately take up the task? Investigations ought to shed new light on sorely vexed questions, but they are not now meeting our peremptory bread-and-butter embarrassments.

We wish to steer clear of questionable issues. We fully realize, also, the importance of having the work in the hands of people who are disinterested, and who know the South. In Dr. T. S. McWilliams[1] of Cleveland, Ohio, we think we have found a high-grade man of this type. An organizer of cool business judgment, forceful earnestness, and with a deep interest in the South and in our people, he seems to be particularly fitted for this enterprise.

We all feel that when you understand what our Association is proposing, you will give it moral support. Dr. Dillard has said that he thinks it represents one of the most important forward steps in the history of educational work among our people. Mr. W. T. B. Williams is of the same opinion. These two men are certainly widely-informed, first-hand investigators. If an organization is to follow up Dr. Jones's findings, why may not this Association do it?

Business men continue to tell us that your co-operation will help us. In the very nature of things, it could not be otherwise. We do not see how great institutions like Tuskegee and Hampton can profit very much in a material way by our program, but the help which they could give to scores of smaller and less favored schools by endorsement and moral support of the joint effort we are now making would seem indeed to be to them a source of comfort and satisfaction.

We hope that we are not wrong in all this, and shall thank you for suggestions. Very truly yours,

Leslie Pinckney Hill

TLS Con. 505 BTW Papers DLC.

[1] Thomas Samuel McWilliams (b. 1865) was the minister of Calvary Presbyterian Church in Cleveland, Ohio. In 1917 he became professor of comparative religion at Western Reserve University.

To Madame C. J. Walker

[Tuskegee, Ala.] May 22nd, 1914

Dear Madam Walker: I have your letter of May 5th.

So that there may be no misunderstanding about the matter, I am proceeding once more to try to state the proposition with reference to the students whom you wish to help here.

The money, that is, the Fifty Dollars each for the five students which you offer to bond will be applied toward the personal expenses of the students, that is, for their board and other expenses. The Fifty Dollars may not pay all of their personal expenses, etc., but what you send will certainly help them in a most satisfactory and appreciable way. Tuition is provided without cost to the student. The help you plan to send, will permit these students to enter the Day School as you suggest.

We shall be very glad whenever it is convenient for you, after the beginning of the next school term, to have you place this money in our treasury for the benefit of the five students you have selected to receive your aid.

I have already written you frankly and fully with reference to placing your work in our course of study; our Trustees and Executive Council do not see their way clear to follow your suggestion.

Thanking you for all of your kindly interest, I am Yours very truly,

Booker T. Washington

TLpS Con. 774 BTW Papers DLC.

To Joel Elias Spingarn

Tuskegee Institute, Alabama   May 23d, 1914

My dear Mr. Spingarn: I thank you very much for your contribution of $25.00 toward our current expenses. We appreciate this more than I can explain in words.

Sometime when I am in New York I will do my best to let you know far enough ahead so we can have a conference if possible.

I hope at some time you may see Tuskegee. Yours very truly,

Booker T. Washington

TLS   Joel E. Spingarn Papers   NN.

To Ruth Standish Bowles Baldwin

[Tuskegee, Ala.] May 25th, 1914

Dear Mrs. Baldwin: If I can possibly find the time for it, sometime during the summer I want to have a meeting probably under the auspices of The Urban League, of the colored men alone, in Harlem. I think I might say something to them that would help them. I do not mean the more prosperous or well-to-do men, but the down and out, discouraged and poorer classes. Yours very truly,

Booker T. Washington

TLpS   Con. 840   BTW Papers   DLC.

To Paul Drennan Cravath

[Tuskegee, Ala.] May 25th, 1914

My dear Mr. Cravath: I am writing briefly regarding Dr. Shedd.[1] After considering the matter very carefully from every possible point of view, I have reached the conclusion that Dr. Shedd is the best man we can get for the presidency of Fisk University. I believe that he will make a success as president. If we place him in this position, however, we must bear in mind one or two things.

First, he will not have an easy task. There is a large and I fear growing element on the grounds and perhaps in the city, against Dr. Shedd. Before going there he would have to make up his mind that it is going to take two or three years to bring this element into sympathy with him and this would require patient, hard work. He ought not to go there with the idea that if he cannot harmonize matters within a few months he would leave.

In the second place, before electing Doctor Shedd, the Trustees ought to make up their minds that they will have to stand by Doctor Shedd through a somewhat stormy period.

Thirdly, Doctor Shedd ought to be cautioned not to be too ready with opinions concerning either Fisk or Southern conditions. Most Northern people coming to the South, I fear, make the mistake of expressing opinions before they have had time to get into the local atmosphere of the community, or of the South.

I repeat, however, that I believe that Doctor Shedd will win out, and will make an effective, strong, helpful president for Fisk and if the Trustees stand by him while he is winning his way. Yours very truly,

Booker T. Washington

TLpS Con. 497 BTW Papers DLC.

¹ John Cutler Shedd (1868–1933) was professor of physics at Olivet College in Michigan from 1909 to 1916, and dean in 1915–16.

To William G. Willcox

[Tuskegee, Ala.] May 26th, 1914

Dear Mr. Willcox: I find that there are approximately 1,517 acres in the two tracts of land and that the parties are asking for the two tracts about $18,000. There is a mortgage of $4,000 on the tracts, which can be taken up or permitted to stand. The income on this land this year should be approximately $1,200. Whether or not the parties will agree to give this year's income to the buyer is a question to be determined.

My main point in writing is to say that there is great danger — and it is increasing every day — of the parties getting an inkling of what we have in mind, and, of course, as soon as they get the least idea of our intention, the price will go up. I have the feeling that if we could be in position to make a cash payment that we could get the two tracts for $500 less than is now being asked for them.

Would you be willing to authorize me to secure an option through a cash payment for two or three months, or to close the trade by an actual purchase? After we are in possession of the land, other matters could be worked out. Yours very truly,

Booker T. Washington

TLpS Con. 989 BTW Papers DLC.

To Carl Kelsey[1]

[Tuskegee, Ala.] May 26, 1914

My dear Mr. Kelsey: Replying to your letter under date of May 21st,[2] bearing upon the question of segregation, I would state, I think great injustice has been done my race in several cities by reason of the segregation measures which have been passed; in some cases, the laws have been declared unconstitutional, in other cases, they are being enforced. I think anything that can be said or done to call attention to this injustice will be of value. It is curious to note that with one or two exceptions, the cities where segregation ordinances have been passed, are the cities where the colored people vote freely, but their ballot does not seem to protect them against these ordinances. This is notably true in such cities as Baltimore and Louisville where there has never been any question about the Negro casting his ballot and having it counted.

In regard to land segregation in the country districts of the South, I am quite sure there is not enough in that movement to warrant any serious or dignified attention. In fact, I think the more attention that is given to it, the more harm will be done. I have followed this movement very carefully from the beginning, and outside of one man in North Carolina, who is the owner of a newspaper and I think is using this agitation largely for the purpose of advertising his paper, I have

33

never been able to discover the slightest foundation for any alarm. The whole matter is so utterly impractical and undesirable on the part of both races that I cannot see how anything would be gained by taking the matter up in a serious way; it would simply be putting a straw man to fight over.

On two occasions recently when I was addressing large white audiences, composed mostly of Southern people, I have gone out of my way simply as a "feeler" to refer to the matter of land segregation and in each case, the audience has applauded what I have said in the way of ridiculousness of any such attempt.

If the matter of segregation in the cities is taken up, I do not believe that much will be gained by simply dealing with the negative side of the question. I think emphasis ought to be placed on the constructive side; for example, I think it ought to be constantly pointed out that colored people are treated very unjustly in most of the cities in the matter of providing them with proper streets, sewerage, lighting and other modern conveniences and necessities. I have found that the colored people are not so much opposed to living among themselves but they know by experience when they are shut off to themselves it means that they are to be provided with fewer of the necessities and safeguards of life, notwithstanding, in many cases, they pay a large proportion of the taxes that provide for the city government.

If I can be of further service, please be kind enough to let me know. Yours truly,

Booker T. Washington

TLpS Con. 511 BTW Papers DLC.

[1] Carl Kelsey (1870–1953) was a professor of sociology at the University of Pennsylvania and vice-president (1912–25) of the American Academy of Political and Social Science.

[2] Kelsey wrote on May 21, 1914, that Oswald Garrison Villard had suggested that the American Academy of Political and Social Science hold a conference on the segregation of farmland in North Carolina. Kelsey asked BTW whether he thought there was warrant for such a conference, "inviting prominent men North and South to take part therein." (Con. 511, BTW Papers, DLC.)

From George Washington Carver

[Tuskegee, Ala.] May 26, 1914

Mr. B. T. Washington: I have just received note, from the Summer Committee and approved by you, to the effect that I am laid off one month. To this I do not agree —

1. Because it is not a question of salary. I saved the school last year in the months of June, July, August, to September 1st, $399.00 by manufacturing things it would have had to pay a much higher price for. I invite you to examine the figures.

2. It is too much trouble to look up work somewhere for one month.

3. Of course, if the school has reached the point where it cannot pay me and doesn't need my services any more, I shall abide by the decision and seek employment elsewhere. I can never consent to work only part of the year as long as I am able to put in full time. Yours very truly,

G. W. Carver

TLS   Con. 653   BTW Papers   DLC.

From Melvin Jack Chisum

Baltimore, Md. May 26th, 1914

My dear Dr Washington: This is just a line to call your attention to an important occurance. The Afro-American is a great supporter of the N.A.A.C.P., I am running a paper in Baltimore. I am making my paper go. I could not allow them to equal my output in reporting that meeting, and at the same time I made all their readers read at the same time about your distinguished self.

I am sending you the front and editorial pages of both the Colored Man & the Afro-American, please observe the two. If you read the Colored Man then I am satisfied for then you know how religiously I am hewing to the Tuskegee line.

Please don't become impatient because of my asking that I be not

35

forgotten when the "pie" is to be passed around. I am, Yours always faithfully

Your Chisum

TLS Con. 496 BTW Papers DLC.

To Oswald Garrison Villard

[Tuskegee, Ala.] May 27th, 1914

Dear Mr. Villard: Replying to yours of May 21st, I would state that for sometime a number of us have been trying to find an effective way to relieve the unsatisfactory condition of things as far as the schools of the South are concerned. After a good deal of effort the Stokes Fund Board of Trustees was induced to undertake the matter of making a survey of all the schools of the South. The Stokes Fund Trustees, as you perhaps know, have plenty of money to do the work well and they have been engaged in this work for a number of months, and while I have not seen any of their reports, I believe that the work is being done in a thorough manner. Dr. Jones with plenty of helpers is covering the whole South, taking in every grade of school. I have a strong feeling that until this survey is completed and the report made that it would not be wise to do the things your letter suggests.

In my opinion it would be a hazardous experiment and a waste of money for such a matter to be put in the hands of anybody except people who are actually acquainted with conditions in the South by reason of actual contact with the schools and their teachers. I cannot for the life of me see why it would be necessary to waste money in making an investigation that has already been made by Dr. Jones and his assistants at a considerable outlay of money.

Every year we are finding that it is a dangerous experiment to bring white people into the Southern schools who have not had the opportunity to get into the life of the South. We have been seeking for many months to find a man for the presidency of Fisk University. Very often many lamentable failures at such institutions as Clark University occur because an attempt has been made to bring people into the Southern work who have had no experience in dealing with conditions.

Certainly it would seem to me to be most unwise to put a man to investigating the smaller schools when we have a man who has been paid for such work and is competent to do it by reason of his long experience in dealing with all classes and conditions of people at the South.

I am quite sure that the Stokes Fund, or some other organization, when Dr. Jones is through with his investigation, will be willing to do something in the way of forming a permanent organization that can look in a large way after the interests of all the smaller schools in the South. If we can find an organization that already has the money and is willing to do this work, I do not think it wise and economical to call upon the public for money that has already been provided. Dr. Jones is so widely known and respected among all elements in the South and his opinion and word will carry weight and I cannot repeat too strongly the point that I have already mentioned, that it will be a grievous mistake to have such investigation of the schools in charge of the officers of the schools that are to be investigated, or looked after. Such work ought to be done by thoroughly and highly disinterested people.

For a number of years Dr. Frissell and I have been constantly appealed to by large and generous donors to Southern education to do something to systematize giving so that donors would know something about the merits of the individual schools. In response to all such suggestions, I have constantly said that it would be difficult to do anything in the way of systematizing the schools until we know all the facts about all of these schools.

I have said to them that as soon as we could get the facts, something would be done in the way of trying to systematize the work so that possible donors would not be so constantly harassed as they are now. Now that we have reached the point where we seem to be likely to bring this work to a head, it certainly would be most silly on my part to agree to throw the results of Dr. Jones's work overboard for something else. I am not advocating that Dr. Jones be put in charge of any bureau that may be established; in fact I do not know that he would accept such a position, but that can be decided upon when the investigation is finished.

First of all, I repeat, as a basis for any intelligent action, we must have facts, it seems to me, with reference to the character of the schools, the kind of work they are doing, their relation to the population, etc. We ought to know, for example, to what extent college work is being done, the amount of technical, industrial and agricultural work being done, etc., and such information as will afford a basis for intelligent suggestion and action.

One of the greatest needs of the South just now is more and better medical schools. It is becoming increasingly difficult for young colored men to get a medical education in the Northern institutions. We have only one school in the South that is doing anything like first-class work in the direction of training physicians. I have been for some time at work on a report covering the matter of medical education, which I hope will induce certain parties to provide adequate means for a first-class, up-to-date medical college somewhere in the South, but even this, I think, ought to wait until the survey is completed.

Dr. Jones was in the South a few days ago, and I had a talk with him as to how and under what auspices such a clearing house as is being discussed should be established and controlled, but he had no opinion at that time; still I feel that the policy I have indicated should in some degree be followed.

The foregoing indicates my reason for any action that I have taken or anything I have said.

Finally, I must repeat what I have said before, that I do not believe that it is the best thing for education in the South to have these smaller schools coupled up with the ideas and activities of the Association for the Advancement of Colored People. I think there is a line of work needed to be done in the South just now that can best be done separate from that organization. I also think there is a line of work needed to be done in the North and elsewhere that can best be separated from the educational work in the South for colored people. Yours very truly,

Booker T. Washington

TLpS   Con. 525   BTW Papers   DLC.

From Byrd Prillerman

Institute, West Virginia, May 30, 1914

My dear Dr. Washington: I have been trying for several weeks to get definite information concerning Mrs. Johnson, but as I have been so pressed with work I have not had an opportunity to go to Malden. However, she came to our commencement Wednesday, May 27th. She took dinner at my house. She is very weak and not herself at all. Her mind is in a rather feeble state. I talked with Miss Clara over the telephone yesterday morning, and she says that the visit here helped her mother very much. I tried all day yesterday to get in communication with Dr. Shirkey of Charleston who is treating her, but was unable to reach him. If there is anything you wish me to do for her, I will be glad to do anything in my power. I really think, however, that you or Mr. J. H.[1] should come to see her at the earliest date possible. Very sincerely yours,

Byrd Prillerman

TLS   Con. 517   BTW Papers   DLC.

[1] John Henry Washington.

To Julius Rosenwald

[Tuskegee, Ala.] June 1, 1914

My dear Mr. Rosenwald: I am sending you by today's mail some photographs bearing upon the completion of the remaining country schoolhouses for which you provided the money. I thought perhaps you would like to have a little time in which to glance these pictures over in advance of my seeing you on the 10th when I can give you the details covering the matter of the erection of these buildings.

Yesterday I spent one of the most interesting days in all of my work in the South. Through our Extension Department under Mr. Calloway, a trip was planned that enabled us to visit four of these communities where the schoolhouses have been completed. We travelled, all told, about 135 miles. At each one of the points visited there was a very large audience averaging I should say a thousand people of both white and black people. It may interest you further to know that two of the state officers from the educational department accompanied us on the entire trip. It was a most intense, interesting day, and the people showed in a very acceptable way their gratitude to you for what you are helping them to do. I wish you could have been present to have noted how encouraged and hopeful they feel; and I repeat, how grateful they are to you. I have never seen a set of people who have changed so much within recent years from a feeling of almost despair and hopelessness to one of encouragement and determination. Yours very truly,

Booker T. Washington

TLpS   Con. 645   BTW Papers   DLC.

To Amanda Ferguson Johnston

[Tuskegee, Ala.] June 2d, 1914

My dear Sister: I am very glad to hear through Clara that you are improved in health and that matters are looking better than they were. I fear the strike there is injuring business.

We are all well. Your brother,

B. T. W.

TLpI   Con. 506   BTW Papers   DLC.

To James Edward McCulloch

[Tuskegee, Ala.] June 3d, 1914

My dear Dr. McCulloch: I hope within a few days to put in your hands the matter covering what I said at Memphis, but I am in an awkward position; I do not have time to write out my speeches, and in the case of my Memphis address I took for granted that it was to be taken down stenographically, hence, I have nothing but the notes left, but I shall try out of these notes to construct an address.

The main point, however, in writing you is to call your attention to a signed editorial by Mr. Clarence Poe in the Progressive Farmer under date of May 30. It seems to me this editorial indicates very clearly that the time has come when we cannot attempt to please all parties; we have got to take a position and stand by that position, otherwise, in my opinion, the Southern Sociological Congress will find itself in difficulties, we will not have the confidence and cooperation of anybody and it will be like any other organization that tries to please everybody and will please nobody. Certainly we owe it to the Southern white people who stand by the organization to let them know in no uncertain terms just where the organization stands.

Mr. Poe's paper has wide circulation in Texas, and I am sure we shall have to do a good deal of explaining before we get the right kind of attention in Texas next year. Yours very truly,

Booker T. Washington

TLpS Con. 841 BTW Papers DLC.

To James Hardy Dillard

[Tuskegee, Ala.] June 3d, 1914

Dear Dr. Dillard: I call your attention to a signed editorial by Mr. Clarence Poe in the Progressive Farmer of May 30.

It seems to me that the editorial indicates one thing that all of us should profit by, and that is that the time has come in all these matters when we have got to take a position and stand by it. We cannot, in my opinion, without great loss to the cause, attempt to please everybody or attempt to straddle. The more this policy is followed the more we are going to get some of our best friends into an embarrassing position. Yours very truly,

Booker T. Washington

TLpS Con. 69 BTW Papers DLC.

From Oswald Garrison Villard

New York June 3, 1914

Dear Dr. Washington: I have your letter of May 27th in which it appears that the assurances I gave you in my letter of April 4th last year (1913) were either not read by you, or my word was not convincing. I wrote you then that the National Association for the Advancement of Colored People had nothing to do with the new Association of Rural and Industrial Schools; it is not in the slightest degree "coupled up with the ideas and activities of the National Association for the Advancement of Colored People" — no more today than when I wrote you a year ago, in fact less so. The only connection that there has ever been was that the idea originated with me and for the first two meetings the National Association extended the hospitality of its rooms. It did not even do this for the last meeting, and as I am not an officer of the Association of Rural and Industrial Schools, or taking any part in it beyond that of an interested friend, there is no connection through me. Is it too much to hope that you will now dismiss this idea from your mind and take my word for it that there is absolutely no connection between the two?

Again I repeat that there is no intention of wasting money to duplicate the work done by Dr. Jones, nor is it planned to "bring white people into the Southern schools who have not had the opportunity to get into the life of the South." As I wrote you — do read my letter again — there are a number of other aims of this Association which have nothing whatever to do with investigation, and these ideas have warmly commended themselves to Dr. Dillard, the late Mr. Bishop,[1] Mr. Clarence H. Kelsey, and many other practical educators and business men.

Meanwhile, believe me, I should be very sorry indeed if we had to go on with this work feeling that we could not bring you to a clear understanding of its purposes and plans.

With kind regards, Sincerely yours,

Oswald Garrison Villard

TLS Con. 525 BTW Papers DLC. A copy is in the Oswald Garrison Villard Papers, MH.

[1] Samuel Henry Bishop (1864–1914), an Episcopal clergyman, after serving several churches in New York City and South Orange, N.J., was general agent of the American Church Institute for Negroes from 1906 until his death.

From Ralph Waldo Tyler

Washington, D.C. June 3rd., 1914

Dear Doctor: Just a note to advise you that "we" can expect little from The Bee, in the way of publicity, for the reason that Roscoe Bruce has it subsidized, as has also the N.A.A.C.P. people The Sun, the new publication here. All "our friends" joined and contributed financially to the N.A.A.C.P., the anti organization, although it was very hard to get them to contribute financially to any movement to conserve your interests. If any one had told me that "our" friends here would join the army of ingrates I would not have believed it. The only one who has not contributed financially to the N.A.A.C.P. is the Judge, although he promised $25. He, as a rule, pays nothing or takes long time to pay. Chase is crowded for money, and as is always with him when crowded feeds from any hand. The Washington Negro knows neither gratitude or honor, and he quickly forgets the hand that fed him, and just as quickly burns the bridge that carried him over, and I include all "our friends" in this, with the one exception of McKinlay. McK. did join and contribute to the N.A.A.C.P., but he was thoughtless as to its real purpose, and largely influenced by his relatives, the Grimke brothers.

Respectfully,
Ralph W Tyler

Had quite a talk with Chase today.

TLS Con. 851 BTW Papers DLC.

To Paul Drennan Cravath

[Tuskegee, Ala.] June 4th, 1914

My dear Mr. Cravath: I am in receipt of yours of June first together with a copy of the letter from Dr. Shedd to you and copy of your letter to Dr. Morrow.[1] I am very glad that you have taken up the matter just in the way you have with Dr. Morrow. I am also glad to have the copy of the letter to Dr. Shedd.

My wife is a pretty keen judge of human nature, and one of the things that led her to favor the election of Dr. Shedd was the fact, as she expressed it, that while he remained in Nashville only a few days, during this time he was able to master the real conditions both in the college and in Nashville.

Nothing could be more unfortunate for the colored people than for them to feel that a man was forced into the presidency of Fisk or into any other important position simply because he was colored without regard to his fitness. I have always said, when the question was asked me, that when the time comes when a colored man shows by actual achievement that he is entitled to the position, I believe the position of the presidency of Fisk will be conferred upon him, but nothing in the way of forcing will help the college or the race.

I think we ought to do everything in our power to discourage any agitation of the color question at Fisk, and I think if we find the party, or parties, who is responsible for originating this question or keeping it alive we ought to get rid of him.

I do not know how well you know Mr. J. C. Napier, of Nashville. I have known him for a number of years and have always found him a level-headed, conservative man. As you know, until lately he was Register of the Treasury, and is now at the head of a colored bank in Nashville. I notice that Professor Fairchild[2] is to resign the position of Treasurer, and I am wondering whether or not it might not be an advantage to consider placing Mr. Napier in Mr. Fairchild's place as treasurer. I am not sure he would accept the position at the salary Fisk is able to pay or that he could give the time necessary to do the work. I thought perhaps you would be thinking of this matter by the time we meet. Yours very truly,

Booker T. Washington

P.S. I refer especially to Mr. Napier, because I believe a level-headed, experienced man of his type would serve as a kind of balance-wheel on the Faculty at Fisk.

B. T. W.

TLpS Con. 497 BTW Papers DLC.

[1] Cornelius Wortendyke Morrow (1855–1923), a Congregationalist clergyman,

became pastor and professor of philosophy at Fisk University in 1902. He was acting president 1914–15 and dean and professor 1915–21.

2 James Thome Fairchild (1862–1947) served as treasurer of Fisk University and professor of Latin at Tabor, Oberlin, and Carleton colleges during a long academic career.

To Emmett Jay Scott

Tuskegee Institute, Alabama   June 4, 1914

Mr. Scott: In view of the rather strenuous year which the stenographers and other helpers in my office have experienced, I am anxious that you arrange a scheme by which each one can have a good vacation before the opening of school, and as far as possible I should like the expenses in connection with these vacations to be shared by the school.

Booker T. Washington

TLS Con. 644 BTW Papers DLC.

To Byrd Prillerman

[Tuskegee, Ala.] June 5, 1914

Dear Mr. Prillerman: I thank you so much for letting me know about the condition of my sister. I [am] sorry she does not get well faster. Will you be kind enough on receipt of this to consult with the doctor and find out if a trip away from home where she might enjoy complete rest for some days will be of help to her.[1] I shall consider the matter very carefully as to someone of us coming to see her. We will arrange this as best we can. Yours very truly,

Booker T. Washington

TLpS Con. 517 BTW Papers DLC.

1 BTW also asked his niece Clara whether a trip to Tuskegee for two or three weeks would help her mother. (BTW to Clara Johnston, June 13, 1914, Con. 506, BTW Papers, DLC.)

To William G. Willcox

[Tuskegee, Ala.] June 5, 1914

Dear Mr. Willcox: Your letter has been received. Mr. Clinton J. Calloway, the head of our Extension Department, has been instructed to secure options on the two tracts of land, in fact, he has already secured an option on the smaller tract and within the next few days I am quite sure will have an option on the larger tract. He already has a promise in writing from the party owning the larger tract that it will be held for a given period, but we are not going to rest with that but will be sure that we get a legal option.

After going over the matter with several of our officers here on the grounds, we have the feeling that it will be well to use Mr. Campbell and his bank in every way possible, especially keeping him and the bank in sympathy with the whole project. We do not, however, believe that it will be wise to put Mr. Campbell or any other Southern white man in just now as one of the incorporators.[1] That may be wise later on. We feel quite sure that nothing will be lost in the way of having Mr. Campbell's sympathy and cooperation by leaving him out.

I have the feeling quite strongly that the active direction and control of the land scheme ought to be in the hands of our Extension Department rather than in the hands of any special committee. The Extension Department is a regular department of the school that is likely to live from year to year, while a special committee is likely to be temporary in its life.

At the head of the Extension Department we have Mr. C. J. Calloway, a man of wide experience who is very conservative and careful. He knows the white people and black people of all conditions in the South, and besides is a successful farmer himself. We feel that the work would be a legitimate part of the Extension Department.

The Extension Department could use some of the members of the committee that has already reported to you in ways to help forward the success of the project.

As to the name, we would suggest: Tuskegee Small Farms Improvement Co., Macon County Small Farms Improvement Co., Tuskegee Farmers Improvement Co., Progressive Small Farms Co., Alabama Small Farms Land Co.

Mr. Logan within the next few days is going to get up an outline for an incorporation, and it will be submitted to you.

After all these details have been attended to and we are in possession of the property as far as we can get in possession of it for this year, it might be advisable to make such arrangements with the tenants as will enable us to have the property thoroughly surveyed and mapped out so as to be ready for sale in the fall. Yours very truly,

Booker T. Washington

By the next mail I am planning to send you a complete report from Mr. Calloway, the head of the Extension Department, covering what has been done about the two tracts.

TLpS Con. 989 BTW Papers DLC.

¹ Willcox authorized the option on the two tracts and suggested that BTW take the option in the name of Campbell's bank or in the names of BTW, Warren Logan, and Campbell as trustees. (Willcox to BTW, May 29, 1914, Con. 989, BTW Papers, DLC.)

To Warren Logan, Jr.

[Tuskegee, Ala.] June 5, 1914

Dear Warren: I have your letter of recent date:

I remember our conversation and have been thinking it over a good deal since I saw you.

Now, let me give you a little piece of my own mind; let me tell you rather frankly what I think about your suggestion though my opinion may not be wise or in accordance with your wishes. I really think you could get a better chance to study what you wish, right here at Tuskegee than anywhere else. There are few colored men anywhere in the country who have the chance to come into contact with real things in accounting or in any other business directions to the extent that our work here offers them. Under the general direction of Mr. Bebbington in the actual doing of things, that is in actual bookkeeping, you could get an experience here which I believe would be worth far more to you than any work you could get in New York City.

You must remember that in the large cities of the North everything is going in the direction of specialties, and a man simply becomes a very small clog [cog] in a very big machine.

I hope you will think of this, and let me hear from you. Yours very truly,

Booker T. Washington

TLpS Con. 508 BTW Papers DLC.

From Isaiah T. Montgomery

Mound Bayou, Miss., May [June] 5th., 1914[1]

My Dear Sir and Friend: I am familiar with the important circumstances and plans that are intended to be considered at a meeting between yourself and our friend Mr. Charles Banks within the next few days; And am sure also that he will fully present the far reaching and extreme importance that the result of our present crucial struggle will have upon the portentious future of our community locally, and upon our people generally throughout the contiguous states and the country at large: Nevertheless I feel it so absolutely essential to contribute everything possible to the success of his mission, that I am constrained to write you.

Realizing some time ago that the bank represented the organizing force and directing power of our settlement, we had Mr. Carter the Auditor from Tuskegee, make a thorough and comprehensive audit from the beginning of business down to December 31/13: Losses from bad debts (nearly 50% of this item was a large check sent to a white bank for collection and the Institution failed before reporting, it only paid 30%) expenditures for public benefit and other sources amounting to something over $4000.00 was charged off to the impairment of capital stock. A few weeks ago when the official representatives of Chas. F. Wermuth & Co., of N.O. public Auditors of National repute, were here in relation to the Oil Mill statement, we had them go over our Bank affairs thoroughly, with the view of adjusting same to meet the requirements of a state Banking law enacted [by] the legislature during the present year; they ruled that the stockholders must make up the above loss and restore the capital; Mr. Banks, understanding that this could not be accomplished at this juncture, voluntarily met this responsibility. Will state here that the Bank had paid dividends amounting to 70% of its capital up to 1912.

I am enclosing herewith copy of the Banks daily statement June 1/14; On the 2nd., and 3rd., inst., the state Bank officers were here and had our officers and directors present while they examined into the Banks' condition; At the close of the work the chief Mr. Anderson, laid down the following requirements: — viz., "Close up the Overdrafts, Pay off the collection account and reduce our holdings of Stocks and Bonds by $10.000.00." The collection account has been paid, the Overdraft has been reduced by 50% and will doubtless be eliminated within the next few days; Leaving the Bond matter, which must be arranged before the close of this month.

This requires the bringing in of $10.000.00 new money; The struggle to do this involves in an inexpressibly important sense, the maintaining of a slowly growing faith and race consciousness of the capacity to develop its own leadership and initiative force in meeting the complex requirements of advancing civilization: In this particular it underlies the whole future of our community, and will extend to every quarter that our history and influence reaches. Before us lies the possibility of conserving with an experience that has been educated and trained under many adverse conditions $22,500.00 of banking capital and between forty and fifty thousand Dollars of Deposits, to the intimate development of the community and the expansion of its business, commercial and social life; This capital and deposits are subject to almost limitless growth, as race faith and race consciousness develops. While our people do not yet know or understand the new banking laws of the state, they do feel and understand that such of their Banks as are able to meet the test, are capable of broadening their field of usefulness: Individually the Negroes control millions of dollars in this state; the Negro Banks are slowing [slowly?] gathering and vitalizing this immense force to the direction of race development and the widening of opportunities for useful endeavor among our young people; And any failure at Mound Bayou at this juncture would inflict an injury that several generations may not be able to overcome.

Our officers and directors have fully empowered Mr. Banks to speak for us as a whole; As a matter of fact he is personally willing to assume all possible responsibility, but I favor inducting our associates into active and vital responsibilities, in order that they may develop power and understanding for future emergencies, when they may not be favored with the present leadership.

Feeling that you will understand the grave matters presented more clearly than I have been able to present them, and that you will generously extend such counsel and assistance as may be within your power; I am   Sincerely yours,

Isaiah T. Montgomery

TLS   Con. 514   BTW Papers   DLC.

[1] The date should be June 5. Montgomery wrote Emmett J. Scott on June 5 enclosing this letter to BTW. Montgomery told Scott that he was anxious for BTW to receive the letter before he met with Charles Banks in Chicago about June 10. The context of the letter also establishes the month as June. (Montgomery to Scott, June 5, 1914, Con. 514, BTW Papers, DLC.)

To George Washington Carver

[Tuskegee, Ala.] June 6, 1914

Dear Mr. Carver: You have been connected with the school for practically 18 years. You have been kept on salary the entire year during all of those years. In the interest of economy, it becomes necessary, from year to year, for us to lay off certain teachers for certain months, and I do not see how you can complain about losing one month within a period of 18 years. I understand Mr. Lee is going to give you some work in connection with the Summer School.

Booker T. Washington

TLpS   Con. 653   BTW Papers   DLC.

To Ralph Waldo Tyler

Tuskegee Institute, Alabama, June 6, 1914

My dear Mr. Tyler: I have yours of June 3rd:

I note what you say regarding the "Bee" and our friends in Washington. Gradually, I find you are coming around to my own position, that public sentiment is not created in Washington because the public refuses to take the average Washington colored man seriously for the reason that he cannot be depended upon: this is known throughout the country. Few persons, if any, who have had experience in dealing with public men and public questions are ever surprised at any turn of affairs that Washington matters may take. It would be impossible for such persons to be creators of public sentiment that had any influence among the masses for the very reason that they are lacking in stability. We shall see, however, how the fight goes and how matters finally turn out.

I told Mr. Scott a few days ago to get from you your plan of work from now until the meeting of the Business League. We shall have to put in some pretty hard and vigorous licks in order to make the Muskogee meeting a great success. Yours very truly,

Booker T. Washington

TLpS Con. 525 BTW Papers DLC.

To Woodrow Wilson

[Tuskegee, Ala.] June 8, 1914

My dear Mr. President: Today I telegraphed you as follows:

For eleven years the Tuskegee Institute has had separate post office from the town of Tuskegee with postmaster appointed by the President. During all this time the business of the Institute office has steadily increased from year to year and most harmonious relations have existed between white people in town of Tuskegee and Tuskegee Institute. One of the objects for the separation was to prevent possible trouble by large numbers of colored students going into the Tuskegee town post office. I understand on good authority effort is now on foot engineered by a few parties who hope to profit financially and politically to have the separate office abolished and made a branch of the office in town. This would prove a great embarrassment and great hardship especially in view of fact that the present arrangements have been working successfully for eleven years. Besides for the peace and good order of the school community it is necessary that a postmaster be appointed who meets with our approval and who acts in accordance with the general policy and spirit of the institution. To make change would probably subject us to having a postmaster appointed who might not meet this qualification. I very much hope for these and other reasons you will give an order that no change be made or at least hold up matter until you can hear from me more fully regarding the matter.

I have little to add to the telegram except the information on memorandum which is attached.[1] You can easily understand how it would disrupt and throw a whole school community out of gear, after eleven years of experience in having our own post office, by having such a change made as I have indicated.

I would not have troubled you with the matter if I did not have very definite knowledge that certain parties for their own personal and political benefit are striving to bring about the change, and I feared it might be done without your knowledge or consent. Yours very truly,

Booker T. Washington

TLcSr   Con. 526   BTW Papers   DLC.

[1] The enclosed nine-point memorandum stressed that the volume of institute mail was so large that delays and inconveniences would result from having it delivered and sorted in town, and pointed out that the University of Alabama and the University of Mississippi had their own post offices. "There is absolutely no objection on the part of the citizens of Tuskegee to our having a separate Office," according to the memorandum. (Con. 526, BTW Papers, DLC.)

To Seth Low

[Tuskegee, Ala.] June 8, 1914

My dear Mr. Low: I am very sorry to trouble you about the following matter, but I find it necessary that action be taken at once. The enclosed copy of a communication to the President explains itself.

I feel very sure if you could see your way clear to take this matter up directly with President Wilson that nothing would be done to change the present status of the Institute Post Office. The danger is that action may be taken without his knowledge or authority.

We are on the most friendly and cordial terms with the white people of the town of Tuskegee and vicinity, and there is absolutely no sentiment in favor of this office being abolished except in the case of one or two individuals who want to have the change made for political and financial purposes. Yours very truly,

Booker T. Washington

P.S. The carrier system if instituted would mean absolutely nothing to us. We have heard it intimated that they are seeking to make this consolidation so as to secure carrier service. We could not have any carrier service that would send a carrier into any of our dormitories.

B. T. W.

I have also written to Mr. Peabody only in this matter.

B. T. W.

TLpS   Con. 70   BTW Papers   DLC.

To Warren Logan

[Tuskegee, Ala.] June 8th, 1914

Mr. Logan: I want to arrange a plan by which Mr. Booker T. Washington Junior will become Mr. Calloway's assistant in the Extension Department. For the present he is to be paid a salary of $65.00 per month. I shall have to work out the details of the fund out [of] which this salary is to be paid on my return, but at any rate, I want the salary provided for. He began work this morning.

[Booker T. Washington]

TLc   Con. 653   BTW Papers   DLC.

From George Washington Carver

[Tuskegee, Ala.] June 8, 1914

Mr. B. T. Washington: I beg to thank you for your very gracious and considerate note of recent date concerning my being lain off a portion of the summer. I trust you will permit me to bring my side of the case to your attention:

1. It is true I have been here nearly 18 years, and feel that I am entitled to more consideration than that of being placed with the ordinary run of people that you let go yearly.

2. I have been working for the same salary that I came here on; I have never asked for a cent more, neither have I received more, while I have seen several and some I have taught go way above that of myself.

3. I have only taken one vacation of the allotted 10 days since coming.

4. I have worked with the hope and feeling that, when my head begins to silver over as it is now, I would have a home. I am not clammering for the mere dollars, but this forces me to seek a place where I can have some assurance of being cared for when I reach the point where I am not so vigorous as I am now. I am sure you will not blame me for this. I promised Prof. Lee to teach in the summer school, and this I will do before looking further. Sincerely yours,

G. W. Carver

TLS   Con. 653   BTW Papers   DLC.

From Ernest Davidson Washington

Tuskegee Institute, Alabama   June 8, 1914

My dear father: In connection with the statement that you have asked me to hand you I wish to say that I received for my services last summer $42.00 per. Month.

It seems to me that since I was not in a position to do the regular routine work of the office owing to inability, and now that I am in a position to demand the recognition of all, the stenographers in the office that it would be certainly no more than just that I receive considerably more than this. Then too, Father you know I shall have more than one to take care [of] after September. I want to be in a position not to bother you any more so far as money is concerned. I am quite sure that I am in a position to make my own way now.

Davidson

TLS   Con. 642   BTW Papers   DLC.

From Woodrow Wilson

The White House, Washington   June 9, 1914

My dear Professor Washington: I have your telegram of June eighth and will take it up with the Postmaster General[1] at once. I had not heard of the suggestion of uniting the post offices again.

In haste   Sincerely yours,

Woodrow Wilson

TLS   Con. 72   BTW Papers   DLC.

[1] Albert Sidney Burleson (1863–1937).

From Hugh Ellwood Macbeth[1]

Los Angeles, Cal., June 9, 1914

My dear Dr. Washington; In obedience to your suggestion made on the eve of your recent departure from Los Angeles, I have been working on the matter of engaging the attention of the white daily newspapers to the worthwhile achievements and general happenings of the colored people of Los Angeles and vicinity. I decided, upon consultation with Mr. Tyler,[2] Mr. Owens and others, that the most useful paper to our race in this particular, is The Los Angeles Times. Accordingly, some ten days ago, by appointment, I took up the matter with the founder, editor and owner of The Los Angeles Times, Gen. Harrison Gray Otis.[3] He was kind enough to give me a most cordial reception and a very frank and open conference at his residence, "The Bivouac," this city.

We have practically agreed upon the proposition of having a regular weekly column in The Los Angeles Times devoted to the interest of the Negroes of this vicinity. We are now working out the details in this matter. I would suggest that you write to Gen. Otis at your earliest convenience, a cordial letter of appreciation and thanks for his kindly attitude to the race in this vicinity, and especially for his decision to dedicate a part of the space of his very valuable paper to the upbuilding of our people here. If you think well of this suggestion, you may address him as follows:

Gen. Harrison Gray Otis, Editor & Publisher Los Angeles Times, "The Bivouac," Park Avenue & Wilshire Blvd., Los Angeles, Cal.

Trusting that you are in continued good health, and that Tuskegee is sailing on to yet larger honors and greater usefulness, I am, Very respectfully,

Hugh E. Macbeth

P.S. Messrs Owens and Tyler join me in kindest personal regards.

H. E. M.

TLS Con. 514 BTW Papers DLC.

¹ Hugh Ellwood Macbeth (b. 1884), a graduate of Fisk University (1905) and Harvard (1908), was a lawyer in Los Angeles.

² Willis Oliver Tyler (b. 1880), a graduate of Indiana University (1902) and Harvard (1908), practiced law in Los Angeles with Hugh E. Macbeth, and was director of the R. C. Owens Investment Co.

³ Harrison Gray Otis (1837–1917), a brigadier general of volunteers in the Spanish-American War, was publisher and editor of the Los Angeles *Times* beginning in 1882.

George B. Ivey to William C. Lloyd

[Tuskegee, Ala.] 6/9th [1914]

The Western Union I understand on good authority has been guilty of holding up and Delaying Messages from the Negro School here for Political Purposes. These Educated Negroes have got to be treated with Business Respect, and Demand the Same Service given to White People. Booker T. Washington filed a Rush Message here with me yesterday June 8th addressed to President Wilson, 232 word message, message filed at 1150 am sent at 1158 am, followed with Request to Show Delivery, no attention was Paid to my 1st 2nd or 3rd Request to Show Delivery. Please Have the Washington office "Show Delivery on Same" as it is important and Probably will Save Suit, these Negros are Due what they Pay for, wires were all ok, yesterday, so there was no excuse for Delay on this message

Geo B Ivey
Mgr

908 am

AWS Copy Con. 517 BTW Papers DLC. Written on the telegram form of the Postal Telegraph-Cable Co., in which George B. Ivey was employed as manager of the Tuskegee Office. Addressed to "W. C. Lloyd, Supt." in Birmingham, Ala.

From Emmett Jay Scott

[Tuskegee, Ala.] June 10, 1914

Dear Mr. W: No developements whatever in the P.O. matter. No letter or telegram in reply has come from Washington. Mr. Hare has heard nothing new. Just before the Inspectors left yesterday they called Mr. J B Washington on the telephone & inquired as to whether he had any proposition to make, etc. He told them he had not: that he w'd simply have to await whatever action the Department might take. Apparently everything is quiet. I have had a report on the Washington telegram & find it was delivered in Washington at the WHITE HOUSE & receipted for one hour after it was filed here. Quick work! Will keep you advised. Yours Truly

Emmett J. Scott

ALS Con. 645 BTW Papers DLC.

James A. Cobb to Emmett Jay Scott

Washington, D.C. 6/10/14

Dear Emmett: The U.S. Atty[1] here informs me that the Atty General has been making inquiry about my appointment and wants to know if it was a political appointment. He told the Atty General that he didn't think it was and he also told him that my services were very necessary to the office. I showed Mr. Wilson your letters leading up to my appointment, none of which say anything about politics. Mr. Wilson thought or rather suggested that I have Dr. Washington write a letter to the Atty General saying that it was a non political appointment as well as urging my retention. If you think advisable I wish you would bring this at your earliest moment to the attention of the Doctor.

Mr. Wilson further says that the A.G. has *no* intention of appointing another colored lawyer in my place, he said he told the A.G. that there are only two colored men thruout the country holding such positions and he thought it would be very discouraging to eliminate us.

Hope you and yours are well. Sincerely,

Cobb

ALS   Con. 10   BTW Papers   DLC.

¹ Clarence Rich Wilson (1874–1923), a Republican, was U.S. attorney for the District of Columbia from Apr. 6, 1910, to Nov. 1, 1914.

Extracts from an Address at the Unveiling of the Harriet Tubman Memorial

Auburn, N.Y., June 12, 1914

In behalf of the race to which I belong, I wish to express my deep gratitude to the Auburn Business Men's Association, the Cayuga Co. Historical Society, and citizens of Auburn for their generosity and liberality in honoring the memory of one of the great members of the Negro race, by placing this beautiful and fitting tablet in one of your public buildings. It is most fitting and proper from every point of view that the name of Harriet Tubman should be perpetuated by means of this tablet so that her memory and deeds can live in the minds and hearts of the present generation, and can be held up as an object lesson for all time to the generations that follow. Harriet Tubman was a unique and great character of which any race and any age should be proud. Here in the city where she spent the larger part of her life, and here where her body rests, is the place of all places where this tribute of love and affection should be expressed. The citizens of Auburn had a chance to know her better than the citizens of any other community. Indeed, she was a prophet not without honor in her own home.

The people of Western New York have gone beyond the people of any other section of our country in honoring the great characters of our race. Not far from here in the beautiful city of Rochester stands a monument erected to the memory of the great leader of our race,

Frederick Douglass, and here in this city you are placing this memorial tablet to honor another great character of our race.

No section of our country is richer in great heroic souls who believed in liberty for all the people this [than] is true of Western New York. As I speak to you tonight, I cannot forget that here lived the great Secretary of State who stood by Abraham Lincoln — William H. Seward. In this section lived Susan B. Anthony. This region was the home for a long period of time of Frederick Douglass, and here, as I have said, was the home of Harriet Tubman. We need not limit, however, the names of the truly useful and great characters to those who have passed away. As I speak to you tonight, I cannot forget that near this same community lives in the person of Miss Emily Howland a woman who through her generosity and interest in all that concerns my race has endeared herself to this and future generations. Indeed these characters have blazed the way and have made the work of those who are left behind much easier than it otherwise would have been. You, then, should count yourselves rich in the possession of the memory of so many great souls who have done their part in bringing freedom and prosperity and union to our country.

. . . .

I will not attempt to dwell upon the details of the life of Harriet Tubman. These you know better than I. Hers was a simple life, a simple mind. Without thought of ambition or praise or glory, she devoted herself to doing her duty as she saw it. There is great power in simplicity. There is no limit to the good that one soul that is really in earnest can accomplish. In her simplicity, her modesty, her commonsense, her devotion to duty, she has left for us an example which those in the present generation of all races might strive to emulate.

In the ten millions of black people scattered throughout this country there are many great souls, heroic souls, that the white race does not know about. Harriet Tubman brought the two races nearer together and made it possible for the white race to know the black race, to place a different estimate upon it. In too many sections of our country the white man knows the criminal Negro, but he knows little about the law-abiding Negro; he knows much of the worst types of our race, he does not know enough of the best types of our race.

. . . .

Was the heroic work of Harriet Tubman worth while? Let me in a few words try to answer this question.

First of all, the Negro for fifty years has survived, from a physical point of view, in a state of freedom, a thing that many said he could not do. Beginning life in this country a few centuries ago with 20 members of our race who were sold into slavery, we increased in slavery until at the end of that period we numbered four millions. We have lived by the side of the white man, a thing that many dark skinned races have failed to do, and have increased in numbers until at the present time we number over ten millions. This means a population that is larger than the entire population of the Dominion of Canada, and means a population of people that is as large as five of the smaller European countries with two millions more.

We have not only survived, but from a material point of view we have supported ourselves. We have not become beggars. We have asked no appropriation from Congress to provide food, clothing or shelter for our race, and it is very seldom that in any part of America a black hand is reached out from a corner of a street asking for personal charity. We have done more, however, than to support ourselves. We have accumulated land and houses; we own and operate business enterprises. The Negro in this country today is the owner of at least twenty million acres of land, a territory that is as large as the State of South Carolina. We have built and paid for over 600,000 houses. We are buying land, especially in the country districts of the South, at a very rapid rate. With no business experience at the beginning of our freedom, we now own and operate about ten thousand grocery stores, drygoods stores, shoe stores. We own and operate nearly 400 drug stores. We own and operate over 60 banks. Progress in these directions will indicate that the work of Harriet Tubman was not in vain.

· · · ·

There were not a few who at the beginning of our freedom predicted that the Negro would not take advantage of the educational opportunities furnished by our country, but we have proven the contrary to be true. Wherever a school house has been opened, the Negro has filled that school house. Unlike many other races in the same relative stage of civilization, education does not have to be forced on the Negro; he seeks education, and is willing to make any sacrifice in order that his children may get education.

When Freedom came to our [race] through the work of Harriet Tubman and others, only three per cent of the American Negroes could read or write; to-day by the official records, it is shown that 69 per cent of the American Negroes can both read and write. This indicates a progress in education which, in the words of the Hon. Henry Watterson, of Louisville, Ky., an ex-slaveholder, is greater than any other race in history has ever made.

· · · ·

It is not true, as some believe and assert, that in proportion as the Negro gets education that he stands still or goes backward from a moral or religious point of view. The fact that today we have about 35,000 churches and Sunday schools, that we have over 30,000 ministers, will indicate that we are going forward morally and religiously as well as in other directions.

Those great anti-Slavery heroes not only wrought the freedom of the Negro race, but they did more, they freed the white race, and to-day through their efforts instead of having one race free we have two races in the South that are free, and we have two sections of our great country that are no longer engaged in strife but in mutual cooperation and to bring about all that is best and noblest in the life of the nation. There never was a period in the history of the country when, all things considered, there were so many evidences of racial friendship and cooperation as exist in the South today. I say this in spite of my knowledge of the fact that there is much wrong, much injustice still perpetrated upon the Negro, but in spite of this we are going forward and we are gaining new and better friends each day. The outlook is not hopeless, but most encouraging.

· · · ·

All, however, is not done. There are many battles still to be fought, many problems still to be solved, and there is a call for heroic work such as Harriet Tubman performed still to be accomplished. There remains a duty for each of us. We must not despair, because Harriet Tubman did not when great serious, perplexing problems confront us, whether these problems are local or nation-wide. We must thank God for problems, and remember always that in proportion as problems come to us for solution that if we face them manfully and heroically that we are made stronger and better by reason of performing our duty. As Harriet Tubman did her duty, may each in his own way find the path of duty and follow it, no matter where it leads.

From this humble and comparatively ignorant black woman we can all, white and black, glean a lesson which will strengthen us broaden us and make us of more service to our community, to our race, and to our nation.

TMc Con. 957 BTW Papers DLC.

Emmett Jay Scott to James A. Cobb

[Tuskegee, Ala.] June 13, 1914

Dear Cobb: Your letter of June 10th is received this morning and is having my attention. I am very sorry to have been out of touch with you during the past three or four months, but I know how irksome correspondence is, and therefore do not seek to annoy you with my correspondence.

The letters which you mention as having shown to Mr. Wilson, on their face, indicate that your appointment was not a political one.

Dr. Washington has had no correspondence with the Attorney General's Office since the change of administration, and we are not on any footing that would permit us to approach the Attorney General in this particular matter unless he should open the way for us to do so. Probably, Mr. Wilson can, in serving you, have the way opened whereby the Doctor may address the Attorney General or some of the powers.

It is unnecessary for me to say how much I regret the possibility of your being "eliminated" from the service. I feel quite sure, in your usual dexterous way, you will succeed in averting this calamity — a calamity, so far as the service to your country is concerned, and what is equally important, a calamity to the purse of James A. Cobb, Assistant United States Attorney for the District of Columbia, Washington, D.C. Sincerely yours,

Emmett

TLpS Con. 10 BTW Papers DLC.

Charles Banks to Emmett Jay Scott

Mound Bayou, Miss. 6/13 1914

My dear Mr. Scott: I am just back from Chicago. Mr R.[1] let us have five thousand, while it is not as much as I wanted, but can & will make it serve the purpose. The Dr stood up for us strongly. I have already written Mr Tulane about the note matter & will keep after it & the Birmingham item until the embarrassment to you is passed. Gradually, but surely the clouds are passing. Just at this time the five thousand was a great relief & enables us to square fully with the new Banking act. Yours truly

Chas Banks

ALS   Con. 9   BTW Papers   DLC.

[1] Julius Rosenwald.

A Press Release

Chicago, Ill., June 15 [1914]

Last week Dr. Booker T. Washington, of the Tuskegee Normal and Industrial Institute, visited Chicago for the purpose of reporting to Mr. Julius Rosenwald, the Chicago philanthropist, regarding the use that has been made of certain monies appropriated by Mr. Rosenwald a short while ago for the purpose of building schoolhouses in some of the rural districts of the South. In each case the people of the community were asked to do as much as they could toward the building of the schoolhouse by making cash contributions, or contributions in materials, or labor. The report made by Dr. Washington was so satisfactory that Mr. Rosenwald has decided to go ahead with the experiment on a large scale, and has agreed to duplicate dollar for dollar whatever sum is raised in any rural district in the South for schoolhouse buildings.

The experiment which Dr. Washington has been carrying out has been kept very quiet for the reason that Mr. Rosenwald was anxious to test out the experiment before making any public announcement regarding it.

One of the crying needs in the South is good schoolhouses in the country districts where a majority of our people live. Until this need is met the masses of our people will in a large measure remain in ignorance.

The securing of these schoolhouses through the generosity of Mr. Rosenwald marks a long step forward in the advancement of our race. Any number of communities in the South will, it is expected, within a few months meet the conditions demanded by this gift. Every time a schoolhouse is built in one of these country communities it will bring new hope and confidence to our people.

TDp Con. 512 BTW Papers DLC. Sent by E. J. Scott to twelve black newspapers.

To Mamie A. Harrison[1]

Rochester, N.Y. June 16, 1914

My dear Madam: Replying further to yours of June 6th, I would state that I am going to take up very carefully the matter of the Confederate monument about which you wrote me, and see if I can find some one to give the money that is still needed. I am very much interested in the matter, and thank you for writing me. During the summer months people with money are very much away from home and it is hard to reach them, so it may be I may not be able to do anything about it until fall.

I want to say again how very much we all appreciated the visit of General Harrison to Tuskegee. We all realize more and more that men like him are the true friends of our race, and that any monument that will keep the fine character of such heroes before the public will prove helpful to both races in the South. Yours very truly,

[Booker T. Washington]

TLc Con. 505 BTW Papers DLC.

[1] Mamie A. Harrison wrote from Opelika, Ala., on the stationery of her relative George Paul Harrison, general counsel of the Western Railway of Alabama. She asked for BTW's help in paying the $300 deficit on Opelika's Confederate monument, erected three years earlier. She suggested that BTW solicit donations from Andrew Carnegie and Thomas Fortune Ryan. (Harrison to BTW, June 6, 1914, Con. 505, BTW Papers, DLC.)

From Charles Banks

Mound Bayou, Miss., June 16, 1914

Dear Dr. Washington: You will see from the above heading that I am back at Mound Bayou.

I am taking this opportunity to thank you most sincerely for your efforts in Chicago the other day in having Mr. Rosenwald come to our relief here. It was not only a great turn to me, but to [the] entire community and incidentally the race. It is not my method of course to attempt to put into words just how I feel over the matter, but I hope to always prove to you by deeds that I am in every way worthy of the splendid support and consideration you have given me, not only in this instance, but from time to time. After all that is said and done by those who aspire to impress the world that their activities and ideas are best and most far reaching in the uplift of the race, yet to my mind, the time that I have been able to observe, and I think I have had some advantages to see and know, there are none in the race who in any way measures up to your usefulness and effectiveness in all the things that affect us as a people upon the American continent. Very truly yours,

Chas Banks

TLS Con. 68 BTW Papers DLC.

James A. Cobb to Emmett Jay Scott

Washington, D.C. June 16, 1914

My dear Mr. Scott: I am duly in receipt of your letter of the 13th instant, in which you traveled out of your way to be facetious at my expense. No, it will not be a calamity to the Gov. if my services are eliminated, tho it may be to my pocket book. However, I fancy that I shall sleep and eat with the same relish. As to letters, I think if you look over your files you will find that I had written to you last. I have reluctantly begun to think that you and the Doctor appreciate lip loyalty more than you appreciate real genuine service. Chase was in to see me the other day and said that he saw the Doctor when he came through and that he intimated that I along with some others based my friendship for him solely for what he could do for me rather than what he is and what he is doing for the race. I am sorry that you both feel that way — all that I can say, is that, yours and the Doctor's association with me has been to little purpose. No individual on earth who knows me other than you two would honestly make such an observation. As for the letter to the President or Atty General — you know best what to do from your standpoint. I thank you just the same [for] what I believe to be your good intentions notwithstanding, you went out of your way to give a mean and unwarranted thrust. Sincerely,

Cobb

ALS Con. 10 BTW Papers DLC.

To James B. Washington

Rochester, N.Y. June 18, 1914

Dear Brother: We are trying to get the post office matter held up and hope we will succeed. This matter, however, ought to teach you a lesson, and that is the importance of trying to save some of your money and invest it in a home. If your salary is reduced or you are thrown out of the office, I fear you would find yourself in a desperate condition. There is no reason in the world why with your large salary you might not buy a home and save something every month. Your brother,

[Booker T. Washington]

TLc Con. 654 BTW Papers DLC.

To Emmett Jay Scott

Rochester, N.Y. June 18, 1914

Dear Mr. Scott: I note what Mr. Cobb says in his letter, and your reply.[1] I think you treated the matter right.

With the present light before me, I cannot manifest much interest in his case for the reason that I do not think he has stood up straight. I confess that I have been a good deal disappointed in him, although I may not have good ground for my feeling. Yours very truly,

B. T. W.

TLI   Con. 645   BTW Papers   DLC.

[1] James A. Cobb to E. J. Scott, June 10, 1914, and Scott's reply of June 13, 1914, above.

From Emmett Jay Scott

Tuskegee Institute, Alabama   June 18, 1914

Dear Mr. Washington: I sent you, this week, a copy of my letter to Cobb. The enclosed letter[1] from him illustrates, in some degree, the attitude of our Washington friends. When we are able to respond to their requests without reservation we are alright; when we are not able to do so then we are *all wrong*. You will see by Cobb's letter that Chase has repeated to him your statement regarding our Washington friends.

Mr. Logan, Mr. Gibson, Mr. Taylor and I are planning to leave here Monday evening, reaching New York, Wednesday morning. Hope you will approve this:

Emmett J. Scott

TLS   Con. 645   BTW Papers   DLC.

[1] Cobb to Scott, June 16, 1914, above.

Emmett Jay Scott to James A. Cobb

[Tuskegee, Ala.] June 18, 1914

Dear Cobb: I have your letter of June 16th. I confess it gave me no pleasure to read it. I have reviewed a copy of the letter which I sent you under date of June 13th, and, for the life of me, I cannot understand why my letter should have so angered you.

67

It is never safe, I find out more and more each day, to attempt to be "funny." It is true that I sought to be "facetious" in writing you, but it was not at all with the intention of going "out of my way" to wound you, or, in any way to stir up your feelings. When you speak of my making a "mean and unwarranted thrust" I confess again, I cannot, for the life of me, understand what you are referring to. Unfortunately, I presumed upon our friendship, to refer to your leaving the Service, but I suppose these things look worse in writing than they do when spoken. I am sure that I have heard you say, hundreds of times worse things to Dancey, Terrell and Tyler, and none of them, apparently, seemed to feel that you were going "out of your way," or making "mean and unwarranted thrusts."

To be perfectly frank about the matter, Old Man, it rather seems to me that you were spoiling for some kind of a fight, and embraced the first opportunity to shoot your little gun this way. I do not know what Mr. Chase has said to you, but I do know that I have not, to anyone, whatsoever, expressed any opinions that in the slightest way challenged your friendship for, and loyalty to the interests represented by us here at Tuskegee.

Of course, you understand, as well as I do, that we have not sent any letters to the White House, or to the Attorney General's Office, in behalf of any positions since the change of administration. Reasons for this are so obvious that I am surprised that you should take umbrage.

I have written you at this length to disabuse your mind of the feeling you have that somebody was seeking to be facetious at your expense, and to assure you that I shall be very careful in the future in the matter of attempting to be "funny" in writing, even with my best friends. If you are not too super-heated, and should decide to write again, I can be reached in New York City, care St. Denis Hotel, Wednesday, June 24th. I leave here Monday Evening. Yours truly,

(Signed) Emmett J. Scott

TLcSr Con. 10 BTW Papers DLC.

To Booker Taliaferro Washington, Jr.

The Biltmore, New York, June 25, 1914

My dear Booker: I have not heard from you for several days. I hope that everything is going well. I am especially anxious that you make a fine reputation for yourself this summer with Mr. Calloway. He is going to have a lot of important things to do this fall, and I want you to have a part in them. I will explain to you about them when I see you, which will be early in July.

Be very careful to report to your work on time, or before time, every morning and in the afternoon. Do not get in the habit of being late. Better be ahead of time than behind time; that is the way to make a good reputation.

I am very anxious to see you all. Please remember me to Nettie and all the members of the family. Your papa,

[Booker T. Washington]

TLc   Con. 642   BTW Papers   DLC.

To Margaret James Murray Washington

[New York City] June 25, 1914

Am planning to be home July twelfth to remain ten days. Am very well. Suppose you saw in papers that Mrs. Morris K. Jesup left the school a bequest of fifty thousand dollars.

Booker T. Washington

TWcSr   Con. 655   BTW Papers   DLC.

To Clinton Joseph Calloway

New York City, June 27th, 1914

Dear Mr. Calloway: I think as a matter of precaution, you should not make too much of a stir in connection with the purchase of those lands until we have actually the deeds in hand. As soon as the property has been turned over to us no time should be lost in having it surveyed and plotted so that we can put it on the market as soon as possible. We went over with Mr. Willcox of having about 50 acres around the railroad station reserved to be sold if necessary in lots. He approved of that policy.

As soon as we are in possession of the property, I think it well for you to see Mr. Wickersham with a view of having the railroad station removed to a more central point.

Of course there is great danger, as soon as the parties learn how the land is to be used, of their trying to back out of the trade. We want to guard that point in every way possible. Mr. Logan has authority to pay the money over as soon as it is safe to do so.

I think it important that you secure deeds to both pieces of property at the same time. We would be caught in a very awkward position if we were to secure the deeds to one piece of property and then for some reason the other parties were to back out of the trade. One part of the land would be of little or no value to us without the other part. It is very easy to get those people excited and to be made to think that a gold mine has been discovered on their property, and for that reason they may begin to haggle for a larger price or to back out of the sale.

Without reaching any definite decision at present, suppose you go ahead and find out what an automobile to hold four people will cost.

Let me know how much it will cost to set up a saw mill on the Connor tract. That is, what outlay we will have to make for a new engine or new saw mill or what we will have to buy. Can we use the new mill at the school? Yours very truly,

[Booker T. Washington]

TLc   Con. 68   BTW Papers   DLC.

To George Edmund Haynes[1]

New York City, June 27th, 1914

My dear Mr. Haynes: From time to time I get hold of information that indicates that a rather unfortunate state of feeling is being permitted to grow up around Fisk by some of the colored people both at the University and in the city. It is to the effect that the colored people should take charge of Fisk University and have a larger hand in governing it than in the past; in a word, the idea seems to be to displace white people.

Now you and I both know that this kind of agitation is most harmful and unwise. Whenever a colored man appears who has the ability to be placed in an important position at Fisk he should be recognized, but nothing would be more unfortunate for us than to place a colored man in any position simply because he is colored.

I am sure that the white people who during all these years have given of their money and of their time, and have suffered much in the way of ostracism, have done so for the sole purpose of helping, and there is no set of people anywhere in the world more inclined to recognize colored people when the time comes when it can be done in a safe, helpful way. The very worst thing that we could do is to indicate that we do not appreciate what has been done and is being done for us.

I very much hope that you and others, both at the University and in the city, will use your influence to get rid of any agitation that may crop out from time to time in the direction [of] agitating the color question at Fisk. It has been almost the one institution in the South that has escaped such agitation, and it would be a calamity at this late date for the policies and reputation of Fisk University to be injured by an agitation that is undignified and out of keeping with the history and character of Fisk University.

I am sure I can depend upon you to do your best in favor of keeping Fisk on the dignified plane that it has always maintained. Yours very truly,

[Booker T. Washington]

TLc   Con. 504   BTW Papers   DLC.

[1] George Edmund Haynes (1880–1960) combined careers of teaching sociology and directing the National Urban League. Born in Pine Bluff, Ark., he graduated from Fisk in 1903 and was the first black to receive a doctorate from Columbia University, in 1912. He published in the same year his sociological study, *The Negro at Work in New York City*. Meanwhile he gained experience as a traveling secretary for the Colored Men's Department of the YMCA from 1905 to 1908, and from 1908 to 1910 he was a fellow in the Bureau of Social Research at the New York School of Philanthropy. In 1910 he became executive secretary of the National Committee on Urban Conditions among Negroes, and when it became the National Urban League he was its chief officer from 1911 to 1916. He established the first department of sociology in a black college, at Fisk in 1910, and stressed preparation for careers in social work among the black migrants to north-

ern cities. In 1917 he became the Urban League's educational secretary, while Eugene Kinckle Jones took over the executive secretaryship. After that, Haynes drifted away from active leadership of the league, but by then he had infused into it his own social ethos and his commitment to interracial cooperation.

From 1918 to 1921 Haynes took leave to serve as director of Negro Economics in the U.S. Department of Labor. He also served for twenty-five years as secretary of the Commission on Church and Race Relations of the Federal Council of the Churches of Christ. For the last nine years of his life, Haynes taught at the College of the City of New York. (Weiss, *National Urban League,* 30–34, 40–43, 63, 65.)

To Thomas Mott Osborne

New York City. June 27th, 1914

My dear Mr. Osborne: I have been so busy that this is the first opportunity I have had to let you know how very much I enjoyed the privilege of speaking to the men in the Auburn prison. I have said to many people since I was there, that I have never addressed an audience anywhere in the country that showed keener appreciation of what I said than was true of the men in the prison.

It must be a matter of great satisfaction to you to be connected with such an institution, and especially to have the opportunity of showing these men that you have a heart as well as a head and that you are determined to do whatever can be done in the direction of making them happier and more determined to live useful, upright lives.

I very much hope at some time we can see you at Tuskegee. Yours very truly,

[Booker T. Washington]

TLc Con. 841 BTW Papers DLC.

To Alexander Robert Stewart

New York City. June 27th, 1914

Dear Mr. Stewart: I did not have time until yesterday to examine with any degree of care the plans for Booker's house. There are several serious defects. In the first place, the whole house is spoiled by reason of the fact that one enters the sitting room directly from the street. This would mean that in the winter the wind and cold would go right through the whole house and it would be impossible to keep the sitting room warm. The little hall is dark instead of having any light in it.

Altogether there are 42 windows and doors in the house. It would require the time of some one to look after these windows and doors. There are so many windows that there is no place left in the bed room, for example, to put furniture. In the room in the hotel where I am staying here, there is only one window.

Some of the rooms, especially the dining room, are entirely too large. In a house of that character they would present the appearance of a barn instead of a comfortable dwelling house. The dining room is as large as my dining room. A dining room of this size with only two people in it would be anything but appropriate.

Fortunately Mr. Taylor is here, and I am taking up the whole plan with him and asking him to make a sketch which I think will be pretty safe for you to go by.

In the meantime, I want just as little time lost in erecting the house as possible. If you can do so, I wish you would go ahead on the grading and have all the rough material put on the ground. Also get a large number of workmen who will be ready to begin work just as soon as the plans are decided upon. I want the house constructed very quickly.

On the whole, my experience in building in the South is that we had better stick pretty closely to the Southern models. These complicated, cut-up houses sometimes built in the North do not answer the purposes of the South. A plain, simple, dignified house is far more satisfactory in the long run. Yours very truly,

[Booker T. Washington]

TLc Con. 644 BTW Papers DLC.

To Wright W. Campbell

New York City, June 28th, 1914

My dear Sir: I want to let you know how very grateful all of us feel to you and Mr. Wright[1] for the way in which you have taken up the post office matter with members of congress. I feel rather sure that the whole movement has been checked largely through your efforts.

I would not object to any change if there was any justification for it, but, as you know, there is none. I will tell you more about the results when I see you.

One of the greatest satisfactions of my life grows out of the fact that we are able to show to the world that it is possible for white people and colored people to live together in the same community in peace and in harmony, each race helping the other.

Enclosed I return to you the letters from the Congressmen.

You will be glad to know that we had a fine trustee meeting. We had a good attendance, and every one seemed greatly pleased with the results of the year's work. All were sorry, however, that you could not be present. Yours very truly,

[Booker T. Washington]

TLc Con. 72 BTW Papers DLC.

[1] BTW sent a similar letter to J. C. Wright, a Tuskegee cottonseed-oil manufacturer, on the same date. (Con. 72, BTW Papers, DLC.)

To Ernest Davidson Washington

[Chicago] June 30, 1914

Think it wisest for you to remain at Tuskegee until I reach home. You can go to New York soon after. Experience and actual work at Tuskegee will do you good.

Papa

TWSr Con. 642 BTW Papers DLC.

An Account of a Speech before
the International Sunday School Convention

Chicago   June 30, 1914

CHANCE FOR
NEGRO, PLEA
OF LEADER

"Bring Old Theology,"
Booker Washing-
ton's Appeal to
Churchmen

AUDIENCE IS THRILLED

Ringing Words of Man Who
Rose from Slavery Stirs
the Sunday School
Workers

"Brother Washington," as they called him, was the whirlwind of the last night session but one of the great Sunday school convention.

The man from Tuskegee took the platform at Medinah Temple at 9:30 o'clock last night and for more than half an hour he was everybody's master — this man who came up from slavery.

He strode before them like a tawny lion. He neither cringed nor palavered.

He hit hard sometimes, hammering home his facts with a vehemence that made a fact take on the color and splendor of the ordinary platform gladiator's brightest purple passage.

There was every token of a tremendous personality — conviction, candor, vigor, sincerity, and the tactful infusion of just enough humor to keep the hammering from getting on people's nerves.

When the Red Sea Froze

Sometimes he told them a quaint story of the old-time southern darky type — told it with the golden accent and the ingratiating drawl, as when he quoted the colored preacher whose explanation that the melting of the ice on the Red Sea had engulfed Pharoah's army, while

75

the children of Israel had passed safely over on solid ice before sun-up, was challenged by the colored schoolboy, who said:

"But, preacher, my geography tells me that within a certain distance of the equator no ice ever forms, and the Red Sea is within that distance."

"Thar 'tis! Thar 'tis!" cried the exhorter. "Thar 'tis! I knew when I was givin' that 'splanation some of you young folks 'ud come along to spile the old theology! But the time I was speakin' of was before there was any jographies — or any equator either."

PLEADS FOR HIS PEOPLE

Before the shout of laughter died away Booker Taliaferro Washington had grown very grave. The man who had so cleverly imitated the old preacher of the cabins and the revival vanished and the prophet of his race stood before that assemblage of white men and women.

"I don't want to spoil the old theology," he thundered in tones of which the passers in the streets could catch every inflection. "That's the theology that I want you to take to my people on the plantations of the South; my people who are close to the soil and who will be better off for staying there if you will take them the Sunday school and all that the Sunday school means. The old theology! Take them that! The old theology, that says thou shalt not kill, thou shalt not steal, thou shalt not commit adultery, thou shalt not bear false witness. That's the old theology I mean."

AUDIENCE IS THRILLED

He launched his utterance of the commandments in a hoarse shout, swiftly, passionately, coming down with a crash on the words "kill" and "steal." The veins in his neck stood out like whipcords. From the roots of his close-cropped, crinkly hair to his massive chin, his deeply lined face was streaming with perspiration. He made Sinai mean something. Falling from his lips that hoarse crying of the commandments made them sound urgent and terrible.

The people whom a few seconds before he had had shaking with laughter at his imitation of the darkey preacher, were looking up at him in awe now.

An instant later he was an old colored woman, bent and quavering, and standing before a judge who was about to pass sentence of death on her boy, whom whisky and drugs had driven to the murder of a white man.

And that old woman was saying over and over again:

"Jedge, jedge, jedge! — my boy — he ain't never had no chance, my boy ain't, jedge — no chance at all, jedge. Jes' remember, jedge, no chance at all in this world! I'd like, jedge, for you to remember that — no chance in this world!"

"Just Want a Chance"

The voice trailed off into a mumble and a sobbing.

The great hall was so still you could hear the footfalls of the people in the streets outside.

That was only a few seconds.

For in a flash the mumbling old woman was gone and the tawny leonine man was commanding the platform again, his hands outstretched, his voice beating upon the ears of the white men and women with the words:

"His chance! His chance! That's what the negro is groping for. He knows he's down and he wants to get up. He knows he's in the dark and he wants the light."

The delegates broke into a storm of applause.

That was the dramatic side of "Brother Washington." It was revealed in brief, infrequent flashes — the more telling because they were so brief. He did not give them the ornate periods of the fluent, clever, imitative colored man who has an inborn gift of gab. It was more a smashing style, and such decorative effect as it produced had its source in the massing and the projection of the matter more than in any studious elaboration.

That lion comparison is a pretty good one — not grandiloquent, as such comparisons usually are.

His voice was leonine. The blazing eyes set in the ochre face were leonine. So was the restless stride of him. So were the words in which he roared his defiance of patronage and "sympathy."

Thankful He's a Negro

"I want no man's sympathy," he said, "because I am a negro. I thank God every day that I belong to the race to which I do belong. I wouldn't change places tonight with the whitest man in America.

"Aye, I thank God that I belong to a race that has been with you a long time on these shores and that means to stay with you, a race that had a man on the spot when the Pacific Ocean was discovered, a race that had a man in the march when the Rockies were crossed, a race that had men with Lewis and Clark when they blazed the trail into Oregon and Washington, a race that had men at Bunker Hill.

"And when the civil war came that race had men on both sides — for the negro never wants to hurt anybody's feelings by being partial."

There was laughter when Booker T. Washington said that — and he laughed, too.

That was the way he would suddenly come down from a linguistic high-flyer and get on intimate terms with his audience again.

He wound up his intentionally mock heroic flourish thus:

"And a white man said 'this is the north pole,' and he turned around, and there was a big black man right behind him.

"We are here and we are going to stay. I suppose we both are going to stay — at any rate I haven't seen any signs of our going anywhere else. We are here to stay — ten million of us negroes, enough to populate five of the smaller kingdoms of Europe and then have some left.

"We are here with our problems. The race to which I belong, and to which I am proud to belong, has got such problems as the white race hasn't got. The white man hasn't got problems enough for me. He hasn't got troubles enough to make excitement enough for me.

"And remember that it is not always unfortunate for a race to have large and complex problems pressing upon it. Such problems turn races into kingdoms and nations.

"When we negroes were in Africa we had no problems — or if we did we didn't know it. And we did not develop a civilization there.

PROBLEMS FOR BOTH OPEN

"But remember, our problems are yours. It is not for my race alone that I want to see the negro rise, but for the white race in the South, too; for unless the race that has been down rises, then it pulls to its level the race that is up. We want our chance to know right from wrong, our chance to develop. The negro is learning and he is developing.

"The trouble with some of our white friends is that they read more and think more about the criminal negro than they do about the law-abiding, God-fearing negro. It's like the time I was a younger man and spoke in a Kentucky town one night. Next morning I looked eagerly in the newspaper in the hope of finding myself considerable of a fellow — perhaps on the first page. But I wasn't there, nor on page 2 nor page 3, but buried in a paragraph at the bottom of page 4.

"It had chanced the night before that a negro had snatched a pocketbook on the street corner. He got page 1 in the morning."

Chicago *Herald*, June 30, 1914, 1, 4. The account was written by James O'Donnell Bennett. It was reprinted in the *Tuskegee Student*, 26 (July 18, 1914), 1, 4.

To Seth Low

Boston, Mass. July 1st, 1914

My dear Mr. Low: I am very sorry to report the most disastrous fire in the history of the school. On night before last the barn containing mules burned, and in some unaccountable way the fire was not discovered by the watchman. The worst part of the fire is the fact that 34 mules were burned and 4 others were so injured that I fear they will have to be killed. Thirty-eight pairs of harness were also burned. Leaving out the value of the building, which will not be very large owing to the character of it, the total loss I estimate at something over $9,000. The building I think will be very largely covered by insurance. I will know definitely very soon how much we shall get back for the building.

I am having a very searching investigation made as to how the fire occurred and why it was not discovered by the watchman. I will report to you the result later. All the buildings and grounds are covered by watchmen with a system of watchman's clocks, and it is inconceivable to me how the fire got such a start and did so much damage without being discovered.

We are right in the midst of our farming. It is most important that something be done to replace these animals. I therefore, have telegraphed Mr. Logan, who has not yet left New York, to get in touch with you at once. I suggest that the local executive Committee at Tuskegee be given authority to deal with the situation temporarily.

As soon as I return to Tuskegee, which will be within a few days, I shall report the matter to you fully, but I have all the essential facts.

I am not reporting this matter to any of the other trustees, thinking you might care to do so yourself if you think it wise.

I can be reached by telegram or letter at any of the following places:

July 3d. Houlton, Me. Snell House.
July 5th. Rockland, Me. Thorndike Hotel.
July 6th. Castine, Me. Arcadian Hotel.
July 7th. Dexter, Me. Care Mrs. J. W. Sawyer.
July 8th. Rumford, Me. Care Mrs. E. W. Howe.
July 9th. Poland Springs, Me. Poland Springs House.

From Poland Springs I shall go direct to Tuskegee. Yours very truly,

[Booker T. Washington]

TLc   Con. 70   BTW Papers   DLC.

To Booker Taliaferro Washington, Jr.

Presque Isle, Maine. July 2, 1914

My dear Booker: Both your mamma and Mr. Scott have told that they have heard you speak to audiences in the country since I left, and each one said that you spoke extremely well.

I am very glad to hear this as it is all very encouraging and makes me feel very proud of you.

Please remember me to Nettie and to all the members of the family.

Your papa.
[Booker T. Washington]

TLc   Con. 642   BTW Papers   DLC.

From Frederick E. Edmunds

Buffalo, N.Y. Jully 4, —14

Dear sir: We are trying to start an industrial association among our-selves as Pullman Porters, because the time has come for us to do something to better the condition of this particular employment for colored men, some who are students of various institutions.

Dr. Washington there are a thousand or more young men who are graduates from some school, or undergraduates who have given up their professions and trades, on account of financial discouragement and ill treatment of those who knew not the burden of their hearts.

We are persecuted on every side, and have been indulging in the illusion of hope for a long time, but the condition grows to our disadvantage every day which gives us cares and burdens too hard to bear.

The boys have a number of petty organizations, but they don't amount to very much in building up for us a reputation as men of efficiency. We mean to have an organization of this kind in every district or Pullman head quarters and then consolidated, working as subdivisions of one great body.

The Pullman Company is our great combat in every feature of this kind.

They are afraid that we will have a union among ourselves to fight them, and discharge every man who starts any helpful movement.

We don't mean to have an organization of that nature, but rather, an organization to create business and positions among ourselves, which will lessen the percentage of humiliation and brutality on the part of our boys. Two or three good men and my-self got together and suggested this proposition, if carried through, to be one of the direct met[h]ods in the solution to the great problem which confronts seven thousand men today.

Dr. Washington, I shall be very thankful if you can help me in some way, if no other than to endorse my movement. If I can get hold of money enough to be independent of the company this movement will be a success. I can't trust my fellow porters, because some one has betrayed me already. Let me hear from you promptly, and I shall give reference as to my standing in next letter. This movement is the burden of my heart and when I think of its necessity my soul cleaveth to the dust.

The longing of my soul is for the strong men of both races to help me with this industrial work.

This is my prayer in faith. Respectfully,

F. E. Edmunds

ALS Con. 501 BTW Papers DLC. Enclosed was a leaflet by Rev. F. E. Edmunds proposing the Industrial Association of Pullman Porters.

To Virginia Mitchell Wheat[1]

Rockland, Me. July 5th, 1914

Dear Mrs. Wheat: My son, Davidson, will be there some day this week to begin his lessons again. I am very anxious that he give especial attention to longhand writing, and shorthand and typewriting, especially the longhand writing.

I shall be careful not to disturb him again until I hear from you in writing that he has finished the work and is ready for his diploma. Yours very truly,

[Booker T. Washington]

TLc Con. 527 BTW Papers DLC.

[1] Virginia Mitchell Wheat (b. 1866), formerly a public school teacher and free-lance writer, founded the New York School of Secretaries in 1912.

From Nannie Helen Burroughs

Washington, D.C. July 8, 1914

Personal

Dear Dr. Washington: For sometime I have intended calling your attention to the fact that I think a number of our men and women, take advantage of the opportunity given them to tell in a simple straightforward way, before the Business League, how they have made their business "go," to exploit their wealth. For sometime I have been suspicious of a great many of the statements made on this particular point, and I think a number of men come to the League with their stock considerably watered.

You know as well as I do, that it is impossible to become tremendously rich by honest methods, in such a short time. There are a great many statements made that cannot be taken on their face value.

There are two effects — first upon members of the race. They live in the community — they know the men and women — and they know what they are saying would be nearer the truth, if taken at half value. They get it into their minds that all of the men and women, who appear before the League to report progress, are over stating the case. Second — the white people who do not analyze the facts, but take them at their face value, simply say if there is so much wealth in the Negro race, these people ought to contribute largely to race enterprises, and relieve the white people of the burden they are now carrying.

I think you know how I stand on this question of self-help. I have tried to make my doctrine practical and have certainly collected and invested more from Negroes, for their own uplift, than any woman of the race. And I do not know that many men have gotten quite as much and have invested it for a definite purpose.

I am not trying to conceal facts in order to get funds, but I would like to believe all I read in the "reports on progress." You have the situation in hand and can make these men tell how they do things, without over stating the returns financially. White men do not get on the platform and exploit their wealth and I think it is bad taste for anybody to do it. A little more modesty would be becoming, even in a business man.

I would like very much to attend the meeting of the League in Oklahoma, but at this time I do not see my way clear to do so. I am so tied up with engagements and work, that I must forego the pleasure of attending several very important meetings during the Summer.

Trusting that this will be the best session of the League, I am   Yours very truly,

Nannie H. Burroughs

TLS Con. 852 BTW Papers DLC.

To Frederick E. Edmunds

[Tuskegee, Ala.] July 8, 1914

My dear Sir: I have your letter of some days ago and make careful note of what you have written regarding the proposed organization of Pullman Car Porters.

I have always believed that our people should organize where such organization is intended to improve their general condition and living conditions generally. There are a great many organizations of a secret character among our people which bring them closer in touch with one another and greatly aid in strengthening them materially, morally and otherwise. It has occurred to me that such an organization among the Pullman porters, while it need not be secret in character, would greatly help in maintaining a higher standard of efficiency, not only as employees but as men.

I am glad that you have written me and hope that the future may see the organization perfected in the way that you have outlined. Yours very truly,

Booker T. Washington

TLpSr Con. 501 BTW Papers DLC. Signed in E. J. Scott's hand.

From Charles Banks

Mound Bayou, Miss. July 9, 1914

Dear Dr. Washington: In keeping with your suggestion of sometime ago for the Negroes throughout the country to take up the matter of better accommodations by the railroads for our people, I am writing to advise, that this was pretty generally done throughout Mississippi.

At Jackson, Miss., a committee headed by Mr. P. W. Howard[1] of that city, took the matter up with the officials, were courteously received and promised full consideration on the matters set forth to them. In this connection however, I am glad to state that in the matter of accommodations for our people on the Yazoo & Mississippi Valley Railroad which is owned and operated by the Illinois Central and on which Mound Bayou is located, we feel inclined to commend, rather than condemn their attitude towards us as a race in the matter of accommodation and general service. The writer has on more than one occasion, taken up matters with them along this line, and in each case they have manifested their willingness to grant any and every request that was in any degree practicable. I have ridden on most of the roads in the south as well as the northeast and west, and it is my deliberate opinion that the accommodations for the Negroes on the line of the Yazoo & Mississippi Valley between Memphis and Vicksburg is equal to that of the whites so far as day coaches are concerned, and as good as can be found anywhere. I regret however, that I cannot make such a statement for the rest of the lines operating in Mississippi, and I am trusting with you, that the concerted action in having our people call upon the representatives of the railroads, and soliciting their favorable consideration of our claims for better accommodation will have the desired results.

I am not sure that it is good judgement for me to embrace in this letter another matter that has given me some little concern, but I will do so anyway. There is a great tendency on the part of some of our people to institute suits against railroads for every little imaginary thing to say nothing of real causes. In a large measure the desire does not originate with them to pursue such a course, but they serve as the instrument. In my opinion we could hardly expect the highest and most favorable consideration from those whom we desire to reach when it is understood that we perniciously and indiscriminately harass the companies with law suits without merit or foundation, and I am hoping that we can in some way discourage those parties. Very truly yours,

Chas. Banks

TLS   Con. 68   BTW Papers   DLC.

¹ Perry Wilbon Howard (1877–1961) was a lawyer from 1905 to 1921 in Jackson, Miss., where he was active in Republican politics. He was special assistant to the U.S. Attorney General from 1921 to 1929, and subsequently practiced law in Washington, D.C., in partnership with James A. Cobb.

To the Editor of the Boston *Transcript*

Tuskegee Institute, Alabama   July 11, 1914

Editor, Transcript, Boston, Mass. According to the record kept by Monroe N. Work, in charge of the Research and Statistics Division of the Tuskegee Institute, there have been during the first six months of the present year 20 lynchings.

This is 4 less than for the same period a year ago, and 16 less than for the first six months of the year 1912.

Of the number lynched since January 1st, one was a white man and all the rest were colored; 2 were colored women, and only 2 of the entire number lynched were charged with rape, or attempted rape. Yours truly,

Booker T. Washington

TLSr   James Thomas Williams Manuscripts   NcD.   Signed in E. J. Scott's hand.

To George B. Ward[1]

[Tuskegee, Ala.] July 13th, 1914

Personal and Confidential

My dear Sir: I understand through the public press that the question of passing a law segregating the colored and white people so far as their residences are concerned in Birmingham is to be considered at an early meeting of the Board.

While I am not a citizen of Birmingham, I am deeply interested in anything that concerns the peace and welfare of the two races in our state.

I think you will agree with me in saying that there is no state in the Union where a greater degree of harmony and friendship has existed in the last few years than in Alabama. This condition has been maintained very largely through the influence of a number of sensible, conservative colored people working in cooperation with the best white people. I am very anxious that nothing be done anywhere to disturb present relations between the races, and I very much fear that the passing of the law segregating the two races in Birmingham will stir up racial strife and bring about bitterness to an extent that will result in discouraging a number of the best colored people in the state.

Of course I do not know just in detail what the local conditions in Birmingham are, but I do know that taking the two races generally in the South that one seldom buys property in a section of a community or city where he is not wanted. The general custom has settled the matter it seems to me, and custom in this case I sometimes think is stronger than a law. I believe if it were made known to a half dozen of the leading colored men in Birmingham that certain things were desired in reference to the purchase of property in the future that the same results could be obtained as by passing a law which I very much fear will be misunderstood throughout the country and, I repeat, stir up racial strife.[2] Yours very truly,

Booker T. Washington

TLpS Con. 527 BTW Papers DLC.

[1] George B. Ward was mayor and president of the Birmingham, Ala., board of city commissioners.

² Ward replied on July 16, 1914, thanking BTW for his arguments and reporting that, after a conference with black leaders, the ordinance was "now in abeyance pending investigation of its working in other cities." (Con. 525, BTW Papers, DLC.)

To Nannie Helen Burroughs

[Tuskegee, Ala.] July 13, 1914

Dear Miss Burroughs: I think you are entirely right in your position with reference to the over-statement in the matter of their wealth being made by delegates before the Business League. We take particular pains to try to hold down these statements so that nothing in the way of over-statement may appear.

I am sending you, under separate cover, today, a copy of the Minutes of the Chicago session. You will notice how the Executive Committee, in a particular case, personally investigated and otherwise sought to put before our delegates an exact statement as to what the situation is.

I very much wish you could be at Oklahoma, so as to say, personally, to the delegates just exactly what you have so splendidly said in your letter to me. Yours very truly,

Booker T. Washington

TLpS Con. 852 BTW Papers DLC.

Emmett Jay Scott to Lyman Beecher Stowe[1]

[Tuskegee, Ala.] July 13th, 1914

Dear Mr. Stowe: I have been up to my ears disposing of accumulated correspondence since my return to the Institute. This must be my apology for failure to write you more promptly in the matter we discussed.

I do not feel that I would be willing to go into the proposition of getting out the book we discussed along the lines proposed by you when I saw you Friday, July 3rd. I have had in mind for several years that I ought to write this particular book myself and acting upon Mr. Page's suggestion, thought we might collaborate, but I do not want to relinquish wholly all claims to authorship in connection with the book. I would not be content to simply get out for you the material to be used. I say this with keenest appreciation of your own point of view.

I still hope that we may have the opportunity of welcoming you here at Tuskegee at some time in the near future. I am sure you will enjoy a visit to this school.

With all good wishes, I am   Yours very truly,

Emmett J. Scott

TLpS   Con. 522   BTW Papers   DLC.

¹ Lyman Beecher Stowe (1880–1963), a grandson of Harriet Beecher Stowe, was the author of non-fiction books and an editor with several publishing firms. From 1913 to 1915 he was secretary of the National Association of Junior Republics. He and E. J. Scott co-authored *Booker T. Washington: Builder of a Civilization* (1916).

To James Hardy Dillard

[Tuskegee, Ala.] July 14th, 1914

My dear Dr. Dillard — I have received both your letters of June 30th and July 6th. I realize fully your perplexity and disappointment regarding the Jeanes Fund money. Very confidentially I want to say that I think we ought to do something in the direction of making a change in the handling of our funds. I do not believe that we are doing justice by letting things remain as they are. In the first place I am sure arrangements can be made by which the teachers can be paid promptly, and in the second place I think the money can be so invested as to yield a larger return. Such a large fund demands the constant care and watching of some competent person.

Now regarding the matter of helping to get some funds to tide over until we get out of the present awkward position, I would state that I think it would be a great mistake to bother Mr. Rosenwald just now in this direction. He is doing a great many things for colored people and I fear may grow discouraged and think we are trying to saddle the whole race upon him. Especially do I fear it would be a mistake to take this matter up with him until we have gotten some definite plan worked out for the erection of small school houses. I fear putting so much before him may tend to confuse and discourage him. Just as soon as I have gotten a rough plan blocked out for the erection of school houses I want to have a consultation with you.

There is a gentleman in New York by the name of Mr. Edward S. Harkness,[1] 26 Broadway, who I think could be interested to give some money for the rural school fund. Soon after Miss Jeanes gave this money he learned about it and something of the methods we were employing, and seemed deeply interested. He is quite wealthy and generous. I think it might be well for you to send him one of your reports and perhaps write him a letter. I am sorry I am not on sufficient intimate terms with him as to permit me to give a letter of introduction. He is quite close, however, to the people at the Teachers College, and I think some of them might put you in direct touch with him.

I am turning the whole matter over in my mind. If I can think of any other source from which money might be gotten, I will be glad to write you.

I think it well for you to keep in constant touch with Dr. Buttrick and Dr. Flexner, especially in view of the fact that they have been relieved from spending so much money for farm demonstration work in the South.

I have actually read the enclosures which you have sent me. They contain a lot of valuable information. I am very glad to see the report which you have sent the Phelps-Stokes people. Yours very truly,

Booker T. Washington

TLpS Con. 68 BTW Papers DLC.

[1] Edward Stephen Harkness (1874–1940) was the son of one of the original partners of John D. Rockefeller in the Standard Oil Co.

To Harrison Gray Otis

[Tuskegee, Ala.] July 14th, 1914

My dear Sir: While in Los Angeles last March I had consultation with a number of leading colored citizens including such individuals as R. C. Owens, Willie Tyler and Hugh E. Macbeth, and suggested that they should make a special effort to engage the attention of the white daily newspapers to the worth while achievements of the colored people in Los Angeles and vicinity.

I am pleased to learn that the idea when placed before you received your favorable consideration. The colored people of Los Angeles are most grateful to you for the kindly attitude which you and your newspaper have always maintained toward the colored people of that section. I very much hope that this idea may still further be carried out. Yours very truly,

Booker T. Washington

TLpS   Con. 514   BTW Papers   DLC.

To Joseph Oswalt Thompson

[Tuskegee, Ala.] July 14, 1914

My dear Mr. Thompson: I think it will please you to know that both the Alabama senators[1] took a strong position on the post office matter and were not afraid to come out and say so in the frankest manner. They really wrote very fine letters which I should like to show you when I see you.

All this of course is confidential. Yours very truly,

Booker T. Washington

TLpS   Con. 658   BTW Papers   DLC.

[1] John Hollis Bankhead and Francis Shelley White.

To Lyman Beecher Stowe

[Tuskegee, Ala.] July 14, 1914

Dear Mr. Stowe: I am writing you regarding a personal and rather delicate matter. Mr. Scott has been placed in somewhat of an awkward position. When he first saw you, he felt so sure that you and he could undertake the writing in the way he first suggested that he made [no]

effort in Boston where he went soon after seeing you, or elsewhere, to get some one there. When he returned to New York and found you had changed your mind, it was too late for him to get any one else. That is one phase of the matter.

Another is this. It will be absolutely impossible for any stranger without Mr. Scott's direct, constant and personal help to do the writing. He knows about matters in a way no other person does or can know.

Having you and Mr. Scott collaborate is not unusual. The best autobiography, in my opinion, ever written was written by Nicolay and Hay,[1] although I am very far from putting myself in the class of persons treated by them. I really believe if you could see your way clear to carry out the first plan that you would be well satisfied with it. You would find Mr. Scott a man of high character, of great ability and intelligence. Your name and his name in my opinion would attract attention in a way that would more than offset any disadvantages in other directions. I very much hope that you will consent to carry out the original plan. Yours very truly,

Booker T. Washington

TLpS   Con. 522   BTW Papers   DLC.

[1] John George Nicolay (1832–1901) and John Milton Hay (1838–1905) collaborated on a biography of Abraham Lincoln (1890) and an edition of *The Complete Works of Abraham Lincoln*.

From William Emory Mitchell[1]

Chicago, Ill. July 14th, 1914

My dear Mr. Washington: I have been connected with the above named organization for the past year, and recently I have interested my self in the progress it is making.

Not very long ago the Board of Directors was discussing the Aswell[2] Segregation [bill] which came up in Congress not long ago, and some of the members seemingly did not understand you[r] position in reference to Segregation. I immediately answered the gentlemen on this subject, by stating that you were against any kind of Segregation, whether in the Postal Service or in Public places, and that you have always fought it in your own quiet way.

I would like very much to have you give me an expression along this line Dr. Washington because as you know we are having a hard fight with the present Congress, on Segregation, and too it would help me wonderfully in impressing upon the minds of the membership of the Phalanx Club which numbers two hundred and fifty, that my statement made some time ago in reference to your position in the matter was correct.

I also wish to state that this information is not to be given out publicly, but is to be used in stimulating interest in our organization and have the membership clearly understand that you are with us in this fight.

I am a member of the '03 class and am striving as best I can to live up to the class' mot[t]o "Bend to the oar though the tide be against you." Respectfully yours,

William E. Mitchell

ALS Con. 509 BTW Papers DLC. On stationery of The Phalanx Club, Organization of Postal Clerks and Carriers.

¹ William Emory Mitchell of Charleston, S.C., graduated from Tuskegee Institute in 1903. In 1911 he was president of the Chicago Tuskegee Club.

² Congressman James Benjamin Aswell of Louisiana was one of the leaders in the movement to segregate the federal government.

To Joseph Oswalt Thompson

[Tuskegee, Ala.] July 15, 1914

Personal

Dear Mr. Thompson: I am in receipt of communications from prominent colored people in the Northern states, asking whether or not it is true that the Progressive party in Alabama has decided to refuse to admit colored people into the councils of that party.

I would not trouble you with the matter except that these communications are from important and influential colored people who have thrown their energy and influence in the direction of promoting the success of the Progressive party. They find themselves, by reason of the news which has been sent out from Birmingham, rather embarrassed not knowing just what to do and how to act. They say that they hardly feel they can support a party in the North which refuses to recognize in any respect the Negro in the South.

I have told these people that I would get what information I could from proper sources in order to set them right as to the policy of the Progressive party in Alabama. I shall be very glad if I might receive a communication from you or anybody else which these people could use in the North and West. Yours very truly,

Booker T. Washington

TLpS Con. 525 BTW Papers DLC.

To Charles Banks

[Tuskegee, Ala.] July 16, 1914

Dear Mr. Banks: I am very glad to make note of what you write regarding the observation of "Railroad Day" in Mississippi: I am sure that splendid results are going to follow throughout the country as an outcome of what has been done by our important men in the various centers. I am particularly well pleased to make note of what you have written regarding the effort of Mr. P. W. Howard and others of Jackson, Mississippi.

I have always heard splendid reports of the accommodations given our people on the Yazoo and Mississippi Valley Railroad.

The other matter to which you call attention is one which all of us should very carefully watch. It will not do to have the railroad authorities get the idea that we are disposed to harass them with suits for damages in connection with every little difficulty which may arise. I shall see what I can do toward discouraging such suits whenever opportunity offers.

Thanking you for taking the trouble to write me so fully as to results in your state, I am: Yours very truly,

Booker T. Washington

TLpS Con. 68 BTW Papers DLC.

To A. G. Plummer

[Tuskegee, Ala.] July 16th, 1914

My dear Sir: Your letter of June 20th is called to my attention on my return to Tuskegee, and I am very much interested in the thorough-going way in which you write with reference to travel conditions for our people in the South.[1] The information you have secured is almost invaluable from a standpoint of a man of the race.

As you state this law is not going to be abolished, and the best we can hope to do is to have conditions changed so that travel accommodations may be at least more nearly equal and more comfortable than at present.

Just now, I know of nothing additional that can be done to carry on the campaign, but I wish that something might be developed of a constructive nature.

I am taking the liberty of sending your letter to Doctor Robert E. Jones, editor of The Southwestern Christian Advocate, of New Orleans, with the request that he read your letter at least for the information contained therein. Yours very truly,

Booker T. Washington

TLpSr   Con. 519   BTW Papers   DLC.

[1] Plummer, a black War Department clerk on his first trip to the South, wrote from Galveston, Tex., of his bitter resentment of the Jim Crow car, but he agreed with BTW that, at least for the present generation, segregation on the railroads was an established feature. The only way to alleviate conditions for black travelers, he concluded, was to press for equal accommodations. He offered to help BTW in any efforts for the betterment of conditions. (Plummer to BTW, June 20, 1914, Con. 519, BTW Papers, DLC.)

From Monroe Nathan Work

[Tuskegee, Ala.] July 16, 1914

Mr. Washington: A careful study of the facts seems to indicate that Prof. E. C. Branson of Athens, Georgia, is not correct when he states that "At present the drift of the Negro population in the South is country-ward." I don't think we should hereafter use this part of his statement concerning Negro progress because of its incorrectness and its tendency to mislead and obscure the facts.

While it is true that in the decade, 1900–1910, the Negro population increased 10 per cent and, the number of Negro farmers 20 per cent; it is not true that the increase in the percentage of Negroes in the rural districts was greater than the increase in the percentage of Negroes in the cities; in fact, the reverse is true.

In 1890, 84.7 per cent of the Negroes in the South were living in rural districts. In 1910, 78.8 per cent or, almost 6 per cent less than 20 years before. From 1890–1900 the percentage of increase in the number of Negroes in the South was: for urban districts, 32.0 per cent; for rural districts, 14.5 per cent. From 1900–1910 the increase was: for urban districts, 35.8; for rural districts, 5.1 per cent. That is to say, the percentage of increase for Negroes in the cities of the South is 7 times as great as the percentage of increase for the rural districts.

We continue to have the problem of checking the movement of Negroes to the cities. In the accompanying sheet, the number and percentage of Negroes in urban and rural districts, for the whole country and for the South is shown in detail. Very truly yours,

M. N. Work

TLS   Con. 653   BTW Papers   DLC.

From Monroe Nathan Work

[Tuskegee, Ala.] July 17, 1914

Mr. Washington: I give you the following to illustrate further what I said in my letter yesterday concerning the fact that there is no special movement of Negroes from the city to the country nor, any apparent checking of the movement of the Negroes to the city. Mr. Branson has not distinguished between the Negroes operating farms and Negro farm population. What he is talking about is the increase in the number of Negroes operating farms which, in almost every state in the South, was greater in per cent than that of the whites.

While it is true that the number of Negroes operating farms and the number of Negroes owning farms increased at a greater percentage than the whites during the decade, 1900–1910; on the other hand the percentage of increase of the whites in the rural districts of the South was greater than the percentage of increase for Negroes in the rural districts. There was a marked decrease, 4 per cent, in the increase of Negro farm population during this same decade.

There are at present about 7,000,000 Negroes in the rural districts of the South. 900,000 of these, or, one in every eight, is operating a farm; 220,000, or, one out of every thirty-two owns a farm. It is those from the 7 not operating farms and the 31 not owning farms who are drifting to the cities. Mr. Hughes, one of the summer teachers from Tennessee, informs me that there is a decided effort in that state to sell Negroes property, both city and farm. This is an attempt by the white people to check the movement of Negroes from the rural districts to the cities and to the North. This, it seems to me, helps to explain why, although the Negro population in Tennessee is decreasing, the number of Negroes owning property is increasing.

It seems to me, it would be worth while to re-emphasize, at the Business League meeting, the importance of the Negroes of the South attaching themselves to the soil. Very truly yours,

M. N. Work

TLS   Con. 653   BTW Papers   DLC.

Lyman Beecher Stowe to Emmett Jay Scott

New York   July 17th, 1914

My dear Mr. Scott, In reply to your letter of July 13th I would say that when I made that proposal to you on July 3rd I did not realize that you had planned yourself to write a book about Dr. Washington, but I had the impression that you were merely seeking some one to undertake such a book with your assistance. Had I realized that such was your intention, I should not have made the suggestion at all. As it is, I should be very glad to collaborate with you in the authorship of such a book if you still wish to have me do so, and if satisfactory arrangements with Houghton Mifflin or some other desirable publishers can be made.

I am going out of town next week for a few weeks vacation, but I can be reached at any time through this office. Cordially yours,

[Lyman Beecher Stowe]

TLc Copy Con. 522 BTW Papers DLC. Enclosed in L. B. Stowe to BTW, July 17, 1914.

From Harrison Gray Otis

Los Angeles, Cal. July 18, 1914

Dear Sir: I have your letter of July 14th.

Several weeks ago a representative of your people (I believe it was a lawyer named Macbeth) came to me in reference to the subject of your letter, to-wit, attention in The Times to the "worth-while achievements" of colored people in Los Angeles and vicinity.

I encouraged the desire and suggestion put forth at the time, though with some misgivings, candidly expressed to my interviewer. I explained very carefully the class of news and facts which I am willing to print in The Times relating to the doings of colored people, and also the class of matter which we will not print.

The practical difficulty will come when the "copy" is sent in. The persons concerned may submit many things that will deserve and receive the blighting blow of the blue pencil, and then there will be grief, and complaints of Gen. Otis and The Times, coupled with a good deal of general and loose shouting among the colored people, and probably direct appeals to you.

I don't want to encounter anything of this sort, and will do nothing under coercion or attempted coercion.

I am willing to print news and facts, not essays, "preachments" or controversies, nor mere "unconsidered trifles."

Nothing has been submitted so far. If the proper course is pursued by chosen representatives of the colored people here, whoever they may be, and my advice and injunctions are respected by them, good results will follow — not otherwise.

I have deemed it expedient and necessary to write plainly on the subject, as I have here done, on the principle that "good understandings make long friendships."

I am in doubt about the good will — the reliable good will — of your people. I, and The Times likewise, have frequently been grossly assailed, ignorantly and bitterly assailed, by colored people because of imaginary grievances on their part — and they have no other sort of grievances against me, a lifelong champion of liberty, law and the freedom of both races. Yours truly,

Harrison Gray Otis

P.S. I will try the experiment because I promised to do so, but I will not be treated with suspicion, indignity or distrust by anybody, white or black, who may seek to "break into" the columns of the Los Angeles Times. You are at liberty to make any use of this letter that, in your best judgment, may be expedient.

I particularly object to people with grievances resorting to the cheap expedient of making hurried tracks for "the shop across the way." I never permit myself to be influenced by menacing tactics of that sort.

TLS Con. 514 BTW Papers DLC.

To Frederick Randolph Moore

[Tuskegee, Ala.] July 20, 1914

Dear Mr. Moore: I think at some time if you will examine the news and editorial columns of The Age you will agree with me that it is possible for The Age to be of greater service to the people by emphasizing both in the news and editorial columns the things which relate to the success and progress of our race along constructive directions rather than dwelling so much upon mere complaint and "getting back" at the white people. I do not believe it pays to give very much attention to all the little discriminations that are heaped upon our people. The calling attention to all these discriminations does more harm than good, one constructive effort in the way of progress does more to blot out discrimination than all the whinings in the world. Your article on Boley will do more good than calling attention many times to the fact that colored people have been refused a sandwich at some time. Yours very truly,

Booker T. Washington

TLpS Con. 71 BTW Papers DLC.

To William Emory Mitchell

[Tuskegee, Ala.] July 21, 1914

My dear Mr. Mitchell: Your letter of recent date received. I am pleased to know that you are endeavoring to promote the interest of the Phalanx Club organization of postal clerks and carriers. I am also interested to know that your club is taking up the subject of segregation in Government Service. This is an important subject and is of vital concern to the whole race.

The discussions of the proposed segregation measure before the Aswell committee indicates that back of the question of the segregation of the races in public service is the still more fundamental one of whether the Negro is to be entirely eliminated from government work.

Although it does not appear that there is any probability in the near future of any of the National segregation bills being enacted into law, nevertheless organizations such as yours should be alert on such matters and should endeavor to do what they can to create sentiment against such proposals and to prevent such measures from becoming law. Very truly yours,

Booker T. Washington

TLpS Con. 509 BTW Papers DLC.

To Emmet O'Neal

Tuskegee Institute, Alabama July 22, 1914

My dear Sir: I cannot find words with which to sufficiently thank you for your thoughtful kindness in sending to this institution such an excellent committee to inspect our work. The committee composed of the following gentlemen:

Mr. Thomas Oliver, Montgomery,
Mr. W. W. Garth, Huntsville,
Mr. W. L. Casy, Ozark,
Mr. W. C. Thomas, Lafayette,
Mr. C. P. Demming, Evergreen,
Mr. Williams, of Dale County[1]

spent the whole day here. They were joined by the following citizens from Macon County:

Mr. W. C. Hurt,
Mr. C. W. Hare,
Mr. J. C. Ford,
Mr. George C. Wright

and others. They went into every feature of our work and spoke acceptably to the student body and others. My only fear is that we worked them too hard while they were here. I have never met a finer set of gentlemen anywhere than this committee was composed of. Of course, I do not know what the nature of their report will be but I will be perfectly satisfied to abide by it.

Regarding the distribution of the money coming to the State of Alabama through the Smith-Lever bill; I am anxious to have it demonstrated to the world that the distribution of such a sum of money is left to our Southern white people and that they will do justice to the Negro without such appropriations having to be restricted at the original source by Congress or any other organization out of the state.

Regardless of the interest and claims of the Tuskegee Institute, I am most anxious that the colored people in the state shall, in some way, receive proper recognition at the hands of the white people. I am quite sure anything that the committee or yourself may decide upon will be most acceptable to the colored people of the state. Yours very truly,

Booker T. Washington

TLS   Governors' Correspondence File   A–Ar.

1 Williams was not a member of the committee. Washington also omitted the name of the chairman of the committee, Reuben F. Kolb, Commissioner of Agriculture, and misspelled the names of W. F. Garth, W. L. Casey, and C. P. Deming.

Report of a Special State Commission on
Agricultural Education at Tuskegee Institute

[Tuskegee, Ala., July 27, 1914][1]

His Excellency Governor Emmet O'Neal, Governor of Alabama: We, the committee appointed by your Excellency to visit The Tuskegee

Institute for purposes of inquiring into and reporting to your Excellency upon the conditions of that school, beg leave to make this report.

In discharge of our commission together we visited the school on Wednesday, July 22nd, and spent the day there inspecting its plant and studying the methods and conditions under which it is operated. Our mission was to report specifically upon the features that referred to the claims of this institution to participate in the appropriation to be administered by the State of Alabama under the provisions of the Smith-Lever Bill. We therefore directed our main attention to the facilities of the institution in services of its agricultural branches. In this line we find it has an efficient and full equipment. Its Department of Agriculture is presided over by eighteen instructors who teach 350 students in this science. In other equipment the institution has a farm of 1,000 acres including pasturage and truck garden of 50 acres, an orchard of 150 acres, a large and well equipped creamery and laboratories for technical instruction. The farm is well stocked with various kinds of live stock and poultry. A short course in agriculture, continuing for two weeks in January of each year is maintained, and we were informed that in the last few years this course has been attended by more than 1,500 people annually. This department has given special attention to improving the grade of farm animals and this is manifest through its large and splendid herd of live stock. The Experiment Station, largely maintained by the State and established in 1896, serves the farmers of that section in various ways. Experiments are conducted at the Stations for the discovery of varieties of plants best adapted to the soil and climatic condition of the section in which the school is located. The results are sent out to the farmers in bulletins issued at intervals through the columns of the local papers. We had evidence that the director of this Station is constantly busy in solving the problems of the individual farmer in his search for instruction upon phases of agricultural economy.

The Extension Department appealed as a feature of interest and study to our committee. This Department is devoted exclusively to the work of bringing all phases of the work of the Institute into active touch with the lives of the colored people in their homes, schools, churches and on their farms. Most of this work is conducted through the Extension Department of the Institute. This Department of the school appeals strongly to all interested in the development of scientific farming practically demonstrated. Through it the negro farmers of

Alabama, and many from other southern states are gathering together each year in conference for the discussion of progressive measures for farm improvement. We were told that as many as 2,000 people annually gathered at this Institute to avail themselves of instruction through the Extension Department. We had evidence of its practical result in the development of school farms and gardens connected with the public schools in that section, and in this way many of the schools for negroes have their farms and gardens through which their pupils receive practical instruction in farming. Boys Corn Clubs, Girls Canning Clubs, Farm Improvement Clubs, Pig Clubs and similar organizations form a part of the regular work of the Department. We were told that during the past few years it has given special attention to the schools and school buildings of Macon County.

The Department of Women's Industries does a considerable part of its work through the Extension Department, doing regular demonstration work in cooking and housekeeping, together with instruction in matters of health, care of children and social life. Through the various agencies mentioned in our report, The Tuskegee Institute has developed its organization for reaching the masses of negroes and materially helping them in their development.

We have been specific in detailing certain features of the course included in the agricultural work of the Institute, to emphasize the claim that, in our mind, this institution possesses all of the consideration that the State in justice and fairness can bestow. There are 100,000 negro wage hands working on the farms in the State of Alabama. Negroes operate 42% of the farm lands of the State. There are 93,000 negro tenant farmers in the State who cultivate a total of 3,600,000 acres. There are 17,000 negro farmers in the State who own and operate a total of 1,500,000 acres. These are statistics which are properly recalled in mentioning any policy of the State towards this class of its citizens, and we feel that where such agencies exist which have a demonstrated power of service, that the Tuskegee Institute has shown, that such agencies appeal as a thing of regardful concern to the administrative and legislative power of the State. We therefore are of the opinion that it is incumbent upon the State in the administration of the appropriation of money that will come, or may come into its control under the provision of the Smith-Lever Bill, to allow a fair proportion of this sum to go in maintenance of its two best known and best equipped schools for negroes. Specifically, we would recommend to your Excellency an allowance of 30% of this fund for these purposes to be divided equally between The Tuskegee Institute and the Agricultural and Mechanical College for Negroes at Normal. We believe that less than this amount would not properly requite the efforts being made at these institutions in the direction of ends that the Smith-Lever Bill mentioned is meant to serve.

While our commission limited us to special lines of investigation and study of the Tuskegee Institute, we deem it not improper to express our gratification at the splendid monument it represents to the Negro race and to commend its founder and principal for the benefaction to his people expressed in his work at Tuskegee. Our service performed on this occasion at the request of your Excellency, was made enjoyable through courtesies and privileges extended by Dr. Washington and members of his faculty which besides aiding us in accomplishing our mission, favored us with opportunities of appraising the magnitude of the plant which constitutes this splendid Negro institution. Respectfully submitted,

R. F. Kolb
Commissioner
Thos W. Oliver
Wm. C. Thomas
W. L. Casey
C. P. Deming
W. F. Garth

TMSr Copy Con. 936 BTW Papers DLC. Signed by R. F. Kolb, who also signed for the other members of the committee.

¹ Commissioner R. F. Kolb forwarded a copy of the report to BTW on July 28, 1914, stating that it had been submitted to the governor on July 27. The report appeared in the Montgomery *Advertiser*, July 28, 1914, 3.

From Richard Carroll

Anderson S.C. July 28th 1914

Dear Dr. Washington: For the second time in South Carolina, I faced a mob today at Iva S.C. Eighteen miles, South of Anderson in a cotton mill town. I am going to write the story out later for the newspaper. Some body had announced "The Booker T. Washington" would speak at the Saluda Association. This Association has forty churches in it. The largest Association in South Carolina.

I arrived on the train at seven oclock with other white delegates. They begin to phone at once that "Booker Washington was in town," and would speak at the White Baptist Church. Gover[nor] Blease[1] supporters begin to make threats, and about 10:30 I went to church, was to speak at 12 oclock. I was waited on by a committee of three poor white men under a big tent jo[in]ing church, and was asked to leave town.

Several prominent white men especially Dr. V. I. Master's,[2] Editor of the Home field of Atlanta Ga. who knew me met the commit[t]ee told them who I was, not Booker Washington, but Richard Carroll of South Carolina. The Committee said it was alright since it was not Booker Washington but in an half an hour they returned and said Richard Carroll shall not speak, and demanded that I come from under the tent, leave town at once, or they would drag me out of the tent. The introduction was being preached at the time. I remained seated some time, refused to go, but a colored man named Ed. Cowans came near the tent, and beckon me come to him. He begged me to get away at once, as another mob was coming in town to kill me. Dr. V. I. Masters saw me as I was walking away with a colored man, beged me return and speak.

The mob then wanted to turn on him. He said Carroll is simply pleading with you for justic for the Negro.

The Blease leaders said dam the Negro, "we want to keep them down." and we demand that this Negro get out of town at once or we take him out in an Automobile and etc. I had to wait in town two hours and a half for a train, and you can imagine how I felt. Twenty five men gathered at the Station to do me harm, but I didn't open my mouth to any of ther remarks. I acted brave, but was scared nearly to death. I did not go there to represent an orphange as stated by an Anderson paper published this evening. I had been invited there by the colored people of the Association simple to speak. The Association I under stand voted. "The mob" did not represents delegates of the Association, but person's where not in any way connected with it. I was to speak on, what is true Christianity. You will notice in this little clipping that Dr. Master's brought the matter up, but I had gone home.

The men that were after me were all Cotton mill men. I write this letter Eighteen miles from the senee. I am on my way to Gaffney.

Thank God for the deliverance. I am to speak to another Association at Due West on the 4th of Aug. also Gaffney. I guess they will get me yet.

I think a newspaper interveiw on lynching of a colored woman some weeks ago when I announced them as murders, had much to do with affair today. I am going to write the whole story in a news paper and send it to you. After the mob wanted me, the colored people were afraid to invite me in their homes. A man came to my rescue before the train left and I think that saved my life. Your Friend truly [?]

Richard Carroll

HLSr Con. 497 BTW Papers DLC. Written "per D. E. W."

¹ Coleman Livingston Blease (1868–1942) was governor of South Carolina from 1911 to 1915 and U.S. senator from 1925 to 1931.
² Victor Irvine Masters (1867–1954) was the editor of several Baptist publications, including the Louisville *Western Recorder*.

To John E. Bush

[Tuskegee, Ala.] August 3rd, 1914

My dear Mr. Bush: I wish to express my sincere thanks to you as well as the thanks of the institution to the Mosaic Knight Templars of America, for their very generous contribution toward the current expenses of this institution.

I assure you that we appreciate all of your kindly interest and wish you to know how much we enjoyed the visit of the Mosaics to Tuskegee.

The white people in town are wild over your organization and want you to come here for every meeting.

It is a matter of genuine pleasure and satisfaction to work with such a man as yourself. I found you among the very few people who can be depended upon in every situation: the average man often yields to the temptation of trying to "toady" to everybody, but I find you entirely different.

With kindest personal regards, I am   Yours very truly,

Booker T. Washington

TLpS Con. 494 BTW Papers DLC.

To Melvin Jack Chisum

[Tuskegee, Ala.] August 3, 1914

Dear Mr. Chisum: In reply to your letter of July 18th addressed to me care of Tuskegee Institute but which was sent to me in the North, I beg to say that I appreciate most sincerely the privilege and the opportunity of subscribing to some of the capital stock of your newspaper when it is incorporated, but I am very sorry not to be in position to make the investment at this time, because I have not the money to spare; but another, and as important reason is that I have positively declined to take stock in any given newspaper property for reasons which must be more or less obvious to you.

Thanking you for your very kind letter, I am: Yours very truly,

Booker T. Washington

TLpS Con. 497 BTW Papers DLC.

To Paul Drennan Cravath

[Tuskegee, Ala.] August 3, 1914

My dear Mr. Cravath: I am feeling exceedingly anxious concerning the future of Fisk. I have seen Dr. Jones twice since our meeting, and I very much fear that Dr. Jones has finally reached the conclusion that he ought not give up his present work for sometime at least. In a talk which I had with him as I came through Washington a few days ago, he did agree, in case he did not accept the presidency, that he would be willing, without expense to the university, to spend three months on the grounds helping the present officers or the new president get the university into better shape. As Dr. Jones is a very tactful man, I think this offer is worth considering very carefully.

In the second place, I got him to agree, if we desire, to become a member of the board of trustees.

One other thing. There is a gentleman at the head of the A. M. A. school in Macon, Ga. about whom I have heard rather favorably. Dr. H. H. Proctor thinks he is the man for Fisk. Dr. Jones, without knowing anything about Dr. Proctor's opinion, mentioned him to me. Dr. Jones has seen both this man and his wife, and thinks very highly of both of them. I am sorry I cannot call his name, but it is some very long and tremendously outrageous name.

I shall be in the vicinity of New York again about September 4th or 5th. Yours very truly,

[Booker T. Washington]

TLp   Con. 497   BTW Papers   DLC.

From Hugh Ellwood Macbeth

Los Angeles, Cal., August 3, 1914

My dear Dr. Washington: In answer to yours under date of New York City, July 28, 1914, would say that I have gone into the matter of having the Los Angeles Times carry some news of our local colored people with some degree of care with General Otis, and while he had given me his consent and certain definite instructions as to the character of the news The Times would handle, I wanted to have him get a word from you with reference to this suggestion before starting in with our news. Accordingly, we shall submit our first copy this week in time for Sunday's issue.

The undecipherable part of the General's letter to you under date of July 18 is very clear to me. For a number of years past, it seems that the General has been the object of much ill advised criticism on the part of a few of our race leaders of the "Eternal Protest Type." In common with the great majority of our worth-while citizens, white and colored, General Otis has little time and no sympathy with the professional complainer. Accordingly, he wants no breachments veiled or unveiled printed in his paper. He is more than glad to print the substantial facts of worth-while achievements as they may occur among our people. In common with myself and others of our colored citizenship, he does not desire any wailings and lamentations because of injustice or prejudice to be voiced through his paper, for as he sees it and as you see it and so ably put it, nobody cares to do business with a sick race or a complaining race. As soon as we get our first copy published, I shall forward you several copies of the publication.

Again I find occasion to thank you sincerely in behalf of our local colored citizens for the tremendous help that you gave us in your recent visit here. And, along that line I wish to add that we are looking forward to a repetition of that visit next year.

Messrs. Tyler and Owens beg to be remembered to you.

With sincere wishes for your personal good health and happiness and those of your family, and the continued growing of prosperity and usefulness of Tuskegee, I am, Very respectfully yours,

Hugh E. Macbeth

TLS   Con. 514   BTW Papers   DLC.

To Joseph Patrick Tumulty

Tuskegee Institute, Alabama   August 4, 1914

My dear Mr. Tumulty: I have taken the liberty of asking Mr. James A. Cobb to see you personally and present this letter.

Mr. Cobb was appointed Assistant District Attorney by Mr. Roosevelt largely at my request some years ago. I think the District Attorney, Mr. Wilson, and other people who have come into contact with Mr. Cobb will tell you that he has conducted himself in a modest, straightforward and helpful manner; in other words, in a way to commend himself to all the people in the office and in the District of Columbia.

If it is in accordance with the policy of the President, I very much hope a way can be found to retain Mr. Cobb in the service, as it will prove very disappointing to the masses of the colored people for a good man like Mr. Cobb to be dismissed on racial or political grounds. Yours very truly,

Booker T. Washington

TLS Woodrow Wilson Papers DLC. A press copy is in Con. 497, BTW Papers, DLC.

To David Franklin Houston

Tuskegee Institute, Alabama   August 4, 1914

My dear Secretary Houston: The whole matter, as you know, of appropriating money to the two races in the South from the Smith-Lever Fund will come before you soon, and I very much hope that in so far as you can, you will use your influence and power to see that the Negro in the South gets a reasonably fair proportion of this fund; without such influence I very much fear that in most of the states, the Negro will get very little if anything from this fund.

I am asking that the Negro be treated justly in this matter not only in the interest of the Negro, but in the interest as well of the white people of the South. I am sure you will agree with me in this: no strong race can treat a weaker race unjustly without the stronger race being hindered as much or more than the weaker race.

A committee of white farmers appointed by the Governor of Alabama, of which the State Commissioner of Agriculture was Chairman, as you will see by the enclosed newspaper clipping, has recommended that the colored people receive 30 per cent of the fund.

Using Alabama simply as an example:

The following funds from the Federal Treasury come into the state of Alabama:

From the Land Grant Funds of 1862....	$20,280	$20,280
From the Morrill Fund..............	50,000	
From the Hatch Fund..............	15,000	
From the Adams Fund..............	15,000	80,000
		100,280

Of the total amount, the colored people receive only $22,500. This, I am sure, you will agree with me, is an injustice.

I am also sure you will also agree with me that it is impossible in a large measure to do any effective and practical work for the colored farmers except as it is done through and by colored people themselves. Yours very truly,

Booker T. Washington

TLS Office of the Secretary of Agriculture, General Correspondence "Lever Bill," RG16 DNA.

To Richard Carroll

[Tuskegee, Ala.] August 5, 1914

My dear Mr. Carroll: I thank you for writing me regarding your interesting experience in connection with the mob.

One of the great things about such an action is that within a few years, you will be glad to look back upon it and wonder how such a state of civilization could have existed. The progress of the world is constant and sure, and within a few years the white people of South Carolina will be ashamed that any such state of affairs could ever have existed in any particular in their commonwealth. The light is breaking in spite of the shadows that are cast temporarily from time to time. What we want to do is to go steadily forward facing obstacles as well as encouragements.

I shall be glad to have you send me a copy of anything that you may print on the matter.

Perhaps you will be interested to know that the white people of Cheraw sent me a very pressing invitation, urging me to be present at their celebration, but I could not go. Yours very truly,

Booker T. Washington

TLpS Con. 497 BTW Papers DLC.

To Seth Low

[Tuskegee, Ala.] August 5, 1914

Dear Mr. Low: I am sorry to trouble you or the executive committee just now about the following matter, but it is a case that requires immediate action, if action is taken at all.

The enclosed copy of letter explains the case fully. It is from Miss Porter, who for a number of years — some 20 or more — has been Dean of our Woman's Department and in other ways connected with the school in most valuable direction. She is one of the most conscientious persons I know anything about, and she would not accept a single dollar for any length of time after she is able to earn her living.

In view of the discussion which we had at the last Trustees' meeting regarding the retirement allowance, the Business Committee is wondering whether you would not be inclined to grant Miss Porter for an indefinite period, one-half of her former salary, which would be in this case Fifty Dollars ($50.) per month. We think this would take care of her. Yours very truly,

Booker T. Washington

TLpS   Con. 71   BTW Papers   DLC.

To Robert Ezra Park

[Tuskegee, Ala.] August 5th, 1914

Dear Doctor Park: Regarding the European trip. I suppose we will now have to wait until the majority of Europeans have succeeded in killing themselves off. The more I see of the actions of these white people of Europe, the more I am inclined to be proud of the Negro race. I do not know of a group of Negroes in this country or in any other country, who would have acted in the silly manner that these highly civilized, and cultured European people of your *race* have acted.

I suppose, however, that everything is in abeyance and we shall have to wait.

I am very much pleased with the article for THE CONGREGATIONALIST. It is all right.

I am also of the opinion, however, that in order to make the European trip of value, that you ought to go there at least three months in advance of my going.

I think Mr. Harris has done very finely in getting that letter from Mr. Carnegie. I shall keep that for use in the future. Yours very truly,

Booker T. Washington

TLpS   Con. 255   BTW Papers   DLC.

To Andrew Carnegie

[Tuskegee, Ala.] August 6th, 1914

Dear Mr. Carnegie: Let me thank you for the fine letter which you have written Mr. Harris regarding my proposed European trip, but all that, I suppose, just now, must wait on the wars.

I cannot for the life of me understand what has gotten into the people of Europe. I had supposed that we were further away from the days of complete barbarism. After all, considering the way these highly civilized and cultured people — or people supposed to be civilized and cultured — of Europe are acting, I think the colored people of the United States deserve great credit for the way that they are acting.

I hope that you and Mrs. Carnegie will not become completely discouraged and disheartened over conditions in Europe. What is now taking place shows all the more plainly that the fine work which you have inaugurated to bring about a peace sentiment throughout the world should have been undertaken one hundred years ago or more.

With all good wishes, I am   Yours very truly,

Booker T. Washington

TLpS   Con. 68   BTW Papers   DLC.

To William Colfax Graves

[Tuskegee, Ala.] August 6, 1914

My dear Mr. Graves: I thank you very much for sending me a copy of Mr. Rosenwald's offer to assist in the construction of the Y.M.C.A. building. I can make it of service in connection with the "Outlook" article.[1]

I am interested in the point raised by Mr. Trotter regarding segregation. While, of course, there is something to be said on both sides, as a practical policy I have found that nowhere in the country do any large number of colored people actually use the Y.M.C.A. facilities except as they have a special building; even in Boston I think an examination would reveal the fact that not more than half a dozen colored men out of a population of some twelve or fifteen thousand have any practical connection with the Y.M.C.A. Just why this is true I do not know. I do not attempt to discuss the justice involved in the matter, but I have observed the matter for a good many years.

I am not sure whether it will be of any value to mention this matter in my "Outlook" article or not; my present thought is I shall not refer to it. Yours very truly,

Booker T. Washington

TLpS   Con. 255   BTW Papers   DLC.

¹ See An Article in *Outlook,* Oct. 28, 1914, below.

To John Hobbis Harris

[Tuskegee, Ala.] August 6th, 1914

My dear Reverend Harris: I am keeping in touch with Doctor Park. In view of all the circumstances, it looks as though we will have to wait until the highly civilized and cultured Europeans of your race have gotten through shooting at each other.

I am writing especially to thank you for the fine letter you have gotten from Mr. Carnegie. Yours very truly,

Booker T. Washington

TLpS   Con. 842   BTW Papers   DLC.

To Andrew Franklin Hilyer

[Tuskegee, Ala.] August 6, 1914

My dear Mr. Hilyer: Replying to yours of July 31st addressed to Mr. Scott, I would state that while I am deeply interested in your case, I am puzzled to know just how to help.

As you know, I am a straight Republican and opposed the election of Mr. Wilson; under the circumstances, it is rather embarrassing for me to ask a political favor of the Secretary of the Treasury. However, I confess that Mr. Wilson and members of his cabinet have been exceedingly kind to me since they have been in office and have refused practically nothing that I have asked. I think the best way to help you is through a friend of mine, who is very well acquainted with Secretary McAdoo, and I am going to pursue this method.[1] Yours very truly,

Booker T. Washington

TLpSr Copy   Con. 505   BTW Papers   DLC.

[1] The letter was docketed in E. J. Scott's hand with the note: "see Bishop Walters."

Emmett Jay Scott to
Margaret James Murray Washington

[Tuskegee, Ala.] August 6th, 1914

Private!

My dear Mrs. Washington: As you know, Mr. Washington is leaving here today to fill his lecture engagements in Indiana and other points. He has just decided to return to Tuskegee after filling those engagements on the 11th, remaining here until time to leave for the Business League meeting.

I have said to him personally that I thought he ought not to do this as he has just made the long trip South from the North and is now going away and then to come back to Tuskegee for three or four grinding days, then to go away again with three or four hard days at the Business League meeting is to treat himself altogether unfairly.

It may be that you feel as I do about the matter, and if so, you may have opportunity to try to influence him otherwise. I do not believe that he should undertake this hard, grinding campaign & return here just on the eve of the Business League meeting. Yours very truly,

Emmett J Scott

TLpS   Con. 655   BTW Papers   DLC.

From Joseph Patrick Tumulty

The White House   Washington   August 7, 1914

My dear Dr. Washington: With further reference to your recent letter, I am sure you will appreciate the conditions with which I have been confronted the last few days and my disinclination now to add to the burdens of the President. I feel it my duty to keep from him all but the most important and urgent matters. I am confident you will appreciate my point of view. Sincerely yours,

J. P. Tumulty
Secretary to the President

TLS   Con. 527   BTW Papers   DLC.

From Robert Ezra Park

University of Chicago, August 8, 1914

My dear Mr Washington: I note what you say about *my* race in Europe, but, as you once said to me when I told you some thing particularly disagreeable about *your* Race, "that makes it all the more interesting."

The letters from Europe continue to pile up here. I have not answered any of them thus far, simply because I did not know what to say. If you intend to come to Chicago soon I think that I better hold them until I see you.

It seems to me that we shall have to postpone the European trip indefinitely now. very truly

Robert E. Park

P.S. Please send me the letter from the North American Review and my suggestion in regard to the article they want. I have only an indefinite notion in regard to the thing now.

I have completed the sketch of yourself for the Torch Press.

TLS   Con. 255   BTW Papers   DLC.

From Seth Low

New York, Aug. 10, 1914

Dear Dr. Washington: Replying to your letter of August 5th, I conferred this morning with Mr. Willcox and Mr. Trumbull. They concur with me in authorizing an allowance to Miss Porter of $50., for the remainder of the academic year. Anything more permanent should be passed upon by the Trustees next February.

It seems to all of us highly important that every unnecessary expenditure at the Institute should be held in abeyance. The ultimate consequences of the war in Europe no man can forecast, but it is already clear that those having money to give away will have many and strong appeals made to contribute to the Red Cross and to personal friends in need. Very truly yours,

Seth Low

TLS Con. 71 BTW Papers DLC.

To Robert Ezra Park

[Tuskegee, Ala.] August 14, 1914

My dear Dr. Park: I see nothing to do but just to lay the European trip aside for the present; that is until white people get a little more civilized. I really think it would be worth while to consider sending a group of black missionaries to Europe to see if something can be done for the white heathen. Yours very truly,

Booker T. Washington

TLpS Con. 72 BTW Papers DLC.

To Joseph Patrick Tumulty

[Tuskegee, Ala.] August 14th, 1914

My dear Mr. Tumulty: I am really glad that you did not put my letter before President Wilson. I do not see how either one of you are able to stand this tremendous strain which has been upon you during the past few weeks. All of us should relieve both of you in every way possible. Yours very truly,

Booker T. Washington

TLpS Con. 527 BTW Papers DLC.

An Address before the
National Negro Business League

Muskogee, Oklahoma, Convention Hall, Wednesday evening,
Aug. 19 [1914]

Throughout the world the ten millions and more of black people in the United States are being observed and studied in a larger measure than is true of any similar group of black people in existence, or perhaps that has ever existed. People from all parts of the world interested in the civilization of black people are coming to the United States to study the condition and the progress of the American Negro; for after all is said, if there is any place where the Negro has a chance to show his mettle, it is right here in the United States.

For this reason, as well as for the sake of ourselves, it is a matter of extreme importance that we not disappoint ourselves nor those who are studying and observing us.

Within the fifty years of our freedom, and even before physical freedom came, great and almost marvelous progress has been made, but we must not rest upon the past; we must continue to go forward.

Hon. John L. Morris, the Secretary of the Treasury for the Republic of Liberia, a man who has come into contact with black people in many parts of the world, after meeting our people in this country in nearly every section for several weeks, remarked to me that the Negro in America is making more progress than anywhere else in the world. I state this not to tempt us to swell with pride, but that we may note the responsibility that rests upon us and to cause us to double our efforts.

The National Negro Business League, under whose auspices we are gathered today in the new state of Oklahoma in such large numbers, is simply one of the many agencies employed to promote further progress among us.

This National Negro Business League has a unique history. Organized by a small group of men and women in the city of Boston, Massachusetts, in 1900, it has grown in power and influence till its spirit is felt and is being carried on in the form of Local Business Leagues, or similar organizations, in nearly every centre of Negro population throughout the United States. Getting its strength and its standing from these Local Leagues, the National Negro Business League at each annual session grows in dignity and influence.

Before beginning the body of my remarks, there are a few simple but fundamental things to which I wish to direct the special attention of each Local League. These things I ask in order that the usefulness of the League may be still further felt among the ten millions of our people.

First of all, do not fritter away too much time in your meetings in technicalities known as "parliamentary rules."

2. Let each Local League study the condition and needs of our people in its community, and devote itself to doing that which will promote the commercial, industrial, educational, professional and moral life of our race in that community.

3. Have a regular time of meeting, and always have a meeting at that time.

4. Strive to have a regular place of meeting, one that shall be attractive and convenient.

5. Have for each meeting a carefully arranged program that shall strike at some definite thing. A general program means little; serving refreshments often helps.

6. Each Local League should strive to gather into its membership every man and woman who is interested in any kind of honorable business, no matter how humble that business may appear to be.

7. Each League should have for one of its objects the bringing of the white man by whose side we live into friendly and sympathetic

contact with the progress of the race. One way to do this is to invite successful white men to visit and speak to the Local Leagues. The white man will help and we will be helped.

8. Try to simulate competition and up-to-date business methods.

Having said this much covering some of the details of this organization, let me give attention as best I may to the main thought in my mind.

I believe that the time has come when we as a race should begin preparing to enter upon a new policy and a new program. In plain but in emphatic words I want to suggest whether the time has not come when we should get off the defensive in things that concern our present and future, and begin to inaugurate everywhere an aggressive and constructive progressive policy in business, industry, education, moral and religious life and our conduct generally. We must follow the teachings of the Master when He said, "Overcome evil with good."

A general, however able, who contents himself with merely holding the territory that he occupies, or merely devotes himself to defending himself against the assaults of the enemy, is not the general who gains renown for genuine leadership or gains the confidence of the world. A general who occupies much of his time in explaining the weakness of the enemy or the unjust assaults or tactics of the enemy is not the general who wins many battles; so it is in business of every kind.

For example, the merchant who merely contents himself with holding his present trade without covering new ground in the way of increased patronage and trading in new territory, is not the merchant who gets much of a rating for success in the business world. The merchant again, who spends his time pointing out the weakness of another's business is not getting very far on the road to business success. All the energy you have to "knock" with, all the energy you have to voice complaints, coin that energy into improved methods of handling your merchandise. And so with general race matters. Damning the other fellow does not push us forward. His damning us cannot permanently hold us back.

Now, having said this much to indicate in a rather general way my thought, let me be a little more definite in applying these ideas to conditions in Oklahoma and nearby states. What is said of these states can be applied, I think, with profit to other states.

I find that of the 1,700 colored farmers in Kansas, 100 of them are without live stock and 350 are without poultry on their farms.

Of the 3,600 colored farmers in Missouri, 230 of them are without live stock and 360 are without poultry on their farms.

Of the 63,000 colored farmers in Arkansas, 8,500 of them are without live stock, and 13,800 are without poultry on their farms.

Of the 54,800 colored farmers in Louisiana, 5,300 of them are without live stock and 12,600 were without poultry on their farms.

Of the 70,000 colored farmers in Texas, 5,000 of them are without live stock and 15,000 were without poultry on their farms.

Of the 20,000 colored farmers in Oklahoma, 1,300 of them are without live stock and 3,300 are without poultry on their farms. Get off the defensive and put the world to wondering how we have been able to secure so much live stock & poultry instead of so little.

Many farmers in this section, and likewise in every section of the South, are not making the most of their opportunities. They are living over riches in the form of chickens, hogs and cattle, which they can possess by simply letting down their buckets where they are. While the Negro farmer is neglecting his opportunity of raising live stock, the prices are continually getting higher. Beef is being imported from Australia and from South America. Eggs by the shipload are being sent to us from China. There is no special color line in stock and poultry raising. If the Negro has cattle for sale, they will bring the same prices on the market that the white man's cattle will bring. The black man's leghorn chickens, if properly cared for, will lay as many eggs as the white man's, and he will get the same price in the market.

In few other parts of the world is there a greater chance for the Negro to get off the defensive through protection from the soil than is true in this section. As I have stated, in no other part of the United States is there greater opportunity for the Negro than in the six states adjacent to Muskogee: namely, Kansas, Missouri, Arkansas, Louisiana, Texas and Oklahoma. These six states comprise the greatest living stock and poultry section of the United States. About one-fourth of all the live stock in the country is in this section. This section is also great for poultry raising. The poultry owned in these six states is worth over $31,000,000, and is one-fifth the value of all the poultry in the country.

My own observations and statistics indicate that this is also one of the greatest farming districts in the United States. Almost 40 per cent. of all the cotton raised in the country is produced in these states and a great amount of corn, oats, wheat, and potatoes is also raised. Here are indeed great opportunities for the Negro farmer.

There are in the six states adjacent to this city 133,000,000 acres of unimproved land. This is an area of over 200,000 square miles. It is equal to the area of all the New England states, New York, New Jersey, Delaware, Pennsylvania and Ohio together.

In this great tract of unimproved land Negroes have the opportunity to settle, and to bring up out of the soil, which is full of riches, cotton, corn, oats, wheat, poultry, horses, mules, cattle and hogs. These six states have a Negro population of 2,000,000. These Negroes have under their control as owners and renters about $300,000,000 worth of farm property. They own about 60,000 farms containing about 6,000,000 acres of land. The total value of the farm property, land, live stock, farming implements, etc., owned by the Negroes of these states is about $200,000,000. There is room, however, for improvement along all lines. For every Negro that owns an acre of land there are 33 who are landless. These 33 ought to get some of the millions of acres of unimproved land which are for sale. Let us get off the defensive and putting the world to talking about the little land that we own, but the much land that we do own. Get off the defensive by putting the world to talking about the 33 that do own land and not about the ones that do not own land.

Let your success thoroughly eclipse your short-comings. We must give the world so much to think and talk about that relates to our constructive work in the direction of progress that people will forget and over look our failures and short-comings. Instead of giving people opportunity to explain why we failed to build a house, let us build so many houses that the world will forget about the house that we failed to build. One big, definite fact in the direction of achievement and construction will go farther in securing rights and removing prejudice than many printed pages of defense and explanation.

It is not well for us or our children that we should dwell so much on the defensive, with the negative side of life instead of the positive side. It is not well that our minds should be so continually centered upon our miseries or upon those who mistreat us. In the future let us emphasize our opportunities more and our difficulties less. Let us talk more about our white friends, and about our white enemies less. We do our children a lasting injustice when we feed them constantly upon the miseries of the race. Let us talk about the man who has got a job, and less about the man without a job. Let our fraternal and secret societies talk less about sickness and death, and more about health and life. Let our societies spend less money in taking care of the sick, and much more money in promoting the health of the race and they will have to spend less on account of sickness and death. Instead of giving the world a chance to discuss the high death rate of the Negro, let us put the world to wondering why the Negro keeps so healthy and strong. Let us make health contagious in every community rather than disease.

I often deplore the fact that so many of our Men's organizations, women's clubs and best newspapers devote so much time to merely resenting something, or "getting back" at some unfriendly critic, instead of devoting more time to constructive and progressive measures. Too often insignificant occurrences and insignificant individuals are given an importance and an advertisement by organizations and newspapers that is unnecessary and hurtful.

Explaining is easy. Construction is difficult. Explaining why we have not built up a business is easier than constructing a business.

Let us, in the future, spend less time talking about the part of the city that we cannot live in, and more time in making the part of the city that we can live in beautiful and attractive. Let us get off the defensive in explaining why the house that we live in so often has the gate off the hinge, the fence palings gone, windows and doors broken out, and plastering knocked off. Instead of this, let us put people to talking about the beauty and attractiveness of the houses occupied by our people. Let us make such progress in these directions that the other fellow will be kept so busy talking about our progress that he will have no time to abuse and misrepresent us. Let us acquire wealth and intelligence so fast that the world will forget our poverty and ignorance. Let us be so thrifty and industrious that people will have no time to talk about our carelessness and idleness. Let us make the Negro so law-abiding that people will talk less about the criminal Negro and more about the one who obeys the law.

Too much time of organizations and of the press is often devoted to not only resenting something, but in criticising the white man in the absence of the white man, or out of his presence.

Everywhere let us talk more about how we can live in peace and harmony with the white man, and less about racial friction and racial bitterness. Let us exalt the white man who treats us with justice, and overlook and pity the little man who would retard our progress. We call too many meetings to resent something, and not enough to construct something. All this is in the direction of progress that will be lasting, and in time remove many of the little difficulties.

In connection with the same line of thought, we must give, as business men and women, less attention to the lines of business which simply cater to miseries and misfortunes, and the weaknesses and follies of our race and more attention to the lines of business that create wealth by dealing with nature at first hand. The fact is to be deplored that so much time and money in the larger cities is being spent in encouraging our young people to spend money instead of save money. The dancing hall, the billiard room, the bar room, the card parties and excursions are not the places where wealth is created. Nothing gets an individual or a race permanently upon its feet except definite, progressive, constructive work.

One of the gratifying evidences of what we can accomplish by concentrated and united effort is in the success that recently attended us in the recognition of "Railroad Day" in all parts of the country; from nearly every part of the South have come reports to the effect that railroad conditions have been bettered by reason of our efforts. I think the National Negro Business League can justly claim credit for inaugurating this movement.

Another gratifying evidence of the strength and growing prosperity of the race is shown in the fact that whereas a few years ago the wholesale merchant either in the North or South scarcely gave the Negro merchant any attention, today, the wholesale merchant in every part of the country is giving as much attention to catering to the trade and good wishes of the Negro merchant as is true of the white merchant; all this in the way of business relationships between the races means better things for both races throughout the country.

If there are those who are inclined to be discouraged concerning racial conditions in this country, we have but to turn our minds in the direction of the deplorable conditions in Europe growing largely out of racial bitterness and friction. When we contrast what has taken place there with the peaceful manner in which black people and white people are living together in this country, notwithstanding now and then there are evidences of injustice and friction which should always be condemned, we have the greatest cause for thanksgiving. Perhaps nowhere else in the world can be found so many white people living side by side with so many of dark skin in so much of peace and harmony as in the United States.

The Negro business and professional men have in the past few years made remarkable progress. Their progress in the future, however, is going to depend more and more upon the progress and development that the Negro who remains on the soil makes. As they acquire more land, raise more cotton and corn to the acre, raise more live stock and poultry, they will be able to support more banks, more drug stores, more dry goods stores and pay the teachers and preachers better salaries.

When the 2,000,000 Negroes of the Southwest have made the most of their opportunities and have let down their buckets deep into the earth and brought up the riches contained therein in the forms of cotton, corn, oats, wheat, potatoes, chickens, turkeys, hogs, horses, mules and cattle, they will be able to support in Kansas, Missouri, Arkansas, Louisiana, Texas, and Oklahoma, 1,000 more grocery stores owned by Negroes, 500 additional dry goods stores, 300 more shoe stores, 200 more good restaurants and hotels, 300 additional millinery stores, 200 additional drug stores and 40 more banks.

Whenever we think of agricultural progress among Negroes we invariably associate it with the mule. The most modern vehicle for transportation is the automobile. It is doing almost as much for the Negro as the mule has done. The business man, professional man, and the planter in all parts of the South are using the automobile. This has necessitated the building of good roads in every section of the South. The building of these roads has brought the country nearer the town and is carrying the town into the country.

The rural free delivery, the parcel post, and the telephone have all helped to bring the remotest sections of the South into close touch with the cities. All this has tended to make conditions in the country better for the Negro. With these facilities for the Negro in the country, with the opportunities for the Negro business man of the city growing brighter, let us press forward to that goal of American citizenship of which not only we and our children shall be proud, but at which the whole world shall marvel and do us honor.

TMd Con. 959 BTW Papers DLC. Both BTW and E. J. Scott made minor editorial changes in this draft.

From Richard Carroll

Columbia, S.C., Sept. 1, 1914

My dear Dr. Washington: I wrote you the day the mob got after me at Iva, S.C. I told the parties that were present to write the story as well as he could. I am going to publish the whole story within the next two weeks.

Governor Blease has been defeated. Hon. Richard I. Manning,[1] I am sure, will be governor. He is a high-class gentleman. Blease was in Iva about two weeks before I went there and stopped with a Mr. McElree a letter carrier. The white Baptist association met there on the 4th of July. Iva is a factory town. I attended the association by invitation. I was met at the station by a colored man who called me Booker T. Washington. I told him I am not Booker T. Washington. It seemed that some white man let fall the expression "The Booker T. Washington of South Carolina will speak here today." Some white people got it into their heads that you were to speak.

This colored man over-heard them making a plot over the telephone to mob me, and prevent me from speaking. Before the association assembled in the church, I was waited on by two or three white men. Members of the association told me that I would be protected as long as I was in the church, but these men told me to leave. I told them that I was to speak at 12 o'clock and would remain.

Later on a colored man called on me at the request of another colored man who sent word that he knew of a mob coming to whip or kill me. I walked about 100 yards from the church and was faced by 15 men who had come for me.

Dr. V. I. Masters #1006 Healy Building, Atlanta, Ga. who was in the church, saw the white men gathering around me and came to see what the trouble was. Dr. Masters made a speech to the mob and among other things he said: "I know Richard Carroll and would rather be Richard Carroll with his black skin than you with your devilish spirit." They replied: "We will make you leave if you take sides with your nigger."

I decided the best to do was to leave and this I did on the first train — a freight train. A crowd of factory boys and men gathered at the train talked in low tones, but said nothing to me. After I left, I was called on to speak. Dr. Masters of Atlanta then stated why I was not there.

It was found that this man who took such a prominent part, was not a member of the church and not connected with the association at all. The association then voted and put it on record that they were not a party to the affair. I trust you are well. I have had much trouble. My daughter is still an invalid. Yours very truly,

Richard Carroll

TLS Con. 497 BTW Papers DLC.

[1] Richard Irvine Manning (1859–1931), a Democrat, was governor of South Carolina from 1915 to 1919.

From Marcus Mosiah Garvey[1]

Kingston, Jamaica, W.I. September 8 1914

Dear Sir & Brother. I have been informed by our Commissioner in London that you are expected to be in Europe during the month of April or May of next year, and that you shall be engaged addressing Meetings in London and other cities of the British Isles on the subject of "The progress of the Negro." Please be good enough to inform me if this is correct.

I have been keeping in touch with your good work in America, and although there is a difference of opinion on the lines on which the Negro should develop himself, yet the fair minded critic cannot fail in admiring your noble efforts. The two schools of America have gone as far as to give us, who are outside the real possibilities of the industrial and intellectual scope for Negro energy. We are organized out here on broad lines and we find it condusive to our interest to pave our way both industrially and intellectually.

The prejudice in these countries is far different from that of America. Here we have to face the prejudice of the hypocritical white men who nevertheless are our friends as also to fight down the prejudice of our race in shade colour.

Our organization is marching steadily on and we hope to extend our scope all over the world within the next few years. I have just returned from a tour in Europe where I spent two years studying the Negro's place there. I am also hoping to be in England about March next year after paying a visit to the U.S.A. I intend lecturing in a few of the European cities on the condition of the West Indian Negro.

I enclose you a Circular Appeal which I feel sure will interest you, and I am asking that you be good enough as to help us with a small donation to carry out our work.

We publish for the first time next week our paper "THE NEGRO WORLD" a copy of which we shall send you regularly. If you publish any journals in connection with Tuskegee please be good enough to send us same in Exchange.

Wishing you well and praying for the salvation of World Wide Ethiopia. Yours in the bonds of Fellowship

Marcus Garvey
President and
Travelling Commissioner

TLS Con. 842 BTW Papers DLC. Written on stationery of The Universal Negro Improvement and Conservation Association and African Communities League.

¹ Marcus Mosiah Garvey (1887–1940) was the Jamaican leader of the back-to-Africa movement in the United States and in other countries of the African diaspora in the 1920s and 1930s. He arrived in the United States soon after the death of BTW, but his correspondence makes clear that the Universal Negro Improvement Association and many of the elements of Garvey's program were formed in 1914–15 under the Tuskegean's indirect influence. Garvey's flamboyant style, nationalist objectives, and business methods, however, were unlike Washington's. Garvey's phenomenal rise as a black mass leader was the result partly of the disillusioning black experiences of the period, but also because of his ability to express the inchoate thoughts of blacks. His equally meteoric fall, following imprisonment for fraud and subsequent deportation, was also the result of the times and the unfriendliness of intrenched white and black interests, but his personal faults, notably poor business policies and refusal to take advice and criticism, were additional factors. Among the biographies of Garvey are E. David Cronon, *Black Moses* (1955), Theodore G. Vincent, *Black Power and the Garvey Movement* (1971), and Tony Martin, *Race First* (1976). See also the forthcoming edition of Garvey's papers by Robert A. Hill.

Charles Banks to Emmett Jay Scott

Mound Bayou, Miss., September 8, 1914

Dear Mr. Scott; Things have been coming so thick and fast until I have not had chance to keep you fully advised, but it seems now that the storm has sufficiently calmed for me to cast around and take time to write you.

I met the Doctor in Chicago by engagement and went over matters pretty thoroughly with reference to reorganization of the bank, so that he knows my intention in that regard.

You already know about the closing of the M. B. A. This is final so far as the old concern is concerned. We meet at Jackson on the 24th to reorganize that department under a new name. While these things are coming thick and fast, yet I do not know that they could have happened at a better time as we are not singled out but the conditions are embarrassing generally; especially in this cotton section. The old Diamond Cox and Redmond contingency at Jackson which fought me in the beginning and all along, took advantage of this opportunity to strike at me through the columns of the paper and I hand you herewith my reply to them which speaks for itself. Fearing that the wrong stuff might get lodged in the minds of the people throughout the country and the wrong impressions created where we did not want them, I had Simmons to come here to do a lot of syndicate newspaper work that will serve to cover the ground in quarters where I want the correct impression made, as I shall be too busily engaged to give any thought to matters in a literary way myself. I am inclosing you some of the stuff which he is preparing.

Suffice it to say that I am not at all rattled, and while I might be battered and scarred in coming thru this, it will come out all right. One thing I am sure will please you and that is, the books are all straight and there is no reflection on me and no criminal proceedings liable. It will require a great deal of hard work, patience and time to properly rehabilitate but that I am willing to do. The whole situation, carries with it advantages as well as dis-advantages. I am at a disadvantage before the public but from a financial and personal standpoint, it presents a distinct advantage. This of course will seem strange and unreasonable, nevertheless it is the case, and were it not for the condition brought on by the War, I should be able to do what I wanted to do personally, easier and quicker now than any former arrangements.

I do not know just what fate will be your father's as I have no place open for him just now, but I have given it some thought and may be able to place him in some way. Of that however I am not certain, but in any event, I shall see that he is not unnecessarily embarrassed until he is placed.

Assuring you of my deep appreciation of your great concern in me and in all things that concern me, I am, Faithfully yours,

Chas. Banks

TLS Con. 9 BTW Papers DLC.

From Seth Bunker Capp

Reading, Penna. September 9th 1914

My dear Mr. Washington, I should very much like to have made a full life size oil painting of you, so that it may be exhibited this fall in Philadelphia at the exhibition of the Pennsylvania Academy of The Fine Arts. After it has been exhibited, it will give me a great deal of pleasure to present it to your institution to aid embellish its walls in a fitting manner. If you can spare the time to come to Reading, Pa for one week this can be accomplished, should it all be entirely agreeable to you.

I am stopping here in Reading receiving Radium treatment to restore my impaired eyesight. I have with me, my companion, and friend, and my protege, a talented young Bohemian American portrait artist, Mr. G. Hruska. My enforced idleness does not mean that he must be idle, therefore, he has his studio here in Reading, Pa., and a collection of over a hundred portraits with him. I enclose his card and also my card which will give you somewhat of an idea who it is that is writing you. I enclose for your information a partial list of organizations in America in which I am identified as a life member.[1]

I am greatly interested in your wonderful work, and I should like very much to present your portrait to your institution as I have described above, allowing it first to be of assistance to my protege in his fall exhibit. I am sure that thousands will be interested to see it, and it should prove an inspiration and a medium of interest to the public, in your great works. I should be delighted to hear from you in the very near future and have your expressions on the subject of having your portrait painted, absolutely without charge to you or anyone else, as it is to be distinctly a gift. With regards, I am, Very truly,

S. B. Capp

TLS Con. 497 BTW Papers DLC.

¹ The list contained the names of thirty-five cultural, scientific, and historical organizations, mostly in Philadelphia, of which Capp was a member.

To Richard Carroll

[Tuskegee, Ala.] September 14, 1914

Dear Dr. Carroll: On my return to Tuskegee, I find here your letters of September 1st and 2d and also a copy of Mr. Masters' letter, which I am returning herewith. I am sure that Mr. Masters expresses the sentiments of the best people of South Carolina and indeed of all the South. These people are becoming increasingly tired of the tyranny and meanness of the elements which threaten and menace you.

I sympathize with you most sincerely in your ill health and in your trouble. Yours very truly,

Booker T. Washington

TLpS Con. 497 BTW Papers DLC.

To George Cleveland Hall

[Tuskegee, Ala.] September 14, 1914

My dear Dr. Hall: I have just telegraphed you as follows: "Find I can be at Coden from September 23d to October 1st. Will this suit you? Hope it will. In that case, hope you will plan to reach Tuskegee one or two days before so we can go together. Answer."

Regarding the Banks matter, about which the clipping you kindly sent me refers, I would state that I have never lent Charles Banks a single dollar in my life, nor has he ever asked me to send him one. I have never endorsed a paper of any character for him, nor has he ever asked me to endorse anything.

The whole matter, as everybody in Mississippi knows, so far as the publication of fabrications is concerned, is due to that man you mentioned to me. He happens to be in with the owners of this white paper and he and the editors concocted the whole scheme in giving these lies out to the public. A man must be pretty low when he will go so far as he has done. At the time this publication was made, Banks was in Mound Bayou.

Now I very much hope that you will let nothing interfere with your coming to Coden. We must leave here on Tuesday or Wednesday, so the people will be prepared for us and we must not disappoint them. I hope you will come early and spend several days with us here in Tuskegee.

Kindly remember us all to Mrs. Hall and the little girl. Yours very truly,

Booker T. Washington

TLpS Con. 505 BTW Papers DLC.

To James Hardy Dillard

[Tuskegee, Ala.] September 15, 1914

Dear Dr. Dillard: I am simply amazed and almost, I might say, disgusted on reading the proceedings of the recent action of the Peabody Fund to find they rescinded their action giving $350,000 to the Slater Fund.[1] Just what is back of this extraordinary action I cannot understand. Yours very truly,

Booker T. Washington

TLpS Con. 69 BTW Papers DLC.

[1] This was a step in Washington's campaign over several years, and without ultimate success, to embarrass the Peabody Education Fund into sharing equitably with black schools in the final allocation of its dwindling funds. Instead, most of the final amount went to the all-white Peabody College for Teachers as the southern white trustees desired, whereas the northern trustees were interested chiefly in merging Peabody with Vanderbilt rather than in equity for black schools. (Harlan, *Separate and Unequal*, 227–28; Dabney, *Universal Education in the South*, 2: 19–22.) According to Dabney, however, the Slater Fund did receive $350,000 in the final distribution of the Peabody Fund. (*Ibid.*, 2:437.)

To Seth Bunker Capp

[Tuskegee, Ala.] September 15, 1914

My dear Mr. Capp: I am somewhat tardy in answering your very kind letter of recent date, but I have been away from home for several days, hence the delay.

You do not know how very much I appreciate the compliment which you pay me in suggesting to have a portrait of myself painted by your friend, Mr. G. Hruska. I would say yes without hesitation but my trouble is to find the time. Practically the only time in the year when I take any kind of a let-up is the latter part of September, but, unfortunately, just before your letter came I had already completed arrangements to spend the last week in September in another part of the country, and I could not, without disappointing and embarrassing a great many people, change this plan.

In addition to my usual work the exigencies created by the existence of the war have multiplied my problems many times, so that every hour is of tremendous value to me.

In case I cannot see my way clear to come there any time soon, would it be possible for the work to be done here or in any of the larger cities of the North — say, New York or Boston. Should no better plan suggest itself, would it be possible to have the purpose answered by my spending a shorter period of time in Reading than a week.

I am afraid that I am expressing in a very poor way the gratitude which I feel to you for your very great generosity. I wonder if you, or your friend, have seen a copy of my Book, "Up From Slavery." I am taking the liberty of sending you a copy by this mail. Both you and Mr. Hruska could be made very comfortable here at any time.

Since dictating the above, I find that Reading is only about sixty miles from Philadelphia, and this simplifies the problem a little, provided the work will be done early in October and in a shorter time than your letter indicated. I shall be glad to hear from you. Yours very truly,

[Booker T. Washington]

TL Copy   Con. 497   BTW Papers   DLC.

To John Hobbis Harris

[Tuskegee, Ala.] September 15, 1914

My dear Mr. Harris: I have your letter of August 17th, which I regret has remained unanswered owing to my absence.

I was in Chicago, a few days ago, and had a conference with Dr. Park on the European trip and he and I both agreed that it would be very unwise to attempt the trip this year. Perhaps a year from next March would be a favorable time. What do you think of it?

How horrible this war is and how much it has upset everything!

If I make the trip next March, I would have to confine it to Great Britain. This I should not like to do.

I hope you will remember me to Mr. Travers Buxton and all the good friends there.

You will find in an early number of The Outlook, published in New York, an article from my pen on the work among the colored Young Men's Christian Association in this country. I think you will be interested in it. Yours very truly,

Booker T. Washington

TLpS Con. 842 BTW Papers DLC.

To Marcus Mosiah Garvey

[Tuskegee, Ala.] September 17, 1914

My dear Sir: I have your very kind favor of some days ago.

I have given up altogether my plans for the European trip which I had planned for next March. Matters are in such unsettled condition in that country that I fear I could not accomplish what I hope to do. I shall keep the matter in mind and hope to be able to make the trip at some other time.

I have read what you say with reference to the advance being made in educational facilities for the Negroes of that section. I hope that when you come to America you will come to Tuskegee and see for yourself what we are striving to do for the colored young man and woman of the South.

I thank you for the printed matter which you sent. I shall give it a careful reading at the earliest convenience. I regret, however, that I am not able now to make a contribution toward your work.

We shall be very glad to receive copies of The Negro World, and shall be glad to send you in exchange The Tuskegee Student, published at this institution. Yours very truly,

Booker T. Washington

TLpS   Con. 842   BTW Papers   DLC.

From John Robert E. Lee

[Tuskegee, Ala.] September 22, 1914

Mr. Washington: I have followed your suggestion of two or three years ago to keep in touch with the Tennessee Coal & Iron Company. Last year seven of our graduates were placed with them. This year out of twenty nine teachers they have only two of our graduates. Some of these who were dropped out, were dropped out for inefficiency; two cases that I know of; others, I think, left of their own accord.

The question which interests me, however, is that Mr. Tidwell[1] has not asked for five others of our graduates to fill the places of the five who have dropped out.

You will permit me to say that from all I can get I am convinced that the great weakness of our students is that of scholarship. In several cases they are able to set a meal for a board of trustees, but when it comes to teaching a group of children 30 or 40 or teaching a grade, they do not measure up as they should. This is not only true in the Tennessee Coal & Iron Company district alone, but it is too largely true.

I am convinced that we are making a serious mistake to allow our young people, especially those who give promise, to pass up and out of the school without covering thoroughly our academic course, and without more definite training for the work of teaching, whether that teaching is to be industries or in the academic class room. Unless it is a question of age on the part of a student, as in the case of Mary Statesman[2] who is over 35; I believe we are doing the students an injustice to have them pass up from one grade to another by vote rather than by covering the work. Yours very truly,

J. R. E. Lee

TLS Con. 641 BTW Papers DLC.

[1] Robert Earl Tidwell (b. 1883) was the superintendent of the Tennessee Coal, Iron and Railroad Co. schools.

[2] Mary Susan (Susie) Statesman, of Philadelphia, first enrolled as a student at Tuskegee in 1905 and graduated in 1915.

From C. Elias Winston[1]

St. Louis Mo. Sept. 23rd. 1914

My dear Dr. Washington: In the last two weeks I have read from several papers, white and colored, what purports to be a declaration made by you with regards to Race segregation in America, in an address delivered before the business men's league. I clipped the alleged declaration from the Central Afro-American, published in this City, it reads as follows: "the Negro should stop fighting segregation and lend his forces towards beautifying the neighborhood in which he lives."

Now I wish to ascertain from you personally if the statement quoted above was made by you in the address referred to, or in any address, at any time? As a Race man who has always had the highest regards for you and your splendid work for the Race and Humanity, as a minister of the Gospel and as the founder and Editor of a Race paper, I do not feel that I would be safe in discussing this matter publicly before ascertaining from you, just what you did say on the subject at issue — I shall therefore await in anxious expectation for a reply before I discuss this matter either pro or con, thru the columns of my paper.

I am sending, by this mail and under another cover a few sample copies of The Western Torch Light, the paper is far from being perfect but it has, I think, a trend in the right direction, as you may be able to glean from its editorials and other matters, Yours for a fair play and "a square deal,"

C. Elias Winston

TLS Con. 523 BTW Papers DLC.

¹ C. Elias Winston was minister of the Tabernacle Baptist Church in St. Louis, Mo.

From Charles Templeman Loram¹

New York City   Sept 28th. [1914]

Dear Sir, I beg to enclose herewith a letter of introduction to you from Mr Maurice S. Evans² of Durban South Africa.

As you will see I am in the United States taking a post graduate course in Education at Teachers' College, Columbia. My chief interest, however is in native education in South Africa,³ and I am naturally anxious to have an opportunity of seeing what you have been able to accomplish for a branch of the same people in this country.

If you would be good enough to send me a copy of your calendar and also inform me when it would be most convenient for me to come to Tuskegee I shall be much obliged. I am hoping that it will be possible for me to visit Tuskegee without interfering unduly with my studies at Columbia, and to this end I am hoping that it might suit you if I came during the Christmas holidays (Dec 21–Jan 2) or after the close of the academic year at Columbia June 9th 1914 [1915]. I am however prepared to come at any other time which would suit you better, and which would give me an opportunity of seeing your institution at work. Yours faithfully

C. T. Loram

ALS Con. 508 BTW Papers DLC.

¹ Charles Templeman Loram (1879–1940), born in Pietermaritzburg, Natal, was educated at the University of Capetown, Cambridge, Yale, and Teachers College, Columbia (Ph.D.). After working as a teacher in Natal, he became inspector of schools (1906–17) and chief inspector of native education (1917–20) of Natal. He was a member of the Native Affairs Commission (1920–29) and superintendent of education (1930) in Natal. In 1931 he became professor of education at Yale.

[2] Maurice Smethurst Evans (1854–1920), a Natal segregationist, wrote in *Black and White in South East Africa* (London, 1911), 112–13, 117, that the education of Africans and Indians should be designed to prevent "overlapping of the races" and consequent friction. Agricultural education was less likely in his view to cause overlapping of the "spheres of activity" than literary or industrial education. He later, after visiting Tuskegee, wrote *Black and White in the Southern States: A Study of the Race Problem in the U.S. from a South African Point of View* (London, 1915).

[3] Loram later published his dissertation, *The Education of the South African Native* (London, 1917).

From William Colfax Graves

Chicago September 29, 1914

Dear Dr. Washington: Mr. Rosenwald, as a member of the Advisory Committee of the National Association for the Advancement of Colored People, has been asked to make suggestions as to the possible candidates for the first award of the Spingarn Medal. This medal, as no doubt you are aware, is offered by Dr. J. E. Spingarn annually "to be awarded for the highest or noblest achievement by an American Negro during the preceding year" upon certain terms and conditions. It is a gold medal not costing more than $100.00. Mr. Rosenwald would very much appreciate your assistance in recommendations to this Committee. Will you, at your convenience, write him what Colored man or what Colored woman, or several of them, who might be considered candidates for the award?

Thanking you, I am Very sincerely yours,

William C. Graves

TLS Con. 255 BTW Papers DLC.

From Seth Bunker Capp

Reading, Pa. October 1, 1914

My Dear Dr. Washington: I received your letter of confirmation of arrangements dated September 26th and have since received the call of your representative, Mr. Frank P. Chisholm, upon his arrival here. He doubtless has written you last night in regards to our agreeable meeting. I find in Mr. Chisholm a most interesting gentleman and a well qualified representative.

I asked Mr. Chisholm for your exact height and weight and he gave the same as about five foot six inches and about 160 pounds, this being his opinion. Will you kindly ask your secretary to drop me a line as soon as possible, giving me accurately these two points, for reasons which I have previously mentioned.[1]

I trust that I shall meet with Mr. Chisholm again before he leaves here and looking forward to seeing you in a few days, I am, Very truly,

S. B. Capp

TLS   Con. 497   BTW Papers   DLC.

[1] E. J. Scott telegraphed Capp that Chisholm's estimate was approximately correct. (Oct. 3, 1914, Con. 497, BTW Papers, DLC.)

To William Colfax Graves

[Tuskegee, Ala.] October 2, 1914

My dear Mr. Graves: Answering your letter under date of September 29, referring to the Spingarn gold medal, I would say in my opinion the person who is entitled to such reward is Isaac Fisher, whose achievement will be found described fully in the September number of Everybody's Magazine.

If I can think of any other person who in any degree approaches Mr. Fisher in achievement in the direction that is sought to be encouraged I shall write you later. Yours very truly,

Booker T. Washington

TLpS   Con. 255   BTW Papers   DLC.

To William Colfax Graves

[Tuskegee, Ala.] October 2, 1913 [1914]

Dear Mr. Graves: In answer to that portion of your letter in which you refer to the kind of statement that ought to be made with reference to the money which Mr. Rosenwald is giving toward building rural schoolhouses, I call your attention to the last paragraph of the enclosed circular which was sent to Mr. Rosenwald for his approval.[1]

This we are giving out in answer to appeals and in other ways we are using it in a way to give correct information as to our plans. I hope this is satisfactory to you.

It is likely from year to year the scope of the scheme will be broadened. Yours very truly,

Booker T. Washington

P.S. — I hope you will note carefully the additions which we have made, in compliance with your wishes and suggestion, in the last paragraph.[2] I think the whole matter is now clear and we are now hard at work trying to get as many new schoolhouses started as possible.

B. T. W.

TLpS Con. 72 BTW Papers DLC.

[1] Enclosed was a typescript "Plan for the Erection of Rural Schoolhouses." It proposed to limit the program for the present to three Alabama counties and to limit the amount Rosenwald would contribute on an equal matching basis to $350 per schoolhouse.

[2] The paragraph stated: "Any publication to the effect that Mr. Rosenwald has promised to give dollar for dollar for rural schoolhouses for colored children in the South without limitation as to the number and location has been made without Mr. Rosenwald's authority or knowledge."

To C. Elias Winston

Tuskegee Institute, Alabama. October 2, 1914

My dear Mr. Winston: I regret the delay in answering your letter owing to the fact that I have been off on a fishing trip for a week.

In your case, I am doing something which I very rarely do, and that is to attempt to correct a misrepresentation of my words. I have found by some experience in public life that if one spends his time in attempting to correct false reports, he will rarely do anything in the way of constructive work, and that the time spent in trying to make such corrections could be better spent, in most cases, in some direct effort in the way of progress.

I am making exception in your case, because you have been kind and thoughtful enough to do that which very few people think of doing, and that is to try to find out directly from the individual, himself, the facts concerning his utterances. In most cases, persons simply hear a rumor, or read a garbled report of one's address and then this report or rumor is passed from one hand to another without anyone taking the precaution to get first-hand, direct information from the person most concerned.

You say that I am quoted in both the white and colored press as making the following remarks: "The Negro should stop fighting segregation and lend his forces towards beautifying the neighborhood in which he lives." Let me say that I have made no such remarks at any time or at any place. On the other hand, I have always opposed the passing of any law to segregate the Negro, either in city, town or country district. I have always said, especially when speaking to Southern white people, that such segregation is unnecessary, unjust, unwise, and from my point of view, illegal, and I have been often surprised at the number of white people in the South who have agreed with my position.

A few weeks ago, when an attempt was made to pass a law segregating colored people in Birmingham, I, in connection with a number of other colored people in Alabama, took the matter up directly with the city commissioners and the law was not passed.

When speaking on the subject of railroad accommodations in Muskogee, I made the following direct remarks to the white people who composed a large part of the audience, "Let us urge upon the railroads throughout this country to provide more equal, more just, more clean and up-to-date railroad facilities for the black people of this country, wherever the law requires such separation. And there is no white man in the United States, no matter where he lives, North or South, who will not agree with us in the statement that, whenever and wherever a Negro pays a railroad fare that is equal to that paid by a white man, he should have accommodations that are just as just and equal, and that are just as clean and decent, as those furnished the white man for the same amount of money. You would not permit the white merchants in Muskogee to sell so many pounds of flour to a Negro customer at a certain price and then sell better flour and more flour to a white customer for the same money; no more should a railroad be permitted to furnish one kind of accommodation to the Negro passenger and another kind of accommodation to the white passenger for the same money."

What I did attempt to say in Muskogee, and what I have attempted on numerous occasions to say when speaking in public, was to urge our people not to become discouraged or disheartened in communities where they were segregated, but notwithstanding such segregation, go forward and make progress. In a word, to overcome evil with good; to make so much progress in the beauty, comfort and convenience of their surroundings that those who have treated them unjustly will be made to blush with shame because of the progress that the colored people are making. In a word, I try to impress upon our people the idea that they should keep a cheerful heart and a strong will and not permit themselves to be continually on the defensive side of life, but to make such progress that the world will admire the rapid strides with which they are going forward.

I realize fully the importance of condemning wrong — such wrongs as segregation, — but I realize, too, the danger of our spending too much time and strength in mere condemnation without attempting to aid our cause by progressive, constructive work as well as condemnation. Condemnation is easy; construction is difficult. The constructive action should employ the major portion of our time. The two lines of thought and work must go hand in hand; condemnation of wrong and constructive effort; overcoming injustice through evidences of progress. On this platform we can make an appeal to every white man in the South and in the North whose goodwill and influence is worth having. More and more, throughout the South, the number of white people who feel and see that it never helps to yield to the temptation of mistreating a black man is increasing; throughout this country, the number of black people who feel and see that it never helps a black man to yield to the temptation of mistreating a white man is increasing.

In proportion as we go forward in all parts of the country, making real progress and asking for fair and just treatment by the hands of all people, North and South, our race is going to command the respect and confidence of all the people of all classes.

You are at liberty to make any use of this letter that your judgment dictates. Yours very truly,

BOOKER T. WASHINGTON

TLSr Copy   Con. 523   BTW Papers   DLC.

To Daniel M. Gerard

[Tuskegee, Ala.] Oct. 4, 1914

Depressed financial condition in South owing to no market for cotton makes it necessary for me to realize something soon as possible on house in Huntington. Is it possible that the house might be sold at reasonable price any time soon or if it cant be sold will it be possible to secure additional loan. If so how much. Answer my expense.

Booker T. Washington

TWSr   Con. 503   BTW Papers   DLC.

To Charles Templeman Loram

[Tuskegee, Ala.] October 5, 1914

My dear Sir: I write to say that it will give us great pleasure to welcome you here at Tuskegee Institute at any time that it would best suit your convenience. I shall be here at the Institute during the Christmas holiday season and of course shall be here the first two weeks in June most likely. We shall be very glad to offer you every opportunity to see the work we are trying to do here at Tuskegee and to make your stay among us as pleasant and profitable as possible.

We recall with great pleasure the visit of Mr. Evans during the meeting of our International Conference on the Negro.

I very much hope you will write me well in advance of your intended visit so that I may plan, if possible, to be here at the school. It is not altogether necessary, of course, that I should be here for you to visit the school as our officers will take good care of you. Nevertheless, I make the above suggestion, because of your mention of the fact that you would like to visit the school while I am here. Yours very truly,

Booker T. Washington

TLpS   Con. 508   BTW Papers   DLC.

An Invitation to a Possum Supper for Teachers

[Tuskegee, Ala.] Oct. 6 [1914]

You are cordially invited to attend
An old-time 'Possum & 'tater Supper and Candy Pulling
Saturday Evening, Nov. 7, 1914
At Mr. Callanan's Place on the Chehaw Dirt Road.
Vehicles to convey the party will be ready
To leave the Court Yard (Boys' Trades Building)
At Seven-thirty P.M.

Booker T. Washington, Principal

TDSr   Con. 635   BTW Papers   DLC.

From Seth Low

Bedford Hills, New York   October 8th, 1914

(Personal)
My dear Doctor Washington: From some of your friends, I learn that they have the impression that you are working too hard and need a rest. May I ask you to let me know confidentially just how you feel about it yourself? Very truly, yours,

Seth Low

TLS   Con. 70   BTW Papers   DLC.

To the Editor of *The New Century*

Tuskegee Institute, Alabama   October 10th, 1914

PIGS AND EDUCATION AND PIGS AND DEBTS

EDITOR THE NEW CENTURY — Our race is in constant search of means with which to provide better homes, schools, colleges, and churches, and with which to pay debts. This is especially true during the hard financial conditions obtaining on account of The European War. All of this cannot be done at once, but great progress can be made by a good strong pull together, in a simple direct manner. How?

There are 1,400,000 colored families who live on farms or in villages, or small towns. Of this number, at the present time, 700,000 have no pigs. I want to ask that each family raise at least one pig this fall. Where one or more pigs are already owned, I want to ask that each family raise one additional pig this fall.

As soon as possible, I want to ask that this plan be followed by the organization of a Pig Club in every community where one does not already exist. I want to ask that the matter be taken up at once through families, schools, churches, and societies, Farmers' Institutes, Business Leagues, etc.

The average pig is valued at about $5.00. If each family adds only one pig, in a few months at the present prices for hogs, $10.00 would be added to the wealth of the owner, and $14,000,000 to the wealth of the colored people. If each family adds two pigs, it would have in a few months $20.00 more wealth, and $28,000,000 would be added with which to promote the welfare of the race during the money stringency created by the European War.

Let us not put it off, but organize Pig Clubs everywhere. Give each boy and girl an opportunity to own and grow at least one pig.

Booker T. Washington

TLSr Mimeographed   Con. 514   BTW Papers   DLC.

To Charles Banks

Reading, Pa. October 13, 1914

Dear Mr. Banks: I have been thinking a good deal about you recently. I am wondering, if you cannot meet your promise, owing to the cotton situation, to Mr. Rosenwald to return his gift in cash, whether or not it would be a practical thing for you to put aside enough bales of cotton to meet the gift when cotton reaches normal prices again. That is to say, if you could say to Mr. Rosenwald when the time comes, that you are ready to place at his disposal enough bales of cotton at normal prices to cover the gift. I think this would be in a measure satisfactory, though of course I am not sure of it. Mr. Rosenwald has ways, of course, of disposing of cotton.

I hope things are going well with you. Yours very truly,

[Booker T. Washington]

TLc   Con. 68   BTW Papers   DLC.

Timothy Thomas Fortune to Emmett Jay Scott

Washington, D.C. Oct. 14, 1914

Dear Mr. Scott: Many thanks for your letter of the 12th instant, and for the enclosure. I am glad that Dr. Washington has taken the trouble to notice the matter of his alleged reference to segregation at Muscogee. It will do good. I will use it current.

We are also using in the current issue a splendid article by Prof. Charles H. Moore backing up my editorial position as to what Dr. Washington meant in the quotation attributed to him, and enlarging on the splendid work Dr. Washington has done for the race.

I am surprised to find Washington a hot bed of Association for the Advancement of Colored People sentiment, and opposition to Dr. Washington, which is generally ascribed in large part to Chase's vile and vacillating support of Dr. Washington and his policies. It would serve us all better if Chase were an out and out opponent of Dr. Washington.

I have been unable to get a settlement with Moore and it has hampered me materially in my work here. I may have to go to law, and stand for the stinking scandal of it.

The paper is gaining in favor, and I am managing to pay the printer. With love for all, Yours sincerely,

T Thomas Fortune

TLS Con. 11 BTW Papers DLC. Written on stationery of the Washington *Sun,* T. Thomas Fortune, Publisher.

To Seth Low

Mansion House, Reading, Pa. October 15, 1914

Dear Mr. Low: I have just received your kind letter of October 8th in which you make inquiry concerning my personal health.

I thank you very much for your thought of me in this respect. At the end of the summer I found myself considerably run down, but after the opening of the school I spent a week fishing down on Mobile Bay and that helped me a great deal.

A friend who lives in Philadelphia, Mr. Seth B. Capp, has been after me for sometime to let a Bohemian artist friend of his, who has a studio at present in Reading, paint a portrait of me, and I have been here in Reading a week giving sittings and this has given me a good rest and agreeable change, so that I now feel from every point of view perfectly strong and in good shape. I shall be returning to Tuskegee at the end of the week in fine condition.

Matters in the South growing out of the cotton situation are in pretty bad shape, but everybody is taking a cheerful view and no one seems to be inclined to oppress the other on account of debts. Yours very truly,

[Booker T. Washington]

TLc Con. 70 BTW Papers DLC.

To the Editor of the Tuskegee *News*

[Tuskegee, Ala.] October 21, 1914

Dear Sir: The Trustees and officers of the Tuskegee Institute are anxious in every way possible to help relieve the financial depression in Macon County. With this in view, we are trying to spend every dollar in the county that we possibly can. In connection with the building of a new steam, light and power plant and other work, aside from what we are paying for material bought at a distance, we are paying out in cash in the county between $1200 and $1500 each week. In order to continue this permanent improvement, which we thought of stopping at one time, our Trustees have recently borrowed $50,000 in New York City, and a large part of this will be spent in Macon County.

In order further to help relieve conditions in the county, I wish to make it known that the Business Agent of the Tuskegee Institute[1] will buy for cash from farmers of Macon County the following lines of produce, subject to his approval, delivered to the Institution as needed, well dried corn on the cob or shelled and sacked, oats, thrashed and sacked, poultry, eggs, butter, and other farm products raised in Macon County.

We are further willing to pay the market price in cash, when in need of same, for good qualities of pigs or beef delivered to the school. Yours very truly,

Booker T. Washington

TLpS Con. 58 BTW Papers DLC.

[1] Ernest Ten Eyck Attwell.

Emmett Jay Scott to J. S. Johnson

[Tuskegee, Ala.] October 22, 1914

My dear Sir: I am very much obliged to you for your kindness in sending me the "Story of Paramount."

Please permit me to trespass further upon your time to request a word with reference to the suggestion submitted in my last letter. Will you kindly name the gentleman connected with the Jesse L. Lasky[1] Feature Play Show, who can advise me as to the picturizing of "Up From Slavery," Dr. Washington's autobiography. Under separate cover, today I am sending a copy of the book for your personal perusal, and I am also attaching a memorandum statement, showing the languages and dialects into which the book has been translated.

From an entertainment point of view, I feel quite sure that "Up From Slavery," if properly filmed, will prove a satisfactory entertainment for presentation by the Paramount Pictures Corporation. Yours very truly,

Emmett J. Scott

TLpS Con. 13 BTW Papers DLC.

[1] Jesse L. Lasky (1880–1958), motion picture producer, organized the Jesse L. Lasky Feature Play Co. in 1914. He merged with Paramount Pictures, and later was associate producer of RKO Radio Pictures, Inc.

To the Editor of *The Independent*

[Tuskegee, Ala.] October 26, 1914

My dear Sir: Replying to yours, under date of October 20th, asking for an expression from me "on the best book I have read for a year,"[1] I would state that the book which has interested me most during the last year has been "V. V.'s Eyes."[2] I have been pleased by this book because it represents the new and fast awakening of the South in reference to the application of education, culture and wealth in relieving and improving the social conditions in our Southern communities. The writer being a Southern man knows Southern conditions and needs and he has by clear and incisive illustrations shown the South how to change conditions and at the same time indicated how public sentiment is growing in the direction of service. Yours very truly,

Booker T. Washington

TLpS Con. 506 BTW Papers DLC.

[1] BTW's letter appeared, with some editorial changes, in *The Independent*, 80 (Nov. 16, 1914), 247.
[2] Henry Sydnor Harrison's *V. V.'s Eyes* (New York: Grosset & Dunlap, 1913) was a romantic novel about a southern tobacco-manufacturing town.

To John Henry Washington, Jr.

[Tuskegee, Ala.] October 26, 1914

My dear John: I have read your last letter with a great deal of interest. I hope you will make good in your new position. Bear in mind that you cannot succeed except as you learn to tell absolutely the truth at all times, and not exaggerate. Then you will have to learn to pay your debts, to not borrow money, to not involve yourself in financial obligations that you cannot meet. I hope you attend some Sunday school and church every Sunday.

All are well at home, and we are giving especial attention to Rev. Mr. Kinchen.[1]

Your uncle,
B. T. W.

TLpI   Con. 526   BTW Papers   DLC.

[1] Elijah Wesley Kinchen was born in Baldwin, La., in 1874. He attended Fisk University and Gammon Theological Seminary (B.D., 1905). In 1906 he became pastor of Wesley Chapel (M. E. Church) in Los Angeles.

An Article in *Outlook*

Oct. 28, 1914

A REMARKABLE TRIPLE ALLIANCE:
HOW A JEW IS HELPING THE NEGRO
THROUGH THE Y.M.C.A.

In the spring of 1910 the Chicago Young Men's Christian Association, during a canvass to raise $1,000,000 for its general purposes, approached Mr. Julius Rosenwald for a subscription. He inquired whether the objects for which the million-dollar fund provided included a building for colored men, and, on being informed that it did not, stated that as soon as the Association was ready to undertake such a project he would contribute $25,000.

Later, encouraged by Mr. Rosenwald's offer, under the leadership of Dr. George C. Hall, the well-known colored surgeon, the Chicago

Association undertook to raise a fund of $100,000 for a building for colored men. More than this amount was raised, and there has been constructed a modern, well-equipped building, costing, with land and equipment, nearly $200,000.

Shortly after the successful conclusion of the Chicago canvass Dr. J. E. Moorland, one of the colored International Secretaries of the Young Men's Christian Association, who with Dr. Hall had directed the canvass of the Chicago Association for subscriptions among colored people, in company with Mr. Messer and Mr. Parker,[1] of the Chicago Association, called on Mr. Rosenwald to explain the successful conduct of the campaign. During the course of the luncheon Mr. Rosenwald made careful inquiry regarding the progress of Association work among colored men elsewhere in the country, and, on learning that the work was of small volume owing largely to inadequate equipment, he, in the most matter-of-fact way, stated that he would duplicate his Chicago offer to any city in America — that is to say, during a period of five years he would contribute $25,000 to any city that raised $75,000 toward a Young Men's Christian Association building for its colored men.

That, as I have heard the story, is the way in which the first announcement was made of Mr. Rosenwald's offer of $25,000 to any city in the United States that could provide the remaining $75,000 toward a $100,000 building for the colored Young Men's Christian Association. This gift has proved to be one of the wisest and best-paying philanthropic investments of which I have any knowledge. In fact, I doubt if there is any single gift to any public institution that has brought a greater return to the community than this one single benefaction, which is all the more interesting because it is the gift of a Jew to a Christian religious institution.

Since that time four buildings, each costing $100,000 or more, have been erected. The one in Washington, D.C., was dedicated in May, 1912. Then followed the buildings in Chicago, Indianapolis, and Philadelphia. In addition to these, funds have already been subscribed for buildings costing upwards of $100,000 each at Los Angeles, California; Atlanta, Georgia; Baltimore, Maryland; Kansas City, Missouri; Cincinnati, Ohio; and New York City. There are to be two Association buildings in the Eastern metropolis, the second being for colored women. In Nashville, Tennessee, the colored people have subscribed $3,000 more than their allotment — $33,000, instead of $30,000 —

and the campaign ended one day ahead of time! The campaign is, as I write, under way among the white people of Nashville to subscribe $45,000 allotted to them.

Mr. Rosenwald has paid out $100,000 already; $175,000 more will be paid at the proper time in the construction period, and, if Nashville completes its fund, $25,000 more will be available there. Facing such a proposition, Mr. Rosenwald's only source of disappointment has been, as Dr. Moorland tells me, that the demands upon him were not more frequent.

First and foremost among the ways in which this gift has helped the Young Men's Christian Association and the colored people has been the giving them an opportunity to help themselves. Since January, 1911, in response to Mr. Rosenwald's offer, not less than $411,500 has been subscribed by the colored people in the eleven cities I have named. In addition to this sum, $53,513.33 has been raised by colored people for the Young Men's Christian Association organizations in smaller towns. This means that, altogether, $465,013.33 has been subscribed by the colored people thus far, mostly in the Northern cities, for the erection of these buildings in which the Christian young men of the race may find opportunities for wholesome recreation, Christian education, and moral guidance.

Some notion of the enthusiasm and interest with which the colored people have gone at this work may be gathered from the fact that, in the campaign to erect the first $100,000 building in Washington, D.C., the campaign committee carried 4,500 different accounts with colored people. Practically one in every twenty of the Negro population of Washington contributed to the $27,000 raised by them for this purpose. Of the remainder, $25,000 was given by John D. Rockefeller, $25,000 by Julius Rosenwald, and $23,000 by the white people of Washington. In the campaign to erect a Young Men's Christian Association building in Chicago the sum of $67,000 was subscribed by 10,000 colored people. This means that about one in every four of the colored population of Chicago, according to the last census, contributed to the erection of a building costing $195,000.

In Philadelphia the colored people started out to raise $25,000, and succeeded in getting subscriptions amounting to $23,000 in six days. In Atlanta, Georgia, colored people raised among themselves $50,000, and among the white people $25,000. In Indianapolis colored people raised $18,000, and among the whites $60,000. In Baltimore the colored people started out to raise $25,000, but finished their campaign with subscriptions amounting to $31,000; the white people contributed $50,000. In Kansas City colored people raised $31,000, the whites $50,000. In Cincinnati it was proposed that the white population raise $60,000 and the colored $15,000. As a matter of fact, the colored people raised $25,000 in ten days. In New York City they subscribed $40,000 toward a $150,000 building. In Nashville Tennessee, as I have said, they raised over $33,000 among themselves, and they did it in nine days. In this campaign the Nashville "Globe," ordinarily published once a week, issued a daily edition announcing the amount of the day's subscription. This was one of the first daily papers ever published by and for colored people.

It is interesting to note the sources from which this money raised by colored people came.

It must be remembered that this is the first time in the history of the world that the Negro race has had an opportunity of handling and of contributing to so large an enterprise. Both those who handled the subscription lists and those who gave realized keenly that the whole race was on trial. Their gifts ran all the way from 25 cents to $1,200 per contributor. The number who gave $1,000 was both gratifying and surprising. Who were they, and how could they respond so liberally to this great cause? The first man to give $1,000 was James H. Tilgham, of Chicago. Mr. Tilgham was born back in the days of slavery, 1844, in Washington, D.C.

For some fifteen years this man was driven hither and thither, seeking work, seeking some place to settle down and make good. Now he was in New Orleans working under the Reconstruction Government; now back in Washington, first in Government work, and then learning the trade of decorator; now in Boston as a waiter in the Harvard diningroom. Finally, in 1881, he went to Chicago and, after some struggle, began his work as messenger, first to Carter H. Harrison, Sr., then to Engineer Clark, of the Lake Shore and Michigan Southern and Rock Island Railroad system, then to the Chicago Telephone Company, with which he has been employed since 1901.

In giving his $1,000 Mr. Tilgham said: "Many years ago, when I left my Eastern home, a mere boy, I landed in Chicago without friends and hardly a dollar I could call my own. I began to search here and there for a home and a place to work. After a time I was successful, but even then I did not get a desirable place where a young man can feel homelike and happy. It was during these times that my mind was formed to make it better for the 'wanderer' who would perchance leave a good home to battle in this broad world to make himself a man and become a respected citizen in the community in which he lived.

"Seeing the door of hope closed to me and to my people, and my hands tied to give millions, I vowed to God that I would take advantage of my disadvantages, and, if ever the opportunity presented itself, I would give largely of my hard-earned means, which were from the sweat of my brow, to the first call that came that was interdenominational, which would help to fully develop the boy and man to fit him, not only for the service of himself, but for his country as well."

Another man to give $1,000 was David T. Howard, of Atlanta, Georgia. Mr. Howard started life as a slave. He, too, tried his hands at many kinds of work. Finally, in a humble way, he started the business of undertaking. During the later years of his success his means have been generously divided with the poor of his race. He takes the widows and children under his care and aids them in getting their business in order. He has financed and instructed many young men who wanted to begin a business of their own. Mr. Howard owns, not only much valuable city property, but a lot of farm land, on which, again, he makes opportunities for his race.

R. H. Boyd, of Nashville, Tennessee, was another ex-slave to contribute $1,000 towards the Young Men's Christian Association in his city. Mr. Boyd owns one of the few big Negro publishing houses in the country. This man went to school — elementary school — after he was grown, married, and had a family of considerable size. To quote a part of his own story:

> I went into Palestine, Texas, and formed a partnership with Dunlap and Smallwood and bought the first printing machinery furnishing Bible leaflets to the young people of the South. I went in partnership with Dunlap and Smallwood because they were white men and experienced printers. I had, at that time, $500, possibly $1,000. I invested it in machinery. I knew nothing of printing. I swindled both Dunlap and Smallwood. I swindled these men out of what they had. When we went into the business, they had the experience; I had the money. When we quit — we were finally burned out — they got all the money and I left Palestine with all the experience. I went to Nashville in 1896 for the purpose of devising some ways and means by which we could print all of the Bible leaflets, Sunday-school and Church literature used or required by our denomination. I secured a secretary, rented a room for $5 a month, furnished it nicely with one or two split-bottom chairs and a second-hand table, which served as my desk; then I bought a few pencils and some paper, opened my office, began business, and reported for work

every morning promptly at or before nine o'clock. The first thing I did — my secretary and I — was to bow down by the side of that table and ask Almighty God to help me to succeed in this work. And I want to tell you that from that day until the present time there has never been a day in the National Baptist Publishing Board but what every employee working there has been ordered to shut down the presses, stop whatever they are doing, and at 9:30 each morning enter the chapel and thank God for his goodness and ask for guidance during that day. When I first started into this printing enterprise at Nashville, I lived in that little room; I had left my family in San Antonio, Texas. There, beside the open fireplace, I slept, I prayed to God for success, and laid my plans for the future. I was my own cook and servant girl. The problem of the Negro servant girl had not entered my household. My breakfast consisted of a cup of coffee, some rye bread toasted on the coals, and a nickel's worth of bologna sausage.

This is the type of life story back of nearly every large as well as small sum paid from the Negro purse in all those campaigns. So it has been with Thomas E. Lassiter, of Atlantic City, New Jersey, again a man who started with nothing, but who now, through hard work and self-control, is worth some $50,000. His wife, a hairdresser, is, I am told, worth in her own name almost as much as her husband.

Again, there is Mrs. C. J. Walker, of Indianapolis, who not many years ago left the farm in Louisiana for the wash-tub, left the wash-tub for the kitchen, and then left the kitchen for business. She, too, was in the $1,000 class of donors. In all these instances of $1,000 Negro donors — in that of Mr. Preston Taylor, a wealthy undertaker of the same city; of the Rev. William Beckam and Mr. Henry Allen Boyd, also of Nashville; of Mrs. Daisy Merchant, of Cincinnati, who gave $1,200; of Dr. E. P. Roberts, of New York; of Mr. Henry T. Troy, of Los Angeles, California — in all these cases the money has been literally wrung from the respective occupations by hard work, under trying circumstances and the greatest amount of personal restraint.

That most of the showing in building Young Men's Christian Associations should have been made among Negroes of the North is to me a matter of marked significance. In the first place, these buildings themselves provide places of welcome where they are most needed. Year by year our boys get into Northern cities. Often they are in schools and work on trains or steamboats in summer to earn their tuition for the next year. The Northern city gets attractive to them. They decide to stay there. But in too many cases this decision is the end of all that was hopeful in the young man's career. He misses the best people and gets among the easy-going. He gets into a hotel, where money comes easily and regularly. Coming easily, it goes easily. The Young Men's Christian Association in these cities will lead him among different companions and keep in him the ambition he set out with.

It is sometimes said that the Young Men's Christian Association weakens the influence of the church. This was not so in the case of the Negro. In many instances the persons who contributed the most in effort and money to make the erection of these buildings possible were men who had not been counted as particularly religious men. In a great number of cases, after the building campaigns were over, they connected themselves with the church again. Men and women who had previously taken little or no part in any organized effort to help themselves or the race were drawn into the movement. Men of all classes and all denominations united and pulled together for the common good as they had never done before. The result of this was that when the work was over and the finished building came to be dedicated, the people felt that it belonged to them to an extent that they could not have felt if it had cost them any less effort and sacrifice.

Another way in which this gift has helped the Negro people has been by enabling the Young Men's Christian Association to teach how it is possible to make religion touch practical life. That "old-time religion," from which the Negro got so much comfort in slavery, turned all attention to the next world. In the Young Men's Christian Association he learns to associate religion with cleanliness, with health, with pure living. He learns to associate religion with the reading of books, with opportunities for study and advancement in his trade or profession. In short, the young colored man learns in the Young Men's Christian Association how religion can and should be connected up with all the ordinary practical interests and wholesome natural pleasures of life.

Another direction in which, it seems to me, Mr. Rosenwald's gift and the Young Men's Christian Association have been a help to the members of my race is in what they are doing to convince the white people of this country that in the long run schools are cheaper than policemen; that there is more wisdom in keeping a man out of the ditch than in trying to save him, after he has fallen in; that it is more Christian and more economical to prepare young men to live right than to punish them after they have committed crime.

Some years ago at Buxton, Iowa, where there is a community of about fifteen hundred Negro miners, the Consolidated Coal Company was persuaded to erect a colored Young Men's Christian Association building at a cost of $20,000. For several years this Christian Association was about the only government that community had. So satisfactory did this investment prove that, after a short time, another building was erected for a boys' branch of the Association. When the manager of this company was asked his opinion as to the value of this work, he said: "The Association has made a policeman and a prison unnecessary in this community."

This work, begun at Buxton in 1903, has now become a regular feature of the Young Men's Christian Association's work. There are similar Associations among the lumber men at Vaughn, North Carolina, and Bogalusa, Louisiana. Recently an Association was started among the five thousand Negroes employed by the Newport Shipbuilding Company, at Newport News, Virginia. At this place night classes were established to give the boys and young men of the community a general education. In addition, there is a social room where members may play billiards, pool, and other games, and an athletic field where they have outdoor games and sports. Thousands of colored men are employed in mines, in lumber camps, iron mills, and construction camps, in which there are neither schools nor churches, nor any other influence that makes for better living. Under such conditions employers see that it is not only human and right, but sound economy, to provide some sort of welfare work for their employees, both white and black. The result is that these Associations are springing up more rapidly than the Association can find competent men to direct them. At Benham, Kentucky, an Association has recently been started for colored miners. At Birmingham, Alabama, the American Coal and Iron Company has recently fitted up a splendid plant for its employees, white and colored. This branch of the work illustrates how the Association has been able to adapt its work to all kinds and classes of men.

The organizing of the colored people for the gathering and collection of subscriptions, the inspiration that comes from labor in common for the common good — all this is in itself a character-building process, and has had a far-reaching influence upon the churches and other religious organizations throughout the country. These efforts have helped not merely the black man, but the white man as well, in bringing the best element of both races together in labor and counsel for the common good. To the South especially, where the best black and the best white people almost never meet and know each other, the struggles, the sacrifices, and the generous enthusiasm which the building campaign has brought out in the black man and white have served to reveal each race to the other and to bring about an understanding and community interest between them that could probably have come about in no other way.

Outlook, 108 (Oct. 28, 1914), 484–92.

1 Francis Warner Parker (1858–1922) was a Chicago lawyer and politician who was active in the work of the YMCA.

From Timothy Thomas Fortune

Washington, D.C. Oct. 29, 1914

My dear Dr. Washington: Thanks for your letter of the 27th instant. In standing by you and your good works I am only hewing to the old lines, from which I have never departed. But, in my own paper, of course, I can speak out more freely than I could in The Age or any other of the newspapers with which I have been associated during the past seven years, and with authority. All the editors I have worked for had prejudices of their own, which I respected, by not writing anything that they might censure or turn down. I helped make your situation, and have no part in the situation built alongside it by others, who have it in for me, as I have it in for them.

I do not expect to convince the fanatics that they are wrong; but I shall show them that they are, and thus spike their guns and keep their supporters and apologists guessing, and at the same time diminishing the enthusiasm of those who want to get on their staff, mainly because they "have white folks for their leaders."

I am fighting it out single handed with The Sun, and I shall win. With kindest regards, Yours sincerely,

T. Thos. Fortune

Prof Moore gives 'em another broadside in this Sun this week on "Who is Responsible for our Disfranchisement?["]

TLS Con. 502 BTW Papers DLC. On stationery of the Washington *Sun*, T. Thomas Fortune, Publisher. Postscript in Fortune's hand.

From Jesse Edward Moorland

Washington, D.C., October 31st, 1914

My dear Dr. Washington: I was very much pleased to see your splendid article on "Association Work" in the current number of the "Outlook." The illustrations are splendid. I am very sorry, however, they left out Mme. Walker as she is one of our strongest supporters.

The reference to Mr. Rosenwald making his gift to the entire country, after the success of the Chicago campaign is, unfortunately, not historically correct. As I tried to make clear in my statement to Dr. Park and in subsequent correspondence to you, Mr. Rosenwald made his gift at a luncheon where Messrs. Messer, Parker, Loeb[1] and I were present before we even organized the campaign; and Dr. Hall came into leadership of the movement after the campaign. He was not a member of the church when we had the campaign and said to me after he had decided to join the church that he did not give much time because he could not afford to look at the young men as a leader not having taken the stand he knew he ought to take himself. I think it would have made the article much stronger on that point, had it been shown that the finest result of the work was the leading of a man like Dr. Hall into the leadership of such a movement. This is according to his own testimony which has been published.

It is almost impossible, however, to get every item just as it should appear from a historical standpoint. It probably may make no difference to most people. There might be some people in Chicago who would take some exception.

I want to thank you heartily for this splendid piece of service which will have a good effect not as regards the Association movement alone, but as regards the Colored people throughout the entire country.

Hoping to see you sometime in the near future and with all good wishes, I am, Very sincerely yours,

J. E. Moorland

P.S. I wonder will it be possible to get the photographs back. I am called upon for photographs for illustrations so much that it is hard to keep a stock on hand.

J. E. M.

TLS Con. 511 BTW Papers DLC.

¹ Probably Jacob Moritz Loeb (b. 1875), an insurance executive, a member of the Chicago school board (1913–22), and a leader in Jewish welfare and relief organizations.

To the Editor of *The Negro Farmer*

[Tuskegee, Ala., ca. Nov. 1, 1914]¹

Editor, The Negro Farmer: From my point of view, Alabama is the very best state in the Union for both white and colored people to live in.

It has a large variety of the necessities of life. It has plenty of good farming land. It has mineral land, including iron, coal and lime and it has large sections of timber land. Aside from this, it has plenty of sea coast with good fisheries. It has a cold climate in the Northern part, a mild climate in the central part and a warm climate in the Southern part.

Aside from all this, it has a fine type of white people. Here one finds the backbone of Southern aristocracy — a class of people who has always treated the Negro kindly and considerately. There is absence of racial friction or difficulty in this state that is very marked. One finds that a black man who lives an industrious, sober, earnest up-right life is given a fair chance.

Alabama, too, has been unusually fortunate in not having the Negro in recent years brought into political discussion. The result is that we have had a class of public men in office that have not stirred up racial friction, as has been true in other states.

There are many other reasons why from my point of view Alabama is the best state in which to live.

Booker T. Washington

TLpSr Con. 512 BTW Papers DLC.

¹ On Oct. 29, 1914, Isaac Fisher, editor of *The Negro Farmer*, asked BTW for a short article on "Why Alabama is a good State for colored people?" He requested that BTW get it to him in about a week. (Fisher to BTW, Oct. 29, 1914, Con. 512, BTW Papers, DLC.)

To Timothy Thomas Fortune

[Tuskegee, Ala.] November 2, 1914

Personal.

My dear Mr. Fortune: I have yours under date of October 29th and am very glad to hear from you. I read with deep interest and satisfaction the policy which you outlined in your letter and I know that it is the same policy which you have always stuck to.

First, I am not deceived by conditions in Washington. Whenever I have been there and spoken directly to the masses of the people, I found that they were with me. They understand me and are loyal. The type of people who are opposing me and criticising me I do not believe would be true to anybody very long.

You strike at the heart of the matter when you refer to white leadership. As you know, I have never aspired to leadership. I have simply tried to do my duty, but there is a type of colored people, and Washington seems to be the headquarters for them, who have been educated by white people usually in Northern institutions, who are never happy unless they are worshiping at the feet of some white man. No matter how insignificant or irresponsible the white man may be, they are perfectly happy if he gives them the slightest attention and they are willing to fall over themselves both in contributing money and in rendering worship whenever a certain type of white man crooks the finger. This type of black people are mad in the first place because God made them black, instead of white, and it is very hard to reconcile them to anything that is rational.

I note with interest what you say about Prof. Moore's article. I shall read it when the paper comes.

I shall hope to see you soon. Yours very truly,

Booker T. Washington

TLpS Con. 502 BTW Papers DLC.

To Hollis Burke Frissell

[Tuskegee, Ala.] November 2, 1914

My dear Dr. Frissell: I am thinking of making an application to the General Education Board for an increase in the appropriation which it gives us annually and I am writing to know if you have any suggestions to make.

You can easily understand how the present war conditions are affecting us rather seriously, so far as our income is concerned and I thought the General Education Board might consider it a great privilege to help out by enlarging the annual appropriation. I shall not make the application without consultation with Dr. Buttrick. As yet, I have not seen him.

I have never seen this part of the South so handicapped and depressed from a financial point of view as it is at present. A year ago, cotton was selling at from 13 to 14 cents. Now cotton is selling from 5 to 6 cents and the worst of it is that people do not want to buy it at any price.

It is very interesting to note, however, what a fine spirit of mutual forbearance and cooperation exists between the white people and colored people in bearing the burden. I have not heard of a single case where a white man has foreclosed on a colored man on account of indebtedness, in fact, I believe public sentiment is such that it would drive out of the community any white man who oppressed a colored man on account of a debt just now. How much longer this part of the South can stand present conditions, it is hard to say. We have not reached the most critical period. That will come sometime after Christmas when the question of planting a new crop is to be considered and the question of getting means with which to grow a new crop is before the people. Yours very truly,

Booker T. Washington

TLpS Con. 255 BTW Papers DLC.

To William G. Willcox

[Tuskegee, Ala.] November 3, 1914

My dear Mr. Willcox: I have your letter of October 30th regarding advertising the Tuskegee Farm and Improvement Company.

I would state that, in the first place, we refrained from advertising the plan very broadly because we feared that if the owners of the property got wind of what we had in mind, they might try to back out from their bargain to sell.

After we secured the land, we took up the matter through correspondence with our graduates and former students, and the result was, more applications came to settle on the place than we could accommodate, this year, hence we felt it necessary not to advertise very broadly; and then, too, we have had the feeling that it would be better before advertising very much to be able to state what had been accomplished rather than predict what we wished to accomplish in the future. I will be sending you within a few days a report showing just what has been accomplished up to the present. The sudden change in the financial condition of the South has, of course, impressed upon us the importance of going very cautiously and very slowly. I do not think that those who are planning to settle there this year will be able to pay as much in cash to begin with as they had planned to pay, owing to there being practically no sale for cotton, and then in the next place, I very much fear that until conditions readjust themselves, those who go there will not be able for a year or two, at least, to get very much out of cotton. We shall have to watch things very carefully while they are trying to change their cotton crop largely to a food growing crop.

It will be very easy to get a lot of people on the place this year who would have to be perhaps supported wholly from the funds of the company during the next year or two. We think rather than to do this, we had better go slowly and get too few rather than too many. As I have stated, there is no trouble about applications and do not think there will be.

Perhaps you failed to note what we said about the colonization scheme in the former issues of The Student. I am sending you marked copies. Yours very truly,

Booker T. Washington

TLpS Con. 989 BTW Papers DLC.

To Timothy Thomas Fortune

[Tuskegee, Ala.] November 4th, 1914

Personal.

My dear Mr. Fortune: The way those fellows treated you in not attending the meeting is a clear indication of their disposition to worship
at the altar of white people. If some cheap, unknown white man had
wanted them to attend a meeting, they would have been there by the
score.

With all good wishes, I am, Yours very truly,

Booker T. Washington

TLpS Con. 502 BTW Papers DLC.

To Jesse Edward Moorland

[Tuskegee, Ala., ca. Nov. 5] 1914[1]

My dear Dr. Moorland: I thank you for your letter regarding my
article in The Outlook.

I would state as to the changes made in the manuscript: these
changes were made for the most part by Mr. Rosenwald. The whole
thing was submitted to him before publication for his criticism. As
to the photographs that were left out, I would say that in all such matters one has to trust himself to the tender mercy of the editors. It
seems for lack of space they were compelled to leave out, as is often
true, a good many of the most interesting photographs, among them
Dr. Boyd of Nashville. I regret very much that Mme. Walker's photograph did not get in.

I am glad you liked the article and hope it will do good. Yours very
truly,

Booker T. Washington

TLpS Con. 511 BTW Papers DLC.

[1] The dateline is obliterated on the edge of the press copy.

To Charles Seymour Whitman

[Tuskegee, Ala.] November 5, 1914

Personal.

Dear Mr. Whitman: Please permit me to congratulate you most heartily on your great and deserving victory. It is a matter of the greatest satisfaction to all of your numerous friends.

This victory, in my opinion, is but a preparation for a still higher promotion, and I want to do my part in bringing about such promotion.[1] Yours truly,

Booker T. Washington

TLpS Con. 526 BTW Papers DLC.

[1] BTW congratulated Whitman on his election as governor of New York, and although the letter was marked "Personal," it found its way into several New York newspapers. The New York *Tribune* interpreted it to mean that BTW would support Whitman for President of the United States in 1916. (New York *Tribune,* New York *World,* New York *American,* Nov. 8, 1914, clippings, Con. 526, BTW Papers, DLC.)

To William A. Harris

[Tuskegee, Ala.] November 6, 1914

My dear Sir: I regret the delay in replying to your letter of some days ago.[1] It has remained unanswered for a longer period than is customary with me.

I would say that one of the causes of prevalence of tuberculosis among the Negroes is due to the poor housing conditions in the congested districts of our large cities. As you may know, it is very difficult for a colored man to secure a decent home in which to live in cities, particularly in the South, and where they are so congested, city authorities are not inclined to surround them with proper sanitary and otherwise living conditions. Statistics will show that Negroes who live in rural districts are not so liable to attack as are persons living in the congested city districts.

I am unable, however, to go into any technical discussion of the case and would refer you to the National Society for the Prevention of

Tuberculosis located in New York City. A letter addressed to them at New York City will reach them. Yours very truly,

Booker T. Washington

TLpS Con. 523 BTW Papers DLC.

¹ William A. Harris, a black physician in Savannah, Ga., asked BTW for an outline of the best way to educate blacks on the prevention, cause, and cure of tuberculosis. (Oct. 18, 1914, Con. 523, BTW Papers, DLC.)

From John Ege

Reading, Pa. Nov. 10, 1914

Dear Dr. Yours of Oct 31 received. In reply will say, I sent you two bottles of radium water yesterday. I was out of strong radium water and therefore could not send it at once. Hope you received it by this time. There are certainly no charges, no matter how much you want. Just Write for it anytime you need it. I'm sure you will find out, as I said in my 1905 article, that it is one of the greatest tonics known, and that not too much is said, if we call it the Elixir of Life.

I received a letter from your doctor and am sorry to say that I mislaid it, and I enclose a note of a few cases, which kindly hand to him and I will write him a long letter with some of my articles *when* I get them reprinted.

I wish your doctor were here for a few days so I could show him what radium can do. There is so much to write about the use of radium I do not know when I will get time. Sincerely yours,

Jno Ege MD.

HLS Con. 501 BTW Papers DLC.

An Address before the
Negro Organization Society of Virginia[1]

Norfolk, Va., November 12, 1914

WHAT COÖPERATION CAN ACCOMPLISH

Mr. Chairman, Ladies and Gentlemen: The Negro Organization Society is so unique and at the same time so practical in its objects and results that it commands the respect, confidence, and support of all the best people of both races throughout Virginia. Not the least important part of the work of this society consists in teaching colored people to work together, and in showing them that they can accomplish more through union than through dissension. It is not only teaching our race to coöperate, but it is furnishing an object lesson in showing how white people can help black people; how we can be and are separate in strictly social matters, but one in all that concerns the fundamental things of the South.

The Negro Organization Society of Virginia is showing us that in the great big fundamental things of life there is no one who can help us except ourselves. That no law of Congress or of the State Legislature can help us as much, in the last analysis, as things that we can do, is being emphasized through this practical and far-reaching organization, which is bringing religious denominations, educational movements, secret and fraternal organizations, business leagues, and civic organizations together for the purpose of seeing that throughout the state of Virginia better educational facilities are provided, better sanitary and moral conditions brought about, crime reduced, and friendly relations between the two races maintained.

Another thing that the Negro Organization Society is teaching is that we have advantages right here in the South in the way of soil and climate and white people who understand us and whom we understand, which are not accorded to any similar group of our people anywhere else in the world. True, we sometimes have evidence of racial friction, but when we consider the large number of black people and the large number of white people scattered over an immense territory, such as we have in the South, the wonder is that there is not more racial friction instead of less. We must remember, too, that when a large territory is occupied by people who are white, they sometimes have trouble. This is manifest in what is now going on in Europe.

The mere fact that the Negro race is in the South in large numbers does not mean that we can always remain here in our present state of prosperity, unless we prove to the people in every community where we live that we can get as much out of the soil and as much out of the natural resources of the community as any other race can. This places upon us a tremendous obligation.

The great bulk of our people are going to live, in my opinion, here in the South, where they are better off in proportion to their numbers than anywhere else in the world. We are going to live here because we do not want to leave and because the white man does not want us to leave.

I am glad that this organization is emphasizing the matter of health, the matter of cleanliness, the matter of better sanitary conditions throughout Virginia. In this work for better health both races can coöperate. When food is being prepared, the Negro touches the white man's life; when food is being served, the Negro woman touches the white man's life; when children are being nursed, the Negro woman touches the white man's life; when clothes are being laundered, the Negro woman touches the white man's life. It is mighty important, in the interest of our race as well as in the interest of the white race, that the Negro woman be taught cleanliness and the laws of health. Disease draws no color line.

If by reason of filth and unsanitary conditions in Norfolk, growing out of ignorance, there come to the black community consumption, smallpox, or any other contagious disease, it is likely to reach, through the Negro community, the mansion of the richest white person in the city. In Alabama, a few years ago, an ignorant Negro woman was employed as cook in an aristocratic white college for girls. Little attention was given to the health or cleanliness of this colored woman. Little attention was given to the place where she slept or the way she lived. In the end, a deadly contagious disease took hold of her body and from her spread among the white girls in the college. The result was that four of the most promising of these white girls were taken away by death and the college was disbanded for the year.

The entire South is dependent upon the Negro, in a large measure, for certain kinds of work. A weak body, a sickly body, is costly to the whole community and to the whole state, from an economic point of view. The average length of the Negro's life in the South is at present thirty-five years. It should be fifty years, and the Negro Organization Society of Virginia can prolong the life of the average Negro working man to fifty years. In India the average length of life is twenty-five years; in Massachusetts, where they have good public schools, it is forty-five years; in Denmark and Sweden, fifty years.

In the city of Norfolk there are practically 35,000 black people. Statistics show that 1,800 of these people are sick all the time; $65,000 is spent every year in Norfolk for Negro funerals alone. All this, in the way of sickness and death, means a net loss to the city of Norfolk of at least $1,370,000. In the state of Virginia statistics show that there are 41,000 black people who are sick all the time. This means a net loss to the white and black people of Virginia, in the way of earning power, of at least $23,000,000.

There are 450,000 Negroes sick in the South every day in the year. The sickness and death of so large a proportion of its population means an annual loss to the South of over $300,000,000. At least $150,000,000 of this amount could be saved by taking measures to prevent disease by the simple precautions which the Negro Organization Society in every way emphasizes. This $150,000,000 saved would furnish six months of schooling for every white and black child in the South and, besides, would build good schoolhouses for every child in the South.

Through this organization the Negro can do his part in ridding the state of the idle and loafing class. We must let our people everywhere understand that we will not hide crime, that the black loafer is a great burden, and that he gives our race a reputation which hinders its progress. Our white people, too, can help us in this matter of better moral conditions by encouraging the colored people who live upright, industrious, economical, and frugal lives by not advertising Negro crime quite so much in the newspapers, and by advertising, instead, more evidences of Negro thrift and Negro morality. While we are trying to do our part in bringing about a higher moral condition, the white people can help us by seeing that the Negro everywhere gets absolute justice in the courts, that throughout the South we get rid of the crime of lynching human beings, and that every man charged with a crime has an opportunity to come before a court of justice where his guilt or innocence can be proved.

The two races in Virginia can coöperate in encouraging the Negro wherever he lives to have a clean, sanitary, healthy community. I do not believe that this can be brought about by any laws meant to segregate the Negro in any certain part of a community or city. Wherever the Negro is segregated, it usually means that he will have poor streets, poor lighting, poor sidewalks, poor sewerage, and poor sanitary conditions generally. These conditions are reflected in many ways in the life of the race to its disadvantage and to the disadvantage of the white race. Happily the Negro here in the South has pretty good common sense, and he is not likely to thrust himself on any community where conditions are not congenial, where he is not happy, and where he is not wanted. Segregation is not only unnecessary, but, in most cases, it is unjust.

I am glad to note that in Virginia, as in most of the states of the South, there is a spirit of coöperation between the two races, which has never existed before in like degree, in helping our race to get education. For a good many years after the Civil War white people were afraid to educate the Negro because they did not know what it was going to lead to, but, just in proportion as the white people throughout the South see that education is used by our people in a way to make them simple, modest, earnest, never afraid to work on the farm or in the shop or in the house — in proportion as they see that education makes a better citizen, millions of dollars are going to be poured out throughout the South for the education of our race.

We must not deceive ourselves, however. The problem of educating the Negro, as well as the white child, in the South is just beginning to be solved. We have scarcely begun to educate. In the state of Louisiana, at the present time, each black child receives $1.59 a year for his education; in Georgia, only $1.42. Fifty-two per cent of all the Negro children in the South of school age entered no school last year. By reason of the poor salaries paid teachers and the short length of the school term, it would require twenty years for a Negro child, under present conditions, to complete a public school education. In several of our Southern states, first-class Negro convicts earn $40 per month for twelve months in the year, while Negro school teachers receive about $25 per month for teaching four or five months in the year. All of these conditions must be faced frankly in the interest of a higher and better civilization in the South. In proportion as we face them, both races are going to be happier and more prosperous. Ignorance cures nothing. We must all unite to blot out ignorance from the South by placing good, first-class schoolhouses for both races in every community in our beloved and beautiful Southland.

We must not become discouraged. Tremendous progress, in all the directions to which I have referred, has been made and is being made. When we consider all the struggles, all the difficulties through which both races have passed during the last fifty years, the wonder is, not that we have accomplished so little, but that we have accomplished so much. Both races are going to live here in the South together. Year by year we are going to understand each other better. There is going to be more racial coöperation, more friendship, more peace, more harmony, more prosperity. Despite evidences of racial friction which crop out here and there, when you get to the bottom of conditions in any Southern community it is found that each individual Negro has his or her white friend; and each white man has his individual Negro friend. The relations which exist between the individual Negro and the individual white man are often closer and better understood and more sympathetic than those obtaining in any community outside of the South. In the matter of facing the trying conditions in the cotton-growing states brought about by the European war, there is a racial coöperation and sympathy which I have never seen before in the South.

Our race is improving in the matter of health. Some ten or fifteen years ago, the death rate was about thirty per thousand; at the present time, through such organizations as the Negro Organization Society and others, the death rate has been decreased. It is now from twenty-four to twenty per thousand.

The Negro began life fifty years ago with practically no property. He owns now in the South 20,000,000 acres of land. Fifty years ago only 5 per cent of the Negroes could read or write. At present 70 per cent can read and write. Twenty years ago, there were in one year 250 cases of lynching; during the past ten months, there have been only 33 cases of lynching. This reduction has been brought about through racial coöperation and better understanding. For these evidences of progress our race deserves great credit; and the white man by whose side we live in the South deserves equal credit for the encouragement and the practical help which he has given us in all these fundamental matters.

We of the black race and the white race here in the South are going to present to the world a great object lesson, showing how two races, different in history, different in color, can live side by side on the same soil in peace and in harmony, neither hindering the other but each helping the other towards a higher and more useful civilization.

TM   BTW Papers   ATT.

¹ The Negro Organization Society of Virginia was founded by Robert R. Moton in 1912 at the Hampton Negro Conference to bring into active cooperation the many black lodges, clubs, churches, and other organizations in the state. Moton suggested its motto, "Better Schools, Better Health, Better Homes, Better Farms," and he was its president until he left the state in 1916. It was intended to promote for rural black people what the Urban League undertook for city dwellers, and BTW encouraged it at every opportunity. (Hughes and Patterson, eds., *Robert Russa Moton,* 60–62.)

From George Perley Phenix¹

Hampton, Virginia   Nov. 13, 1914

My dear Mr. Washington: I felt quite anxious about you all the afternoon and evening up to the time you began to speak.² Knowing what a very hard day you had Wednesday and your subsequent illness, I was afraid that meeting such an audience would be too much, but after you began to speak, I had no further anxiety.

I always enjoy hearing you speak and I have always admired your masterly power over an audience, but last night it seemed to me you met a difficult situation amazingly well. I never heard you speak better. It was splendid! Very truly yours,

George P. Phenix
Vice Principal

TLS   Con. 516   BTW Papers   DLC.   Written on stationery of Hampton Normal and Agricultural Institute.

¹ George Perley Phenix (1864–1930) was director of academic work and teacher training at Hampton Institute from 1904 until 1919. He was vice-principal from 1908 until 1930.

² See An Address before the Negro Organization Society of Virginia, Nov. 12, 1914, above.

From Ruth Standish Bowles Baldwin

[New York City] Nov. 14. 1914

My dear Mr. Washington: I have just been reading with deep interest your last report to your Trustees.

It has made me feel a renewed eagerness to visit Tuskegee again, for it is fully five years since I was there, & to see for myself something of the splendid things you have been doing — & to catch again some thing of the wonderful Tuskegee spirit that is after all the most splendid of all your achiev[e]ments at the Institute.

But I shall not get down this year I fear, the dollars it would take must go to help actual need here and elsewhere in these distracted times.

As I am writing now, I enclose the check which I usually send in January, adding a trifle lest some body else be obliged to cut off $10. in these days of diminished incomes.

And now I have a *great* favor to ask of you — which I most earnestly hope that you will grant.

We have long wanted you on the Board of the National Urban League. You will remember our talk about it last year perhaps, & we are about to elect members to take the place of those whose terms expire this year. Will you permit us to put your name up for election to the Board on Dec 2nd? *Please* say yes!

The Board meets in October, February & May — & the annual meeting comes in early Dec. I think it can be arranged so that the times of the meetings will fit in with your usual visits to N.Y. & at any rate we can have your counsel & advice more freely if you are a member than at present, tho' you are ever generous in your sympathetic interest in all efforts for your people. May I ask to hear from you at your early convenience.

Please give my regards to Mrs. Washington and believe me, as always, Yours sincerely,

Ruth S. Baldwin

May I have Davidson's address? I understand that he has been recently married.

ALS Con. 767 BTW Papers DLC.

To George Perley Phenix

[Tuskegee, Ala.] November 16, 1914

My dear Mr. Phenix: You do not know how very much I appreciate your thoughtful and kind letter concerning the matter of my address in Norfolk. Such words, coming from you, will always be remembered and cherished by me.

My general health is very good. In fact, I have seldom felt better. A hard day's work such as I went through on Wednesday does not, as a rule, affect me unless I am careless. I got upset on Wednesday night simply because I foolishly ate something which I ought not to have eaten. If I am careful, I usually keep in good health.

As I look back upon it now, it seems to me that the opportunity of speaking to those students at William and Mary College was really worth the trip to Virginia. Of all the addresses which I tried to make during my visit, I think the one at William and Mary College was the most satisfactory. I care nothing for what the world calls eloquence except as a tool to be used in the accomplishment of some good purpose. I am going to show your letter to my wife, and I am sure she will appreciate it as much as I do.

One other thing — a very good friend of Hampton had a son to graduate some years ago in the Agricultural Department. This gentleman tried three Agricultural Colleges, later, one in the North and two in the West, to enter his son in the regular course but, in each case, he was not admitted to even the lowest class in the Agricultural College. This friend was especially grieved because he said, just previous to his son's graduation from Hampton he heard one of the most eminent educators in the country remark that no white students receive such fine instructions as the colored students receive at Hampton. He could not make this statement, and the outcome on the part of his son reconcile themselves to each other. I am wondering if Hampton cannot use its influence to break through this artificial barrier. That is, I am taking for granted that I am stating the case correctly.

Please remember me to all the good friends there who made it so very pleasant for Mrs. Washington and myself all the while we were there. We shall hope to have the privilege of seeing you at Tuskegee some time in the near future. Yours very truly,

Booker T. Washington

TLpS   Con. 516   BTW Papers   DLC.

To William Anthony Aery

[Tuskegee, Ala.] November 16, 1914

Dear Mr. Aery: I have asked Mr. Scott to send out some special notes regarding my speaking at William and Mary College. I am thinking it would be a good thing for you to do the same thing.

I am not actuated by any selfish motives in this, but I think the fact that I have been asked to speak at a typical Southern white college will serve to give strength to many timid Southern white people, and also will encourage our Northern friends to feel and see that real progress, after all, is being made in the South. I think the wider publicity this matter could be given, the better it would be for both Hampton and Tuskegee, and general education in the South.

Please let me thank you again for your great kindness to me while I was in the State. Yours very truly,

Booker T. Washington

TLpS   Con. 491   BTW Papers   DLC.

To John Ege

[Tuskegee, Ala.] November 16, 1914

My dear Dr. Ege: The two bottles of Radium Water have been received, and you do not know how very grateful I am to you for your generous kindness.

Our Doctor was saying to me only a few days ago that he had not heard from you. I shall be glad to put your letter in his hands, and I feel quite sure that if he is in that part of the North at any time he will call to see you. He is in Texas just now, on a special case, but will be returning within a few days. I am sure he will be very glad to see the communication which you have sent him, and will be writing you, himself.

By this mail, I am sending you one of my books, called, "My Larger Education." I hope you will find time to glance it through. Yours very truly,

Booker T. Washington

TLpS Con. 501 BTW Papers DLC.

To Thomas Jesse Jones

[Tuskegee, Ala. ca. Nov. 16, 1914]

Personal and Confidential.

My dear Dr. Jones: I think that you are in a position to perform a great service for Negro education in the South in connection with the Smith-Lever bill. Unless some strong influence is brought to bear, and that very soon, the colored people are going to receive practically nothing from this fund, except in the case of one or two states.

I am wondering whether you could not get hold of the Secretary of Agriculture and impress him with the need of standing by the colored people in this matter. He has a veto power on the use of the fund. Perhaps if he would indicate in a strong definite way to the Heads of the Agricultural Colleges that he wishes the colored people to receive a fair share of the fund, it would result in having these colleges themselves take the initiative in doing something for the colored people. Without any some such suggestion, I fear that little or nothing will be done. Of course if you desire more facts before approaching the Secretary, I think I could get these facts into your hands. I had thought once or twice of approaching President Wilson on the subject, but I have not decided whether this is wise or not. Please study the whole situation and let me hear from you. Yours very truly,

Booker T. Washington

TLpS Con. 506 BTW Papers DLC.

To Seth Bunker Capp

[Tuskegee, Ala.] November 17, 1914

My dear Sir: Thank you for yours of November 7th, which I regret I have been somewhat delayed in answering owing to absence.

I am sorry that Col. Roosevelt was not able to see the picture, but I feared that he would not be able to do so owing to pressure of time. I am very glad that you gave the ministers an opportunity to see the picture. The Reading Eagle was received and I am very grateful for it. The extra copies we used to good advantage.

I am very sorry that the relationship between you and Dr. Ege has not been improved. The plan which you suggest of placing a goal in front of him seems to be worth considering. When you get to the point, will you be kind enough to give me some idea as to the probable cost of such a plan? I suppose the more persons who joined in it, the cheaper the price ought to be. It is too bad that a man with such great talent cannot have his business systematized so that humanity may reap the best results. I realize all the benefits that might come from a number joining in with the same end in view.

Now regarding Colonel Roosevelt. I fear that we would not succeed in getting him to agree to sit for a portrait unless he could be convinced by some friend of his, in whose judgment on matters of art he has faith, that Mr. Hruska could paint a creditable picture. In other words, I think we should have to go at him in a matter of this kind rather indirectly. In other matters I think he would take my word, but I am quite sure he would feel that my judgment on matters of art was very limited. One other thing has occurred to me that might possibly pave the way toward getting Colonel Roosevelt's portrait and that is for Mr. Hruska to try to get an opportunity to paint the picture of Mr. George McAneny, who up to last year was President of the Borough of Manhattan, and at the present time, is Vice-Mayor of New York City and President of the Board of Aldermen. He is a very prominent figure in New York City and throughout the state and is a coming young man. I am quite well acquainted with him and I believe I could help Mr. Hruska to make arrangements with him. If he painted a good picture of Mr. McAneny, who is well known and has a host of friends, I think this would pave the way to his getting to Mr. Roosevelt.

Will you kindly remember me to Mr. Hruska. I often think of my pleasant stay with you and him at Reading. Yours very truly,

Booker T. Washington

TLpS   Con. 496   BTW Papers   DLC.

To Ruth Standish Bowles Baldwin

[Tuskegee, Ala.] November 18, 1914

My dear Mrs. Baldwin: I am answering your very kind and generous letter very hastily, for the reason that I am taking a train within a few hours to visit the Snow Hill Normal and Industrial Institute, in Southern Alabama.

It was very kind and thoughtful of you to send us Sixty Dollars instead of Fifty Dollars at this time. You are very much right in presuming that quite a number of people have been compelled to hold their annual contributions. I hope some of them, at least, will make up for their withholdings later on in the year.

These are very strenuous and pinching times in the South. A year ago, cotton was selling at from 12 to 14 cents. At the present time it is between 4 and 7½ cents, and one has to almost beg persons to buy it at any price. I fear there is going to be much suffering this winter. People who have been planting cotton for years have made up their minds not to plant cotton next year. What will become of the renters, I do not know.

We are so sorry that you cannot come to Tuskegee again this year. We hope, however, that you will not forget us, and that you will come next year.

Davidson's address is here, in care of the Institution. He is working in my office, and has a beautiful little home here. He and his wife seem very happy. I am sure he will be very glad to hear from you.

Now, regarding the Urban Society — I shall be very glad to have you use my name in the way that you mention. In order to make our plans fit into each other, better, I give you a list of definite engagements, which I have in New York or vicinity within the next few months, thinking that some of your meetings might be held about the same time. Yours very truly,

Booker T. Washington

December 16 — Newark, N.J.
January 23 — New York City.
February 5 — Washington, D.C.
February 8 — New York City.

TLpS Con. 767 BTW Papers DLC.

To Robert Elijah Jones

[Tuskegee, Ala.] November 18, 1914

My dear Dr. Jones: I thought you might care to see the enclosed letter from the General Superintendent of the Pullman Company, Chicago.[1]

I think it well from time to time to suggest to our travelling friends, when they do receive courtesies from the Pullman people, they should write to the general office at Chicago and thank them for kindnesses shown by their various conductors. I believe that it will strengthen the backbones of the conductors and make them stand up for us more satisfactorily, if they know that the office in Chicago is backing them as is true in this case.

Please return this letter after you have had opportunity to read it. Yours very truly,

Booker T. Washington

TLpS Con. 506 BTW Papers DLC.

[1] BTW had commended the behavior of Pullman conductor W. H. Waite to L. S. Hungerford, general superintendent of the Pullman Co. Hungerford replied that he was gratified to note the commendation, and would see to it that "suitable entry is made on his service record." (Hungerford to BTW, Nov. 12, 1914, Con. 517, BTW Papers, DLC.)

From Thomas Jesse Jones

Washington   November 21st, 1914

Dear Dr. Washington: I have consulted Commissioner Claxton[1] as to the Smith Lever Bill and the interests of the colored people. He suggests that you send all the facts that you have in hand and that we can then take up the matter on the basis of the information already at hand together with that which you will submit. I have had this matter under consideration for some weeks. About a month ago Mr. Geo. Foster Peabody and I visited Commissioner Houston[2] and urged upon him the importance of assistance for the colored schools, calling his attention to the favorable attitude of the Alabama committee toward Tuskegee. A little later Dr. Frissell called on Mr. Bradford Knapp.[3] At the same time he called on Secretary Houston. I gathered from all the information that has come to me thus far that the tendency is to entrust the expenditure of this money to one white Agricultural School in each State. The feeling is that the land-grant schools have made such poor use of the money given to them that it is not wise to trust them with any more money at present. While I agreed that the majority of the land-grant schools are below the standard, I am strongly of the opinion that there is, in almost every State, one school to which a part of this money can be entrusted. At least the money should be given with a definite understanding that adequate consideration is to be given to the colored people.

I wish that you could stop in Washington some time. I would like to discuss this matter in detail. I am not sure but that it will be wise for you to take some personal part in the final presentation of this matter. Very sincerely

Thomas Jesse Jones
Specialist

TLS Con. 506 BTW Papers DLC. Written on stationery of the Department of the Interior, Bureau of Education.

[1] Philander Priestley Claxton (1862–1957) was professor of education at the University of Tennessee (1902–11), a member of the Southern Education Board, and U.S. Commissioner of Education (1911–21).

[2] David Franklin Houston, Secretary of Agriculture.

³ Bradford Knapp (1870–1938), son of Seaman A. Knapp, succeeded his father in 1911 as chief of the Cooperative Demonstration Work of the U.S. Department of Agriculture. He was president of Oklahoma A. & M. (1923–28), Alabama Polytechnic Institute at Auburn (1928–32), and Texas Technological College (1932–38).

To Clara J. Johnston

[Tuskegee, Ala.] November 23, 1914

Dear Clara: I have just received your letter, also, one from Albert telling about your mother's condition.

Will you be kind enough to write me at once telling me if there has been any change for better or worse concerning her condition.

I am still hoping to come by there during the fall or winter.

Please let me know how much it will cost to put the piping around the kitchen, also how much will be necessary to buy the coal. I sent a check a few days ago to cover the matter of insurance. Yours very truly,

B. T. W.

TLpI Con. 506 BTW Papers DLC.

To George Perley Phenix

[Tuskegee, Ala.] November 23, 1914

Confidential

My dear Dr. Phenix: Please treat the following as confidential.

The young man to whom I referred was the son of Dr. Adkins of Winston-Salem. He said that after his son graduated from the Agricultural Department at Hampton, he could neither enter the lower class in agriculture at Cornell or at the University of Wisconsin, and he also mentioned one other school which I cannot remember.

I shall be glad to know how the matter turns out. Yours very truly,

Booker T. Washington

TLpS Con. 516 BTW Papers DLC.

From Robert Russa Moton

Hampton, Virginia Nov. 23, 1914

My dear Dr. Washington: I am enclosing herewith copies of a letter I wrote to President Wilson[1] and his reply. I did not, of course, mean to give the impression to him that I approved of segregation in Washington, but I think he is [in] such a condition now that we may be able to make an impression on him.

I have been surprised and pleased at the attitude of the many Northern papers regarding the Trotter incident. The New York "World" for example took grounds against Mr. Wilson on this segregation question, while it did not excuse Mr. Trotter, and many of the leading papers have done the same thing.

I am glad you got home safely and enjoyed the trip to Virginia and Hampton. I spoke at Williamsburg on Monday evening to a packed house and afterwards talked with Prof. Bennett[2] and a number of the leading white people and they were very enthusiastic over your address. Your being at William & Mary was one of the most significant incidents that has happened in the State for many years. The Virginians are very conservative as you know and William & Mary has been especially so.

I am sending you under separate cover your pipe and tobacco which you left at our house. Sincerely yours,

R. R. Moton

TLS Con. 511 BTW Papers DLC.

[1] In the enclosed copy of his letter to Woodrow Wilson, Nov. 16, 1914, Moton wrote that Wilson's letter had been read at the meeting and encouraged the black people. He added: "Your letter has been copied in several editorials within the past few days to show your kindly feeling toward Negroes, as contrasted with the very unfortunate incident of Mr. Trotter, and I want to say that the Negroes, generally, do not in any way approve of Mr. Trotter's conduct at the White House." He expressed, he said, "the regrets of ninety-nine percent of the thoughtful Negroes of this land at Mr. Trotter's attitude and words." Wilson replied on Nov. 18, 1914: "It is particularly delightful to me that my real temper and disposition in matters of this sort should be understood by those who themselves have the interests of the negro people most at heart, and I shall be happy at any time to render such assistance as I can in furthering the development to which you are devoting yourself."

[2] Henry Eastman Bennett (1873–1941) was professor of philosophy and education at the College of William and Mary from 1907 to 1912 and head of the department of education from 1912 to 1925.

To Charles Ellis Mason

[Tuskegee, Ala.] November 24, 1914

My dear Mr. Mason: I do not know anything regarding the Washington incident except what I have seen in the papers. I know, however, something of Trotter's hot-headed and unreasonable disposition. In this matter, I think it was simply a case of an indiscreet and unreasonable man having a good cause to present. Trotter, as you perhaps know, belongs to a very unreasonable and hot-headed element of colored people and in my opinion, does not do the race any good.

The democratic party has carried the matter of racial separation in Washington to an unreasonable extent and there is a good deal of resentment all over the country among the best classes of white and colored people.

I have been rather careful to not seek inside information on th[e] subject for the reason that I do not care to be drawn into the controvers[y] or to permit the people at the White House to draw me into it. Yours very truly,

Booker T. Washington

TLpS   Con. 936   BTW Papers   DLC.

From Anson Phelps Stokes

New Haven, Conn., November 24, 1914

Dear Sir: I have the honor to inform you that at a meeting of the Trustees of the Phelps-Stokes Fund held at 100 William street, New York City, November 18th, 1914, the following appropriation was made:

> "$500   To be expended under the direction of Dr. Booker T. Washington in inaugurating a negro health day movement throughout the South, this money to be used in meeting the expenses of a publicity and educational campaign in the interest of better health conditions."

The following vote was also passed at the same meeting:

"Voted, to direct the Secretary in informing institutions of grants as above, to state that the grants made are for one year only without expectation of renewal."

Sincerely hoping that this appropriation may prove of real benefit to your work, I am, Very truly yours,

Anson Phelps Stokes

P.S. The appropriation will not be available until after January 1st next.

TLS   Con. 73   BTW Papers   DLC.

To G. Douglas Wardrop[1]

[Tuskegee, Ala.] November 24, 1914

Dear Mr. Wardrop: You asked me to give you some idea of my impressions and feelings at the time I made my maiden speech. This is not an easy thing to do, because though I have tried to do so since receiving your letter, I am not sure that I can recall with any degree of definiteness the occasion or time when I made my first speech.

I rather think, however, that the first time I ever tried to stand on my feet and make what might be called a speech or recitation was when I was in a small public school in Malden, W.Va., my former home. At that time, Friday afternoon was usually given up to hearing recitations from pupils, or if we did not have a recitation on Friday afternoon, we usually had an old-fashioned spelling match, which was always enjoyed.

My first recitation or speech was taken from one of McGriffay's [McGuffey's] readers and the subject was "Try, try again." The lines ran something like this: "If at first you don't succeed, try, try again" and I remember that after getting in the midst of this speech, I forgot the lines, broke down and in the opinion of myself, as well as others, made a failure. I resolved, however, that I would follow the advice given in the recitation and would try again and I kept at it week by week until I was able to hold the lines in my mind and speak them with some degree of credit.

From this beginning, I have gone on trying to improve my speaking up until the present and I might add here that almost from the beginning, I have never made an address without making special preparation for that address. I try to study the audience to be reached and not yield to the temptation of having a stereotyped speech, which would fit any audience. The public speaker who yields to such a temptation soon grows stale and mechanical and his words lose weight. I have learned by some experience and observation that each individual audience has a personality or individuality just the same as each individual whom one talks to has an individuality and personality and everyone should prepare to speak to each different audience just as he prepares to speak to different individuals. This has been my policy.

I have been often asked, and it seems to me that this thought might prove of some interest to your readers, what method I pursue in the preparation of my addresses. First, I was undecided and tried different methods of preparing and delivering my addresses. I used to commit everything to memory. That I soon found was a nerve racking and head racking task, and in the effort to remember what I committed to memory so I could speak it word for word and line for line, all of the naturalness and force of the address disappeared in the attempt to keep the exact words and lines in my mind, so I gave up that habit.

Then I tried to read my addresses. That I soon found unsatisfactory, as there is a stiffness about it that prevented me from reaching the souls of the audience directly.

Then I tried speaking without committing to memory, or the use of manuscript. After some experience with this method, I found that my mind was so continually at work trying to put together the speech in proper form while I was delivering it, that the result was, I had not reached and influenced the audience in the way I wished.

After years of experience, I have discarded all of these methods and now my general plan is, from which I seldom deviate, to determine what subject I shall speak on — and the subject is usually determined by the character of the audience — sit down, think the subject through, make a careful analysis and then get information through conversation and through reading on the subject until I feel that I have mastered it from bottom to top, from center to circumference. After I have done that, I make an analysis, make certain notes or head lines which I keep before me while speaking. After I have made these notes or headlines,

I usually from these headlines dictate a speech, which I hope to deliver, to a stenographer.

This practice I have found has two values. First, the dictating of the speech fixes the words and sentences in my mind. Secondly, I can give such dictation to newspapers in advance of my speaking. I have found, by a good deal of practice, that after making these headlines and dictating the speech to a stenographer, I can follow almost word for word, sentence for sentence, the dictation. This practice of delivering a speech has several advantages. First, one is never afraid that he is going to get lost because his headlines will guide him. Then he does not have to tax the mind with remembering certain words and sentences, and he is free to face his audience and attach importance to the condition and needs of his audience. In a word, there is a freedom and satisfaction in speaking after this fashion that I have never experienced in trying to follow any other method. Yours very truly,

[Booker T. Washington]

TLp   Con. 506   BTW Papers   DLC.

[1] G. Douglas Wardrop, born in Scotland in 1890, was at this time on the editorial staff of *The Independent*. A graduate of the University of Glasgow, he was later a foreign correspondent and the editor of *International Aeronautics* and *Radio Merchandizing*.

To Charles Allmond Wickersham

[Tuskegee, Ala.] November 25, 1914

Personal and Confidential.

Dear Mr. Wickersham: On last Friday morning, a number of people from Tuskegee took the train leaving Selma for Montgomery at 5:10 o'clock. It was a very cold, disagreeable morning; but nevertheless we found the car well lighted, well heated and perfectly clean and everything was finely arranged.

The only "fly in the ointment" was this, and I thought you might like for me to speak to you frankly about it. A number of us tried to get a cup of coffee at the lunch room near the station. The man in charge of the lunch room seemed to feel that it was his duty to drive patronage away from the railroad, instead of inviting it. He refused, of course, to let any colored person drink a cup of coffee on the inside of the lunch room, which was not surprising, but he refused to let anyone of the party bring a cup of coffee into the car where it might be drunk. Finally one of the party did succeed in paying a porter to permit the lunch counter keeper to let some coffee be brought out of the lunch room in a tin cup.

I believe you will agree with me that if the same amount of time and energy were spent in trying to be courteous to people, instead of discourteous, it would serve a much higher purpose and bring about a greater degree of success on the part of individuals.

I hope you will find it possible to make some arrangement for colored people to be served at all of the eating houses where there is any considerable number of colored people patronizing the road. Yours very truly,

Booker T. Washington

TLpS   Con. 526   BTW Papers   DLC.

To Emmet O'Neal

[Tuskegee, Ala.] November 25, 1914

Dear Governor: You do not know how very much I appreciate your kindness in sending me a full copy of your opinion in which you commuted the sentence of Irwin Pope to life imprisonment.[1] I have seen extracts from your opinion, but they were very far from giving all the facts in the way that they are brought out in the opinion which you sent me.

In the first place, I wish to say that colored people throughout Alabama, including myself, have followed this case with the deepest interest and we know something of the courage it has required on your part to stand by this colored man and see that he was not executed unjustly. You have acted in this matter as you have in every matter concerning our race, or any other race, that is, tried to see that justice was rendered regardless of the condition of the individual, but in this particular case, all of us realize something of the tremendous influence that was brought to bear against this man and this makes our obligation to you all the greater. I do hope that at sometime in the future, when the passions of the people have somewhat cooled, that there may be an opportunity to bring the whole case again before the courts in order to see if the man had any connection with the murder. Full vindication in that case of Pope would, of course, strengthen the position which you have taken. I had no idea that you were taking all the pains that you have taken to go so thoroughly into the case and bring out every detail that might have any bearing upon the charge brought against Pope.

I am going to take the liberty of letting some of the influential colored people see the full opinion, so that they may be kept informed of what you have done.

Thanking you again for your deep interest in this matter, I am

Yours very truly,

Booker T. Washington

TLpS   Con. 515   BTW Papers   DLC.

[1] According to reports in the Montgomery *Advertiser*, Ervin Pope, a black man, had been tried and convicted five times for the murder of James McClurkin, a white Calhoun County farmer, the state supreme court having reversed the lower court's decision four times. Repeatedly sentenced to be hanged, Pope was respited three times by Governor Emmet O'Neal, who finally after careful investigation commuted the sentence to life imprisonment. "The weight of the evidence was not such as to justify the death penalty," the governor concluded. Blood-stained shoes found under Pope's porch turned out to be more than two sizes larger than Pope's foot; the blood type could not be positively identified. Discrepancies were found in the testimony of John Body, a black witness who disappeared after the initial trial. The governor dismissed financial need as a motive, since Pope owned his own farm. (Montgomery *Advertiser*, Nov. 8, 1914, 22; Nov. 19, 1914, 2; Nov. 20, 1914, 1, 2.

To Robert Russa Moton

[Tuskegee, Ala.] November 25, 1914

Dear Major Moton: I am planning to start a little agitation in the way of a National Health Day among our people.

I do not want to interfere with your own plans, but rather to emphasize what you have been doing so well in Virginia. Will you be kind enough to let me know what day you propose to use in Virginia? I think we could hinge this national movement on what you have done and are doing in Virginia.

I have a little money at my disposal which I can use in the way of publicity and I think much can be gained by cooperation. Yours very truly,

Booker T. Washington

TLpS Con. 255 BTW Papers DLC.

To Thomas Jesse Jones

[Tuskegee, Ala.] November 25, 1914

My dear Dr. Jones: You do not know how very grateful I am to you for the information which your letter of November 24th contains bearing upon the recent action of the Phelps-Stokes Fund. This is all most interesting and encouraging. Of course, I shall treat it all as confidential. I am quite sure, however, that we are deeply grateful to you for helping to bring about this favorable action.

I am deeply interested, also, in what you write concerning Mr. Claxton and the Smith-Lever bill. I have read carefully all that you say concerning Dr. Claxton, Mr. Peabody, Dr. Frissell, Dr. Knapp and Secretary Houston in their relation to the Smith-Lever bill money and, after considering the matter very carefully, I agree with you that it would be well for me to come to Washington and spend a day there, if possible. I think according to my present program, that I could be in Washington sometime between the 3d and 5th of December. How would that suit you? Of course I should want you to be present and want the whole situation to be thoroughly understood before I saw any other parties. I shall be sending you whatever information I can get hold of in any way bearing upon the administration of this fund. I might add that one of the principal men controlling this fund and connected with Auburn College has notified us that he is coming here next Friday to take up matters with us and it may be that we shall reach some satisfactory arrangement. The Governor and State Commissioner of Agriculture[1] are thoroughly on our side.

The most satisfactory information, however, in your letter is that which covers the matter of the Board deciding definitely to retain you in its service for three years after the present investigation has been completed. I am wondering if there would be any objection on the part of yourself and the Board to my giving this to the public. Yours very truly,

Booker T. Washington

TLpS Con. 506 BTW Papers DLC.

¹ James Aaron Wade succeeded the long-time incumbent Reuben Francis Kolb as Alabama commissioner of agriculture on Nov. 3, 1914.

To William G. Willcox

[Tuskegee, Ala.] November 25, 1914

Dear Mr. Willcox: Enclosed, I send you a report signed by Mr. Calloway and Mr. Bridgeforth indicating something of what has been done at the Tuskegee Farm and Improvement Company.

There is no trouble in getting applications from people who want to settle there. The only trouble is to be sure that we sift them out and get the right ones and do not try to put too many on the place this year in view of the unsettled financial conditions.

In addition to building new houses, we are planning to repair for permanent use several of the old houses that are already on the place. Yours very truly,

Booker T. Washington

TLpS Con. 989 BTW Papers DLC.

To Robert Russa Moton

[Tuskegee, Ala.] November 27, 1914

My dear Major Moton: I have read the copies of the correspondence sent me in your letter of November 23rd.

I am sure, as you say, that you did not mean to give the President any impression that you were favorable toward segregation, but he is being "pounded" so severely in various quarters that I imagine he was glad to have a word from some member of the race less stinging than some of those he is at present reading. Yours very truly,

Booker T. Washington

TLpS Con. 511 BTW Papers DLC.

To Len G. Shaw[1]

[Tuskegee, Ala.] November 28, 1914

Dear Sir: Your letter of recent date received. I have examined with care the very interesting booklet dealing with the evil of cigarette smoking among boys which you kindly sent me. In answer to your request I will say that we have had some interesting experiences at Tuskegee Institute with boys who smoke cigarettes, for every year in the thousand or more young men assembled here there are, of course, a few who are addicted to this habit. We have a rule prohibiting smoking by our students.

For disciplinary purposes our students are organized on a military basis with a commandant. Major J. B. Ramsey, who for many years has held this position, states that it is generally the students who have the cigarette habit who give the most trouble with reference to discipline. Their will power is broken down, their moral sense is blunted, and it is very difficult when inveterate smokers before coming here to make anything out of them; they will go to any length, take any sort of risk to get an opportunity to smoke a cigarette. It may also interest you to know that in connection with our hospital the boys addicted to the cigarette habit are given regular treatment for its cure. Very truly yours,

Booker T. Washington

TLpS Con. 775 BTW Papers DLC.

[1] Len G. Shaw, of Highland Park, Mich., worked for Henry Ford on a series of booklets for boys on the evils of smoking cigarettes. He asked BTW for information that could be used in the series. Shaw sent BTW sample pages of "The Case

Against the Little White Slaver," including a copy of a letter Thomas Edison wrote to Henry Ford, dated Apr. 26, 1914. Edison stated that smoking cigarettes caused "degeneration of the cells of the brain. . . ." Furthermore, Edison concluded, "I employ no person who smokes cigarettes." (Shaw to BTW, Nov. 20, 1914, Con. 775, BTW Papers, DLC.)

From Stephen Frink Dana

Cincinnati, O. Dec. 1, 1914

My dear Mr. Washington: I am enclosing you herewith my check for $100.00, which I know you will appreciate, and have delayed sending it because of the War. As you understand, it is a pleasure to me to know that you are going ahead notwithstanding the bad times, and bad business due to the effect of this War. When I think back of the time when you and I lived on the Kanawha River, and I saw you running around doing errands, I wasn't looking very closely at you, but you seemed to be a nice little boy who always kept out of trouble, and looked for something to do. But now when I know what you have done I realize that you are doing some of the best work to be done in the United States. Yours sincerely,

S. F. Dana

TLS Con. 769 BTW Papers DLC. Written on stationery of The Campbell's Creek Coal Co.

From William Junior Edwards

Snow Hill, Alabama, Dec. 1st, 1914

My dear Dr. Washington: A little more than a year ago Dr. Thomas Jesse Jones of Washington, made an investigation of this school for the Phelps Stokes Fund. I was under the impression that after this investigation something of material aid would be forthcoming from this fund. In fact, I wrote several of the trustees at the time and they assured me that when the investigation, which was then on foot, be completed, something would be done for the colored schools. Just now, we are in great need of funds to enable us to continue the work here. The new building which was dedicated the other day, is costing us upwards of $50,000, and the hard time having overtaken us before we could complete it, with the additional financial stringency, made by the European War, has made this the hardest year that we have experienced in the history of the school. During the entire year we have been following a plan of retrenchment and cutting off every possible expense that we could. Still I find we are greatly in need of $10,000 immediately. Without this, I hardly see how we can continue the work here. If ever there was a time we needed aid, it is now. If ever there was a time a good cause was short-handed, it is now. I sincerely appeal to you to help us in any way you can. I have done my utmost to get some of the Northern Trustees to visit us at the time of the dedication, and I also tried to get some of our friends, but in both efforts I was not successful. Our donations have fallen off practically two-thirds since the hard times begun, and just now I see very little signs of any improvement.

I feel sure that we are in a good cause and believe that we are doing reasonably well under these trying circumstances. What we need now is a little money, and I earnestly appeal to you for help in any way you can.

With best wishes, I remain as ever   Most gratefully yours,

W J Edwards

TLS   Con. 501   BTW Papers   DLC.

To William Junior Edwards

[Tuskegee, Ala.] December 2, 1914

Dear Mr. Edwards: I am very glad to tell you that all those who visited Snow Hill on the occasion of the formal opening and dedication of your new building, Robert C. Bedford Hall, were very much impressed by the earnest effort being put forth by your officers and teachers to build up a creditable and effective institution. We were not only impressed by the loyalty and earnestness of your teachers, but by the promising set of students in attendance.

On the other hand, one could see the need of more money for your work and how much better things might be done, if you had sufficient means. It is also very evident that you, your teachers and students had stinted themselves and economized to the very limit going without ordinary comforts and conveniences in order to keep the school alive.

Of course we found many directions in which improvement can be made. This is true of any institution, in fact when an institution gets to the point where there is no way in which it can be improved, the interest in carrying on such work ceases.

Snow Hill has the advantage of being located right in the heart of a dense black population and it has not only a great opportunity to lift up these thousands of black people, but to do that which is equally important, get the sympathetic interest and cooperation of the Southern white people and let them see and feel the value of Negro education. Yours very truly,

Booker T. Washington

TLpS Con. 501 BTW Papers DLC.

A Press Release

Tuskegee Institute, Alabama. December 2, 1914

Dear Sir: Some weeks ago, through our Southern papers, I made a suggestion that each Negro family raise one or more additional pigs this year in order to help bring about more prosperity in the South. I have been surprised to note how well the suggestion has been received, and how many are following it; one minister in Uniontown, Ala., went so far as to organize a Pig Club in his church.

Now, I want to make one other suggestion, that, in my opinion, is of still greater and more practical importance. For months the great cry has been all through the South to stop growing cotton or reduce the acreage.

Chambers of Commerce, Business Leagues, State Legislatures, and other bodies have passed resolutions without number urging that we in the South stop growing so much cotton. To stop growing cotton is very easy; in fact it is always easy to stop work, but merely to stop growing cotton is a mere negative proposition and will not, I fear, leave the South much better off than it is at present. If we destroy, or cripple a great industry, we should be very sure to have one, or a number equally good to put in its place. In this connection it should be kept in mind as a matter of great importance, that if the labor once leaves the farm by reason of changing crops it will be very difficult to get the labor to return to the farm in after years.

The great cry is to grow food crops. That is well, but one must keep in mind that the great masses of Negroes who have actually grown the most of the cotton in the South for years, and who live upon the most valuable land in the South do not hear of the resolutions that are passed by these various bodies. These people have been trained to grow nothing but cotton and do not know how to grow anything else. In fact, in many cases, they have not been, permitted and are not now permitted to grow anything else!

We must also bear in mind that the largest land owners seldom visit their plantations — some not more than once or twice a year, and hence can be of little service in teaching these Negro tenants how to change all at once from a cotton-producing crop to a food-producing crop.

If permanent results are to be secured, the Negro who actually cultivates the land must be reached and trained into growing a food-producing crop. How can this be done? My answer would be, by putting a Negro Farm Demonstration Agent into every county of the South where there is any considerable number of Negro farmers. This Negro Demonstration Agent should be a man of good common sense. He should be a man who knows the characteristics of the colored people, who knows how to reach them in and through their societies, their churches and their various organizations of one kind and another. He should be a man required to travel from one farm to another throughout the country training the Negro farmer how to produce a food crop. Wherever these Demonstration Agents have already been at work in the South, they have done work which has been most helpful and commendable.

If this important work is to be done, no time should be lost in selecting these demonstration agents. The cost should not be very large. Either through county appropriations or from some part of the State funds appropriated for agricultural purposes, a portion of the money for the salary perhaps could be provided. Appropriations are also being made by the United States Government to encourage and promote various kinds of agricultural work. Some part of this money, I feel sure, might be secured from the Smith-Lever Fund or from the United States Demonstration Fund administered through Dr. Bradford Knapp. While I am not in position to suggest just where the money may be secured, I think that if an earnest effort is made, some portion of it can be secured from some of the funds or agencies here mentioned.

Booker T. Washington

TMSr Copy   Con. 514   BTW Papers   DLC.   This copy was addressed to the editor of the Twin City *Telegram,* New Decatur, Ala.

To Stephen Frink Dana

[Tuskegee, Ala.] December 5, 1914

My dear Mr. Dana: You do not know how very grateful I am to you for your check. It helps the school at this time more than you can realize.

As you intimated in your letter, the war has made it very difficult to get money, but we are still forging ahead and making progress.

It is very kind of you to refer to my boyhood days on the Kanawha river. I often look back with a great deal of pleasure and satisfaction to the days I spent on the Kanawha river and I also remember with satisfaction the interest you all manifested in our people and in me.

Perhaps you will remember my older brother, John, who used to work for you. He is now here and has been almost since the founding of the school, acting as General Superintendent of Industries. I go to Kanawha once in a while to see my sister, who still lives in Malden. I hope I may be able to go there sometime this winter.

I do hope that if you are ever in this part of the South, you will come to see us. We extend you a most hearty welcome.

By this mail, I am sending you a little pamphlet which will give you some idea of what we are accomplishing in the way of extension work. Yours very truly,

Booker T. Washington

TLpS   Con. 769   BTW Papers   DLC.

To Emmet O'Neal

[Tuskegee, Ala.] December 7, 1914

My dear Sir: We were all very much pleased to hear, through the persons who went to see you a few days ago, that it was possible for you and Mrs. O'Neal to visit Tuskegee sometime before you go out of office.

We are more than anxious to indicate in some definite way how much we owe to your deep interest in our race and how much you have done to help forward our progress in this state. We feel, too, that you would see some things that would interest you and please you. In connection with your visit, we are working with the white people in Tuskegee through their Commercial League, of which Mr. W. C. Hurt is President. You will be hearing directly from him within a few days regarding the matter.

As to the time that would best suit us, we could name the following dates; from which we hope you will be able to make a choice: from December 26th to December 31st; from January 2d to January 12th. We hope that some one of these dates will suit your convenience. Yours very truly,

Booker T. Washington

TLpS Con. 515 BTW Papers DLC.

To William Colfax Graves

[Tuskegee, Ala.] December 7, 1914

Dear Mr. Graves: Replying to yours of November 30, I would state that I do not want you and Mr. Rosenwald to feel that any such large proportion of the money for schoolhouse building is going into promotion expenses as your letter would seem to indicate. It is my highest ambition to reduce the overhead expenses to the very lowest, and I hope before many months pass away to put practically all the money into building schoolhouses and practically nothing into expenses. I am maturing this plan as fast as possible. I shall send you reasonably soon, however, such a detailed statement as your letter calls for.

Just now you can understand that it will be rather difficult to state just what proportion of the money used in promoting schoolhouse building has been spent on an individual schoolhouse for the reason that a good deal of time and effort has been incurred in aiding the people to collect money and start schoolhouses that are not yet completed, and will not be for several months. It will be unfair of course, to saddle this expense on schoolhouses already completed.

But for the unfortunate condition brought on by the war in the cotton growing sections, there would be no trouble in getting all the schoolhouses built practically almost without any expenses for promotion.

And then, again, if we were to pursue the policy of placing schoolhouses where they are asked for instead of pursuing the policy of placing them where they are needed whether they are asked for or not, we could get on much faster and without expense. The letters which have passed through your office indicate that we could spend all the money in communities where the people feel the need of a schoolhouse rather than in the communities where they do not feel the need as keenly. But I think the better plan is to keep the schoolhouse building for the present, within a reasonable restricted territory and let the colored people and white people come in contact with the influence of first class schoolhouses in rural communities. This will help the whole cause of education.

We have just completed the erection of three fine schoolhouses in Lee County, and are planning a formal dedication of them very soon. Yours sincerely,

Booker T. Washington

Not the least encouraging feature in connection with the building of these schoolhouses is to note the awakened interest on the part of Southern white people. In many cases white people have now become interested who hitherto have manifested no interest in anything concerning Negro education.

Enclosed I send you receipt for $1540 on account of schoolhouse building. Yours very truly,

TLpS Con. 255 BTW Papers DLC.

To Ruth Standish Bowles Baldwin

[Tuskegee, Ala., ca. Dec. 10, 1914]

My dear Mrs. Baldwin, Perhaps I ought to have spoken to you about the following matter earlier and perhaps I ought to have asked your permission about that which I am going to explain.

The enclosed small slip will explain the farm colony that is being established near here largely through the generosity of Mr. Willcox, one of our Trustees.

Among ourselves and with Mr. Willcox's consent it was decided to name the place "Baldwin." A station is to be built on the place and is to be named as mentioned. Mr. Willcox did not want the place to bear his name, but thought it most fitting for the place to bear the name of "Baldwin" in memory of Mr. Baldwin.[1]

With best wishes, I am Yours very truly,

Booker T. Washington

TLpS Con. 493 BTW Papers DLC.

[1] Ruth Baldwin replied that she appreciated this remembrance of William H. Baldwin, Jr. (Dec. 14, 1914, Con. 493, BTW Papers, DLC.)

From Eugene Kinckle Jones

New York City December 11th, 1914

My dear Dr. Washington: You probably received several days ago notice of the meeting of the Executive Board of the National League on Urban Conditions among Negroes, which is to be next Wednesday afternoon at four o'clock at this office. I presume that you understand from that letter that at the last meeting of the League you were elected to membership on the Executive Board. I am not sure that Mr. L. Hollingsworth Wood,[1] the Secretary of the Board, notified you of your election, and I cannot ascertain this fact because he is now in the City of Washington, D.C. and cannot be easily reached. Sincerely yours,

Eugene Kinckle Jones

P.S. A copy of this communication has been sent to you at the Biltmore Hotel.

E.K.J.

TLS   Con. 506   BTW Papers   DLC.

[1] L. Hollingsworth Wood (1874–1956), a white Quaker, was chairman of the board of the National Urban League from 1915 to 1941. A specialist in estate law, he was an active pacifist, a founder of the American Friends Service Committee, president of the Howard Orphanage and Industrial School, and a trustee of Fisk University for forty years.

Lyman Beecher Stowe to Emmett Jay Scott

Long Island [N.Y.] Dec. 14, 1914

Dear Mr. Scott   I am sending forward to you the Synopsis of our book. I decided to make it very full thereby obviating the necessity of a model chapter which really ought to be unnecessary as both the publishers we have in mind are perfectly familiar with my ability or inability to write.

How do you like the alternative title, "Builder of a Civilization"? At first I thought it perhaps too pretentious but am coming to like it and prefer it to the other and more commonplace one. If you like it and the publishers have nothing better to suggest I think it better stand.

Please read this over both with a view to its accuracy in statements of fact and with a view to the material which will be needed to amplify it. The first few paragraphs are suggested as the opening of the book just as they stand or with only slight alteration. I think it would be well if we did not show this to Dr. Washington nor indeed confer with him any further in the matter. In this case we would be free to state in the introduction (which he says no one ever reads) that he had had no part in the preparation of the book and was not responsible for anything in it. That would let him out in case anything should be adversely criticised and would put us in the relation of real biographers rather than quasi-publicity agents. I think Dr. Washington has sufficient confidence in your judgement to be willing to let us work it out on this basis. Please tell him, by the way, that I gave my first talk on his life and work before an audience of working girls yesterday afternoon in Manhattan.

After you have been over the outline and made what corrections are needed and what changes you see fit please have it typed for submission to Arthur Page. I suppose you will send on the material which you were to dig out for each chapter piecemeal as you have opportunity from your heavy tasks.

With best wishes of the Season

Lyman Beecher Stowe

I am also returning the Lynch book[1] which gave me a new point of view and which I greatly enjoyed.

L. B. S.

Personal

I am a candidate for a position with the Carneige Foundation for the Advancement of Teaching and Dr. Pritchett told me he might be able to use me in connection with a projected campaign to study the religious life of American colleges or in a campaign to aid your race through the establishment of medical schools and the aid of those already established. This latter campaign, as I understand it, is not scheduled as is the other but is merely a personal idea and desire of Dr. Pritchett's which he may recommend to his Board and Mr. Carneige. I thought the latter idea would interest you and Dr. Washington and as far as I am concerned a word from him would materially help me to connect with either campaign and should be the most influential recommendation in the country in case of the second scheme. It is possible that Dr. Pritchett told me of this Negro college plan in confidence, or thinks that he did, so I would request that for my protection you bear that possibility in mind in using the information. Cordially yours

L. B. Stowe

ALS Con. 14 BTW Papers DLC.

[1] John R. Lynch, *The Facts of Reconstruction* (1913).

Emmett Jay Scott to Lyman Beecher Stowe

[Tuskegee, Ala., Dec.] 17, 1914[1]

My dear Mr. Stowe: I have received the synopsis of our book. I think you have made splendid use of the material placed before you. I shall proceed to get it in shape as early as convenient — in fact, I am going over it at once and will try to have it in your hands within the next week.

I very much prefer the alternative title "Builder of a Civilization." I am sure, in every way, it will be more satisfactory than the more commonplace one we first decided upon.

I am altogether in agreement with your thought that we should not confer further with Dr. Washington in connection with the publication so as to leave us free to state that he had no part in its preparation and is in no way responsible for anything in it. It so happens that as I write this letter, he is in New York City, at the Biltmore Hotel, and it may be that you might care to confer with him while there with reference to the Carnegie Foundation matter. I have telegraphed you to this effect today so as to save delay and so as to serve you in bringing about this connection.

I am very much interested in the proposed study which opens up many possibilities which I shall want to talk with you about when I have opportunity.

We are fundamentally interested in the matter of more medical schools for Negroes and Dr. Washington has emphasized this fact within the last year or two in a very pronounced way. What you have written will of course be regarded confidentially.

I have quit "whining" about my various tasks and responsibilities, but the truth of the matter is I have been so thoroughly overwhelmed during the last two or three months that I have hardly known where I was going to get off. Sincerely yours,

Emmett J. Scott

TLpS Con. 14 BTW Papers DLC.

1 The typed letterpress copy is dated Nov. 17, but it is clearly a reply to Stowe's letter of Dec. 14, 1914, above. See also Stowe to Scott, Dec. 22, 1914, below.

Lyman Beecher Stowe to Emmett Jay Scott

[Long Island, N.Y.] Dec. 22, 1914

My dear Mr. Scott   Your letter came yesterday and I was glad to learn that you thought well of the synopsis of our book and also that you liked the new title. Thanks to your telegram I have seen Dr. Washington and secured his approval of the idea to leave him out of our councils regarding the book and also his assistance in the Carneige Foundation matter. He agreed to speak to Dr. Pritchet[t] in my behalf when he saw him yesterday morning. Also he introduced me to Dr. Jones and Dr. Jones and I breakfasted together at the City Club yesterday morning and discussed our book among other things and he very kindly offered to read over the synopsis and make suggestions regarding the development of our facts and ideas. I think it will be very valuable to have the point of view of an outsider who is a specialist in our field and a very discriminating friend and admirer of Dr. Washington and hence my telegram to you of last evening requesting you to have an extra carbon copy made and sent to Dr. Jones in Washington.

I shall look forward to discussing the Carneige Foundation matter with you when we meet. I hope it may come to something and that I may have a part in it. Cordially yours

L. B. Stowe

ALS   Con. 14   BTW Papers   DLC.

From Felix von Luschan[1]

New York City   23.12.14

Dear Sir, though I have not the honour of your personal acquaintance, I still hope, that you have perhaps once heard of me in connection with the "First Universal Races — Congress" in London, where you were expected, and where I read a paper on racial anthropology, which is printed in the volume published on this Congress and which you have certainly in your Library.

I do now ask for your helpful advice. I would like to study some Problems of Heredity that might perhaps proof to be of general social interest. To get a valid Basis for my work I would like to study the exact pedigree of some hundred coloured families for 3 or if possible 4 generations and to note some anthropometric and other data on bodily and mental qualities of every single available member of these families. Mrs. v. Luschan and I are intimately familiar with this kind of work and we have studied in this way 320 Greeks on the Island of Crete, a short time ago. But this work can only be done with the support, and I may even say, only with the enthusiastic support of the coloured people and their leaders and teachers. I therefore first write to you, before I go to work.

My idea had been, to work in Hampton, in Tuskegee, in Baltimore and in Washington but I would be very thankful for every advice also as to the best places for my studies. I may be allowed therefore, to state, that we have not much interest now, in studying single individuals, what we want to study are *families* in at least two generations. Three or four would naturally be much better still. If such material should be scarce already the study of brothers or sisters would be of some use.

Hoping you will excuse me, a stranger, in asking you for assistance and with the compliments of the Season   I am, dear Sir, very truly yours

> Dr v. Luschan
> Prof. of Anthropology in the
> University of Berlin.

ALS Con. 945 BTW Papers DLC.

¹ Felix von Luschan (1854–1924) was an Austrian anthropologist and ethnologist.

To William Colfax Graves

[Tuskegee, Ala.] December 26, 1914

My dear Mr. Graves: I thought Mr. Rosenwald and yourself would be interested to know that in connection with the building of the schoolhouses we are using as far as we can Sears and Roebuck material, as the enclosed letter from the Rural School Agent will show.

We are going to push this policy because, as Mr. Sibley states, we not only show our appreciation to Mr. Rosenwald, but save money at the same time. Yours very truly,

Booker T. Washington

TLpS Con. 255 BTW Papers DLC.

To Charles Francis Meserve[1]

[Tuskegee, Ala.] December 28, 1914

Dear Dr. Meserve: I find myself in rather an awkward position regarding the request contained in your letter of December 8th. I like to be frank and straightforward in all of my dealings. I am in an awkward position for this reason:

I find that many of the colored people in North Carolina and many of the graduates of Shaw University do not speak well of the policy that now controls Shaw University, in fact there is quite a good deal of feeling against it.

I know nothing definite myself, but you can easily see that it would place me in an awkward position not living in the state or being connected with the University to go over the heads of these people and give a recommendation of the kind you ask for.

If you have any further suggestions to make, I shall be very glad to consider them. Yours very truly,

Booker T. Washington

TLpS Con. 941 BTW Papers DLC.

[1] Charles Francis Meserve (1850–1936) was president of Shaw University from 1894 to 1920, after an earlier career that included superintendency of an Indian industrial school in Lawrence, Kan., and service as an agent of the National Indian Rights Association.

To Melvin Jack Chisum

[Tuskegee, Ala.] December 28, 1914

Dear Mr. Chisum: I recall our conference with reference to your attendance upon the next meeting of the Tuskegee Negro Conference.

I am enclosing herewith printed matter which gives information with reference to the coming session.

On account of the great financial depression caused by the European War, we have been compelled to retrench in our finances in many directions, and I fear that for this year it will not be possible for us to undertake to arrange for your traveling expenses from Okmulgee to Tuskegee.

I feel quite sure that in that new country you will have ample opportunity to grow and develop a strong influence. Yours very truly,

Booker T. Washington

TLpS Con. 943 BTW Papers DLC.

From Charles William Anderson

New York, N.Y. December 29, 1914

PERSONAL.

My dear Doctor: The enclosed letter bears on the subject discussed with you during your recent visit to this city. You will recall that I wrote to "our friend" at Washington[1] and informed him that both you and I were blamed for having the Trotter meeting called off. I clipped the advertisements of the meeting from the New York News and the Amsterdam News, and I also clipped the announcement that it would not take place from the same papers and forwarded them with my letter. I requested Mr. T.[2] to lay the matter before "our friend," which he undoubtedly did. It won't hurt to have "our friend" know that we were able to serve in this connection.[3] Yours very sincerely,

Charles W. Anderson

TLS Con. 75 BTW Papers DLC.

[1] Woodrow Wilson.

[2] Joseph P. Tumulty.

[3] Anderson wanted Woodrow Wilson to know that he managed to squelch a meeting in New York planned by William Monroe Trotter to reveal the substance of his interview with Woodrow Wilson. Anderson told Joseph P. Tumulty that a group of black leaders met at his home and persuaded Trotter's committee to call off his scheduled appearance. Anderson later said that "several of the democrats, who curiously enough were the most noisy advocates of the Trotter meeting, were accusing me of a lack of race loyalty and were threatening to organize a movement for my displacement as Collector of Internal Revenue." (Anderson to Tumulty, Dec. 22, 1914, Woodrow Wilson Papers, DLC.)

To Eugene Kinckle Jones

[Tuskegee, Ala.] December 30, 1914

My dear Mr. Jones: I note carefully what you say regarding the meeting in New York. Since I wrote you last or saw you, I have taken the matter up with Mr. Moore again.

January 24 is impossible, but I think it possible to select a date sometime in the late winter or early spring that will be suitable.

In my talk with Mr. Moore I suggested that the best use of my time would be for me to put in the full day in making a vigorous campaign through Greater New York, something in the same way that I do in the Southern states. I am quite sure that I ought to cover five or six different meetings, making the men's meeting in Harlem the most important one, perhaps the central one.

Will you be kind enough to talk the whole matter over with Mr. Moore and see if your ideas agree with what he and I have in mind, and let me hear from you again.

I congratulate you upon the work which the Urban League is doing. Yours very truly,

Booker T. Washington

TLpS Con. 841 BTW Papers DLC.

To Felix von Luschan

[Tuskegee, Ala., ca. Dec. 31, 1914]

Dear Sir: Your letter of recent date received. I have noted with interest the fact that you are in America to make some studies in racial anthropology. I read with interest what you had to say before the Universal Races Congress in London on this subject. Judging from the outline in your letter of the work that you propose to do, it appears to me that it would be best for you to make your study in places where you could find several generations of the same family. The best places for this are in the following cities: Baltimore, Washington, New York, Boston, Savannah, Georgia, Mobile, Alabama, and New Orleans, Louisiana. In all of these cities that I have named you will be able to find families who have information concerning themselves for several generations. At Hampton Institute and Tuskegee Institute it would be difficult to find such families for the family ties in these particular sections were broken up by the slavery system, whereas, in Savannah and the other cities in our Southern States which I have mentioned there were in the days of slavery a considerable free Negro population which, if I understand the purpose of your study, have the elements as to heredity, race mixture, etc., which you desire to get hold of.

We will be pleased, however, if you have the opportunity during your stay in this country, to have you make a visit to Tuskegee Institute. Very truly yours,

Booker T. Washington

TLpS Con. 945 BTW Papers DLC.

A Press Release

Tuskegee Institute, Ala. [ca. Dec. 31, 1914]

To Editors: I am sending in this form a report of lynchings in this country during the year of 1914. I very much hope you may be inclined to use it in your valued newspaper morning of January 1, 1915.

Booker T. Washington

THE LYNCHING
RECORD FOR 1914

Tuskegee Institute, Ala., Dec. 31, 1914. I find according to records kept by the Department of Records and Research of the Tuskegee Institute that during the year that has just passed 52 persons were put to death by mobs. Of this number 49 were colored and 3 were white. The number of persons lynched in 1914 was apparently the same as for 1913 and is the smallest number for a year since records of lynchings have been kept.

Although the number of lynchings has not increased, there appears to be an increasing tendency to lynch for any cause, however trivial, and also to disregard sex. Of the 52 persons lynched in the past year only seven, or 13 per cent, two white and five colored, were charged with rape. Three of those lynched were women. One of these women was only seventeen years old, and was charged with killing a man who, it was reported, had raped her. Another of the women lynched was accused of beating a child to death; while the third woman and her husband were charged with setting fire to a barn. In the presence of their four-year-old child they were put to death.

The crimes charged against the persons killed were: murder, 13; robbery and murder, 6; robbery and attempted murder, 1; suspected of murder, 1; rape, 6; attempted rape, 1; killing an officer, 5; wounding officer, 1; murderous assault, 3; alleged murderous assault, 1; biting off a man's chin, 1; accused of wounding a person, 1; killing person in quarrel, 4; beating child to death, 1; trying to force way into woman's room, 1; stealing shoes, 1; stealing mules, 1; setting fire to a barn, 2; assisting man to escape who had wounded another, 1; being found under a house, 1.

I find that lynchings occurred during the year in fifteen States as follows: Alabama, 2; Arkansas, 1; Florida, 4; Georgia, 2; Louisiana, 12; Mississippi, 12; Missouri, 1; New Mexico, 1; North Dakota, 1; North Carolina, 1; Oklahoma, 3; Oregon, 1; South Carolina, 4; Tennessee, 1; Texas, 6.

Booker T. Washington

PDSr Galley proof   Con. 514   BTW Papers   DLC.

To the Editor of the New York *World*

Tuskegee Institute, Ala., Jan. 2 [1915]

Fair Play for Negro Aliens

To the Editor of The World: Through your newspaper I desire to appeal to the American Congress and to the people of the United States in favor of fair play and justice in connection with the Immigration Bill now pending before the United States Senate, which by amendment excludes from coming into this country any person of African descent.

The bill, in my opinion, is unjust, unreasonable and unnecessary. It is unnecessary because only a few thousand people of African descent enter this country annually. Practically all of these that do come are mainly from the West Indies and almost none from the continent of Africa. It is evident that many of those who come into this country do not remain permanently, but I find, according to the census of 1910, there were in the United States only 40,319 negroes who were foreign born and only 473 of these had come from Africa.

The bill puts an unnecessary slight upon colored people by classing them with alien criminals.

The bill in its present form would seem to prohibit citizens from the Republics of Liberia, Cuba and Hayti, and also from Porto Rico and Santo Domingo, entering this country, thus placing an unnecessary hardship upon these smaller countries, which would not be done, in my opinion, if they were stronger.

In a personal conversation with a high officer of the Panama Canal Commission he told me that the services of the Jamaican negroes were invaluable in building the Panama Canal. Now that we are celebrating the completion of this great canal, it seems most unjust and unreasonable that the people who contributed in so large a measure toward it should be slapped in the face and told that they cannot enter this country even when they meet the requirements of our Government.

An investigation will show that the colored people who have come to this country from the West Indian Islands and from other foreign countries have proved as a whole to be a law-abiding, intelligent, industrious class. They have never become Anarchists or as a class given trouble to the Government.

Let me repeat that it is unfair at this time, when we are all striving to bring about racial harmony and peace, to raise a question which is calculated to stir up needless strife, and I cannot feel that the best people in the South approve of any such bill.

Lastly, the passing of such an unjust law will cripple the missionary and educational work which we are trying to do in Africa and elsewhere. For a number of years some of the brightest young people from Africa and elsewhere have been coming to this country to receive training to fit them to go back and help their people, and this they have done in an effective manner. All this, I understand, will be stopped by the passing of this law.

This measure is not political or sectional, and I hope that all people will see the justice of asking Congress to refrain from perpetrating this unjust act upon my race. Certainly we have enough to contend with already without having this additional handicap and discouragement placed in our pathway.

Booker T. Washington

New York *World,* Jan. 6, 1915, 8. The letter appeared in several major newspapers. The headline was added by the New York *World.*

From Harvey Johnson[1]

Baltimore, Md. January 2nd., 1915

Dear Sir: I have just now finished reading your most deeply interesting, carefully kept, and very important record of mob violence in this country. Dr. Washington, let me thank and congratulate you, for I believe that this record kept by you, and sent forth throughout the world by the Associated Press, will do more to call attention to the great crime of mob law, called lynching, than anything within my recollection that has been put forth as a remedy, since records have been kept. There have been other[s,] many of them, carefully prepared, but they were not from Tuskegee, nor were they by Dr. Washington. Doctor, I have always admired the great work that you have done, by way of the phenomenal achievements made in the building up of that great institution over which you have the honor to preside, and over which you have presided so long, and so honorably, and achieved so

much for the betterment and uplift of the colored race: for this also,
let me congratulate you. But dear Dr. Washington, there is one thing
to which I must call your attention, that has always given me pain, and
always made me feel that Dr. Washington in his itineracy and speech-
making, to my mind, so often negatives and largely neutralizes the
splendid work he is doing at Tuskegee, and the splendid addresses he
makes because of certain recommendations and advice to our people.
The manner of putting them; the words in which they are clothed,
and the equivocality of a large number of them — that is, I mean
they can have two significations, a good and a bad one; and as I know
that, Dr. Washington knows that the white man is going to take the
bad one. I call his attention to this, because I do not know that he is
conscious of the fact, or of the harm that follows his advice, especially
with reference to the educational system. The impression, Doctor, (and
this is not hearsay) is wide-spread, that your attitude toward our institutions is that the normal, academic, collegiate or higher grades
ought to be brought down to the industrial form. It is said that the
great lessening of higher education in South Carolina, Charleston particularly, you were quoted as being the cause of the reduction. That,
it is true, is a report. In this State the effort has been on for a number
of years to lessen the grades in the curriculum of our High School, and
even of the Normal School. No longer than the year just passed,
(1914) did Prof Koch,[2] the Assistant Superintendent of the city
schools, seriously put before the Board the cutting out of about all the
higher grades in our High School, bringing them down to what is
known as the industrial system, and this was done on your name, in
language like this: That this is the advice and recommendation of Dr.
Booker Washington, the greatest negro among you. And we, as citizens
of this city, had to fight, and that strenuously too, in repudiating that
idea and act, and then it was only tentatively put aside because it is
held that Dr. Washington's idea is the idea for *our* schools, (of course,
not for the whites — No; Never! the curriculum of theirs is advanced
right along.)

Dear Doctor, this is the first time I have ever written a line about
you or your views to any public or private individual, to my knowledge,
and so I hope you will receive this in the spirit in which it is written.
I have seen in public print, again and again where in different parts
of this country you were being quoted, when the white man desired

to deprive us of the advantages of higher education where the State or City had to bear the cost of the same.

Just another thought Doctor: I had the pleasure of listening to your address at the National Baptist Convention in Philadelphia, and the text of it was that we should cease, as a race, being on the defensive. Now Dr., that is what I consider one of those equivocal statements and ideas. I am quite sure that you meant that we were to make the best of our condition, with as little restiveness as possible, and as little irascibility and contention as possible. But Docter, when you say that we are to get off the defensive, and take what you call the progressive — going forward with what we have, to get more — I say, my dear sir, that can mean, and to the white man does mean that Dr. Washington is advising his people to just let the white man go ahead, and ride right over us rough-shod, and say nothing about it; whereas I am sure you did not mean anything of the kind, in your heart of hearts. But the white man is taking your words, and not what you feel; because as a race man you cannot but feel grieved at what we are bearing, so I think the advice is wrong when you tell us to get off the defensi[ve] for we have got to defend ourselves and our rights that have been gained, and you know Dr., they were gained on the defensive side, and the progress has been made in keeping with the aggressiveness with which the defence has been made, and not with an humble submission making the best of our condition. No, Dr., battles have been fought against great odds, and we are where we are because we fought, and we will go back rapidly to where we were, when we cease to fight. The theory that every man is to let down his bucket where he is, is well enough, but he can't let it down unless he can get to the well, and you know that the well is always surrounded with the enemies to our progress and achievements.

I will close by thanking you again for the record I have just read in this morning's Baltimore American, and wishing you a Happy New Year; many of them, and continued success in the building up of Tuskegee. I am   Yours sincerely,

(Rev.) Harvey Johnson

TLS Con. 940 BTW Papers DLC.

[1] Harvey Johnson was born in slavery in 1843 in Fauquier County, Va., and graduated from Wayland Seminary (D.C.) in 1872. He was minister of the Union Baptist Church in Baltimore for many years.

[2] Charles J. Koch.

To Whitefield McKinlay

Tuskegee Ala   Jan 3 1915

The immigration bill which is before Congress by amendment prohibits all people of African descent from entering the United States in the future.[1] The final enactment of such a law is unnecessary unjust and unreasonable. Not the least injustice is in the fact that only a comparatively few black people enter this country each year and that the law classes our race with original aliens. The passing of such a law will exclude not only persons from Africa but from the West Indian Islands including the Republic of Haiti San Domingo and Cuba. Without the services of the West Indian Negroes in digging the Panama Canal it could hardly have been completed in such a satisfactory and quick way. Now that the canal is completed it is unjust to prohibit the colored people who have been largely instrumental in building it from entering this country even when they meet the strict requirements of our immigration laws. The whole matter seems an unnecessary and unfair slap at the colored people the bulk of whom are in the south. I have discovered no sentiment among the white people in favor of such a law. It is not a sectional or political question and I am urging you to use all the influence you can through Negro business leagues colored newspapers and through our various organizations that you can reach to bring about the defeat of this unjust measure. I hope you will also communicate at once with your senator and representatives.

Booker T Washington

TWSr   Con. 4   Carter G. Woodson Collection   DLC.

[1] In the first days of Jan. 1915, when a general immigration bill was before the U.S. Senate, Democratic Senator James A. Reed of Missouri proposed and secured passage of an amendment barring all persons of African descent. Then the bill with this amendment was passed and was sent to the House of Representatives for consideration. BTW hastily organized a campaign of arguments and constituent pressure against the amendment. He wrote letters to the editors of the Atlanta *Constitution* and the New York *Evening Post*. He wired many of his lieutenants urging them to write to their congressmen or visit them in their offices in opposition. (See, for example, BTW to George C. Hall, Jan. 2, 1915, new series, Con. 58, BTW Papers, DLC; BTW to Robert R. Moton, Jan. 3, 1915, ViHaI.) The House defeated the African exclusion measure by 250 votes to 77, and BTW was generally credited with a central role in the defeat. He later said that if the bill had passed the House, he would have "gone direct to President Wilson and ask[ed] him to veto the bill." (BTW to Henry A. May and others, Jan. 18, 1915, Con. 656, BTW Papers, DLC.)

To Andrew Carnegie

Tuskegee Institute, Alabama   January 4, 1915

Dear Mr. Carnegie: Thank you for so kindly sending me a copy of your New Year's greeting, "War Abolished — Peace Enthroned."[1]

I have read what you have written with sincerest approval, and the fervent prayer that your plea for permanent peace may not fall upon deaf ears. Yours very truly,

Booker T. Washington

TLS   Andrew Carnegie Papers   DLC.

[1] Carnegie's open letter called upon the belligerent nations to employ the Hague Tribunal to bring about an armistice, and a vaguely conceived league of nations to keep the future peace and make armies and navies unnecessary. (PD, Con. 75, BTW Papers, DLC.)

From Robert Russa Moton

Hampton, Virginia   January 4, 1915

My dear Dr. Washington: Your night letter[1] I received and we are taking up the matter of the Immigration Question with vigor. Dr. Frissell is communicating with all of our Trustees as well as with our representatives in Congress. I am doing the same thing.

We have put Dr. Thomas J. Jones in Washington on the job also and we are sending a representative up to-night to pull every possible string that can be pulled to defeat this unfortunate clause. I agree absolutely with you.

If you think of any other suggestion I wish you would let me know. Yours sincerely,

R. R. Moton

TLS   Con. 77   BTW Papers   DLC.

[1] Probably the same as the telegram to Whitefield McKinlay, Jan. 3, 1915, above.

From Whitefield McKinlay

[Washington, D.C.] 1/5/15

Grimke, Miller, myself saw Borah[1] and Madden.[2] Borah fa[v]ors amending bill exempting students and merchants. Madden objections kept bill from going to Conference to day and hopes tomorrow to eliminate measure. We plan to see Gardner[3] and others tomorrow. We feel hopeful but not sanguine.

W M

HWIr Con. 4 Carter G. Woodson Collection DLC.

[1] William Edgar Borah (1865–1940), Republican senator from Idaho from 1907 until his death.
[2] Martin Barnaby Madden (1855–1928), Republican representative from Illinois from 1905 until his death.
[3] Augustus Peabody Gardner (1865–1918), Republican representative from Massachusetts.

To Cleveland Hoadley Dodge[1]

[Tuskegee, Ala.] January 6, 1915

Personal and Confidential.
My dear Mr. Dodge: I am venturing to do something which I have not done in connection with any other individual during the present administration, and that is, speak of the fitness of an individual for a presidential appointment. I am doing this wholly on my own action.

I have heard that President Wilson is considering the fitness of Governor O'Neal of Alabama for a position on the Federal Trade Commission.

I want to say without hesitation that of all the men from this section who have been discussed for this position I believe that Governor O'Neal is eminently fitted for a position on this Commission. In addition to being a lawyer of high standing, he has given special attention to the study of economics and has the confidence of all the business men of high standing, who know him.

In addition to these qualifications, I want to say that during all the years that he has been Governor of Alabama he has proven himself to be a just, honorable and brave man seeking to do justice to all people regardless of race condition or color. I believe he is just the kind of man that the President would like to have on such a Commission.

While I do not want to seek to advise or influence you in this matter, if in your own way and at your own time you can see your way clear to call the Governor's claims to the attention of the President, I should feel that you are performing a good service.[2] Yours very truly,

Booker T. Washington

TLpS Con. 944 BTW Papers DLC.

[1] Cleveland Hoadley Dodge (1860–1926), son of the capitalist William Earl Dodge, was vice-president and director of the Phelps Dodge Corp., director of the New York Life Insurance Co., the National City Bank, and many industrial and railroad corporations. He was a trustee of the John F. Slater Fund, the Carnegie Institution, and the Carnegie Peace Foundation.

[2] The same letter, on the same date, was sent to Jacob H. Schiff and George F. Peabody. A similar letter of the same date went to George McAneny. BTW endorsed O'Neal on Jan. 9, 1915, in a letter to Paul M. Warburg (Con. 944, BTW Papers, DLC.)

From George Cleveland Hall

Chicago   Jan 6 [1915]

My Dear Dr. Washington   Your letter concerning the mens meeting at Oak Park at hand. I think you would make a mistake to attempt a Sunday mornings meeting out there. I think the Oak Park meeting one of the most important, aside from the Chic[a]go Men's club — that you could have in this State in point of influence and future profit and I would advise that you give them as early a date as possible and a special night address. I hope you wont suggest the other proposition to Mr Hill.[1]

I think the letter to Bishop Fallows is all right and the advance of the money a very timely notice as Swan[2] has used nearly all of it now, and their credit will soon be Nil.

I have had lots of fun with Mr. "Woodrow" Trotter my new name for him. He gave me this clipping and said that for once you two were agreeing upon the same thing and he wished it could continue. I told him it could if he could see his way clear to stop his bitter personal attacks upon you — I told him that I thought he was crazy upon the subject and that he was hurting not only himself, but everything he touched by his spirit of vilification. When he left me he said that he hoped that through the immigrations bill all factions might learn to stand on a common platform — He thought what a fine thing it would be for *You,* DuBoise & *Himself* to appear in Washington arm in arm, fighting against the measure. he was willing to agree to an Armistice until the fight was won, at least. I put him after Bentley and got them going — Trotter meeting at orchestra Hall was a frost. They closed the doors upon the people until Ida got a white woman to stand for $200.00 — his audience was just 180 people by actual count. Ida is holding 15 ct. admission meeting to get him the hundred dollars she promised him and he has had to resort to an old trick "pass the hat" programme — Never saw a Man so hungry for money and cheap notoriety —

I saw Senator Lewis[3] and telegraphed the entire Ill delegation and stirred up the "NAACP." and had a number of influintial white people telegraph both congressman, Senators & the President.

With the hope that I may see you soon and that "Woodrow Trotters" Dream may come true. I am   Sincerly

G C Hall

Mrs. Hall sends best wishes to you and Mrs Washington

ALS   Con. 939   BTW Papers   DLC.

[1] Richard Hill, Jr. (b. 1887) was a graduate of Fisk University and the University of Michigan Law School (1911). He practiced law in Chicago beginning in 1912, and was active in the West Side Colored Protective Association, the Illinois Colored Democracy, and other civic and political organizations.

[2] Thomas Wallace Swann, a black journalist, was the principal organizer and secretary of the Illinois Commission on the National Half-Century Anniversary of Negro Freedom.

[3] James Hamilton Lewis (1863–1939), Democratic senator from Illinois (1913–19).

To James Carroll Napier

Tuskegee Institute, Alabama, January 7, 1915

My dear Mr. Napier: I am putting the following matter before you as a member of the Executive Committee of the National Negro Business League:

I have secured a small sum of money to be used in assisting and promoting a National Health Week in connection with various state and national organizations which have already been giving some attention to the health of the race.

My present thought is to inaugurate the National Health Week under the auspices of the National Negro Business League, but I do not wish to do so without the consent of the majority of the members of the Executive Committee. Whatever is done in this respect will entail no additional cost to the League because, as I have stated, I have money to defray the greater part of the expense. The date that we have in mind is March 21 to 27 inclusive.

The enclosed pamphlet will indicate something of the importance of doing something to better the condition of the health of our people. Unless the people have good, strong, healthy bodies and increase in numbers it is impossible to have successful business and other enterprises.

In order to save time, will you be kind enough to telegraph me at my expense your opinion regarding the matter. Yours very truly,

Booker T. Washington

TLpS Con. 942 BTW Papers DLC.

To the Editor of the Montgomery *Journal*

[Tuskegee, Ala.] January 7th, 1915

Dear Sir: In your issue of January 4th 1915, there appeared a news-story to the effect that I had purchased 10,000 acres of land on the West Point Route for colonization purposes. This is an incorrect statement and I am taking the liberty to request a little space in your valued columns to give your readers a clear and more accurate description of the agricultural experiment which we have located about twelve miles below Chehaw.

I will state, first, that the tract of land consists of 1750 acres instead of 10,000 as stated in the Journal and it was purchased by the Tuskegee Farm and Improvement Company and not by me. Instead of Adamsville, it has been decided to name the place Baldwin Farms in honor of the late Mr. William H. Baldwin, Jr., of New York City, whose untiring zeal and faithfulness to Tuskegee contributed so much in helping us lay a substantial foundation for our present work.

Recently, some friends of Tuskegee Institute who were visiting the school made the suggestion that some plan might be evolved which would provide an opportunity for the graduates of our Agricultural Department to get a little start by helping them to get a home and a farm and allow them to pay for it by putting the lessons taught them in their classes, into actual and profitable practice. It was shown that this method of helping them would inspire enthusiastic work, since the result of their struggles and sacrifice is a home and a farm paid for and clear of debt.

Accordingly, after arrangements were made and the soil carefully investigated, the tract of land was purchased. It has been cut up into smaller farms and is now being assigned to our graduates and former students who care to join the movement, under the following plan. Simple and yet comfortable homes will be erected for the tenants and every encouragement given to get them started in the proper direction. The first payment for the place is to be made after the first crop has been harvested.

It is our hope that Baldwin Farms will develop into a model Negro farming community and we are confident that the results will justify the experiment and furnish a valuable object lesson in selling farm-lands to trained Negro workers.

As to the proposed railroad, I wish to say that we are not planning to construct a railway line of any kind from Baldwin Farms to the town of Tuskegee nor to the Tuskegee Institute. We have not at any time considered the construction of such a line for we have no money in hand nor shall we have any for that purpose.

I am obligated to you and your columns for many considerations in the past and am only too sorry that an incorrect statement in the original account has made this letter necessary. Yours very truly,

Booker T. Washington

TLpS Con. 941 BTW Papers DLC.

From Whitefield McKinlay

Washington DC Jany 7th — [191]5

The objectionable measure was overwhelmingly defeated. Grink [Grimké] and Miller deserve heartiest credit for their tireless fight. If convenient see you when you next pass through Washington.

Whitefield McKinlay

TWSr Con. 946 BTW Papers DLC.

From Cleveland Hoadley Dodge

New York January 8, 1915

My dear Dr. Washington: I have your valued favor of January sixth, and note what you say regarding Gov. O'Neal. I have heretofore been very chary about recommending anybody to President Wilson, but I hope to see him in the near future, when I may have an opportunity of telling him what you say regarding Gov. O'Neal. With best wishes, Yours very truly,

C H Dodge

TLS Con. 944 BTW Papers DLC.

From Emmet O'Neal

Montgomery, Alabama   January 12, 1915

(Personal)

Dear Dr. Washington: I write to express my sincere appreciation of the many gracious courtesies which you extended to myself and party on our recent visit to your institution.[1]

No one can fully appreciate the splendid work you are doing without a personal visit and inspection of your great institution. I was therefore sincere when I stated that my visit to your splendid school was both a revelation and an inspiration. It will always be a source of congratulation for me to know that during my administration, the relation between the races was never more friendly or amicable.

If the colored race would follow the teachings of such a man as yourself and if they could be equipped for the duties of citizenship by institutions which follow your ideas, there would be no race question in the South.

In my address I stated that although the State does not select the governing board of your institution, yet it contributes to a small extent to its maintenance and was proud to recognize it as one of the brightest stars in our educational firmament. You wisely stated in reply, that whenever the management and policies of the Tuskegee Institute were opposed to the dominant sentiment of this State its usefulness would cease:

While I am not vain enough to believe that I deserve the ovation tendered me at your institute, it is, nevertheless, extremely gratifying to know that I have earned the confidence of that class of my fellow citizens whom you represent and whose good opinion I so highly esteem. Very sincerely yours,

Emmet O'Neal

TLS   Con. 944   BTW Papers   DLC.

[1] Governor and Mrs. O'Neal and their daughter, with a party of about twenty state officials, visited Tuskegee Institute on Jan. 9, 1915.

To Wyatt Rushton[1]

[Tuskegee, Ala.] January 14, 1915

Dear Sir: I am not at all opposed to European emigrants coming to the South. What I have said from time to time in advising the colored people to see to it that they must take advantage of their opportunities in the South or else they will be crowded to the wall by others who will come in and get more out of the soil than they get out of it. I have some personal feeling, however, as to how well European emigrants and our native Southern people will get on together, but this has nothing to do with the direct matter of European emigrants coming into the South.[2] Yours very truly,

Booker T. Washington

TLpS Con. 945 BTW Papers DLC.

[1] Wyatt Rushton was a senior at the University of Alabama and an associate editor of the *Crimson-White* in 1914–15.

[2] BTW wrote in reply to Rushton's request for a clarification of BTW's position on immigration to the South. He was under the impression that BTW opposed immigration. (Rushton to BTW, Jan. 7, 1915, Con. 945, BTW Papers, DLC.) Rushton later pressed BTW for more particulars regarding his views, especially BTW's opinion of how native southern whites and immigrants would react to one another. BTW replied that he was "unable to offer any opinion" on the subject. (Rushton to BTW, Jan. 19, 1915, and BTW to Rushton, Jan. 22, 1915, Con. 945, BTW Papers, DLC.)

From William H. Walcott[1]

Tuskegee Institute, Alabama January 14, 1915

Dear Sir: I rejoiced quietly the other night when you read in the chapel the telegram from the National Capital which stated that the bill that had for its object the debarring of Negro aliens from this country had been defeated.

Yesterday I found in the Library a copy of The New York World in which your splendid letter to the Editor and to the American people was published. That letter confirmed the opinion I held that you would not permit so grave an injustice to be perpetrated upon all the Negro peoples without vigorous protest. Permit me to say that your protest was statesmanlike too, for I think it a blind and unfortunate policy that would permit the National Legislature to pass a law which carried such destructive forces.

This note is to express to you my personal thanks for your action in the matter and I am sure I but give expression to the hearty sentiment of the foreign students at Tuskegee, and the others in all institutions of learning in this country.

I feel also that those persons of Negro descent who come to these shores for the purpose of bettering their condition in every way are equally grateful to you.

I pray that you may long live to champion our causes, for where there is infringement of justice and righteousness against the Negro there we are sure to find you aligned against the forces of destruction. Respectfully yours,

W. H. Walcott

TLS Con. 663 BTW Papers DLC.

[1] William H. Walcott, a graduate of Hampton Institute (1907), was assistant commandant in the military department of Tuskegee Institute beginning in 1907.

To Ruth Standish Bowles Baldwin

[Tuskegee, Ala.] January 15, 1915

My dear Mrs. Baldwin: I am answering only a portion of your letter.

It is now practically settled that we will elect a new President of Fisk on the 8th of February. I am sorry that I cannot give you his name, as it is to be held in confidence until the election takes place, but he is a man whom I am sure you will like and who will get on well and make a strong, vigorous President for Fisk.[1]

I shall hope to see you when I go North, which will be toward the latter part of this month. Yours very truly,

Booker T. Washington

TLpS Con. 937 BTW Papers DLC.

[1] Fayette Avery McKenzie (1872–1957), born in Montrose, Pa., a Ph.D. in sociology from the University of Pennsylvania, was president of Fisk University from 1915 to 1925. He raised an endowment of a million dollars and modernized

the curriculum but was less successful in dealing with students and the increasing militancy of blacks. His autocratic administration and "southernization" of Fisk precipitated a student strike of two months and his ouster as president. (Lamon, *Black Tennesseans*, 274–93; Wolters, *New Negro on Campus*, 29–69.)

To H. R. Williamson[1]

Tuskegee Institute, Alabama January 16, 1915

My dear Sir: Mr. Rosenwald has given no intimation in this matter, about which I write you, but nevertheless I think it would very much encourage him if you will act upon the suggestion:

You will find that his firm, Sears, Roebuck and Company, Chicago, Illinois, handles school furnishings and I think it would very much encourage him if, in connection with the building of Rosenwald schoolhouses, you would order as much material as possible from his firm for the furnishings of the Rosenwald schoolhouses being built under your general direction.

In connection with this matter, I wish that all orders might be sent directly to Mr. Max Adler, manager of the furniture department, Sears, Roebuck and Company, Chicago, Illinois.

I am enclosing under separate cover a booklet which gives information with regard to schoolhouse supplies which Sears, Roebuck and Company furnish. Yours very truly,

Booker T. Washington

TLS Con. 946 BTW Papers DLC. Returned to BTW with the reply: "Will try and have these schools buy desks ect — as suggested when they are ready to purchase. Respt H R Williamson S of E."

[1] Superintendent of schools of Hayneville, Ala.

To Emmet O'Neal

[Tuskegee, Ala.] January 16, 1915

My dear Sir: I have not as yet received replies to all the letters I sent away, but the enclosed one from Mr. Dodge and the other from Mr.

Warburg I thought you would like to see, especially the one from Mr. Warburg. I have also received a reply from Mr. Peabody in which he said he would keep the matter before him and would use the information I have given him in case he has opportunity to do so. Please return the two letters which I enclose.

Later. A letter has come from Mr. Peabody and contains the following extract. The rest of the letter refers to a personal matter.

"I have your letter of the 6th of January and I note your judgment respecting Governor O'Neal is the same as heretofore. I recall that Mr. Edgar Gardner Murphy thought very highly of him before he was elected Governor. I do not fancy that the matter will come before me at all, but I am very glad to have the knowledge in case occasion should arise for my being of any service in that direction." Yours very truly,

Booker T. Washington

TLpS Con. 944 BTW Papers DLC.

To Harvey Johnson

[Tuskegee, Ala.] January 16, 1915

My dear Dr. Johnson: I am fulfilling in part, at least, the promise to write you further in reply to your kind letter of January 2d.[1]

First, I make it a rule from which I do not depart never to give advice concerning the educational affairs in any special community. What I say in regard to education is general and I leave it to the individual communities to apply my suggestions or not as they please. Hence, you can be perfectly sure that I have never given any advice directly or indirectly concerning the schools in Baltimore.

I have realized very fully that my position regarding education is often misunderstood by our people and I think will be misunderstood for some years to come. For this I am perfectly willing to pay the penalty.

My life has been given to educational matters just as yours has been given to the preaching of the Gospel, and in studying the trend of education throughout the world, I have noted from year to year that there is a growth everywhere in the direction of the application of the general principles of what is called the old-time higher education to the things of life right about us and all that I am doing and saying in connection with industrial education or technical education is simply in the direction of trying to get our people to keep pace with what is going on in every part of the world among white people. My present trouble grows out of the fact the Negro is being left behind in the matter of industrial and technical education.

I think if you will measure the amount per capita being spent in your own city for industrial or technical education among white people as compared with that spent for colored people for the same kind of education, you will be surprised that the amount spent for white people far outreaches that spent for colored people. In the state of Georgia, where a few years ago, industrial and technical education was despised and looked down upon by white people, today the state is spending for the industrial and technical education of colored people less than $25,000. For the same kind of education they are spending for white people about $400,000. From my point of view, anything that strengthens the mind, gives character and usefulness to the individual is education of the highest kind. Anything that fails to do that is lower education.

I am sure that while we may differ as to the method to be pursued in education, there is no difference between us as to the results to be attained. I have always advocated and now advocate that a proportion of our people should be educated for the professions: law, medicine, the ministry and what not, and that the majority of our people need book education, the same as other people, but in our case and in a special degree, it is necessary that this education be applied to the things of life about us. This is what I mean by industrial or technical education. As I have stated, the sad thing to me, however, is to see the white people in every part of the country taking up the idea of industrial education and leaving our people far in the rear.

I am sorry that my words are so often misunderstood. I presume this is one of the penalties that any public man has to pay, but I have never meant, nor do not mean, in any of my references to advise our people not to resent wrongs or refer to them, but I have advised and now advise our people not to depend upon the resenting of wrongs wholly for the success that is to come to them, but to follow the teachings of the Bible, which you and I both believe, which says in effect: Overcome evil with good. That is, overcome evil through progressive, constructive efforts. If there is any . . .² out of the wilderness, I have not been able to discover it.

One other thing: whenever you see anything in print from me that you think is injurious, please call my attention to it directly and frankly. I am not thin-skinned and realize fully that one danger a public man is constantly confronted with is the danger of being over-flattered by friends and the failure to heed those who would criticise him adversely.

I hope at sometime we may see you here at Tuskegee.

By this mail I am sending you a copy of one of my books, "My Larger Education," which I hope you may find time to glance through. Yours very truly,

Booker T. Washington

TLpS Con. 940 BTW Papers DLC.

¹ BTW first replied to Johnson's letter on Jan. 9, thanking Johnson for being so frank in his criticism, and promising to write a full reply when he returned from Chicago. (Con. 940, BTW Papers, DLC.)
² Part of one line obliterated in press copy.

To the Editor of the New York *World*

Tuskegee Institute, Ala., Jan. 16 [1915]

Booker T. Washington Declares
No Lynching Has an Excuse

As an American citizen, proud of his country and its history, I am shocked beyond measure to learn from your telegram of the lynching of two colored men and two colored women for whipping a policeman at Monticello, Ga.

You ask me for an expression of opinion. I can only say that I feel such acts of lawlessness are unfortunate and hurtful in the highest degree. They cast a blot upon our civilization. I feel there can be no excuse for such an outrageous and unlawful act. The community or State that permits such lawlessness is bound to suffer before the public opinion of the world and it is useless to invite and encourage immigration into any section of our country when such lawlessness is permitted.

Every such lynching keeps away hundreds, if not thousands of good people, who otherwise might be induced to settle in such States or communities. In my opinion, there is needed in every community and in every State law abiding men who will fearlessly stand for law and order. This is necessary in the interest of white people and black people.

Even as outrageous as the Monticello lynchings are, I cannot feel that the negro is the one most injured, but instead those guilty of perpetrating such outrages against law and order. I always condemn, as I now do, lawlessness on the part of my own people, but I have never felt that breaking the law on the part of one person justified other persons also in breaking the law.

We have gone a long way to lynching women for whipping a man, and I can but believe that the courts would have punished these people after regular and proper trial. The conscience of the American people, North and South, will be stirred by such offenses as the one here referred to, and I am glad to say there are brave and liberal men in all parts of the South, such as Gov. Emmet O'Neal of Alabama and others who represent a growing disposition to condemn and prevent the lynching of human beings.

BOOKER T. WASHINGTON

New York *World,* Jan. 17, 1915, 4.

Extracts from an Address
before the Twenty-fourth Annual
Tuskegee Negro Conference

[Tuskegee, Ala.] January 20, 1915

Notwithstanding the strenuous financial experiences through which most farmers of this section are passing, I am glad to note many evidences of continued progress on your part.

First of all, the farmers' parade in which you took part this morning is evidence of a high character that the Negro farmers are not discouraged, that they are learning to produce that on their farms which is making them independent and more useful.

While we are passing through these strenuous, trying days growing out of the financial depression because of the war, we must keep in mind that striking illustration in the Bible of the man running a race. You remember that the Bible suggests that one engaged in running a race should throw off every weight. So I want to help our black farmers throughout the South, especially during the next few months and years, to throw off every weight that hinders their running successfully the race, and in helping you and suggesting to you how to throw off these weights, I must be very frank, almost brutally frank, but I have learned by long experience that in the long run frankness is an exhibition of the greatest kindness.

One of the weights that our people should throw off is the habit of carrying pistols, of keeping pistols on the body and in the home. I know many colored people who spend more on a pistol every year than they do on the education of their children. The pistol, in nine cases out of ten, not only does not protect the individual, but it leads him to trouble. One of the weights, then, that we can throw off first is the expense of buying and keeping a pistol and avoiding the trouble the use of a pistol will lead us into.

Now I know that the pistol habit and much else that I am going to say does not relate directly to the members of this Negro Conference, but through you, I want to send a message to the people of our state that will help them to throw off this weight and others which I am going to mention.

Another weight that we should get rid of is the reputation which our race is getting altogether too fast, especially this year, of stealing, of pilfering. Perhaps there has never been a season when there have been so many cases reported in town and country districts of people attempting to steal or pilfer. I am aware of the fact that this, by no means, is confined to the Negro race. The same charges are being brought against white people, but the doing of wrong on the part of white people does not help our people and I am talking just now especially to the Negro. We should make up our minds everywhere that rather than steal in the slightest degree, we should be willing to go hungry, to go half-clothed, to go without proper shelter, to suffer every degree of bodily discomfort rather than steal. We should teach this lesson constantly around the fire-side, teach it in Sunday School and day school, preach it from the pulpit everywhere that we should grow up a race of people that are absolutely honest in regard to money and property.

We must get rid of this weight and it will require all the help and all the encouragement that members of this Conference can give to the common people, especially during this year, to enable them to withstand the temptations that they are going to be surrounded by, especially because of the hard times.

Still another thing that we can throw off is that of supporting and patronizing "blind tigers." There are not a few petty officers of the law who make their living by arresting colored people who are charged with patronizing the "blind tiger." Let us throw off that weight and wherever the law prohibits the selling or buying of whiskey, let us comply with the law at any cost.

Still another weight that we can throw off is the habit, in too many of our country and farming districts, of gambling. Gambling leads to a loss of time, to a loss of money, to a loss of character, and in many cases, it leads to murder and finally to the prison and often to the gallows. Gambling, then, is a weight which we should get rid of in every farming district.

Another weight which we can easily throw off is the habit of spending so much money and time in useless law suits — law suits that are founded upon some trivial matter that could be settled in five minutes by the minister, by the teacher, or by somebody else, or some honest person in the community. Often weeks are spent and much money is spent in hanging around a court house in connection with some little law suit not worth five minutes discussion. Let us throw off that weight during this year and put the same time and the same money into a better farm, a better home, to the education of our children and the strengthening of the church.

Still one other weight that holds back our people, and while it is a delicate matter to refer to, I am going to be bold enough to refer to it in frankness but with all kindness. It is the weight that is holding back not only the black people, but the white people in many of the farming districts of the South and I mean the habit of white men living in immoral relations with colored women in too many of our farming districts. Wherever we can control this weight, let us throw it off. We should make an appeal to the best white people in the community and in the county to use their influence and the power of the law to see that such unholy living is broken up. It injures the white people and injures the black people and often leads to unlawful lynchings and other unlawful outbreaks between the races.

Finally, as you go home from this Farmers' Conference carry in your minds a firm resolve that this year, more than ever, you will raise everything necessary to keep you and your family at home. Raise it in your garden, raise it on your farm, raise your own poultry, your own stock, your own fruit, and in proportion as you do this, you will have better homes, better schools, better churches and better racial relations and a more righteous and law-abiding community.

TMc Con. 989 BTW Papers DLC. Another copy is in Con. 943, BTW Papers, DLC.

To Wallace Buttrick

[Tuskegee, Ala.] January 23d, 1915

Dear Dr. Buttrick: We have just been having for a week a meeting of state rural school agents and county supervisors and county superintendents representing the states of Alabama, Georgia, Mississippi, Florida, Tennessee, etc. I have never seen such a fine, helpful spirit of cooperation as I have seen during the past few days. I never expected to live to see the time when I could witness Southern white men and women working together with colored men and women in the way these have worked. Several of the white county superintendents brought their wives with them, and it seemed as much like an old fashioned revival service as perhaps an educational meeting.

I want to thank the General Education Board most heartily for the $5,000 which it has given Dr. Dillard for supervisor work; and I want to add, if the Board can see its way clear to give an additional $5,000 making the total amount $10,000 a year, I do not believe that a wiser use for money can be found for the South. The idea of putting these state rural agents into the South is the wisest and finest and most fundamental action that has been taken in connection with education in the South for a long while. It is the key to the whole situation.

I shall be in New York sometime near the 30th. Yours very truly,

Booker T. Washington

TLpS Con. 77 BTW Papers DLC.

To E. H. Gamlin

[Tuskegee, Ala.] Jan. 23, 1915

Mr. Gamlin: I find that the store which you are using is getting such a reputation that I must consider seriously the matter of letting a piece of my property be used in a way to get such a reputation as your store is getting.

To be very plain, it seems that your store has become the headquarters for a certain number of people around here who loaf, use loose language, gossip about people, and drink whiskey. The people who have been reported to me by reliable persons as getting whiskey in your store and using it there, whether it belongs to you or to them, are the following — Mr. J. B. Washington, Charlie Washington, Mr. T. J. Murray, and Tracy Brannum. I am putting the facts before you that you may be made aware of the situation. You are at liberty to show this letter to all those parties if you desire.

I think the question for you to decide is, whether you consider the friendship of these people of more importance and value to you than your business itself.

I understand on good authority that one of these parties in an intoxicated condition shot a pistol off several times in the store the other night. You can easily see what a hurtful influence this kind of thing has in a community like this.

I am sure that a good many of the best women refrain from trading at your store because they do not care to be brought into contact with men who have the reputation of loafing and making low remarks about women. You can easily see that this is hurting your trade.

I am not saying from my own knowledge that all these parties are guilty of purchasing whiskey at your place, keeping it there or using it, but I do know that this is the continual report that comes to me, and I have stated very clearly the reputation that your store has gained.

[Booker T. Washington]

TLc Copy   Con. 664   BTW Papers   DLC.

From James Carroll Napier

Nashville, Tenn., Jany. 24th, '15

Dear Mr. Washington; I have just read your interview in the New York World on the Monticello, Georgia, lynching. I am writing to congratulate you upon the bold stand you have thus taken upon this important phase of our life here in the South. Your position is a strong one, your argument convincing and your conclusions that such procedure is hurtful to the white man of the South as well as the black cannot be denied. I think that the cause in this instance was the flimsiest excuse for which the crime of lynching was ever perpetrated. If it is allowed to go on things will shortly reach a point where black men will be lynched for even *looking* at the whites.

Immediately upon the receipt of your "Immigration telegram" I addressed a letter to each one of our Congressman requesting that he vote against the measure. The defeat of this vicious measure, I think, was attributable to your prompt and effective action.

I hope to see you in New York next week. Very truly yours,

J. C. Napier

ALS   Con. 942   BTW Papers   DLC.

To Isaiah T. Montgomery

[Tuskegee, Ala.] January 25th, 1915

Dear Mr. Montgomery: It has been a long time since I have received a letter which has brought me such comfort and happiness as is true of your letter under date of January 20. I am so glad that the people of Mound Bayou are realizing the importance of getting together and working together. Outside of Tuskegee, I think I can safely say that there is no community in the world that I am so deeply interested in as I am in Mound Bayou. There is no community whose success would bring me more happiness outside of Tuskegee, and there is no community whose failure would bring me more sorrow outside of Tuskegee than is true of Mound Bayou.

I want to congratulate you and all the people there for the fine, unselfish and patriotic stand you have taken in holding the mass meeting. I want to urge over and over again that at any cost and at any sacrifice all personal grudges and animosities be forgotten once and for all and that all stand together with a determination to make Mound Bayou a good, clean, moral community, and a community that will prove a success from a commercial and financial point of view as well as prove a model in education.

Above all things, I hope you will let nothing stand in the way with of the reorganization of the bank just as soon as it can be done with safety. In any way that I can I want to help you. Just now of course the hands of most of us are more or less tied, but that does not mean that we should not go forward and do all we can to help each other.

I have the fullest confidence in your fellow-worker and fellow-citizen, Mr. Charles Banks, and have the highest respect for him. I have worked with him under many difficult and trying circumstances and I have always found him loyal and true. I will go further, I have not only a respect for him but a deep affection for him. I am sure he will be willing to do anything in his power to help the people there carry out the plans which they have inaugurated. I hope you and others will keep me fully informed on the situation. Yours very truly,

Booker T. Washington

TLpS   Con. 941   BTW Papers   DLC.

To William G. Willcox

[Tuskegee, Ala.] January 27, 1915

Dear Mr. Willcox: I thought you and Mrs. Willcox might be interested to know that the railroad station at the Tuskegee Farm and Improvement Company is nearly completed, and the railroad authorities have decided to put in a colored man as ticket agent and station agent. This will be the first case of the kind that I know of in Alabama.

There has been some little complication and delay regarding the name. We hoped to have the station called Baldwin, but it has been discovered that there is another station by that name, and we are now trying to get the railroad authorities to agree to the name, "Baldwin Farms."

We are looking forward anxiously to seeing you and Mrs. Willcox here next month. Yours very truly,

Booker T. Washington

TLpS   Con. 81   BTW Papers   DLC.

From Emmett Jay Scott

Birmingham Ala   Jany 29–15

Remained in conference last night with officials of both institutions[1] until very late hour following my telephone to you at Atlanta. Our friends here including Mason and Tulane feel it most important that this situation be saved. I am assured by the white capitalist[2] whom I mentioned last night he will pass upon collateral and guard any resources provided for this purpose. He is personally protecting situation until can hear from New York but is under great pressure with conditions here such as I described last night. I mentioned what has happened to one of the largest in district. It would permanently discourage our people here to have this threatened calamity occur. The effect would be very far reaching. Telegraph Dr Mason what can be done.

Emmett J Scott

TWSr   Con. 80   BTW Papers   DLC.   Addressed to BTW "Care Mr Samuel Woolverton, Hanover Natl Bank, New York."

[1] On Jan. 25, 1915, preliminary steps were undertaken to merge the two black financial institutions in Birmingham, Ulysses G. Mason's Alabama Penny Savings Bank of Birmingham, with branches in Montgomery, Selma, and Anniston, and the Prudential Savings Bank. Scott had gone to Birmingham to aid the heads of the two banks in completing the merger and saving themselves from bankruptcy. (BTW to Mason, Jan. 25, 1915, Con. 941, BTW Papers, DLC.)

[2] The black bank received a temporary loan from Thomas Octavius Smith (1859–1925), vice-president of the Birmingham Trust and Savings Co. In the promotional leaflet the bank prepared to encourage long-term investment, it also reported that William G. Willcox, the Tuskegee trustee and New York capitalist, "after looking into the matter quite carefully has agreed to take $10,000. of such a loan, if the remaining $30,000. can be secured." (Typescript, undated, Con. 81, BTW Papers, DLC.)

To Emmett Jay Scott

Biltmore Hotel, New York, N.Y. February 1, 1915

Dear Mr. Scott: There were three points in connection with the Birmingham Bank which I fear worked against the bank. 1st. Mr. Woolverton[1] showed me a statement which proved that the Birmingham bank had an average [of] ten dollars in his bank during the last few months. These New York banks stick pretty close to the policy of helping out banks that keep a deposit with them. 2nd: Mr. Smith[2] in his telegram made it rather plain that he was very anxious to get the money from New York in order to reimburse him for the money lent the Colored bank. 3rd: Neither Mr. Woolverton nor myself liked the effort which was apparent in the telegram of placing the responsibility of saving the Colored bank on me. I will tell you more about it when I see you. Yours very truly,

B. T. W.

TLI Con. 658 BTW Papers DLC.

[1] Samuel Woolverton (1865–1952), president of the Gallatin National Bank of New York City.
[2] Thomas Octavius Smith.

To Monroe Nathan Work

[Biltmore Hotel, New York City] Feb. 6, 1915

Aside from what they pay in taxes about how much do the colored people in the South contribute annual[ly] in all forms towards their own education.

B. T. W.

TWcSr Con. 664 BTW Papers DLC.

From Monroe Nathan Work

Tuskegee Institute Ala Feb 6th, 15

When amount that Negroes pay in every form in taxes the amount that they give directly for support of colleges and normal schools and for improvement of public schools it is probable that they contribute every year more than eight million dollars for their own education.

Morris [Monroe] N. Work

TWSr Con. 664 BTW Papers DLC.

An Entry in a Notebook of Ray Stannard Baker

[New York City] Feby 9 1915

I spent the evening with Booker T. Washington. He is stopping at the Biltmore Hotel — one of the palatial new places. He is older — seems older — than when I last saw him, his hair growing thin on the top of his head: but gives the same impression as ever of bigness of character, patience, humor. After talking with these agitating negroes of the North — very sharp & able they are, too, — he appears like some big-natured peasant, so busy with his own work that he has no time to be worrying about his rights. He dismisses the negro people of northern cities very easily & speaks for the 8,000,000 — the great masses of the colored people of the South, who are slowly rising. Among these there is plenty of work & not much trouble about the "problem." He even asked me: "Have you ever seen a suffering negro?" & commented on the fact that no negroes were to be found in the bread-lines, & that he had almost never seen a hungry negro. Someway they manage always to live. "I sometimes think," he said, "though it would never do to say it publicly that a little real suffering would be good for the Negro. It would make him struggle harder."

He is one of the comparatively few men I have met who always impresses me as being great — somehow possessing qualities beyond & above the ordinary. He is very simple, very homely in his stories, with a sublime sort of common sense. It is a real inspiration to meet a man of a despised and downtrodden race who remains a tower of strength, humor, hope.

AD   Notebook 6 (1914-15)   Con. 122   Ray Stannard Baker Papers   DLC.

To Robert Elijah Jones

[Tuskegee, Ala.] February 11, 1915

My dear Dr. Jones: I have read with much interest your suggestion to have a Vigilance Committee at Washington to look after the interests of the Negro of the country. As you have pointed out, such a Committee, if composed of the proper persons, would do a vast amount of good to our race. The legislation in Washington in the past few months has demonstrated the need of such a Committee.

There is, of course, the danger that such a Committee might become simply an organization for promoting the political interests of individuals. I believe, however, that this danger could be obviated.

I very much hope that this suggestion may be fully considered and favorable action taken with reference to it. You have my cooperation. Very truly yours,

Booker T. Washington

TLpS   Con. 940   BTW Papers   DLC.

To Warren Logan

Tuskegee Institute, Alabama   Feb. 13, 1915

Mr. Logan: If necessary I wish you and the Business Committee to lay aside other matters and give prompt attention to the following matter:

I want to find out how much we can save by paying cash in the way of discounting bills or paying up promptly old bills. I feel quite sure that we can save the price of three or four scholarships if this matter is taken up promptly and handled with care, and I wish the matter attended to and a report made to me as to results.

As an example, I have just called the Bessemer Coal, Iron and Land Company people on the telephone and asked them what they would deduct provided we would pay cash to them, and they said two per cent. This means the saving of $30 or nearly the price of a scholarship. I stated to the Bessemer firm that a check would be sent them on this basis, and I wish you would attend to it.

I am sorry to find a number of letters here from people with whom we deal in several parts of the country, calling attention to our delay in settling with them. As I have said before, this is the kind of thing that hurts us. It is the kind of thing that white people are always expecting when they are dealing with a colored individual or a colored institution, and I have tried to pursue the policy of acting in a businesslike prompt way especially when we are able to pay. I wish you would take up all these small accounts that are overdue and settle them.

It is doubly necessary that an institution that depends for its living on begging money should keep a good business reputation. It is much more necessary than for an institution doing a strictly commercial business. It does not take long for a rumor to get circulated in any community to the effect that we are not businesslike, and this hurts us in getting in funds. For all these reasons it is very necessary that all the matters I am referring to in this letter be carefully, systematically and promptly attended to in your office. Some of the letters regarding bills that I refer to I enclose.

[Booker T. Washington]

TL   Con. 665   BTW Papers   DLC.

From John Andrew Kenney

[Tuskegee, Ala.] February 15, 1915

Mr. Washington: Yesterday morning during the clinic hour in the presence of one of the gentlemen teachers and two student boys, Dr. King[1] handed me an excuse from drill for one of the girls asking me to sign it, stating that she was menstruating. It was said in such loud tones that not only the persons in the room heard him, but the pharmacist and the assistant head nurse in the drug room adjoining also heard it.

I called him to the office to speak to him about it. His whole manner and attitude with reference to the matter was unsatisfactory. I told him that we were not accustomed to such language in our hospital. He remarked that perhaps I had never had a Northern man before. I asked him if he used this language generally. He said that he did not know, that he had not thought about it and had spoken in a plain, natural way.

In this connection I also had to speak to him about conducting a lady teacher into the internes' bed room to see one of the internes who was sick. Even tho the matron states positively that she saw him take the lady in the room, he denies it, but said in connection with it that if he did do it, what of it? That they were men and not students and if he wanted a lady carried in it was his privilege and that he did not wish any further discussion about it and if I wished to say anything else about it I could say it to you.[2] Very truly yours,

John A. Kenney

TLS   Con. 662   BTW Papers   DLC.

[1]Drue King, a graduate of Tufts Medical College, was an intern at the Tuskegee Institute hospital beginning in the fall of 1914.

[2] On Feb. 14, 1915, the day of his offense, Dr. Drue King resigned. Kenney urged acceptance, and sent to BTW eight counts of complaint against the intern. (King to Kenney, Feb. 14, 1915, and Kenney to BTW, Feb. 17, 1915, Con. 662, BTW Papers, DLC.)

To Seth Low

Tuskegee Institute, Alabama   February 16, 1915

Dear Mr. Low: I have taken the liberty of sending Dr. Fayette A. McKenzie a telegram, copy of which I enclose you. He is at present connected with the Indian Department at Washington, but has recently been elected to the presidency of Fisk University, Nashville, Tennessee. Mr. Paul D. Cravath, the president of the Board of Trustees of Fisk University, is very anxious to have Dr. McKenzie come here with the friends from New York and get somewhat acquainted with our work. You will find him a very cultivated and agreeable man in every way.

Dr. Frissell, as I understand, is also to join the party in Washington, but I presume he has already notified you.

I want to thank you for what you said in a recent letter regarding my letter published in the newspapers regarding the bill which was introduced in Congress looking to prevent colored people from emigrating into this country. I am glad to say that the letter seemed to have quite wide influence among the members of Congress and elsewhere. I think no such law will be introduced in the future. Yours very truly,

Booker T. Washington

TLS   Seth Low Papers   NNC.

From Victor H. Tulane

Montgomery, Ala., Feb. 16, 1915

Dear Doctor: I am sending you under separate cover the mortgages and other securities as agreed upon in securing the loan of Five Thousand Dollars for the Alabama Penny Savings Bank, of Birmingham.

After the loan has been put through, please place the money to the credit of The Alabama Penny Savings Bank, Montgomery, Alabama. If it is needed by Birmingham, we will draw on it, but in case it is not needed, why we will not draw it.

Everything is moving on smoothly with us. Trust that you will have no trouble in putting the deal through, I am, Very sincerely yours,

V. H. Tulane

P.S. Am also enclosing herewith my credentials.

TLS   Con. 80   BTW Papers   DLC.

From Clinton Joseph Calloway

[Tuskegee, Ala.] February 18, 1915

Mr. B. T. Washington: I was at Baldwin Farms yesterday. Mr. Chandler is in charge of the depot.

The four new cottages are painted in brown and trimmed in white. Prof. Carver's stain was used. The whitewashing is pretty well completed. We are hoping to have things cleared up a little better around the depot and some decorations, green, etc. when Mr. Wil[l]cox arrives. The community around Baldwin Farms, as well as the colonists, are planning to greet Mr. Wil[l]cox and his party Tuesday afternoon at 2:00 o'clock.

Mr. Darden and Mr. Thurston are planning to move down this week. I am pushing them in every way I can. I feel quite certain that they will be there before Mr. Wil[l]cox arrives. Yours truly,

Clinton J. Calloway

TLS Con. 989 BTW Papers DLC.

To Charles Banks

[Tuskegee, Ala.] February 19, 1915

My dear Mr. Banks: Writing you further regarding Mr. Rosenwald, I would state that there are two reasons why I do not think it wise for me to approach Mr. Rosenwald directly on your matters.

1st — I always make it a rule never to ask people for money while they are on our grounds as our guests.

2d — I have seen both Mr. Rosenwald and Mr. Graves within the last few weeks and neither said anything to me about your affairs and I took that to mean they were satisfied with the way things were going, and since this seemed to be true, I did not think it wise to raise the question.

One thing troubles me a little and that is a possible law suit in connection with the oil mill. It is a pretty good policy to avoid a law suit and I am wondering if you could not accomplish the same results through some other method. A law suit is tiresome, long and expensive and I fear you in the end would get the worst of it.

I have read with interest the suggestions made by the Buckeye Cotton and Oil Company and also the party from Leland, Miss.

I am sure Mr. Rosenwald would shrink from anything involving his name in a law suit. If while Mr. Rosenwald is here a proper opportunity arises for discussion of the whole question, I am going to take it up with him. One other thing that makes me hesitate to take up your matter with him is the fact that I have had to take up some other matters with him recently of a business nature, which I will explain to you later on when I see you. Yours very truly,

Booker T. Washington

TLpS Con. 75 BTW Papers DLC.

Trustees of Tuskegee Institute
to Woodrow Wilson

[Tuskegee Institute, Ala.] Feb. 22, 1915

The Board of Trustees of the Tuskegee Institute have heard with profound regret that the proposed appropriation of $101,000 for Howard University has been stricken out in the House of Representatives on a point of order. Assuming that an appropriation which has been made for twenty-five years more or less in some amount has been constitutionally made, this board earnestly asks you to use your influence to restore this item to the proper appropriation bill.[1] The cause[2] of training leaders for the ten millions of Negroes of the United States will suffer serious injury if this be not done.[3]

> Seth Low, Chairman
> Booker T. Washington, Principal
> Frank Trumbull
> Julius Rosenwald

TWSr Copy Con. 80 BTW Papers DLC.

[1] Wilson forwarded the telegram to Joseph P. Tumulty with the note: "Please send this to the proper Senator, saying that I have asked you to do so and that

the matter has given me some concern. The President." (Woodrow Wilson Papers, DLC.)

² This phrase was garbled, in the copy President Wilson received, as "because."

³ Copies of the telegram were sent to Frank S. White and J. D. Bankhead in the Senate, and Oscar W. Underwood and Champ Clark in the House. On February 23, the House restored the Howard University appropriation.

From Kelly Miller

Howard University   Washington, D.C. February 24, '15

My dear Dr. Washington: Your telegram came duly to hand and we all wish to thank you for your prompt action in behalf of Howard University. The day has been saved and the appropriation has been secured for this year at least. With many thanks, I remain, Yours truly,

Kelly Miller

TLS   Con. 941   BTW Papers   DLC.

From Seth Low

on Pennsylvania Train #68 — February 25th, 1915

Dear Dr. Washington: I am sorry that Mrs. Low and I were obliged to leave Tuskegee before the rest of our party but you understand, I am sure, why it was unavoidable. I am particularly sorry to have been obliged to leave without the opportunity of saying good bye to your wife. I hope you will give her this message and say to her that I appreciate always the good care that she takes of Mrs. Low and me when we are at Tuskegee.

In common with all with whom I talked, I thought the exhibition which was given on Monday evening of the results of the Tuskegee extension work was very remarkable. I can recall nothing of the kind in my life so interesting and so inspiring. It constituted a life story of surpassing interest told with the artlessness of children but with the understanding of men and women. I understand now better than I have ever done before how it is that the negro race can have made the wonderful strides which it has made in this country during the short period of fifty years since it was emancipated.

I got a little sense when at the Institute that the student body, and perhaps the teaching body, were a little tired. Perhaps this was the result of preparing to meet and care for so large a party of visitors at one time. If my impression was correct, I hope you will find it possible to lessen the strain upon them all for a little while. I know that one must work hard to succeed in anything but it is not worth while to work so hard that one can not work long. In other words, after periods of special effort, a little let-up is often useful.

With best wishes for you and Mrs. Washington; for all of your associates in the work of the school and for the students from us both, I am, Sincerely yours,

[Seth Low]

TLc   Seth Low Papers   NNC.

From Ulysses Grant Mason

Birmingham, Ala. February 28, 1915

Dear Dr. Washington: I can not express to you how deeply grateful I am for your assistance and helpful offices in bringing about the relief which has been worrying the Negro business interests of this state for the past thirty days. Indeed it would have been utterly impossible to have accomplished this without you.

In expressing myself I also voice the sentiments of those who are connected with the proposition and I shall endeavor to show to the gentlemen who came to the relief the spirit which was shown by the Colored man to Collis P. Huntington upon a certain occasion, as stated by you.

The white banks of this city are deeply in accord with what is being done and Mr. Parsons[1] received all the encouragement necessary. I might say in this connection, I took him over and had him to inspect both institutions and he found physical values as stated by our committee. I have enclosed to Mr. Scott copy of agreement which, I think

245

is helpful. I have insisted that Mr. Tulane be put upon the boards and I do not apprehend anything to the contrary along this line.

I will very much appreciate if at some early convenient time you will drop Col. Tom Smith a line regarding this transaction. He is a very rich man and appreciates kind expressions.

I want to thank you for the pleasant stay while at Tuskegee and for the uniform courtesies shown me by both you and Mrs. Washington and your co-workers there. This I always appreciate. While I do not wish to burden you with a long letter, I wish to make a suggestion that probably would be helpful, not only to the Institution but to the colored doctors throughout the state. That is that the Colored State Medical Association have their annual meetings in February at Tuskegee during the time that the clinic is held at your hospital. It would certainly be advantageous to them and I believe it would be advantageous to that part of the institution. I shall think over this matter and shall be glad to discuss it more fully, if it meet your approval. I feel that there would be no trouble in getting the consent of the State Medical Association to adopt Tuskegee as a permanent place of meeting in the future. The clinic held there would, in a measure, be rather a post course for many of the doctors who are anxious to do extra study during the year. It would attract greater attention to the hospital and I believe in many ways be helpful. With my best wishes for your continued prosperity and good health, I am   Very sincerely yours,

U. G. Mason

TLS   Con. 941   BTW Papers   DLC.

¹ Frank J. Parsons was a vice-president of the United States Mortgage and Trust Co. in New York.

From Alfred Charles Sam

Ayirebi Western Akim via Salt Pond
Gold Coast W.A. [ca. Feb. 1915]

Dear Sir: I am sure you have read of me "Chief Sam" several times. God has been able and I am at home now. He has enabled me to carry my plans. I am at home with my people from America. Various tribes have received them than what they expected. Kings and Chiefs are sending their welcomes and their presents of sheep & cows foods and fruits of the lands to their Brethren the American Negro. I have given them 64 sq. miles and the tribe has given them all the land they can be able to settle. We will start our City next week it will be built on the Bank of River Birim.

I shall ask you to introduce me to your white friends when I get back to America. I will start our Ethiopian Institute before I go back to America. Faithfully yours

Alfred Sam

ALS Con. 944 BTW Papers DLC.

To Seth Low

Tuskegee Institute, Alabama   March 2d, 1915

My dear Mr. Low: Your kind letter written aboard the train was received Sunday, and read to the teachers and student body at the usual Sunday evening service, and I cannot describe to you the interest which they manifested in your words.

It is worth working a whole year and putting in the hardest licks that one can possibly do to have the compensation of receiving such a letter. Such expressions give heart to all of us, and we all rejoice that we are permitted to work with and under such a fine spirit.

We are so glad that both you and Mrs. Low enjoyed your trip here, and that you did not feel tired.

What you say about Monday evening is of the greatest interest to us all, especially to the teachers who worked so hard to make the occasion worth while. I find that it takes harder work to get people to be themselves than it does to be artificial sometimes, but all those who had a part in the Monday night program did so well because their heart was in it and they were acting a natural part.

I was very much interested when in Boston lately, to have Mr. Wallace L. Pierce,[1] whom you remember, tell me about a letter which you wrote on the occasion of the anniversary of Major Henry L. Higginson. He said that while a great many letters were received and read on the occasion, yours stood out as the letter which sensed the spirit of the occasion and put in words that which others felt in a more perfect way than any other letter that was read.

Mrs. Washington is always happy, with me, when we can be of any service to you or Mrs. Low.

On Wednesday after the departure of the Chicago friends, we gave the students a half holiday, and now in response to your own suggestion I am going to ask the Executive Council to give them another half holiday next Saturday. This I am sure you feel they deserve, and I shall let them know it is at your own suggestion.

I shall be writing you about several other matters soon. Yours very truly,

Booker T. Washington

TLS   Seth Low Papers   NNC.

¹ Wallace Lincoln Pierce (1853–1920), a Boston grocery merchant, banker, and philanthropist.

Emmett Jay Scott to George Eastman

[Tuskegee, Ala.] March 2, 1915

My dear Sir: At the Mid-winter meeting of the Board of Trustees held here at Tuskegee Institute, February 22nd–23rd, the Board by formal resolution accepted the Veterinary Hospital for which you have given Five thousand ($5,000.00) Dollars and has recorded a Minute of appreciation on the records of the Board of Trustees.

I am directed, by the Board of Trustees to express to you its thanks for this generous contribution and to assure you of the help the building will be to the Institute in connection with its agricultural work.

It is understood, of course, that your name is not to be published in any way in connection with this gift. Yours very truly,

Emmett J. Scott

TLpS   Con. 780   BTW Papers   DLC.

To Charles William Anderson

[Tuskegee, Ala.] March 5, 1915

Dear Mr. Anderson: It looks very much at this distance as if the axe is going to fall, but I hope it is not. I do not believe that your successor can be confirmed at this session. What this would mean in the way of delay, you know better than I do. Will you not let me know?

I regret very much that I did not meet you at luncheon on the day and hour appointed. I was there, but I presume that something kept you away.

The main purpose of this letter is to make the following suggestion: In case you do have to get out, I believe that with the fine record back of you in dealing with finances, that if the proper pressure is brought to bear, the President would be inclined to put you on one of the Haytian commissions that are to be appointed to deal with Haytian finances to reorganize and re-civilize the country generally. What do you think of it? I see that Ex-Governor Fort[1] and a Commission have gone to Hayti to reorganize the finances of the country. It may be that it could be worked out for you to become one of the fiscal agents or representatives in charge of this work in Hayti. That might prove a good occupation while you are waiting for some other opening. Yours very truly,

[Booker T. Washington]

TLp   Con. 75   BTW Papers   DLC.

[1] John Franklin Fort (1852–1920), Republican governor of New Jersey (1908–11), was a delegate to the national conventions of both the Republican and Progressive parties in 1912. President Wilson appointed him as a special envoy to the Dominican Republic in 1914 and to Haiti in 1915.

To Mary L. Hay

[Tuskegee, Ala.] March 6, 1915

Dear Madame: I write to say that I am altogether in favor of woman suffrage and am perfectly willing to have you quote me in the forthcoming suffrage edition of the Pittsburgh Sun which is to appear under the auspices of the Equal Franchise Federation of Pittsburgh.[1]

    With kindest regards, I am, Yours very truly,

Booker T. Washington

TLpS Con. 939 BTW Papers DLC.

  [1] Mary L. Hay, chairman of the press committee of the Equal Franchise Federation of Pittsburgh, thanked BTW for his endorsement but thought "an article from you, altho quite short, would carry much more weight." (Mar. 17, 1915, Con. 939, BTW Papers, DLC.)

To Thomas Jesse Jones

[Tuskegee, Ala.] March 6, 1915

My dear Dr. Jones: After thinking the matter over very carefully, I am convinced that you ought to prepare a statement showing just what you are doing in the direction of investigation of schools and just what you propose to do in the future. I feel that there is need for such a statement being published in some of the white papers and some of the colored papers.

    My reason for it is this: I find that a fake organization is at work and a good many people are likely to be led into it innocently because they do not know of any other organization. A good many schools are likely to be led into it because they do not know of anything else being done and a good many donors are likely to be induced to recognize it for the reason that they do not know of any other source to appeal for information.

    The organization that I am referring to is composed, for the most part, of nondescript little schools, those that are either humbugs or are doing the poorest work. I understand that they are to have a meeting in New York or somewhere during this month and I think it might not be a bad plan to get Mr. Taylor to go into their meeting and get on the inside so as to know what is going on.

    If you agree that some kind of publication ought to be made, if you will draw it up I will help you get it circulated in the press. I think among other papers that it ought to get into The Survey. Yours very truly,

Booker T. Washington

TLpS Con. 940 BTW Papers DLC.

From Charles William Anderson

New York, N.Y. March 8, 1915

Personal

My dear Doctor: I want to thank you for your good favor of the 5th instant and for the assurance of your continued interest and friendship. Of course, I did not need it but it is comforting just the same.

As you may have heard, I took to my bed with acute gastritis on the very day I was to lunch with you, and remained there, with two intermissions, until last Wednesday.

The new man, Mr. John Z. Lowe, Jr.,[1] comes from Norfolk, Virginia. He was confirmed on Tuesday and will take his office this week. He called on me on Thursday and from his conversation I rather got the impression that he thoroughly understands a colored democrat.

When I was asked to resign, instead of coming out in an interview as did the Collector of the 3rd district here, I took my medicine gracefully and wrote the Commissioner of Internal Revenue[2] a letter informing him that I was grateful to him for the many courtesies that I had received at his hands, and wished him a successful administration in the internal revenue service. I wrote a similar one to the Secretary of the Treasury. When my successor called on me I informed him that I was always at his service whenever he might need me. I tried to take my licking standing up like a man rather than lying down like a dog. This seems to have made friends for me among the administration forces.

I am enclosing herewith a copy of a letter from the Commissioner under date of February 5, 1915, and one under date of January 4, 1915. Both will show that he regarded me as not an altogether unprofitable servant. He wrote me on March 3rd, on the receipt of my letter of farewell and said "Your letter is an exceedingly manly one and I appreciate it. I hope your future will be contented and prosperous. Sometime when I am in New York I will try and let you know. With warmest regards, I am, Truly yours, W. H. Osborn, Commissioner." Thus you see I am leaving good odor behind me.

The other day I wrote Otto T. Bannard,[3] President of the New York Trust Company and one of the five governors of the Clearing House, who practically control the banking system of this country, asking him for permission to use his name as one of my vouchers. I am herewith enclosing his reply to that letter under date of March 5, 1915, which speaks for itself.

I wish you would let me know when you are in this neck of the woods for I have many things to say which cannot be committed to paper.

With warm regards and many thanks, I remain, Yours very sincerely,

Charles W. Anderson

P.S. The suggestion you make is a good one and I sincerely hope it can be put into operation. More anon.

C. W. A.

TLS Con. 75 BTW Papers DLC.

[1] John Zollicoffer Lowe, Jr. (1884–1950), for many years a New York City lawyer, was collector of internal revenue for the second district of New York beginning in 1915. He resigned to serve as a major in the American Expeditionary Force.

[2] William H. Osborn.

[3] Otto Tremont Bannard (1854–1929), a Yale classmate of William H. Taft, was the Republican candidate for mayor of New York City in 1909.

To Kelly Miller

[Tuskegee, Ala.] March 9, 1915

My dear Professor Miller: I regret very much several of the colored papers have carried the news item referring to the action of our Trustees in helping Howard University secure its usual appropriation from Congress giving the idea in their headlines that this Institution was wholly responsible for getting the appropriation.

Our Trustees, nor anyone connected with the Institution, claim any special credit for the continuation of the appropriation. I asked the School Correspondent to give the action of our Trustees to the public, with a view of showing how institutions are working together and can work together in a way to help each other.

Our Trustees in a most willing and glad spirit entered into the matter with the greatest earnestness and were glad to feel that we might be of a little service to Howard. I am sure that when all the facts are known, I guess no one individual or set of individuals are wholly responsible for the continuation of the appropriation, but it was the success of the outcome of the united factors of the race and friends of our race.

This is a fine illustration indicating what can be done by working together, instead of working against each other.

I very much hope that the Trustees of Howard University will find a way to increase its endowment from year to year to such an extent that the Institution will not be so wholly dependent as it is now upon the good will of Congress.

The telegram which you sent regarding the appropriation was immediately read to our full Board and the action referred to was carried unanimously. Yours very truly,

Booker T. Washington

TLpS   Con. 941   BTW Papers   DLC.

To Charles Ellis Mason

[Tuskegee, Ala.] March 11, 1915

Dear Mr. Mason: It will interest you to know that since I wrote you regarding the amount due on the new power plant, Mr. Willcox has subscribed $10,000 on condition that $100,000 be raised by July first. We are going out to get that amount, and I believe we will succeed. Yours very truly,

Booker T. Washington

TLpS   Con. 77   BTW Papers   DLC.

To Charles William Anderson

[Tuskegee, Ala.] March 12, 1915

My dear Mr. Anderson: Those are certainly splendid letters written to you by Mr. Bannard and the Commissioner of Internal Revenues.

The Commissioner, if one may judge from his letter, has very great appreciation of your services and it seems a pity that under our peculiar method of doing things a man who has been rendering the best service possible in a position should be asked to retire just after he has rendered such big service in the interest of the Government.

I am in doubt as to what action to take regarding the Haytian matter. Perhaps you can suggest something. At present, as I understand it, the Commission headed by Governor Fort is in Hayti and until that Committee returns and makes some kind of report, I do not know whether anything definite can be done.

If you have not done so, I advise, too, that you write the President the same kind of letter that you wrote Mr. Osborn; that is, a letter thanking him for letting you stay in office two years after he came in power. I think such a letter will have a good effect. Yours very truly,

Booker T. Washington

TLpS Con. 75 BTW Papers DLC.

To Charles Winter Wood

[Tuskegee, Ala.] March 13, 1915

My dear Mr. Wood: We must in some way give the public a different idea of the work of the quartet from what it now has. The impression seems to be that the quartet is out for the purpose of giving "entertainments" or "concerts" and that a few dollars thrown in the collection box amply pays for the work of the quartet and means a contribution to the school. All this is misleading. We must give the public to understand that the quartet is out for the purpose of holding meetings with the serious purpose of getting scholarships and donations for the school and not merely entertaining somebody or giving concerts.

The Hampton singers, for example, are making a tour just now of the hotels in Florida and are having great success in getting scholarships. At one hotel they got seven scholarships.

So far, the work in Southern California has brought in practically no individual gifts in the form of scholarships or otherwise. You see unless we can get individuals to give, it seems that all the work that you are now doing is practically lost, for the reason that we cannot get contributions from the hotels or churches again unless you go for them, while at the same time if you get an individual to give only Ten Dollars ($10.00) he is likely to keep it up from year to year.

I would not any longer refer to the gatherings as entertainments or concerts, but refer to them everywhere on all occasions as meetings in the interest of Tuskegee. For example, the Manager of the hotel Hollywood refers to the meeting as a "performance" of the Tuskegee singers.

I am sending a copy of this letter to Mr. Stevenson. Yours very truly,

Booker T. Washington

TLcSr Con. 535 BTW Papers DLC. Addressed to Wood in Los Angeles, Calif. Copy for Executive Council.

To Charles H. Fearing

[Tuskegee, Ala.] March 15, 1915

Dear Mr. Fearing: Your letter under date of March 11th has been received, and I am very much interested in what you say about Miss Bethune's school.[1] Your impression conforms with the impression Mrs. Washington got when she was there several days ago. I wonder if it would not be worth while for us to consider taking this school somewhat under our control and treat it in the same way as we treat Snow Hill, etc. Supposing you "feel" Mrs. Bethune on this point, if you are there.

I sent you a telegram, some days ago, to Ormond Beach, Florida, reading as follows:

"Note possibility our making campaign with quartette among South-

ern hotels next year same as Hampton is doing. Also see what success
Hampton is having."
I am not sure that you received it.

I hope you are making progress. Yours very truly,

Booker T. Washington

TLpS Con. 657 BTW Papers DLC. Addressed to Fearing in Miami, Fla.

¹ Fearing had written from Daytona, Fla., that he was greatly impressed with
Mary McLeod Bethune's school, the Daytona Educational and Industrial Training
School for Negro Girls. He reported: "The school is doing a splendid work, not
alone for the immediate student body, but it is reaching out and touching the
lives of the rural people." He commented favorably on the plant, farm, hospital,
quality of teaching, and support of local black and white people. (Mar. 11, 1915,
Con. 657, BTW Papers, DLC.)

To John William Beverly¹

[Tuskegee, Ala.] March 17, 1915

All of us here at Tuskegee sincerely regret to learn of Mr. Paterson's
death. His work in behalf of the colored people of Alabama will be
remembered for many and many a year. Please express to teachers and
students and to the members of his family the regrets of the officers,
faculty and student body of this institution.

Booker T. Washington

TWSr Con. 944 BTW Papers DLC.

¹ John William Beverly was a faculty member at Alabama State College and
William Burns Paterson's successor as president.

From Charles William Anderson

New York, N.Y. March 17, 1915

(PERSONAL).

My dear Dr. Washington: Enclosed please find a copy of letter to
Governor Whitman in behalf of Mr. Moore, to whom I gave it on the

day before yesterday, and who took it in person to Albany on yesterday. I made it good and strong because I am anxious to see Fred land something.

Relative to your proposition, I am afraid that we will have to wait until the return of Governor Fort. You may be interested to know, however, that I am trying my best to leave good odor behind me. My successor is a gentleman, originally from Norfolk, Va., and has treated me with every personal courtesy. I am separating from the service with the best of feeling and although I have worked like a galley slave at his oar for the past ten years, I think I can say in the lines of Kipling:

> "Today I leave the galley. Shall I curse her
> service then?
> God be praised whate'er comes after, I have
> lived and toiled with men."

Hoping you are very well, and expecting definitely to see you when you are again in this City, I remain, Yours faithfully,

Charles W. Anderson

P.S. The U.S. Marshals and others who were appointed by the Prest. the day my successor was named have all taken office, but the department instructed me to turn my office over on April first — thus giving me an extra month's pay. My resignation was requested on March first & my successor was confirmed at once without democratic opposition. It looks as though I am leaving the service with the respect of my superiors.

The merchants of this dist. are raising a fund to give me a present. Enclosed is a copy of the invitation to subscribe. Look at it and tear it up as I am not supposed to know anything about it. This was handed to me by a close friend. It is "under the rose."

C

TLS Con. 75 BTW Papers DLC. Postscript in Anderson's hand.

From Margaret James Murray Washington

[Tuskegee, Ala.] Mar. 18, 1915

Mr. Washington: When Mrs. Rosenwald was here this last time she asked me what we wanted for Dorothy Hall. I told her that we did not want anything at all. I afterwards remarked to her, however, that I would like to have some rugs for the new practice dining room and some shades for the new practice kitchen and dining room. She is giving both of these. I thought you would like to know this, because it means quite an item.

You remember some years ago Mrs. Rosenwald said she would give the Domestic Science division, One thousand ($1000.00) dollars; she afterwards changed and said that she would give us what we needed, or that we could order what we needed from Sears, Roebuck and Co. I imagine that it was quite a good deal less than One thousand ($1000.00) dollars, but we got a great many things that we needed.

Mrs W

TLI   Con. 655   BTW Papers   DLC.

Emmett Jay Scott to Henry Hugh Proctor

[Tuskegee, Ala.] March 23, 1915

Dear Mr. Proctor: What I now write is personal and confidential.

Dr. Kenney, our Medical Director, is most anxious that no arrangements be made in connection with Dr. Washington's visit to Atlanta for him to attend any meetings other than the regular scheduled meeting. This refers particularly to banquets and entertainments of that character. We are most anxious to conserve his strength in every way. I am sure that you will act upon this suggestion. Yours very truly,

Emmett J. Scott

TLpS   Con. 846   BTW Papers   DLC.

To Page Aylett Royall Hamill[1]

[Tuskegee, Ala.] April 7, 1915

Dear Madam: In compliance with your request of some days ago, I am sending you the verse which follows, with the hope that it may prove satisfactory.

I very much appreciate the privilege of contributing toward your book for children to be entitled, "Big Names and Little Verses."

The Tuskegee Institute stands for the training of Head, Hand and Heart.

> To think with head, to work with hand,
> To love with heart that's true,
> Are all that God and men demand —
> Are all that one can do.

Yours very truly,

Booker T. Washington

TLpS Con. 537 BTW Papers DLC.

[1] Page Aylett Royall Hamill, formerly of Richmond, Va., was the wife of Barker G. Hamill, a Trenton, N.J., banker.

To Charles William Anderson

[Tuskegee, Ala.] April 10, 1915

Dear Mr. Anderson: On my return to Tuskegee I find here your letter of March 31st. I am very glad indeed that you have sent me a copy of Commissioner Osborne's letter. It is a magnificent testimonial to the splendid relationship you established with the Commissioner, and, as you say, you are leaving such a "pleasant odor" behind you.

As early as possible I hope I may be able to get a line on the Haitian situation, as developed by Governor Fort.

I have been reading in The New York Age of the team work that you and Mr. Moore are doing together. I read of the addresses made at the Lafayette Theatre in behalf of the Howard Orphanage, and I am particularly well pleased to read of your action in forestalling that crowd with Mayor Mitchel. As your letter indicates, I had already read that Mayor Mitchel advised the Committee that he had already given orders to cut out certain scenes in connection with the film "The Birth of the Nation." This apparently took some of the wind out of their sails. Yours very truly,

Booker T. Washington

TLpS Con. 75 BTW Papers DLC.

To Margaret James Murray Washington

[Tuskegee, Ala.] April 10, 1915

Mrs. Washington: My understanding is that your department has charge of the Senior girls' Practice Cottage. I have just inspected the grounds and nothing could be further from a model cottage than these grounds. The whole thing needs careful and immediate attention.

B. T. W.

TLpI Con. 665 BTW Papers DLC.

Emmett Jay Scott to Joseph S. Clark[1]

[Tuskegee, Ala.] April 10, 1915

Dear Dr. Clark: Just one other request in connection with Dr. Washington's visit. Please be good enough to arrange a regular pulpit stand, something strong and substantial and about that height, for use in connection with his visit. He is not able to speak under satisfactory circumstances unless some such arrangement is made. Yours very truly,

Emmett J. Scott

TLS Con. 845 BTW Papers DLC.

[1] Joseph S. Clark, president of Southern University, Baton Rouge, was in charge of BTW's speaking tour of Louisiana in 1915. For a recent scholarly account of the tour, see Vincent, "Booker T. Washington's Tour."

From Marcus Mosiah Garvey

Kingston, Jamaica, W.I. April 12 1915

Dear Doctor Washington: Some time last year I wrote to you inform-ing you of my proposed visit to America to lecture in the interest of my Association and you were good enough to write to me inviting me to see your great institution.

I am expecting to leave for America between May and June and I shall be calling on you. I intend to do most of my public speaking in the South among the people of our race. I enclose you a manifesto of our Association which will give you an idea of the objects we have in view. I am now asking you to do your best to assist me during my stay in America, as I shall be coming there a stranger to the people.

I need not reacquaint you of the horrible conditions prevailing among our people in the West Indies as you are so well informed of happenings all over Negrodom.

Trusting to be favoured with an early reply   With best wishes   I remain   Your Obedient Servant

Marcus Garvey

P.S. I take the opportunity of enclosing you Patron's tickets for our concert to which we ask your patronage — as also envelope.

M. G.

ALS Con. 939 BTW Papers DLC. Enclosed was a leaflet and membership application blank of the Universal Negro Improvement and Conservation Asso-ciation and African Communities League, founded Aug. 1, 1914.

From Philip J. Allston

Boston, Mass. April 12th 1915

Dear Dr. Washington: I am informing you that on last saturday while talking with Mr. David W. Griffith,[1] in the lobby of the Tremont Theatre, immediately after viewing "The Birth of a Nation" which he is the producer of, he said before Dr. Cox[2] to me Mr. Allston what do you think of my reproducing in pictures Tuskegee,? and he is considering the matter very seriously.

I am writing you at this early date because I want you to know, this, and that I feel no one should be allowed to make capital of Tuskegee, without some financial benefit to the Institution in return financially. I send under another cover matter touching the drama, and also enclose clipping. My tickets were presented me by the manager. Yours Sincerely

Philip J. Allston

ALS Con. 75 BTW Papers DLC.

[1] David Lewelyn Wark Griffith (1875–1948) was an innovative pioneer in the art and technology of motion pictures, but in movies such as *The Birth of a Nation* he also brought to his work the pro-southern and anti-black bias of his native Kentucky. He was the son of a Confederate brigadier general. He used Thomas Dixon's racist novel *The Clansman* as his principal source, and his depiction of black characters was stereotypical. (Cripps, *Slow Fade to Black,* 26–27, 41–74.)

[2] William Alexander Cox (b. 1872) was a black dentist and lawyer with offices in Cambridge and Boston.

Extracts from Three Addresses
Delivered in Louisiana

April 13-16 [1915]

In accepting the invitation of Dr. Robert E. Jones, Mr. Walter L. Cohen, Professor J. S. Clark, and other prominent citizens of Louisiana, to spend some days in this State, I have but one object in view and that is to see for myself some of the progress that the Negroes of Louisiana are making. Let me say right here, from what I have already been able to see I feel that the people of Louisiana of both races have good reason to congratulate themselves upon the progress which the Negroes of Louisiana are making.

In many ways the Negro in Louisiana has done well; I repeat he has done well, but he can make himself still more useful in the future than he has in the past and my object in coming here, as I have said, is to see something and as far as I am able to suggest something that will make the Negro more useful to himself, more useful to the State, and to the Nation than he has been in the past.

As I have said, I have sought to keep in close touch with the progress of your State, but one who lives outside of Louisiana is at a certain disadvantage in learning about what that actual progress has been.

Both races in the South suffer at the hands of public opinion in one respect, and that is by reason of the fact that the outside world hears of our difficulties, hears of crime, hears of mobs and lynchings, but the outside world does not hear of, neither does it know about the evidences of racial friendship and good will which exist in the majorities of the communities of Louisiana and other Southern States where black and white live together. I do not believe that one can find another section of the Globe where two races which are dissimilar in many respects dwell in so large numbers where they get on better in all the affairs of life than they do in our Southern States.

Negro Problem Is Labor Problem

To a very large extent the problem of the Negro in the Southern States is a labor problem. In order to secure effective and satisfactory labor from any race, two things have got to be borne in mind. First, people must be taught a love for labor, must be taught the dignity of labor and at the same time given proper methods in the direction of skill. Secondly, they must have their minds and their ambitions awakened so that their wants will be increased. No individual labors except as he has a motive for doing so. The ignorant, untrained Negro in South Africa works for only one or two days in each week. He quits and returns to his little hut at the end of that time. The white man in South Africa wonders why this is true, grows impatient and angry with the African for this kind of conduct.

The white man in South Africa forgets that he ought to do the same thing with the Negro that has been done with the Negro in the Southern States — that he ought to educate the Negro so that he will want more. The knowledge of the South African is so limited, his ambitions are so low, that he can satisfy all the wants that he knows anything about by working only one or two days in each week. When he has satisfied those he quits. Human nature is much the same way all over the world. In the case, however, of the Southern Negro, he works four or five days in each week because he has been educated by contact with the white man, educated through the church, the Sunday School, the day school, so that his wants are increased, are multiplied in many directions.

The Southern Negro wants land, wants a house with two or three rooms in it, wants some furniture, books, newspapers, education for his children; wants to support the minister and the Sunday school, and in proportion as those wants are increased he is led to work an increasing number of days in each week in order to satisfy them.

If we would make the Negro still more useful as a laborer, we must increase his wants, we must arouse his ambition, we must give him something to live for, to hope for, and just in proportion as his wants are multiplied, are increased in many directions so that he will want better homes, better furniture, better churches, better schools, more books, more newspapers, in the same degree will he be led to work with more regularity and a greater number of days in order that the increased wants may be satisfied. The mere matter of paying a high wage to an individual, unless his wants have been increased along sensible and rational lines, does not solve the problem.

NEGRO NEEDS WHITE HELP

In all that concerns the welfare of the Negro in the South, there is no person in the world who can be so helpful to him as his white neighbor. For instance, our white friends will agree with me, I am sure, that they can help the people of my race in preventing migration in so large a number to the cities. Our white friends can help us in this respect in several ways. First, by seeing to it that life in the country is made just as attractive and safe as life in the city. The Negro wants education for his children. He has an ambition to improve the life of his family. If he finds in the city, as he usually does, a school well equipped with good teachers either by missionary effort or by public school funds that is in session eight or nine months in the year, and if he finds in his own community the public school taught in a broken down log cabin with a poor teacher and the school term not longer than four or five months in the year, the Negro is tempted to move to the city where he can educate his children.

This is natural, and any other race would yield to the same temptation under the same circumstances. Our white friends can help the

Negro, and help themselves at the same time, by seeing to it that the Negro family is provided with just as good school accommodations in the country as in the city. In my opinion it would pay in the matter of dollars and cents for every white man who owns a large plantation in this State to see to it that on that plantation or near that plantation there is a good school provided and a good church, with a good teacher and upright minister who are encouraged to remain in that community. This will mean that labor will come to that plantation, will be satisfied there, that the individual who owns such a plantation and makes these provisions for school and church will not have to seek labor but labor will seek him.

RACE MUST SETTLE DOWN

There are some things in the life of every race that must be settled as speedily as possible before they will be able to make any real permanent progress. One of them is the matter of permanent abode, a definite place to live. A race can not make the highest progress, become in the highest degree useful, until it makes up its mind to settle down somewhere on the soil and become a useful part of the community in which it lives. We must get rid of the habit, which in a very large degree still clings to the race, of being an unsettled people. Some portion of our race moves every year. People live on one plantation this year, on another next year, and on still another the following year. Some portion of our race lives in a kind of haphazard manner in one town one year, and moves to a new town another year. Some have been doing this for a period of twenty years. We cannot make progress, we cannot make ourselves respected as we should be, until this habit is changed.

While I am speaking upon the subject of a permanent abode for the Negro race, I wish to repeat here the advice which I have given privately and publicly in every part of the country in which I have been, and that is, in my opinion, there is no place in this country where the Negro is better off, or in any other country, all things considered, than in our Southern States, and particularly in the country districts. I have had the privilege of traveling pretty extensively throughout this country as well as in foreign countries, and I have no hesitation in stating that taking the matter on the whole, there is no place where the masses of Negro people are doing so well, are so healthy in mind and body as they are in the country districts of the South. I may say, also, in my opinion the mass of my people have definitely determined to stay where they are in what is known as the black belt of the Southern States.

PRINCIPAL BOOKER T. WASHINGTON
ADVISES RACE TO SETTLE DOWN AND ECONOMIZE

In the Southern States there are between nine and ten millions of Negroes. In my opinion they are here to stay. They are going to stay because this is the best country for them. They are going to stay because the white man does not want them to leave. In order, however, that my race may remain in the South and prosper, I want to call the attention of my people to some simple, but fundamental things in connection with our future.

First, the time has come when we must settle down and cease yielding to the temptation of moving so often and in so many directions. The fall of the year or winter season is the time when a very large portion of our people move from one farm to another farm, or from one community to another community. We are now far enough along in our freedom to decide where we are going to live and settle down and become a permanent, helpful part of some community, making a reputation in that community for sobriety, industry and faithfulness. We must not let the disadvantages, which often surround us, close our eyes to the advantages which we enjoy here in the South. We like every other race have our disadvantages, our troubles, but it is with the race as with the individual — the one who prospers dwells more upon his advantages than upon his disadvantages. We have the advantage of living in one of the most inviting climates, on the best soil in the world. While people outside of the South are constantly in search of labor, here labor seeks the man instead of his having to seek labor.

Here in the South the colored man can buy property in practically every section, and on easy terms, even if it is true that in some cities it has been thought proper to pass laws preventing the Negro from buying property in certain sections, but such laws from my point of view are not only unjust, but useless, because every black man in the South is able to use good common sense in selecting the place where he will live. Here in the South we are surrounded by a class of white people whom we know and who know us. I have studied the white man in many parts of the world and I am free to say that in all that is said, the Southern white man here in the South, in all that concerns the Negro's life, is willing to give the Negro a chance that is seldom afforded him by any white man outside of the South. This I say despite the fact that I know the Negro is often imposed upon and treated with injustice.

The mere fact, however, that we occupy certain territory in the South in large numbers does not mean that we can continue to occupy this territory except as we conform to certain fundamental conditions of growth. To be very plain and direct the black man in a state like Louisiana is the main dependence for certain classes of labor. The average white man prefers the black man for certain classes of labor, but we can only hold our place in the world of labor in proportion as we learn to put as much skill, as much intelligence, as much conscience into the work as is true of any other race. 50% of the people who cultivate land in Louisiana are black people. Almost half of the land cultivated in Louisiana is cultivated by black people. The mere fact that we have so large a territory in our charge as owners or as laborers places upon us a tremendous responsibility, that is, of seeing that we get as much out of this soil as the man of any other color or race can get out of it.

Then we must learn to economize. We must get rid of the old idea that labor with the hand for an educated man is disgraceful. We must not only learn to save our money, but what is equally important, to save our time, especially during the fall and winter months. I think I am not far wrong in saying that the average farmer in this section of Louisiana does not work more than half the days in the year. When he reaps his cotton crop, he is likely to yield to the temptation of doing practically nothing until he begins planting another crop in the spring of the year. The farmer must learn that the farm is his business place and it is just as important for him to keep the doors of his business place open every working day in the year as it is important for the banker, or the merchant, or the lawyer, or the doctor to keep his business place open every working day in the year. Too much money is thrown away in the fall of the year after the sale of the cotton and other crops. The result is that we have to mortgage the crop in advance of its being planted at a high rate of interest and go without many of the comforts and necessities of life simply because in the fall of the year too much money is wasted on things that we can do without.

I wish, too, to impress upon the farmers of my race the importance of growing a variety of crops. Have something growing on the farm every day in the year, something in the way of grain or vegetables, or fruit, or fowls. In a climate like this something can be kept growing all the time. In the State of Louisiana I find that there [are] 24,000 Negro farmers with no cattle, 18,000 Negro farmers with no hogs, and 13,000 without any poultry. The census figures indicate that almost one-third the Negro farmers of Louisiana raise no vegetables. Now let us go home determined that we are going down deep in the soil, that we are going to work every day, and that we are going to prove to the outside world that we are not wholly dependent upon the growing of cotton for making a living.

NEGROES ARE URGED TO COOPERATE WITH WHITES
FOR THE IMPROVEMENT OF THEIR HEALTH CONDITIONS
BETTER EDUCATIONAL FACILITIES FOR NEGROES
ARE ASKED FOR

I am glad that under the leadership of Doctor Dowling,[1] Louisiana is taking the lead in the matter of improving health conditions and that as a result, in this State so much attention is being paid to cleanliness and sanitary improvements. I am, also, glad to know that both races are so heartily cooperating. Disease knows no color line. When food is being prepared, the Negro woman touches the white man's life; when food is being served, the Negro woman touches the white man's life; when children are being nursed, the Negro woman touches the white man's life; when clothes are being laundered, the Negro woman touches the white man's life. It is mighty important in the interest of our race, as well as in the interest of the white race, that the Negro woman be taught cleanliness and the laws of health. If by reason of filth and unsanitary conditions growing out of ignorance: consumption, smallpox, or any contagious diseases reach the black community, it is likely to strike from this community to the mansion of the richest white person.

In my own State of Alabama, a few years ago, an ignorant Negro woman was employed as a cook in an aristocratic white college for girls, but little attention was given to the health or cleanliness of this colored woman. Little attention was given to the place where she slept or how she lived. The result was that a deadly contagious disease took hold of her body and from her body this disease spread among the white girls in the college and the result was, several of the most promising of these white girls were taken away by death and the college for the year was disbanded.

The entire South is dependent, in a large measure, upon the Negro for certain kinds of work. A weak body, a sickly body is costly to the whole community and to the whole State from an economic point of view. The average length of a Negro's life in the South is at present 35 years. It should be 50 years and this health movement points out the way by which the life of the average Negro working man can be prolonged to 50 years. In India, the average length of life is 25 years; in Massachusetts, where they have good public schools it is 45 years; in Denmark and Sweden, 50 years.

In the State of Louisiana, statistics show that there are 44,400 black people who are sick all the time, and every year some 14,500 die. This means a net loss annually to the white people and black people of Louisiana in the way of earning power of at least $15,800,000.

There are 450,000 Negroes sick in the South every day in the year. The average black man loses 18 working days in the year because of sickness. The sickness and death of so large a proportion of its population means an annual loss to the South of over $300,000,000. $150,000,000 of this amount could be saved by taking measures to prevent disease by the simple precautions which the Health movement in every way emphasizes. This $150,000,000 saved would furnish six months' schooling for every white and black child in the South and besides would build good schoolhouses for every black and white child in the South.

There are, I understand, some 60,000 Negroes operating farms in Louisiana. These Negro farmers can not cooperate with the white farmers in the campaign which the State is carrying on for crop diversification unless they are made intelligent. The time has come when ignorance cannot compete with intelligence. Everywhere I am glad to see, however, evidences of the passing of the old idea that the education of the Negro is going to hurt him, is going to make a fool of him. The Negro has learned how to use education and all the nonsense in connection with the educated Negro is fast disappearing. In proportion as we can show that we can use education in a sensible direction, we want to urge the white people to give us longer school terms and better schoolhouses.

In the State of Louisiana today the Negro child is having spent on him for his education from the public school fund about $1.60. This keeps him in school about 4½ months during the year. At this rate it would require a Negro child 26 years to get a public school education. Ignorance is the most costly thing that can be produced in Louisiana. Ignorance means inefficiency; ignorance means crime. It is cheaper to conduct schools than it is to furnish criminals.

In spite of the present depressed feeling in many sections of the South, growing out of our present financial condition, I have never lived through a period in the history of the South when there were so many evidences of good feeling between white people and black people, when there was so large a proportion of the white people ready to help the black people. Referring to the property our people own, to the amount of education our people have, everybody who lives in the South knows that it would be impossible for the Negro to have gotten property that he now owns and the education that he is now in possession of without the encouragement and help of white people in the South, and the time has come when the Negro is resolved to advertise his enemies less, if he has them, and his white friends more.

All this is an indication of what is going on. Do not become discouraged. Resolve day by day that in spite of hard times and handicaps we will go forward to a still higher degree of success. We will still teach the South how it is possible for two races, different in color, different in history, to remain upon the same soil and each prosper and live in peace and happiness.

TM Con. 845 BTW Papers DLC.

[1] Oscar Dowling, a physician born in 1866 in Montgomery, Ala., began in 1910, as president of the Louisiana State Board of Health, a "cleaning-up" campaign, touring the state in a special train with a health exhibit and inspecting the food and water supplies of various communities. He was a director of the American Public Health Association and vice-president of the Southern Sociological Congress. He founded and edited several medical journals. He served on the Louisiana State Board of Health from 1906 to 1925, and was professor of public health at Tulane University.

From Charles Banks

Mound Bayou, Miss., April 14th, 1915

Dear Mr. Washington: Replying to your favor of the 12th, inst relative to matters here at Mound Bayou, I beg to advise that on the whole, the situation is gradually and substantially clearing up; that it can be but slow is expected and understood. The matter of indicting the officials of the late Bank came up before the Grand Jury, and they took the position that since our accounts were correct, no shortage or irregularities existed, we had committed no criminal act and turned down the Examiners' suggestion of an indictment. We are therefore relieved of anxiety in that direction.

The Examiners' complaint that the securities are worthless is based on the fact that they are in a Negro settlement, the Whites will not buy them as long as we protest and ask for a chance and the Negroes have not the money to take them over, therefore he cannot realize on them. As to this whole proposition of the affairs of the failed bank, my plan is to prorate the securities among the depositors, exchanging them securities for their deposits. I am already at work on this line and practically control two thirds of the deposits for this purpose; I calculate that if my plan carries the depositors would get all their money within about twenty four months. I shall charge no fees or commission for this service.

A new bank, The Mound Bayou State Bank has been organized and will open sometime in June. On account [of] the people here needing their money to make their crops this year as well as all they could borrow, I have arranged to raise the $10000.00 (ten thousands dollars) necessary to open the New Bank on my own securities and am taking the notes from those who are taking stock payable in the Fall to me. I am pushing the opening of the New Bank earlier than they will be in position to help me for the reason that to obtain the best results the Institution should be open and running by time cotton begins to move.

As to the Oil Mill, the Lessee B. B. Harvey[1] failed, or rather his Memphis Mill failed and he will automatically be forced out of the mill here. I have taken out new insurance, placing $25000.00 (twenty five thousand dollars) worth in Mr. Rosenwalds name so as to protect his bond. I have about effected arrangements by which we shall operate the Mill ourselves this Fall. Those who have taken stock in it can at least know that we kept faith and built it as we said, it has been demonstrated that it can be run here successfully and profitably and when out of debt will yield a fair dividend on their money. Under favorable management it should pay a dividend three seasons hence and meantime their investment is rising in value. We are having the hardest time of our existence to get advances to make the crops, but in my opinion this will be best in the end, as they will not owe it all when harvest time comes, as in the past. Touching the Boston Meeting I have not done any work in that direction because my hands were full here, and right now it is my idea that the greatest service I can do you, the League and the Race is to "Come back" on this Mound Bayou proposition, and I am bending all my efforts to that end.

If I can do what I have in mind the other things will follow. Very truly yours,

Chas. Banks

We will begin some work for the League, when crops begin to develop and the feeling or outlook is better developed and begin to afford encouragement. Your[s]

I. T. M.[2]

TLS   Con. 75   BTW Papers   DLC.

[1] Benjamin B. Harvey, a Memphis cotton broker and president of the Memphis Cotton Oil Co.

[2] Isaiah T. Montgomery added this postscript in his hand.

From Charles H. Fearing

[Tuskegee, Ala.] April 16, 1915

Dear Mr. Washington: I stopped by Mrs. Bethune's school on my return from Florida to talk with her further about her school. She left for New York the day before my arrival there, but I had a very pleasant talk with Mr. Harrison Rhodes,[1] the Vice-President of her Board of Trustees.

Mrs. Bethune had already talked quite freely with Mr. Rhodes about the following matters, which he spoke of to me:

They are anxious to secure Tuskegee's backing in the work. They want you brought into closer touch with the school. Mr. Rhodes suggested very frankly that they would like for you to become one of their trustees and asked me what I thought of this suggestion. I told him equally frankly that I could not speak for you on this point. Personally, however, I wish you might give very careful consideration to this request when formal invitation comes to you. Mrs. Bethune is surrounded by a very strong and helpful board of trustees, the President of which is Mr. John Gamble,[2] President of the Ivory Soap Company. Mr. Harrison Rhodes is their Vice-President, whom you know. These men not only give of their time but of their means to help the work.

I can only repeat what I wrote you from Florida that Mrs. Bethune's school, it seems to me, is an almost perfectly conducted institution of its size and kind and I feel that she ought to be encouraged in her efforts. Her school is free of debt and they are to begin soon to make some permanent improvements in the plant in the way of more substantial buildings.

They have made application to the General Education Board for some help, and Mr. Rhodes wonders if you are willing to write Dr. Buttrick concerning this.

Mr. Rhodes also discussed with me the matter of your going there next year, in February or early March for a general meeting, and at the same time to meet with their Board of Trustees. I told him that I thought you would give very careful consideration to this matter. There is a large population of Northern people who spend the winter in Daytona, some of whom are wealthy, and a visit on your part to Daytona would be very helpful, not only to Mrs. Bethune's work, but to your own work as well.

The statements I have made about Mrs. Bethune's work are entirely voluntary and without solicitation from any source whatsoever.

Chas. H. Fearing

TLS Con. 657 BTW Papers DLC.

[1] Harrison Rhodes (1871–1929), author of *Ruggles of Red Gap* (1915) and other popular novels, also wrote a guidebook to Florida.

[2] Probably James Norris Gamble (1836–1932), who was connected with Procter and Gamble beginning in 1862 and was vice-president after 1891.

From Samuel Edward Courtney

Boston   April 19th 1915

My dear Dr. Washington: Doubtless you have heard ere this of the wild unrest of the colored people and their sympathisers over the photo play the "Birth of a Nation" now being shown at our Tremont Theater. It is said not since the Civil War times have such demonstrations been seen here in Boston. The Negroes are a unit in their determination to drive it out of Boston.

I am sending you a few headlines clippings that you may see what happened Saturday night and of the great meeting at Faneuil Hall yesterday.

My chief object in writing you is due to the embarrassing position in which our Business League has been placed by Phillip Allston and Dr. Alexander Cox, who have posed as the representatives of the National Business League. These two men voluntarily called upon the management of this photo play and endorsed it, and the general impression is that they represented *you* and *your* sentiments. Read Cox's Reliance of April 17th and you will see what I mean.

Last week Allston called a private meeting of the executive committee to which I was not invited. I have been informed by Mr. Johnson,[1] Pres. of the local league, that Allston & Cox tried to force a resolution through the Ex. Com. endorsing "The Birth of a Nation," in the name of the Business League, and but for the good judgement of Lovett[2] & a few others, we, the Business League, would have been disgraced.

Indignation runs high against these two men, who claim they represent you and the Business League. I am afraid if these two men are not asked to resign from the management of the August meeting, Boston will be a cold spot for us at our National Meeting. Mr. Washington, I cannot adequately describe to you the intensity of the feeling against these men to-day. Since Saturday night it has been considered dangerous for them to show themselves on the street. Not only are they condemned by the colored people but by the whites as well.

Standing alone they represent nothing and are of little importance, but I do not like to see such insignificant Negroes use you as a stepping stone in such a matter as this. I would like a little advice from you as to my course at our next meeting. Personally, I think, for the good of

the cause, they should be asked to resign. Bill Lewis shares my feelings.
Very truly yours,

S. E. Courtney

ALS Con. 75 BTW Papers DLC.

¹ W. Alexander Johnson was president of the Boston Negro Business League
No. 1.
² William C. Lovett, treasurer of the Boston Negro Business League No. 1.

To Byrd Prillerman

[Tuskegee, Ala.] April 21, 1915

Have just heard indirectly my sister very sick. Please see she gets every
attention possible my expense. Hope you can go up there and telegraph
me after you have seen her.

Booker T. Washington

TWSr Con. 944 BTW Papers DLC.

To Byrd Prillerman

[Tuskegee, Ala.] April 21, 1915

Albert Johnson leaving for Malden today or tomorrow. Mrs. Washington or some other member of family likely to reach there within
few days. Keep me informed my expense.

Booker T. Washington

TWSr Con. 944 BTW Papers DLC.

From Byrd Prillerman

Malden, West Virginia, April 21, 1915

Mrs. Johnson had stroke of paralysis. Critically ill. Night letter follows.[1]

Byrd Prillerman

TWSr Con. 944 BTW Papers DLC.

[1] Prillerman wrote BTW that Amanda Johnston was unconscious and that her doctor saw no hope for her. (Apr. 22, 1915, Con. 944, BTW Papers, DLC.)

From Julius Rosenwald

Fortress Monroe, Va. Apl 21/15

Dear Dr. Washington: If you had the opportunity of dividing $5000.00 among the staff of Tuskegee how would you do it.

I am not sure that I shall do what I have in mind but in case I do, would be grateful for your advice. In each case I would like to know whether married or single & family if any & how many years in service. If you will mail it to me marked personal at Chicago, so it will reach me Wednesday I expect to be home then.

Please treat this in strict confidence as my plan may not be carried out. We arrived at noon today. The New York party arrive this evening. Yours

Julius Rosenwald

ALS Con. 78 BTW Papers DLC.

To James Carroll Napier

[Tuskegee, Ala.] April 22, 1915

My dear Mr. Napier: I have yours of April 19th and I have read it with care.

My present feeling is that the matter of organizing an agricultural department at Howard University had better go on entirely independent of me. Of course those people naturally feel that I want to industrialize the institution and it would be far better for somebody else to take the lead in this matter than myself. As you know, I have already suggested that they are not complying with the charter and this is very true.

I am going to do my best to be present at the Trustee meeting which I understand takes place on June 1st.

I hope you and Mrs. Napier are well. Yours very truly,

Booker T. Washington

TLpS Con. 942 BTW Papers DLC.

To Samuel Edward Courtney

[Tuskegee, Ala.] April 23, 1915

Dear Dr. Courtney: I have just received yours of April 19th and am sending you the following telegram which expresses my views regarding the play.

"Have just returned from educational campaign through Louisiana. Did not know Birth of Nation being played in Boston until very recently. From all can hear is vicious and hurtful play. If it cannot be stopped it ought to be modified or changed materially. Best thing would be to stop it as it can result in nothing but stirring up race prejudice. Do not believe play will be permitted in its present form in any of our Southern states. Glad to hear people in Boston are against play and hope their efforts to stop it will be successful. Particularly unfortunate to have this play at present time when we were entering upon era of good racial feeling throughout country such as we have not experienced lately."

In trying to stop this play, I hope our friends will be very careful not to be used in a way to advertise the play and in the end not accomplish the result which they had in mind, that is, of stopping the play. I am satisfied that the same crowd of people who are handling this play were the ones who got up "The Clansman" and in that case I

277

happen to know in New York and other places they actually paid some colored people to oppose the play for the sake of advertising. For instance, our good friend Mr. Payton, was given money to be used in getting out circulars to oppose the play. Of course Mr. Payton did not know the man who gave him the money to oppose the play was a publicity agent in "The Clansman." Our friends in Boston want to be very sure that the same trick is not played on them.

Another thing ought to be kept in mind. These people have put thousands of dollars into the films and you can be very sure that they did not do so without getting the very best legal advice as to what they could do and what they could not do. This means that our friends should spare no pains to see to it that they get the best lawyers they can get to take the matter into the courts.

Now as to the other matter to which you refer. I should like to think it over. I have found it always safe not to act in the midst of excitement. When one enters the domain of trying to control one's individual utterances or actions, he is treading upon rather dangerous ground. Freedom of opinion and action is rather tenaciously held to in most parts of the country. I do not think it wise to attempt to take any action in regard to the individuals referred to at the present, certainly not until after the excitement has died out.

Notwithstanding I have just returned from this long campaign through Louisiana, I am leaving this afternoon for Malden, where my sister, Amanda, is very sick and not expected to live. Yours very truly,

Booker T. Washington

TLSr Copy Con. 75 BTW Papers DLC.

To George Washington Albert Johnston

[Tuskegee, Ala.] April 24, 1915

Have Mr. Prillerman arrange for team to meet me and Davidson at Charleston Sunday evening so I can go direct to Malden without stopping in Charleston.

Booker T. Washington

TWSr Con. 940 BTW Papers DLC.

To Julius Rosenwald

[Tuskegee, Ala., ca. Apr. 24, 1915]

Personal and Confidential.

My dear Mr. Rosenwald: Your kind letter, under date of April 21st written from The Chamberlain Hotel, Fortress Monroe, has just been received and you do not know how grateful we are to you for your thought of us in the direction that you outline, even though what you suggest might not, for some reason, mature.

The suggestion of dividing Five Thousand Dollars ($5,000.00) among members of our staff would prove a most timely, practical and helpful one from several points of view.

In the first place, it would bring a reward — in many cases a much needed reward — to individuals who have spent some of their best years in the service of the school at a small salary. In many cases, these individuals have increasing families and relatives who are dependent upon them. In several cases, they have found it very difficult to meet their personal expenses, and in a few instances, have been several times embarrassed by personal debt.

Second — It would prove a great incentive for persons to remain in the service of the school rather than go away when they are offered salaries that are much more tempting than any we can pay. It would make all feel, in a word, that their services were appreciated and that even remaining here at a sacrifice is worth while. I can think of few things that would prove helpful to us just now in so many directions and I very much hope that you can see your way clear to carry out the plan.

Now as to the details: I hesitate to go into details just now for the reason that I am compelled to take the train within a few hours for Malden, W.Va., where I have a sister who is very sick and not expected to live. I think, owing to the short time at my command before leaving, I had better not attempt to go into details as to names, but would suggest a general plan which I am sure would prove helpful and practical. A little later on, I could supply you with the individual names, that is perhaps after my return here, which I think will be about the 3d or 4th of May, but I am not sure whether in order to carry out the general plan you have in mind you would want the names in advance. In that case, I can get them together before I return.[1]

First, I would suggest that a time limit, say, 15 years be made and that the money be divided among teachers who come within this limit on a percentage basis. I mean by a "percentage basis" according to the number of years they have stayed here within that limit. That I would suggest as the general policy and then, in addition, I would suggest that wherever it is thought wise, that we make an exception among persons who have rendered exceptional service, or are for some reason, in especial need. I think these exceptions would not be many. It might be well, too, to encourage, say, two or three of our oldest employees, who are not classed as teachers with something. For example, we have a cook who has been in the service of the school practically ever since it was founded and is a very worthy, fine man. Something, however small, would put a great deal of heart into him and make him feel that we had not overlooked his fine service. I should suggest that the money be divided among the staff regardless of whether they are married or unmarried. As a matter of fact, most persons you will see on the list are married.

If we make the limit 15 years, as I have suggested, I find by rough calculation that about [blank][2] individuals would be helped.

Perhaps you may feel that the time limit is too narrow. In that case, of course, it would be very easy to extend it and include a larger number of individuals.

I am sending this off so it may reach you by Wednesday and in the meantime, I will be considering the individuals. By the time I hear from you, I think I can have the name[s] ready. While I shall be at Malden, W.Va. for a few days, anything sent to Tuskegee will reach me.

I very much hope that all of you had a fine time at Hampton. Mr. Willcox and Mr. Trumbull told me that they were going and I am quite sure they must have had some great days there.

I hope you will remember us to Mrs. Rosenwald and the rest of the family. If Mrs. Washington were here, she would be glad to be remembered, too, but she is now in Malden with my sister. Yours very truly,

[Booker T. Washington]

TLc Con. 78 BTW Papers DLC.

¹ Attached is a "Suggested Grouping as to Length of Service & Needs," proposing amounts ranging from $275 to $25 to thirty-four individuals.
² Figure omitted in press copy.

An Account of Washington's Tour of Louisiana in the Chicago *Herald*

Tuskegee, Ala., April 25 [1915]

Booker T. Washington, accompanied by Emmett J. Scott, secretary of the school, and several others of his force, have returned to Tuskegee Institute from an educational tour of Louisiana. This is the eleventh pilgrimage the great race leader has made through the southern states, he having toured Virginia, West Virginia, New Jersey, North Carolina, South Carolina, Tennessee, Arkansas, Mississippi, Texas, Florida and Louisiana.

In Louisiana, as in other states, the one purpose of the educator was to establish a more friendly understanding between the two races, teaching by eloquent appeals, happy anecdote, picturesque narrative, the everyday life of the black man and the white man, that the two races are really friends.

The tour began at New Orleans Tuesday morning, April 13. On Dr. Washington's arrival traffic about the station was blocked for a time, while both white and black crowded about to shake his hand and welcome him to the city. At the home of Walter L. Cohen, one of the leading negroes of the country, Dr. Washington met the distinguished colored men of New Orleans.

. . . .

The sight in the Cohen home was most imposing. Negroes of wealth, college presidents and professors, doctors and lawyers, mixed here and there with the stately figure of an ex-judge or ex-governor of reconstruction days, mingled and buzzed about the "Moses of their race" to do him honor.

Then, as if to show how universally the black people appreciate the negro orator, an old ex-slave, his hair white and woolly, speaking almost in a whisper, pushed his way through the throng, peering up into the eyes of each one he accosted, and said: "Whar Booker? Whar Booker? I want to see Booker."

The scene was typical of those in the dozen Louisiana towns and cities visited. Everywhere the woman from the wash tub, from the kitchen and from the field seemed to think Booker one of her own, as did also the rough fellows from the levees, from the sugar plantations and the rice fields.

"Which is Booker?" "Is dat Booker settin' up dar?" "Hurrah for you, suh," were common expressions.

.   .   .   .

From a sumptuous creole breakfast at the Cohen home the party made a short trip into the country to the parish of St. Bernard, where the black folk were by hard struggling completing a rural school. The speech here struck the keynote of all the speeches of the tour. Booker T. Washington, as every one knows, is at his best before a southern mixed audience. No other man can so pit one set of people against another and yet keep all in the best of humor. To the black people he said:

"Stay on the farm; educate your children; get rid of the lazy negro, the loafer, the gambler, the immoral leader; share your confidence with your wife, as you do your toil and responsibility; cultivate the good will of the white neighbor; talk to him, not about him."

To the white people he pleaded for a chance to educate the black boy and girl.

"In my opinion," he said, "it would pay in the matter of dollars and cents for every white man who owns a plantation in this state to see that on or near that plantation a good school is provided."

Next to providing good schools, he pleaded for the just protection of the law. At New Orleans, at Shreveport, at Lake Charles, indeed all along the line, he exclaimed, "I believe that the South has reached a point where civilization is going to run the mob and not the mob run civilization. There is near, it seems to me, no excuse for a band of lawless men rushing in and taking the law into their own hands."

.   .   .   .

Upon the 9,000 school children in the arena at New Orleans, upon the college boys of Southern University at Baton Rouge and at Gibsland, he urged the responsibility of putting education to some use. He urged them to go back home with their knowledge, to lighten the burden of the mother and father on the farm and to take happiness to their home towns.

To the negro farmer he said, "Get away from draw day. Draw out of your garden peas, onions, corn, tomatoes, beets, cabbages; draw chickens, turkeys, butter, milk, pigs, draw these from around your own home, and not from the grocery store. So shall you rise in your own esteem as well as in the good will of your white neighbor."

In all places the white people vied with the black to do honor to Dr. Washington. The best white citizens were present in large numbers. In eight out of nine places he was introduced by the mayor of the city. In Shreveport he was introduced by ex-Governor Blanchard.[1]

"His words," said the county superintendent of schools at Crowley, "are words of wisdom. He has done more for useful education for his race than any other man living."

The trip is looked upon as one of the most useful made in the state. Speaking of Dr. Washington editorially, the Lake Charles Daily American Press said: "Dr. Washington is devoting his life to the building up of this class of colored citizenship; to the training of more farmers, more efficient workers, and to elimination of the type of worthless negro, who drift from idleness to vice and from vice to crime. He has inspired and directed a movement among his people that has not only elevated them mentally, morally and commercially but which gives the white citizens an increasing sense of peace and security, and the community more efficient producers and increasing wealth."

Chicago *Herald,* Apr. 26, 1915, 6.

[1] Newton Crain Blanchard, Democratic governor of Louisiana from 1904 to 1908.

From Charles Ellis Mason

Boston, Mass. April 26, 1915

Dear Dr. Washington: I wish to thank you very much for your letters in regard to "The Birth of a Nation." If you have not already heard it, I am sure that you will be very glad to know that a bill has been introduced in the Massachusetts legislature to prevent photo-plays being produced which are likely to arouse race prejudice. I have not seen a copy of the bill, but will try to obtain one, and will send it to you. As I understand it, power has been given to the City officials to stop any play which in their opinion is likely to arouse race prejudice. It is a good deal of responsibility to put on the City officials, and a great deal depends on the calibre of the men in office.

I am extremely sorry to learn that you have been called to Malden, West Virginia, on such a sad errand. I hope that you will accept my sincerest sympathy. Sincerely yours,

Charles E. Mason

TLS Con. 77 BTW Papers DLC.

To Marcus Mosiah Garvey

[Tuskegee, Ala.] April 27, 1915

My dear Mr. Garvey: I have yours of April 12th advising of your proposed tour of this country and of your plan to visit Tuskegee Institute while in the South.

I am very glad indeed that you have decided to come here and it will give us all very great pleasure to make your stay as pleasant and as profitable as we can. Certainly I shall do what I can to help you while in this country.

I thank you for sending me the statement outlining the aim and purpose of the Negro Improvement Association. Yours very truly,

Booker T. Washington

TLpSr Con. 939 BTW Papers DLC.

From Jesse H. Harris

Boston Mass. May 3rd 1915

My dear Mr Washington — You have heard of our fight here against "The Birth of a Nation." We are still fighting and the best thing of all to my mind is that for the first time during my 27 years in Boston the entire Negro population is a unite. Now while at one of the hearings last week — as I looked over that vast crowd of Negro men & women — this thought came to me; this is a united people though in the manority now they are going to win. Why not enlarge this so I saw in my mind a meeting in this city in the Old Liberty Hall — the speakers Washington, Walters, Du Bois — Trotter and others — where all things of the past would be buried. And a race of Ten Millions of Negroes would be united. A Nation would *really* be *Born*.

This union together with those of the best blood of the White race — would be a force against which no power in this Country could prevail and our just dues would be secured. This was my dream. I have mentioned it to only two others, both as I am; members of our local Business League — the matter may be taken up — by our League — if others think well of it.

Knowing the many cliques here in Boston I am sending you this note. So that if the matter should be presented to you later you know of its very origin. I am hoping that I may live to see this dream come true; it would be a great day for us in this Country.

So you can realize that your telegram — came during the play — and endorsing our fight has been a great source of comfort to me.

I am enclosing herewith a circular we had distributed yesterday Sunday in all of the Negro Churches of the community. I am very respectfully   Yours

J. H. Harris
Hampton '88.

ALS   Con. 75   BTW Papers   DLC.

From Byrd Prillerman

Charleston, W.Va. May 4th 1915

Mrs. Johnson died at 7 : 20 A.M. Wire answer.

Byrd Prillerman

TWSr   Con. 941   BTW Papers   DLC.

To Clara J. Johnston

[Tuskegee, Ala.] May 4, 1915

Have just reached home. We are all very sorry to hear of death of your mother and sympathize with you deeply. It is impossible as Mrs. Washington has already explained for me to leave here at present. Albert starts for Malden tonight. He has arranged everything and will tell you all about our plans when he sees you. Call on Mr. Prillerman for anything you want.

Booker T. Washington

TWSr Con. 940 BTW Papers DLC.

John Henry Washington to Clara J. Johnston

[Tuskegee, Ala.] May, fourth 15

You all have our deepest sympathy in the death of your mother and our dear sister.

Booker is on the train between here and Chicago and I am sick which prevents us from being present. See that everything necessary is done to properly put the body away.

J. H. Washington

TWpS Con. 940 BTW Papers DLC.

To Gladwin Bouton[1]

[Tuskegee, Ala.] May 6, 1915

Dear Sir: Your letter of recent date making inquiry concerning the steps that are being taken to train American Negroes for service in Africa and expressing your appreciation of such efforts received.

From Tuskegee Institute two groups of graduates and former students have been sent out to Africa to teach cotton raising to the natives.

One group went to [. . .]² Eastern Sudan and another to Togoland. The latter was under the auspices of the German Government. Both of these expeditions went out something over 10 years ago and remained there several years. We received from the Colonial Office of the German Government a number of commendatory letters concerning the good work that these representatives of Tuskegee Institute did.

In addition to these American Negroes that went out from Tuskegee to Africa, a considerable number of Africans are being trained here and in other institutions for service in Africa. In my opinion, these native Africans who have received their training in America will do equally as good if not better work for their people than American Negroes trained and sent out; for these natives will have advantages in many ways that Negroes from America will not have.

In a recently issued volume, "The New Voice in Race Adjustment," by the Student Volunteer Movement, 25 Madison Avenue, New York, you will find an interesting report of a commission "On the Enlistment of Educated Negroes for Work in Africa," also a number of addresses on "Africa as a Mission Field." Very sincerely yours,

Booker T. Washington

TLpS Con. 537 BTW Papers DLC.

[1] A "friend of the colored people," Bouton wrote BTW from Bloomfield, N.J., urging the training of black Americans for service in Africa. (Apr. 18, 1915, Con. 537, BTW Papers, DLC.)
[2] An illegible insertion.

To George Washington Albert Johnston

[Tuskegee, Ala.] May 6, 1915

Before you leave Malden be sure arrange for good iron fence to be put around grave. See that suitable tombstone is erected, also see that suitable arrangements are made for Clara. Sorry cannot be with the family today.

B. T. W.

TWIr Con. 940 BTW Papers DLC.

An Account of the Funeral of Amanda Ferguson Johnston

Malden, West Virginia [May 6, 1915]

MRS AMANDA JOHNSTON'S FUNERAL

The funeral of Mrs. Amanda Johnston, the only sister of Dr. Booker T. Washington, was conducted in the Presbyterian Church (white) at Malden, West Virginia, at 10:30 Thursday morning, May 6, 1915. The services were conducted by Rev. B. A. Brooks, pastor of the African Zion Baptist Church, of which Mrs. Johnston has been the clerk for several years. Rev. Mr. Brooks was assisted by Rev. B. R. Reed, pastor of the First Baptist Church; Rev. J. Sylvester Carrell, pastor of the Simpson M. E. Church; Rev. F. Herman Gow, pastor of the A. M. E. Church, and Rev. Edward Humbles, all of Charleston. Among the host of other persons present were Rev. Wallace Page, Dr. W. L. Jones, Rev. R. M. Mahew, Mr. James M. Canty, and Mr. Albert G. Brown, graduates of Tuskegee Institute; Miss Martha Hughes, Mrs. Martha Lovely, Prof. and Mrs. H. B. Rice, Mr. George Smith, brother of Dr. Washington's first wife; Mrs. Sallie Poe-Vaughn, cousin of the deceased; Mrs. J. W. Lovette, Mr. G. W. A. Johnston, oldest son of the deceased, of Birmingham, Alabama; Mr. and Mrs. Archie McKinney, A. W. Slaughter, and Samuel Clark of Montgomery; President and Mrs. Byrd Prillerman, of the West Virginia Collegiate Institute; Mr. G. W. Clair, of Charleston; Mr. and Mrs. Anderson Rotan, and Miss Eva Rotan of Fayetteville.

One whole side of the church was occupied by white friends from Malden and Charleston. The services were simple and impressive. The floral tribute was beautiful. Rev. F. Herman Gow, who presided at the organ, was a graduate of the Tuskegee Institute. The instances have been rare in which so many highly respected citizens of the State have assembled on a funeral occasion.

This unusual tribute was paid because of the high regard in which Mrs. Johnston's distinguished relatives are held by the people of West Virginia and partly because of her own worth and useful career in the community in which she has lived so long. Soon after her demise, the minister and congregation of the White Presbyterian Church offered the use of their house of worship for this funeral occasion for the reason that they knew that the colored Church was too small for the large host of friends that would assemble on this occasion.

Mrs. Johnston leaves a daughter, Miss Clara, and three sons — G. W. A. Johnston, and Scoville Johnston of Birmingham, Alabama, and B. H. Johnston of Malden; two brothers — J. H. Washington and Dr. Booker T. Washington of Tuskegee Institute.

No other person has better heeded the teachings of her distinguished brother than herself — "Let down your buckets where you are." She was left a widow in Malden several years ago, and here she continued to live a life of usefulness and honor among the people where she grew up.

When Mrs. Johnston had a stroke of paralysis Wednesday morning, April 21, her son, G. W. A. Johnston, in Birmingham, Alabama, and Dr. Booker T. Washington were immediately notified. Dr. and Mrs. Washington and his son, Davidson, hastened to the bedside of the deceased, where they remained until there seemed some hope of recovery. A few days after they left Malden, however, Mrs. Johnston became suddenly worse and before they could reach her bedside, she expired, Tuesday morning, May 4, 1915.

Tuskegee Student, 27 (May 15, 1915), 1.

To Byrd Prillerman

[Tuskegee, Ala.] May 10, 1915

My dear Mr. Prillerman: I cannot find words with which to express the deep gratitude which all of the members of our family feel to you and Mrs. Prillerman and others there for your very great kindness to my sister during her illness and in connection with the funeral and burial. We shall never forget you. I am only sorry that it seemed impossible for me to be there at the burial, but I found it impossible to make a second trip.

I am attending to the Laidley[1] matter today. Yours very truly,

Booker T. Washington

TLpS Con. 944 BTW Papers DLC.

[1] George S. Laidley, superintendent of schools in Charleston, W.Va.

To George S. Laidley

[Tuskegee, Ala.] May 10, 1915

My dear Sir: I am in receipt of yours of May 3d asking me for my opinion concerning the work of the West Virginia Institute and my opinion concerning Mr. Prillerman, the present President of that Institution.

In reply I would say that I think I have visited within the last few years every State College in the state assisted by Federal funds and under State control and I have no hesitation in saying that from what I have actually seen of the work of the West Virginia Institute and its influence on the masses of the people in that state, the West Virginia Institute ranks among the first. It is far better organized, is doing much more effective work than is true of the majority of the other State schools.

Unfortunately, in many of the states there is a want of co-operation between the teachers and in some cases, politics has crept into the management of the school and all of this has served to hinder and weaken the influence of an institution, but it seems to me that the West Virginia Institute is remarkably free from this kind of thing.

As I have visited the state from time to time, I have been gratified to see how Mr. Prillerman has grown in his grasp upon the Institute and upon the conditions and needs of the masses of our people in West Virginia. I consider Mr. Prillerman a very remarkable man. I do not consider him a brilliant man. He is lacking in certain superficial elements that often attract attention, but in real substantial character and in common sense, he has, in my opinion very few superiors and I think the people of West Virginia are remarkably fortunate in having such a man at the head of their Institute. Certainly, if I were seeking a man for an important position here at Tuskegee or elsewhere, I should consider myself fortunate to get Mr. Prillerman. Among his other qualities, he has the rare quality of modesty in not letting his head be turned by reason of success or by reason of promotion — a very rare quality.

I do hope at some time that you can come and see our work in this part of the South. I remember with a great deal of satisfaction my connection with you when I was teaching in West Virginia. Yours very truly,

Booker T. Washington

TLpS Con. 941 BTW Papers DLC.

To the New York *World*

Tuskegee Institute, Alabama, May 11, 1915

In reply to your telegram, would say that, in spite of extreme provocation, the United States has a rare opportunity to teach the world how to settle grave questions by common sense and moral suasion, rather than by physical force. By exercising self-control, our country is and will continue to be in a position to exercise great influence as a mediator when the present European war ends. Consider too that to both victor and vanquished war is barbarous; that questions settled by combat are settled for the time only, while issues settled upon a high moral plane remain permanent. President Wilson is exhibiting more courage in fostering peace than are the rulers in Europe who are promoting war.

Booker T. Washington

New York *World*, May 12, 1915, 4. The printed version varies somewhat from two different copies of the telegram found in containers 537 and 942, BTW Papers, DLC. The sentiment, however, is the same.

To Seth Bunker Capp

[Tuskegee, Ala.] May 11th, 1915

My dear Mr. Capp: The portrait of myself painted by Mr. Hruska has come to hand in good shape. No portion of it was broken or in any way disfigured. You certainly took particular pains to see that it should come through in the very best possible shape, and I am glad to say that it reached us without blemish.

You have certainly placed me under very many obligations to you in having such a splendid portrait painted of me, and in having it framed and sent forward in so thoroughgoing a way as to insure its safety.

I want you to please express to Mr. Hruska for me, my own sincere thanks and at the same time the thanks of my entire family.

I must say, also, that the picture when it first reached here was placed on exhibition at the entrance to our Carnegie Library where it was inspected by practically our entire student body and teaching body, composed of some sixteen hundred persons.

The picture, I notice, is presented to the Tuskegee Institute, and as Principal of the Institution I am writing to express not only my personal but my official thanks as well to both you and the artist for your extreme kindness and generosity in donating this portrait of the Principal of the Institute to the school. Yours very truly,

Booker T. Washington

TLpS   Con. 938   BTW Papers   DLC.

From Mary McLeod Bethune

Daytona, Florida, May 25 1915

My dear Dr. Washington; I am trying hard to raise some money for our work. I want you to help me some. Will you personally donate $100.00 to help us out? Is it possible for you to assist us in getting some money from any of the Funds? I am doing my best and want you to help me. I am trying to raise $12000.00.

I hope you are well and all goes well with you. Very sincerely yours,

Mary McLeod Bethune

ALS   Con. 937   BTW Papers   DLC.

To Charles Harry Anderson[1]

Tuskegee Institute, Alabama   May 26, 1915

Personal.

Dear Mr. Anderson: The papers report that the State Legislature of Florida has passed a bill to prevent any colored person from being admitted to the bar to practice law.

If this is true would this not be a good chance for your Business League of Jacksonville to do something in the way of defeating the object of this unjust measure. Would it not be well for you to take this whole matter up and discuss it and see if you cannot bring about a plan to have the law declared unconstitutional.

Something ought to be done at once in case the report is true. Please write me. Yours very truly,

Booker T. Washington

TLpS   Con. 937   BTW Papers   DLC.

[1] Charles Harry Anderson (b. 1879) was proprietor of the Charles H. Anderson Fish and Oyster Co. in Jacksonville, Fla., and cashier of the banking firm of Anderson and Co.

To Julius Rosenwald

[Tuskegee, Ala.] May 26th, 1915

Dear Mr. Rosenwald: I was in Rochester a few days ago and saw our friend, Mr. Eastman. He gave his usual ten thousand dollars, and this in addition to the five thousand dollars which he gave some months ago for the veterinary hospital.

He referred to you, and said he came near seeing you a few days ago but missed you by a narrow margin. He still hopes to come to Tuskegee at some time.

But this point of this letter is to say that Mr. Eastman has seen some reference to the schoolhouses which you are building in the South, and he wants us to send him a plan by which he can build one of these same kind of schoolhouses on or near a farm which he owns in North Carolina. Perhaps this may prove the entering wedge to greater things on his part in this direction. Yours very truly,

Booker T. Washington

TLpS Con. 78 BTW Papers DLC.

To James Longstreet Sibley

[Tuskegee, Ala.] May 26th, 1915

Dear Mr. Sibley: One thing that I had in mind in connection with the cost and character of the schoolhouses is this:

I think we will have to be very careful in putting up this large number of schoolhouses, not to put so much money into a building that it will bring about a feeling of jealousy on the part of the white people who may have a schoolhouse that is much poorer. I think of course, the feeling of jealousy will gradually disappear in proportion as the white people themselves get better school buildings, but I can easily see how the white people who might have a very poor school building would have a feeling that the colored people are getting ahead of them, therefore something might be done to bring about an awkward position regarding the Negro school. I think this is worth thinking about. I think the more modest our school buildings are at present at least, the more we are likely to avoid such a difficulty. Yours very truly,

Booker T. Washington

TLpS Con. 536 BTW Papers DLC.

To Pinckney Benton Stewart Pinchback

[Tuskegee, Ala.] May 27, 1915

My dear Governor Pinchback: You do not know how very much I appreciate your thoughtful kindness in writing me under date of May 10th concerning the Louisiana trip. I confess that trip furnished us more evidences for encouragement than any trip I have ever made. I went into the state expecting very little. I came out with the feeling of hope and optimism such as I have seldom experienced. I was not prepared for the wide open kindness shown by the people to those who composed my party. There was not a single case where we were not received with the utmost generosity and courtesy by the leading white people. I was especially surprised at the tone and character of Governor Blanchard's speech at Shreveport. You know they have had more lynchings in that community than perhaps any other place in the South recently. I spoke out against lynching and the mob rule generally. Governor Blanchard was even more outspoken on this point than I was, and I noted that the two or three thousand white people present cheered his remarks. The railroads, without exception, went out of their way to furnish every protection and show every courtesy. We travelled from the beginning to the end of the trip in a Pullman car. In several cases trains were held up for us in order that we might make the proper connection.

Everywhere in the state I heard many good things concerning you and everybody rejoices with us here at Tuskegee over the fact that you are still in such good health and spirits. I hope we will see you at Tuskegee again before long. I shall gladly. . . .[1]

With highest regards, I am   Yours very truly,

Booker T. Washington

TLpS Con. 944 BTW Papers DLC.

[1] One line of press copy illegible.

To Charles Ellis Mason

[Tuskegee, Ala.] May 28, 1915

Dear Mr. Mason: I thought you would be glad to see the enclosed clipping which Mr. Rosenwald has sent me from Chicago, bearing on the "Birth of the Nation."

We are certainly to be congratulated that Mr. Rosenwald and our other friends in Chicago have been able to prevent the play opening in Chicago, and I believe that the same action is likely to take place in other cities.

I am delighted to hear through your letter of May 24th, about the passing of the bill through the legislature.[1] The play is so vicious that I believe if this play can be thoroughly squelched that no other parties will be encouraged to put money into such a play.

When I was in New York a few days ago, I was surprised to learn that the moving picture people are not keeping faith with Hampton and do not show the Hampton pictures regularly. It seems they do not show them only when the spirit moves them. Several people went to see the Hampton pictures but they were not exhibited. Yours very truly,

Booker T. Washington

TLpS Con. 77 BTW Papers DLC.

[1] Mason had reported that a new censorship bill giving more latitude to the mayor of Boston had been passed by the Massachusetts legislature and signed by the governor. (May 24, 1915, Con. 77, BTW Papers, DLC.)

To Julius B. Ramsey

[Tuskegee, Ala.] May 29, 1915

Major Ramsey: In all my experience at the school, I have never heard so much complaint about students sleeping in the Chapel and I must take immediate and, if necessary, unusual and strict measures to break it up once for all. This matter has been spoken of before.

I am, therefore, writing to ask you to take whatever measures you want to, beginning with tomorrow, to stop the boys from sleeping in the Chapel. You can use for this purpose any teacher or teachers, or use the boys in whatever way you desire, but at any rate, we must stop the sleeping.

Booker T. Washington

TLpS Con. 663 BTW Papers DLC.

To Mary McLeod Bethune

[Tuskegee, Ala.] May 31st, 1915

Dear Mrs. Bethune: I wish very much I could help you in the way you suggest, but the fact is I am not able. You have no idea how many demands there are upon my personal purse. We are surrounded here by fifteen or sixteen hundred students, many of whom are in need all the time. This calls for help, and there are demands in other directions that keep me drained.

I have been under the impression lately that the expenses of your school were being taken care of by an organization in New York of which your school is a member; that is, I understand that the organization has agreed to be responsible for all the current expenses so that the principals of schools will not have to spend their time in traveling about seeking money for their individual schools. If an organization is to be supported with headquarters and then each individual is to travel and incur the same expense as heretofore in getting money for schools, I can see no advantage in the organization. But, as I have stated, my understanding is that in the future you are to be relieved personally from collecting money and traveling in the interest of the school. Perhaps I have not gotten the right information, but this certainly is my impression. Yours very truly,

Booker T. Washington

TLpS Con. 937 BTW Papers DLC.

The Principal's Report to the
Board of Trustees of Tuskegee Institute

Tuskegee Institute, Alabama, May 31, 1915

Gentlemen: During the past year, this part of the South, especially the cotton growing section, has been passing through one of the most trying and difficult experiences it has been called upon to pass through since the Civil War. This condition has, in the main, been occasioned by the low price of cotton caused by the European War. Conditions have been serious among both white and black people.

Because of these conditions, this institution has been going out of its way to do an unusual amount of work and spending an unusual amount of money in trying to teach the people how to overcome these conditions by planting something to eat. The gratitude of the white and black people for our efforts in this regard has been most emphatic.

The United States Congress recently passed a bill known as the Smith-Lever Bill, by which a certain amount of money was given to each state in proportion to rural population, for the purpose of training the people in better farming and better living. We have entered into arrangement with the Alabama Polytechnic Institute for white people, at Auburn, Alabama, by which we are to become responsible for the expenditure of a portion of this money in helping the colored people in the rural districts of Alabama. We have been during the year engaged under this plan for a number of months in conducting what are called "Movable Schools." I have every reason for knowing that these movable schools accomplished great good. County superintendents of education as well as officers of various counties have written in the most cordial terms with reference to the good results secured in their several counties. The newspapers have also devoted considerable space to them.

Not less than 7,540 colored people were reached through these Movable Schools, and in addition to this work, of course the Annual Short Course for Negro Farmers has been held here at the Institute, and the Annual Tuskegee Negro Conference which meets each year. The amount of money coming to us with which to operate these Movable Schools is likely to increase year by year.

Although the attendance at the Annual Tuskegee Negro Conference was not as large as in other years, the reports indicate quite clearly that the teachings which have been carried on here for a number of years through our Extension Department, through our Agricultural Department, and through these Annual Farmers Conferences, are having a wholesome influence.

ENROLLMENT. Conditions in Europe just preceding the opening of the school term led us to fear a great falling off in attendance of students. The price of cotton, as you know, dropped to the lowest point, and since most of our students come from farming communities it has been harder this year than ever before for the parents of these students to find the money with which to pay their expenses in school. Nevertheless, there has been no faltering in connection with our work, and students and teachers alike have, if anything, worked even harder to make the present school year's work altogether successful.

As stated, I have devoted considerable time during the year, both in Macon County and in other counties in the State of Alabama, and in various portions of the South, in urging the Negro people to diversify their crops and get away from present hard conditions always to be expected when a whole race or a section is more or less dependent upon one crop for its sustenance. Despite these conditions, our enrollment has remained at about the same figure as last year. The school term for 1914–15 began September 8, 1914, with an enrollment in excess of the enrollment of September, 1913. The total enrollment of the year, however, as I have said, is about the same as the enrollment for last year, 907 boys and 630 girls, a total of 1537, from 32 states and territories. Ninety-six students have also come from 19 foreign countries or colonies of foreign countries. This number does not include the 200 in the Children's House or practice school.

I must not fail to call attention to the successful Summer School which is being held every year at Tuskegee Institute under the supervision of Mr. J. R. E. Lee, Director of our Academic Department. Last year 380 teachers registered from 15 states, and there is every indication that the Summer School of 1915 will be as largely attended. No part of our work at Tuskegee is more satisfactory than that which is being done through our Summer School.

IMPORTANT GATHERINGS AT TUSKEGEE. We have never passed through a year when so much deep interest in what we are trying to do has been manifested by Southern white people. As an evidence of this, I call attention to the fact that individuals representing nearly every part of the South are constantly visiting the school. In December, 1914, we had a visit from the Governor of Alabama, Hon. Emmet O'Neal, and his wife, together with a number of prominent state officers and other white men and women, including the State Superintendent of Education and members of the State Supreme Court. They spent the whole day on the grounds and seemed favorably impressed with our work.

I mention, also, the meeting of the Jeanes Fund Supervisors which was held on our grounds the week of January 17th. This meeting was called by Dr. J. H. Dillard, President of the Jeanes Fund Board. There were present about 50 colored supervisors representing various counties of the lower South. There were present at the same time a number of State Rural Superintendents of Education, and about a dozen County Superintendents of Education representing the States of North Carolina, Georgia, Tennessee, Mississippi, Alabama and Florida.

MEETING OF UNIVERSITY COMMISSION. Just a few weeks ago there was also held on our grounds a meeting of the University Commission composed of a member of the faculty of each of the State Universities in the South. With the Commission, Dr. Dillard, to whom I have already referred, also met. Among those present at the meeting were Professor R. J. H. DeLoach,[1] Acting Chairman, University of Georgia, Athens, Georgia; Professor James J. Doster,[2] University of Alabama, University, Alabama; Professor William L. Kennon,[3] University of Mississippi, University, Mississippi; Professor Josiah Morse,[4] University of South Carolina, Columbia, South Carolina; Professor James D. Hoskins,[5] University of Tennessee; Professor William O. Scroggs,[6] University of Louisiana, Baton Rouge, Louisiana; Dr. J. C. Bell,[7] University of Texas, Austin, Texas; Professor William M. Hunley,[8] University of Virginia, Charlottesville, Virginia; Dr. W. D. Weatherford, Y.M.C.A. Secretary, Nashville, Tennessee; Mr. James L. Sibley, State Supervisor of Rural Schools, Montgomery, Alabama; Mr. Wyatt Rushton, Senior Student, University of Alabama, Tuscaloosa, Alabama; Mr. Sam James Smith, Y.M.C.A. Secretary, Alabama Polytechnic Institute, Auburn, Alabama, and Mr. Jackson Davis, in charge of Rural School extension work for the General Education Board.

MIDWINTER MEETING OF THE TRUSTEES. I must not fail to record the appreciation of the officers and teachers of the Institute to our Trustees for their kindness in holding the Midwinter Meeting of the Board on our grounds. When the President of our Board, the Hon. Seth Low, first suggested these midwinter meetings, we had no idea they would prove of such far-reaching value as they have. The coming of Mr. and Mrs. Low and the other Trustees with their friends each year proves a constant benediction to all connected with the school. The meeting held February 21st to 24th, last, brought to us some 75 persons — one party starting from New York composed of our Eastern Trustees, Mr. Low, Mr. Willcox, Mr. Mason, Mr. Trumbull, and their friends, including Mrs. Wm. H. Baldwin, Jr., wife of the former Chairman of our Board of Trustees — and the other from Chicago headed by Mr. Julius Rosenwald, a member of our Board, including in it Miss Jane Addams,[9] Judge E. O. Brown,[10] Dr. Jenkin Lloyd Jones, Judge M. W. Pinckney,[11] Judge George A. Carpenter,[12] and other notable Chicago and Western friends.

Referring again to the visitors who come to see us, some idea of the good will of the people of Alabama toward the Tuskegee Institute may be found in the fact that each year finds large crowds of white visitors from surrounding villages and the larger cities of the state attending the Annual Commencement Exercises. This year, in addition to other visitors, the Automobile Club and the Chamber of Commerce of Montgomery came in a body to the school.

The following letter was received from the Secretary of the Chamber of Commerce on his return to Montgomery:

Chamber of Commerce,
Montgomery, Alabama   May 28, 1915

Dr. Booker T. Washington, Tuskegee, Alabama

Dear Dr. Washington: I want you to know that the members of the Chamber of Commerce who accompanied me to Tuskegee Thursday enjoyed every moment of our stay there. I was happy over the success of the trip because it enabled me to show many of my friends the institution, who had known so little of it before. I am grateful to you especially for your kindly reference to our organization and to the work I am trying to do for the development not only of Montgomery but of our State. It was a pleasure to me to observe the progress the school is making and it gave me inspiration to witness the efficiency of your industrial training.

Many of our men and women have asked to join with me in expressing appreciation of your management of the occasion and of the courtesy and kindness shown to our party. With all good wishes, I beg to remain,

Yours very truly,
Bruce Kennedy, General Secretary

A letter equally appreciative was also received from Mr. T. T. Greil,[13] President of the Chamber of Commerce, and Mr. J. S. Pinckard,[14] President of the Montgomery Automobile Club.

In my reports I have several times referred to the fact that the Tuskegee Institute does not confine its work to what is done on the school grounds. A very large part of the time of the officers and a large amount of money is spent in an unusual kind of extension work that makes the cause of education better understood and more appreciated by both races in the South and in the North.

Let me give one or two illustrations of this kind of extension work: some months ago an invitation was received by the Principal from the Governor of Louisiana[15] and the State Superintendent of Education[16] together with invitations from other leading white people and colored people to make a tour of education through the state for the benefit of the colored people.

The tour was well and thoroughly mapped out by the leading colored people of the state, so that the most important centers of Negro population were covered. In the party were Major R. R. Moton of the Hampton Institute, and about twenty other prominent colored men from within and without the state. The trip occupied four days. From three to five meetings were held each day at railroad stations, in parks, in halls, fair grounds, churches, court houses, etc. At every point the meetings were attended by hundreds and in some places thousands of people. At several of the meetings it was said that as many as 10,000 people were present. At every point hundreds of the best white people of both sexes were present. In most cases the mayor of the city presided or some other important official. At Shreveport, Former Governor Blanchard presided and made a magnificent speech. Nearly all of the expenses in connection with the trip were borne by the white and colored people of Louisiana.

Reference to the trip ought not to close without mention of the liberality of the railroads in arranging schedules, running special trains and even holding regular trains for the convenience of the party as well as in making everything on the train so comfortable that members of the party were spared the usual hardships of travel.

Since this Louisiana trip was completed, numerous letters have come from both white and colored people testifying to the good that was accomplished.

Without exception so far as one could discover, the newspapers, especially the daily papers, were most liberal in helping to make the trip both successful and helpful.

Another series of meetings was held in Greater New York under the auspices of the National League to Improve Conditions Among Negroes. Meetings were held in most of the large centers of Negro population in Greater New York with a view to help encourage and inspire them to better living. Few people realize how large a number of colored people are located in large northern cities, and that in proportion to their numbers they are surrounded by problems that are just as serious as those in the South. In Greater New York there are some 100,000 colored people. At one of the meetings where Hon. Marcus M. Marks, President of the Borough of Manhattan, presided, over five thousand colored people were present. There were many evidences that much good was accomplished through these meetings. Invitations are already coming in for similar meetings to be held in other northern centers of colored population.

NATIONAL HEALTH WEEK. I will tax your patience with only one other illustration of work done away from the grounds of the school. It is a well known fact that the death rate among colored people and proportion of sickness is entirely too high, the death rate in one year reaching as high as 30 per 1,000 of the Negro population. In order to bring about better health conditions, we assisted the Hampton Institute in promoting a National Health Week with a view of reaching a large proportion of the ten million colored people. An appropriation of $500 was secured from the Phelps Stokes Fund, to cover stationery, printing, postage, etc. We were able to use our Extension machinery in interesting nearly every important organization among the Negro people in this Health movement.

The especial matters emphasized in connection with this National Negro Health Movement were the following: The organization of clean-up committees, special health sermons by colored ministers, health lectures by physicians and other competent persons, the thorough cleaning of premises, including dwellings, yards, outbuildings, and making sanitary springs and wells. Everywhere the colored people responded most heartily to the appeal to join in this movement to improve their health condition.

I am also pleased to report that throughout the country, and especially in the South, this Health Week movement received the cordial and active co-operation of the white people. State and City Boards of Health, state departments of education, county superintendents of schools, white women's clubs, and other organizations assisted in making this movement for improving the health condition of the colored people a great success. I give one or two examples of what was actually done.

At Atlanta, Georgia, the observance of Health Week was under the auspices of the Young Men's Christian Association and the Colored Board of Trade. A mammoth mass meeting was held on Sunday afternoon, March 21, at the Colored Odd Fellows' Auditorium. Dr. Claude Smith of the Anti-Tuberculosis League, and Dr. Thomas H. Slater, a well-known colored physician, were among those who spoke at this meeting. During the day the ministers in the several churches preached health sermons. On Tuesday, March 23d, all the children in the colored schools were, at the order of the Superintendent of Schools, assembled in the colored churches nearest to their respective schools where they listened to talks on health subjects.

Also, among the notable meetings held during Health Week was the Public Health Conference of the colored people of Maryland. This conference was under the auspices of the Medical and Chirurgical Faculty of Maryland, the Colored State Medical, Pharmaceutical and Dental Association, representing white and colored citizens of Baltimore and the state. In connection with the conference a health exhibit was prepared, and each evening moving pictures showing conditions that are disease-breeding as well as those that make for health were exhibited. This conference had for its special purpose the arousing of the colored people of Maryland to make a persistent fight against tuberculosis and, also, to call to the attention of the public how little provision is at present made by the State for Negro tubercular patients.

ROSENWALD SCHOOLHOUSES. Through our Extension Department we have been aiding this year, as last year, in building rural schools, the arrangement being that the people shall, themselves, give a certain amount of money, in some cases the state and county, etc. In this way 90 schools have been started or completed, and through the generosity of Mr. Rosenwald, an additional helper has been provided for, so that we hope during this year to build and equip at least 100 rural schoolhouses throughout the South by October 1st.

I would also like to call to the attention of the Board another recent act of generosity on the part of Mr. Rosenwald, a member of our Board, and Mrs. Rosenwald. In celebrating the twenty-fifth anniversary of their marriage, they distributed five thousand dollars among the teachers of the Tuskegee Normal and Industrial Institute, Alabama, on the basis of faithfulness, length of service, etc., with fifteen years of service as the minimum limit. This is probably the first instance in the history of the country where any such sum of money has been distributed among teachers in white or colored schools in recognition of long and faithful service. A warm and cordial letter of appreciation was sent to each of the teachers so recognized, concluding with these words: "Tuskegee can only continue to prosper and grow and prove an effective influence for usefulness to the nation and to the Negro race as the workers are earnest, sincere and sympathetic; and I am sure you will in the future, as in the past, do your part to strengthen and uphold the hands of those charged with the responsibility of carrying on the work." This thoughtful recognition will help and inspire our teachers to better service. It was interesting to note that the teachers who were not entitled to any portion of the money seemed to be equally as happy over the good fortune of their fellow teachers.

ELECTION OF NEW TRUSTEES. I wish in this formal way to call attention to the election last year as new members of the Board of Trustees of Hon. George McAneny, President of the Board of Aldermen of the City of New York, Mr. Edgar A. Bancroft,[17] General Counsel of the International Harvester Company, Chicago, and Dr. Alexander Mann,[18] Rector of Trinity Church, Boston. The sympathetic help of these distinguished gentlemen will count for much, I am sure, in connection with the work of our school.

NEW CENTRAL HEATING PLANT. I must not close this report without some particular reference to the central heating plant. This is the largest and most important single piece of work ever done on our school grounds, and it is well on the way toward completion. The plant includes, as you know, power distribution, rewiring of buildings, building for new power plant; boilers, chimney, engines, generators, electric wiring, transformers, power piping and steam conduits; sewerage system and disposal plant; ice plant; cold storage plant; railroad extension; engineering and superintendence.

Through the kind arrangement of Mr. Frank Trumbull, a member of our Board of Trustees, Mr. A. L. Humphrey,[19] Vice-President of the Westinghouse Air Brake Company, Pittsburg, and the Chief Engineer of the Westinghouse plant, Mr. W. V. Turner,[20] visited Tuskegee Institute for the purpose of inspecting and reporting on the steam plant. By inducing Mr. Humphrey to make this inspection, Mr. Trumbull has rendered a service to the school that has a most far reaching value. Not only are we indebted to Mr. Humphrey for what he has done, but I am sure the Trustees will want to express their gratitude to him for his generous offer to visit the school once or twice a year without expense to us, for the purpose of inspecting the plant. Their visit was altogether helpful to us, and their report will probably be communicated to you in another way. I very much wish that the Trustees might take the time to hear Mr. Humphrey's report read in full.

I call attention to the importance of making provision, while we are engaged in this kind of work, for completing the cold storage plant and the sewerage system.

During the greater part of the present school year we have been engaged in shifting from the old system to the new, so that we have not experienced the benefits that are to come in reduced operating expenses, I am sure, when the system is completed. In fact, for this year the rather upset condition has added to our expenses.

We will doubtless have, when completed, one of the most up-to-date steam heating and power plants in this part of the country.

The Trustees, I think, will be interested to know to what extent our students have taken part in the construction of the new power plant. In a report from Mr. R. R. Taylor, Director of Mechanical Industries, he advises me that they have assisted in connection with the following:

The galvanized iron work which includes skylights, down spouts and the tar and gravel roofing was done by the Tinsmithing Division. The ornamental iron work which includes the iron stairs, iron platforms, etc., has been done by the Machine Division. All the cast iron manhole covers and frames were made by the Foundry Division. All the forging for the wrought iron rollers and other blacksmithing has been done by the Blacksmithing Division. The machine work on the wrought iron rollers, cast iron manhole covers and other such machine work has been done by the Machine Shop Division. All of the electrical wiring inside of the building and the lines extending over the school grounds has been done by the Electrical Division. A large part of the carpentry work was done by students and former students of the school. Mr. Jailous Perdue,[21] who is one of our instructors in Carpentry, was the foreman in charge of the work. With some exceptions nearly all the brick work was done by our students and former students.

It is important that the Trustees keep in mind that the opening of the Warrior River in Alabama to navigation gives added value to our 20,000 acres of mineral land, a large proportion of which either borders on the Warrior River or is in that vicinity. This improvement of the Warrior River makes it possible to transport coal to the Gulf at a very cheap rate. This fact will bring our coal lands in demand, and makes it doubly important that we be continually on the lookout to see to it that we do not lose any of these lands by reason of squatters, and that they are protected from depredation of every character. Several inquiries concerning the price of these lands have recently been made.

(Mr. Gilreath's report)[22]

WESTERN CAMPAIGN. Early in the fall we had a series of meetings in California, in southern California particularly, at which a group of Tuskegee singers appeared. I am pleased to say that, while perhaps no great sum of money was secured, the singers nearly covered their expenses; but what is more important they have called the work of the school to the attention of a particularly fine group of people. Everywhere they were received most warmly, and the expressions of appreciation which have come to the Principal of the Institute indicate that their presentation of the work of the school has been cordially appreciated.

A friend has provided the money with which to build and equip a Veterinary Hospital. Five thousand dollars will be spent in connection with this new building, the plans of which were approved at the midwinter meeting of the Board last February. This hospital is now rapidly being constructed by student labor.

I am pleased to call attention to the fact that Messrs. C. B. Cottrell & Sons Company, Westerly, R.I., and Chicago, Illinois, through the kindly good offices of Mr. Rosenwald, have donated to the school one of their No. 3, Four Roller Revolution Printing Presses, thereby balancing the printing plant in a most satisfactory way.

I am convinced that the time has arrived when we must give closer and more systematic attention to the condition and needs of the smaller schools that have either grown out of the Tuskegee Institute, or are doing similar work. I refer especially to such schools as the Snow Hill Institute, the Utica Normal and Industrial Institute, the Voorhees Normal and Industrial School, and other Tuskegee off-shoot schools. Most of these institutions have had a very hard time during the past year. Through the generosity of one of our Trustees, we are to be permitted during the following year to arrange for visits in groups of two and three of our faculty to the various offshoot schools of Tuskegee Institute, the purpose being in each case to inspect the work of these smaller schools in every way possible, and to make reports, with recommendations, as to how the efficiency of such schools may be increased. Three such visits have been made during the year now ending, to the Snow Hill Normal and Industrial Institute at Snow Hill, Alabama; the Utica Normal and Industrial Institute, at Utica, Mississippi; and the Mt. Meigs Industrial School at Mt. Meigs, Alabama. The principals of these schools have expressed most warmly their appreciation of the help which these visits on the part of our teachers have given them. The total cost of the visits to be made next year will amount to practically $1500 and, as above stated, the money is to be provided by one of our Trustees.

At the February meeting of the Trustees, Mr. Trumbull and others suggested that it would be a wise thing for us to publish a circular showing just how a hundred or more of our graduates located in different parts of the country are using their education. We are now engaged in making an investigation and hope with this in view to publish such a circular early in the fall.

In the inaugural address, as the new president of Tufts College, a few days ago, Dr. H. C. Bumpus[23] made a suggestion which I want to ask the Trustees to permit me to put into practice at Tuskegee. The suggestion was to the effect that in most of our colleges and universities there is too great a gap between the teaching body and the board of trustees — that something ought to be done to bring about a little more human touch between the board of trustees and the teaching body.

At the Tuskegee Institute, as in most institutions, the teachers can bring their work, as a rule, before the trustees only through the Principal. Providing a way by which the teachers can put the work of their departments directly before the Trustees, in my opinion, will enlighten the Trustees and deepen their interest, and at the same time encourage and help the teachers. My suggestion is that beginning with the coming midwinter meeting of the Trustees, in February, we permit one or more Heads of Departments to come directly before the Trustees and state the condition of his department, and that other Heads of Departments be heard at successive midwinter meetings of the Board.

Since my last report we have experienced the most disastrous fire in the history of the school. The burning of a portion of our horse barn caused a money loss of $11,432.92 including damage to building, harness, and the loss of 26 animals. We have received from insurance on the building and animals $6,312.52, leaving the net loss $5,120.40. We have not attempted to replace these buildings in any permanent way, because it is thought well to bring the whole question of a new dairy and horse barn as well as new location before the Trustees for consideration and action. The present buildings are unsuited for their purpose, and besides the location is such as to detract from the appearance of the Hospital and endangers its safety. Besides this, also, the flies and odors from the barns affect and neutralize the usefulness of the Hospital.

THE BALDWIN FARMS COLONY. Persons often inquire as to what extent our graduates and former students become actual and practical farmers. I am glad to say that an increasing number are becoming farmers. Especially is this true in the counties near the institution. One element that has hindered a larger number of our students from becoming farmers is that it requires considerable capital after graduating for them to get hold of land, implements, animals and food upon which to live while their crop is being raised and the farm paid for.

In order to overcome this difficulty to some extent and at the same time show what our students can do in the use of their farming knowledge, some months ago Mr. William G. Willcox, one of our Trustees, and a number of other friends purchased 1800 acres of land, about nine miles from the institution located on the Western Railroad of Alabama. A selected number of our graduates and former students have been given an opportunity to purchase farms in tracts averaging 40 acres of land, and have been given a long period in which to pay for the land and the improvements. I am glad to say that the scheme has started out in the most encouraging way. Already some 40 people representing nine families have actually settled on this tract of land and are purchasing their farms. These farms have been inspected several times this year, and on the whole they present an encouraging condition. We already have applications from a number of other persons who want to settle on the land during the coming year and the outlook is that all the land available will be taken up within a few months.

It may interest the Trustees further to know that the Western Railroad of Alabama, on whose line this farm colony is located, has recently built a neat attractive railroad station at a cost of $3,000. One of our graduates is in charge of the station as ticket and freight agent. The colony has been named Baldwin Farms in memory of the late Mr. William H. Baldwin, Jr., of New York City, who was for so long a time devoted to the best interests of the Tuskegee Institute.

FINANCIAL. I now briefly refer to our financial condition, complete details of which are shown in our Treasurer's report.

The Trustees allowed a budget for the year for current expenses and improvements amounting to $288,303.51. I regret to state that we have overspent the budget for current expenses, but am glad to say that we have underspent the budget for improvements, so that the net over-expenditure in these two accounts amounts to $7,452.22.

This over-expenditure came about not through carelessness, but owing largely to the fact that a large proportion of our industrial and extension operations are of such a nature as to prevent our making a definite estimate of their cost. This is especially true of our farming operations. Then, too, this year in addition to the loss sustained in this department by the fire at the barn, we have suffered loss because of disease among our dairy herd and swine.

As of May 31st, we have received from all sources for current expenses $268,825.17; for buildings and improvements $28,919.47; for endowment $28,102.09; from undesignated legacies, $53,858.10, making the total receipts for the purposes named for the year $379,704.83.

Taking for granted that the Trustees will use the $40,773.07 now in the undesignated legacy account in reducing our obligations, the net indebtedness, including what was brought over from last June, is $137,140.21. About one half of this is on account of the construction of the new heating plant. This takes no account of recent gifts and unpaid pledges received during the month of June. When the Trustees met in February, the amount necessary to meet the debt on the heating plant and to pay for its completion was $97,520. Since the February meeting, including what has been received in gifts and pledges during June, we have secured in gifts and pledges toward the amount needed, $[blank].[24] $27,000 of this amount, however, is conditional upon our getting the whole amount needed, and $10,000 more on condition that all is got by July 1st. There remain to be secured to obtain these pledges and clear up the cost of the heating plant, $[blank].

If we clear off the indebtedness on the heating plant, the school will be free from debt except for about $77,000, all of which is due the Investment Committee and little or nothing to outsiders. In view of this condition, I strongly recommend that our efforts for the coming year be mainly in two directions, namely, the securing of money for current expenses, and getting the $[blank] due the Investment Committee.

The gifts to the Endowment Fund for the year amounting to $28,102.09 now make the fund stand at $1,970,214.17.

The budget recommended for your consideration for the new year calls for an expenditure for current expenses, repairs, renewals, and equipment of $291,567.92. Toward this we have the interest from our endowment and from other assured sources, including the $50,000 five year guarantee fund which expires next year, of $186,500, leaving $105,067.92 to be secured from other sources. This means that our present endowment ought to be greatly increased or a larger income assured from some source. It is not possible to describe in words what a relief and help this $50,000 guarantee fund has proven during the four years it has been in operation.

The Trustees will note that while the amount of money secured for current expenses, etc., this year is larger than it was a year ago, we should not overlook the fact that it has cost more per dollar to get this money than it did last year. I would especially call the attention of the Trustees to the generous action of the General Education Board in increasing its appropriation this year from ten thousand dollars to twenty thousand dollars.

Notwithstanding the depressed financial condition of a large part of the country, I feel it would be a great mistake for us in any degree to slacken our efforts to keep the school before the public or to get funds. I believe, as Dr. H. B. Frissell, Principal of the Hampton Institute, has often expressed it, that a large part of the mission of both Hampton and Tuskegee is to keep the cause of Negro education before the country, and that the benefits coming from such efforts of publicity do not confine themselves alone to Hampton and Tuskegee, but benefit all the schools in the South. With this end in view, I very much hope that the Trustees may see their way clear to encourage and help us as far as possible in holding a number of large public meetings during the coming year.

I think it worth while mentioning that one of the hardest tasks that have to be performed is to secure new donors to take the place of those who for one reason or another, from year to year drop out. Efforts are continually being exerted in this direction. By hard and persistent effort this year, I am glad to say that we have succeeded in securing a larger number of individual new donors than has been true for the same period, perhaps, in the history of the school. These donations as a rule have been small, but they nevertheless represent a growing interest in our work.

In this connection, also, I would call attention to the fact that next year will be the end of the period of five years for which a number of our Trustees and friends made a definite promise to give a certain sum of money each year on the five year guarantee plan. We shall have to begin now to consider some method of replacing these donations. The relief which has come to us because of this guarantee fund has been most marked and far reaching.

Some of our present and most urgent needs are the following:

1. $50 a year for annual scholarships for tuition for one student, the student himself providing for his own board and other personal expenses in labor and cash.
2. $1,200 for permanent scholarships.
3. Money for operating expenses in any amounts, however small.
4. $2,000 each for four teachers' cottages.
5. $40,000 for a building for religious purposes.
6. $16,000 to complete the Boys' Trades Building.
7. $50,000 for a boys' Dormitory.
8. $50,000 for a Girls' Dormitory.
9. An addition to our Endowment Fund of at least $3,000,000.

SPECIAL NEEDS

Our needs are so many and varied it is difficult to single out any special ones, but our daily experience and observation convince us that the effectiveness of our work would be many times increased if we could secure the funds for a much needed new dormitory for boys to cost about $50,000, and Horse and Cow Barns, Silos, Piggery House, Feed and Supply House including Mill Room, Poultry Houses, Meat House, the whole to cost about $90,000.

I wish to again thank the Trustees for their constant help and encouragement. Respectfully submitted,

[Booker T. Washington]

TMdc Con. 80 BTW Papers DLC. A printed version, with many of the sections rearranged and with some minor changes of wording and substance, is in the Albert Shaw Papers, NN.

[1] Robert John Henderson De Loach (b. 1873), a botanist, was director of the Georgia Experiment Station 1913–17.

[2] James Jarvis Doster (b. 1873) was a professor of education.

[3] William Lee Kennon (1882–1952), professor of physics and astronomy (1909–52).

[4] Josiah Morse (b. 1879) was a psychologist.

[5] James Dickason Hoskins (b. 1870), a teacher of mathematics, history, economics, and other subjects at various times in his career, became a dean at the University of Tennessee in 1911.

[6] William Oscar Scroggs (b. 1879) was an economist.

[7] James Carleton Bell (b. 1872) was a psychologist.

[8] William Muse Hunley, a political scientist, taught at the University of Virginia (1914–15) and at Virginia Military Institute (1915–49).

[9] Jane Addams (1860–1935) founded, with Ellen Gates Starr, the social settlement Hull House in Chicago in 1889 and was its head resident for the remainder of her life. She was the acknowledged leader of settlement work in the United States, and was active also in welfare, civil rights, women's, peace, and progressive political movements. In 1909 she signed the call for the conference that formed the NAACP, and served on its first executive committee.

[10] Edward Osgood Brown (b. 1847).

[11] Merritt Willis Pinckney (b. 1859).

[12] George Albert Carpenter (b. 1867).

[13] Terry T. Greil, manager of Greil Bros. Co., a wholesale grocery, drug, and liquor business.

[14] James Steptoe Pinckard (1859–1926), a lawyer in Montgomery, Ala.

[15] Luther Egbert Hall.

[16] Joseph Marr Gwinn, born in 1870 in Warrensburg, Mo., was professor of education at Tulane University (1907–10), superintendent of schools of New Orleans (1910–23), superintendent of schools of San Francisco (1923–33), and professor of education at San Jose State College (1936–40).

[17] Edgar Addison Bancroft (1857–1925), a prominent Chicago corporation lawyer, was general counsel of the International Harvester Co. from 1907 to 1920.

[18] Alexander Mann (1860–1948) was rector of Trinity Episcopal Church in Boston from 1905 to 1923.

[19] Arthur Luther Humphrey (1860–1939) became vice-president of Westinghouse Air Brake Co. in 1910 and president in 1919.

[20] Walter Victor Turner (1866–1919) was an English-born engineer and inventor.

[21] Jailous Perdue became a member of the department of mechanical industries at Tuskegee Institute in 1910–11.

[22] The trustee Belton Gilreath possibly supplied the information in the preceding paragraph.

[23] Herman Carey Bumpus (1862–1943), a biologist and authority on museums, was president of Tufts College from 1914 to 1919.

[24] The amount is left blank here and in two other places in this draft. The financial statement in the printed version of the principal's report differs from the draft version in omitting reference to any funds received after May 31.

To Alfred Tredway White[1]

[Tuskegee, Ala.] June 1, 1915

My dear Mr. White: I am replying to yours of May 25th regarding the Association of Negro Industrial and Secondary Schools. This is for your personal information.

I have known about this organization from its beginning.

In the first place, I think it very unfortunate that good earnest and sympathetic men like Mr. Kelsey and Mr. Villard do not take pains to get information concerning conditions through people who are actually at work in the South and who have had experience in the South among colored schools.

Three years ago, Mr. Anson Phelps Stokes, the Secretary of Yale University, asked Dr. Frissell how in our opinion some of the interests of the Phelps-Stokes Fund could be used in helping out conditions in the South and we advised, among other things, that the Trustees devote a part of their money to an examination of all the schools in the South, with a view of classifying them and getting accurate information regarding them. Mr. Stokes and the Trustees followed our advice and the result is that during the last two years a corps of investigators, under Dr. Thomas Jesse Jones, have been at work at an expense of

One Thousand Dollars ($1,000.00) per month visiting and investigating practically every school in the South of any size. In a few months, their report will be completed and a portion of it will be published. It is the further intention of the Stokes Trustees, after the report has been completed, to set up some kind of headquarters that will be the means through which information regarding schools in the South can be obtained.

When Mr. Villard and others asked me to join in this new movement, I objected on the ground that here was an organization that had the money already to do this work without saddling on the public another paid official and more office expenses, but Mr. Villard and Mr. Kelsey did not seem to agree with me and went ahead and formed another organization.

This organization may accomplish some good, but I doubt it. In the first place, it is largely a paper organization. Within the last few days, I have spoken to the heads of schools whose names they are using and in each case I was told by the Head that they did not know they were members of this organization. In the matter sent you, they use the name of the Virginia Union University. This is an old college, founded, supported and controlled by the Baptists and this Association of Negro Industrial and Secondary Schools could not exert the slightest control or influence over this institution. The same is true of the half dozen other schools named. I do not believe that in a single case the Heads of these schools would be willing to turn over the collecting of money to Mr. Burnet and if they do not, the result will be that the public will have Mr. Burnet's expenses to bear and also will have to support his office. I do not know who Mr. Burnet is. I have never heard of him in connection with Negro education. Certainly he would have to first himself get acquainted with Southern education.

Several of the schools mentioned are totally unworthy, as Dr. Jones' report shows. I do not see how any effective work in the direction you have had in mind can be done by a mere paper organization of this kind. If you can spare the time, when I see you again, I will give you more details about this. I am returning the correspondence.

I am glad to say that we are making some progress in the direction of getting the money to pay for our permanent improvement. When I come North again, I shall hope to have something encouraging to report, but in the meantime we are going forward in reducing the amount needed. Yours very truly,

Booker T. Washington

TLpS Con. 97 (new series) BTW Papers DLC.

¹ Alfred Tredway White (1846–1921) was a Wall Street merchant with the firm of W. A. and A. M. White. He was a leader in the movement for improved housing for workers and wrote several books on the subject. Beginning in 1868 he was director of the Brooklyn Children's Aid Society, and was active throughout his lifetime in other charitable and philanthropic organizations in New York City.

To the New York *World*

Tuskegee, June 1, 1915

Germany's reply to President Wilson's note was a great disappointment to me. At a time of world wide horror because of the Lusitania tragedy, I had felt that the mature deliberation of cooler heads in Germany would have brought forth an expression of deep regret for the loss of American lives and emphatic assurance of the safety of non-combatants traveling on the high seas. The very fact that her attitude of evasion might be mistaken for an attitude of defiance is all the more cause, I am sure, for disappointment to the American people. As yet I am unwilling to believe that Germany is anxious to disrupt past friendly relationships with America. I think however nothing would be lost by giving to Germany whatever direct information we have on the points she has raised. I trust that a sentiment of cool headed self-possession shall prevail in our country during these days of anxious thought on the part of the President of the United States.

Booker T. Washington

TWSr Con. 946 BTW Papers DLC.

To George Eastman

[Tuskegee, Ala.] June 2, 1915

Dear Mr. Eastman: Fulfilling my promise, I am sending you by this mail a blue print indicating the character of the one-teacher rural school building that we are erecting in Alabama and in some other Southern states largely through the generosity of Mr. Julius Rosenwald. We have had to make these plans according to the direction of the state authorities. If it had been left to my own personal judgment, I should have left out a lot of the "frills" that in my opinion make the matter more complicated. We have been able to put up a building of this kind for Eight Hundred Dollars ($800.00), Mr. Rosenwald supplying $300, and the people and the County authorities supplying the remaining portion. In a good many cases, a good deal has been contributed in the form of labor and material. I found it of great advantage to let the people do all the work in the community that they can. It stimulates their pride in the building, as well as teaches them a useful lesson.

I have spoken to the man in charge of admitting our students and told him to admit the young colored man, about whom you talked to me, in case you decide to send him here to take a course in farming.

Thanking you again for all your deep interest in our work, I am

Yours very truly,

Booker T. Washington

P.S. — Of course if I can be of further service to you in regard to the school building, I hope you will let me know.

TLpS Con. 780 BTW Papers DLC.

To William Hale Thompson[1]

[Tuskegee, Ala.] June 3, 1915

My dear Sir: Permit me to thank you most heartily for the action which you have taken in regard to the appearance of "The Birth of the Nation" in the city of Chicago. I feel quite sure that your action in this respect will meet the approval of the majority of our best people of both races throughout the country.

I have studied and watched the influence of "The Birth of the Nation" very carefully ever since it was first put on exhibition and the result seems to be, almost without exception, that it intensifies racial prejudice, and besides misrepresents historical facts.

Again let me thank you most heartily for what you have done. Yours very truly,

Booker T. Washington

TLpS Con. 80 BTW Papers DLC.

¹ William Hale Thompson (1869–1944), a Republican, was twice mayor of Chicago (1915–23 and 1927–31).

To Charles Jackson Ryder

[Tuskegee, Ala.] June 5, 1915

Personal and Confidential.

Dear Dr. Ryder: A bill has been introduced into the Legislature of Alabama which has for its object the preventing of white people from teaching in any of the schools controlled or supported by the state. There is no public sentiment in favor of such a bill seemingly. A number of us think it important that this bill be smothered and permitted to go no further. If it comes before the Legislature, it may be amended so as to include all kinds of schools. The danger grows out of the fact that it is the kind of measure that people who are really opposed to it would vote for because of fear, so our only safety is to kill the bill before it goes further. It seems that the man who introduced the bill did so for the purpose of preventing a Southern white woman, who has been teaching a colored public school in his own county for a number of years, from teaching. It seems that he has a personal grudge against her.

A number of us have talked the matter over and we think it wise to concentrate on a movement in the direction of killing the bill, and if you are willing to trust the matter to my judgment, I feel quite sure that the bill can be killed. In order to do so, it will be necessary to expend some money for a lawyer. I cannot say just now how much the amount will be, but it will not be a great deal, I am sure, unless the bill should get in the open House. I am wondering if your organization[1] would feel like paying your share of the assessment.

Above all things, I urge that the thing not get into the newspapers and that too many people do not begin working for its defeat. Yours very truly,

Booker T. Washington

TLpS Con. 538 BTW Papers DLC.

[1] The American Missionary Association.

To Ernest Davidson Washington

[Tuskegee, Ala.] June 5, 1915

My dear Davidson: I cannot insist too strongly upon your being very careful in regard to your health while you are doing this work. Do not run about too rapidly in the sun. Do not expose yourself too much to the hot sun. Do your work quietly. Be sure to get a good place to sleep every night where you will get plenty of fresh air. Do not sleep in a crowded room. Get plenty of good food and take plenty of time to eat it.

Your reports are very encouraging.

Your Papa,
B. T. W.

TLI Con. 655 BTW Papers DLC.

To William Colfax Graves

Tuskegee Institute, Alabama   June 16th, 1915

Dear Mr. Graves: I have made note on my return to Tuskegee of the various clippings you have sent me from Chicago papers, editorials and news items, bearing on The Birth of the Nation.

I am very sorry that this objectionable film is to be shown in Chicago. I feel quite sure that no particular good will be accomplished by it. Yours very truly,

[Booker T. Washington]

TLd   Con. 78   BTW Papers   DLC.

From Herbert Croly[1]

New York City   June 18th, 1915

Dear Mr. Washington: I have in my office an article written by Mr. Louis B. Wehle,[2] of Louisville, Kentucky, in which he discusses the question of negro segregation in the Southern cities in a dispassionate way, but with a tendency to favoring segregation. I am loath to publish such a paper without running at the same time an article which looks in another direction. If I send you Mr. Wehle's manuscript would you consider writing such an article for us?[3] Sincerely yours,

Herbert Croly

TLS   Con. 529   BTW Papers   DLC.

[1] Herbert Croly (1869–1930), a journalist and political philosopher, was founder and editor of *The New Republic* (1914–30).

[2] Louis Brandeis Wehle (1880–1959), a nephew of Justice Louis D. Brandeis, graduated from Harvard in 1902 and from Harvard Law School in 1904. He practiced law in Louisville (1904–17) before moving to Washington and New York. He served the Wilson administration in several posts, and was a close friend of Franklin D. Roosevelt.

[3] See An Article in *The New Republic*, Sept. 13, 1915, below.

An Account of Washington's Louisiana Tour
by William Anthony Aery

June 19, 1915

LOOSENING UP
LOUISIANA

The story of a missionary
junket carrying the gospel
of co-operation, educa-
tional and economic, to
black folk and white

Georgia now stands alone. This spring, for the first time, a group of Negro leaders, under the head of Booker T. Washington, accomplished an "educational tour" through the black parishes of Louisiana.

The general feeling had been that public opinion in neither Louisiana nor Georgia had reached the stage for the mass meetings and the general gospel of co-operation, educational and economic, which characterize these missionary junkets out from Tuskegee and Hampton. But on the invitation of not only representative Negro citizens, but of the governor of Louisiana and mayors of several cities, the venture was made; and for the first time in their lives hundreds of white men and women listened to Negro speakers.

Mr. Washington confessed that he and his party of twenty-five colored men, when they started on their pilgrimage, had something of the feeling of the little girl whose family were going on a trip. The night before she prayed as usual:

> "Now I lay me down to sleep
> I pray the Lord my soul to keep.
> If I should die before I wake,
> I pray the Lord my soul to take."

Then she added, "Good-bye, Lord, for two weeks. We are going down to Louisiana."

Great outdoor audiences of thousands upon thousands, however, white and colored, all friendly, prosperous and orderly, convinced Mr. Washington and his associates that the Negro in Louisiana is making progress in the essential things of life and that sympathetic contact of the races in Louisiana is more widespread, if less widely reported, than the spirit of modern violence or racial antagonism.

In this tour of the state these objects were kept in view: (1) to observe conditions among Negroes; (2) to say a word to promote greater progress among Negroes; (3) to bring about, if possible, more helpful and sensible relations between white and black.

Within four days, Mr. Washington spoke to over 50,000 of his own people, and hundreds of interested white men and women listened eagerly to his helpful message of progress and co-operation.

Meetings were held in New Orleans, St. Bernard Parish, New Iberia, Crowley, Lake Charles, Lafayette, Southern University, Baton Rouge, Alexandria, Gibsland, Shreveport, and Mansfield. Everywhere Mr. Washington and his party were met at railroad stations by crowds of black people; other crowds of white citizens gathered to see him and to hear him expound his gospel of industrial opportunity and racial good-will.

Negroes came on mule back, in carriages, and in wagons, long distances — ten, twenty, thirty, and even forty miles. They gathered in thousands at railway stations to see the "wizard of Tuskegee." They stood for hours to get a chance to hear the most distinguished member of their race tell them of progress and of the opportunities in the Southland. There were literally miles of people and vehicles. Good-natured policemen were sometimes nearly carried off their feet in the effort to keep a path open through the eager throngs, but there was no trace of disorder. Everyone was happy, sober, receptive.

Equally encouraging was the attitude of white people — men and women of distinction in southern life. Mayor Behrman of New Orleans said to Mr. Washington: "The work you are doing for the uplift of your people means untold good to the great state of Louisiana and to the whole country. Nowhere has your race greater opportunities than in Louisiana. If the people of the Negro race will follow your teachings, they will help materially to bring about a condition that will mean much for Louisiana, the South and the nation."

N. C. Blanchard of Shreveport, an ex-governor of Louisiana, said in introducing Mr. Washington to an audience of over 10,000 white and colored citizens: "I am glad to see this goodly attendance of white people, representative white people at that; for his honor, the mayor, is here, and with him are members and officials of the city government and other prominent citizens of our community. They are here to give encouragement to Mr. Washington, to hold up his hands, for they know that he is leading his people along right lines — lines tending to promote better feeling and better understanding between the two races. . . .

"Our country needs to have white and black people, sober, honest, frugal and thrifty. Booker T. Washington stands for these things. He advises and counsels and leads toward these goals. Hear him and heed his words."

At Violet, a country settlement about eleven miles from New Orleans, visited at the invitation of leading officials, representative men of both races sat patiently in the hot sun on the temporary platform listening to Mr. Washington's message given to the white men concerning his race's need of the best possible education in scientific farming, etc.

At the invitation of Superintendent Gwinn, the school children of New Orleans were given a half-holiday to hear Mr. Washington, and the Dauphine Theater (seating 3,000) was lent by its white owner to the colored committee for the meeting which Mr. Washington addressed.

Fully 3,000 people assembled at Cape Charles, many of them northerners who have made their homes in the rich South.

At Baton Rouge, Mayor Grouchy said: "Nowhere else in Louisiana are the Negroes more respected than in Baton Rouge. Here they are law-abiding and honorable. Religious and civic institutions take a deep interest in their welfare and a civic league for Negroes has been organized."

Especially noteworthy was Mr. Washington's reception at schools.

Six miles out from Baton Rouge, the state of Louisiana is building for Negro youth a well-planned, well-equipped, and well-manned school which gives promise of training useful, level-headed leaders. Here at Southern University, Mr. Washington was received amid vigorous cheering by a happy lot of colored boys and girls who showed that under the direction of President J. S. Clark, they were being educated to be happy as well as useful, self-active and not repressed.

D. B. Showalter, superintendent of schools in Rapides parish since 1908, referred to Mr. Washington as "the Negro who is doing more to dignify labor among his own people than anybody else in the United States."

Coleman College at Gibsland, La., represents the earnest work of a black man, who, with few words and no false promises, has built up in the open country an institution which is useful, sane and attractive.

"The appearance of Mr. Washington," said Mayor W. H. Lazarus, "is especially appreciated by the white and colored people of Gibsland, because of President Coleman, who is making a complete success of his educational work. There has never been any race trouble since Coleman came to this community. Coleman is to us all a guarantee of peace between the two races. Coleman has taken raw, gawky, unpromising country boys and made men of them."

T. W. Oxford, superintendent of Arcadia Schools, approved the policy of promoting industrial education for the masses of the colored people. He referred to the fine work that has been done by Prof. R. U. Clark, a colored man working for the Jeanes Fund, in building comfortable school buildings, introducing industrial work, and securing the active co-operation and hearty good-will of the Parish School Board.

A representative of the Crowley City Council said frankly that he advocated the idea of educating Negroes rather than supporting Negro criminals.

Everywhere along the line of this triumphal march found the Negro population making progress, wearing good clothes, enjoying good health and leading sober lives. Mayor Behrman of New Orleans paid tribute to the share which Negroes had taken in the fight for better health in that city: "We have been fighting a great many battles in this community, battles against disease and pestilence; and I want to say that the colored people of New Orleans have lent every bit of assistance they could in this work."

Dr. G. C. Chandler, of the Shreveport Board of Health, referred with gratitude to the national movement for the improvement of Negro health, which Mr. Washington, acting for the National Negro Business League, has been promoting.[1]

---

[1] The national health movement is the outgrowth of the health work developed by the Negro Organization Society of Virginia under the leadership of Robert R. Moton, John M. Gandy, A. A. Graham, and other hard-working colored men and women.

C. E. Byrd, superintendent of schools, declared that the colored people as he knew them, have shown rare devotion to their children, civic righteousness and industrial economy. "Their cleanliness," he said, "is worthy of commendation."

In several cities substantial portions of the city taxes are paid by Negroes. In Iberia parish they paid the taxes on half a million dollars worth of property; at Crowley, on a total of over $150,000 worth. Apparently, like their white friends, they have not given the commissioner of revenue any excess values on their holdings!

Stories drawn from the every-day life of Louisiana Negroes were effectively told by Mr. Washington. Full of good humor and wisdom, they opened the way for the teaching of important lessons — lessons applicable alike to white and black citizens, but especially useful to Negroes who, while they are making rare progress, must face with determination and courage trying conditions and win for themselves a permanent place in the economic life of the South.

The soil, the rain, and the sun draw no color-line — except that in July and August, when the sun gets really busy, the line is drawn in favor of the Negro.

In the country the black man may enjoy the pleasures of earth. On Sunday morning, for example, he can have fresh eggs, fresh butter, fried chicken, and buttermilk. In the summer, he can have blackberry cobbler. In the winter, he can have sweet potatoes and opossum. Why, then, should the Negro leave the country and yield to the temptation of going to live in the city or the town? Mr. Washington said:

"Be efficient, skilled and reliable in all matters of labor. Put conscience into all your work. Make a good reputation for sobriety, thrift, honesty and righteous living. Get ahead by doing your duty and then doing some more. Put money in the bank or out on mortgage. Have your money work for you twelve hours in the day and twelve hours at night.

"A great many Negroes have all of their land, their livestock, their money — in fact, all their property, in a knapsack. Whenever they move, their knapsack moves with them. Plant yourself in one place and quit living in a knapsack. Stop moving from farm to farm, from county to county, from state to state. Negroes must hold on to their jobs and get property. Otherwise European laborers, who are land-hungry and job-hungry, will soon push them aside. The mere fact that a race controls certain industries or is an important economic factor today is no indication that it will always have the same position.

"Negroes themselves must help to get rid of idlers, gamblers, drunkards, and those who live on the earnings of unfortunate women. They must learn to draw the line hard and fast between the clean and the unclean, the moral and the immoral. The Negro is on trial and is judged not always by the best members of the race but largely by the loafing, idling class.

"Race friction is usually found where there are loafing white men and black men; where bad whiskey is sold and gets into the stomachs of idling black and white men.

"The success of the minister, the doctor, the lawyer and other Negro professional and business men depends finally on the success of the humblest day-laborer.

"The white man has been carrying the Negro on his back for nearly fifty years. He is beginning to get tired. . . .

"Negroes now have draw-day or ration-day once a week or once a month. I want you to have ration-day every day in the year — at home, in your own garden. I want you to draw peas, onions, tomatoes, potatoes, pigs, chickens, and geese, for example, out of your own garden.

"Whenever you come to town bring something in to sell. If you have nothing else, bring half a dozen eggs or a pound of butter. Give your wives more time at home and they will save for you more than you can earn.

"Some Negro farmers want to have their wives with them when the crop is being planted, when the land is being worked, when the harvesting season is at hand — in fact, every day in the year except one — and that is when the crop is sold. Then the Negro farmer says: 'Now, old woman, you stay at home.' "

These quotations show the thoughts which Mr. Washington is constantly offering to Negro men and women. There is also an important message which Mr. Washington gives to Negro boys and girls:

"Ask yourself this question: How can I use at home what I am getting at school? You are being carefully watched by your hard-working parents. Your mother gets up early in the morning, washes and cooks all day, saves all she can, so that you may remain in school. Your father plows day by day and goes without a great many things to give you a chance to get an education. Go back home and give your parents some old-fashioned rest.

"Use your manual arts at home in making repairs and getting rid of such earmarks as the missing fence palings, the gate off the hinge, the loose door-knob, the broken window-pane, and the rotten steps.

"Use your domestic science in better cooking, better dishwashing, better ironing, and better scrubbing. Help put your community on its feet.

"After you receive your education, your conduct will be closely watched by white people and by black people. Remember you are on trial. Education teaches men to love labor. It does not make of a man a dude or a fool. It makes him a useful citizen. Education makes you love the community in which you live. It makes you love your race and honor your father and mother. Education is meant to make a person modest; simple in language, polite; and love God.

"Don't be ashamed to work. With all your education just be an ordinary, useful human being. Be of real service to somebody. Remember that an educated man is simple, honest, humble. Don't advertise your troubles over-much."

Booker T. Washington advises his people not to talk *about* the southern white man but to talk *to* him. Since there is that wonderful, sympathetic contact throughout the South between white men and black men, it is possible for every Negro to have a white friend (indeed, some Negroes keep several white friends for use in troublesome times) to whom he can go and talk very freely.

Mr. Washington himself carries this idea into practice. To several thousand white men and women of Louisiana, he recently brought the following frank and appealing message:

"You have encouraged, advised and aided with your money thousands of Negroes who, during the past fifty years, have bought farms, homes or businesses for themselves. You have been willing to do almost anything for my people — to help pay their debts, to get them out of jail, to go on their bond, to bury their dead, to help them buy homes and farms.

"When, however, you are asked to vote money for Negro education you scratch your heads — scratch them real hard. You have in your mind a vivid picture of a so-called educated Negro that you saw twenty-five or thirty years ago — a Negro who was different from everybody else in the community. This educated Negro wore, perhaps, red socks, a gay necktie, patent-leather shoes, a silk hat, carried a walking stick, smoked a big cigar, and talked a language which nobody else understood — and which he himself did not quite understand.

"Negroes have passed through their 'silly' period. They now know how to use their education. It will pay southern planters to give Negroes good rural schools and good homes. Many good Negro farmers are leaving the plantations and moving into a town to secure better school accommodations for their children. If you will give Negroes training in scientific farming, manual arts, cooking and sewing, you will be well repaid.

"It is better to spend money to educate Negroes than to take care of criminals. Louisiana has done well to put the stamp of her approval on Southern University and to back up this institution with her money.

"You have been so busy educating white boys and girls that you fail to realize that Negro children in many Louisiana parishes receive only three or four months schooling in the year.

"Indeed, 78 per cent of the Negro children of school age in Louisiana did not enter school last year. About $1.60 a year is spent on each Negro child's education in Louisiana. You pay too high a compliment to the intelligence of Negro children. Theoretically, it would take a Negro child about twenty-six years to finish a school education in Louisiana.

"Both races in the South suffer at the hands of public opinion by reason of the fact that the outside world hears of our difficulties, of crimes, mobs and lynchings, but it does not hear of or know about the evidences of racial friendship and good-will which exist in the majority of communities in Louisiana and other southern states where black and white people live together in such large numbers.

"Lynchings are widely reported by telegraph. The quiet, effective work of devoted white people in the South for Negro uplift is not generally or widely reported. The best white citizenship must take charge of the mob and not have the mob take charge of civilization.

"There is enough wisdom, patience, forbearance, and common-sense in the South for white people and black people to live together in peace for all times."

From New Orleans to Mansfield, traveling over a thousand miles by rail and by automobile, Mr. Washington and his educational pilgrims saw clearly: (1) what Negroes are doing for themselves to improve their conditions; (2) what Negroes need to do to make them a permanent force for good; (3) what white people can do to help their colored neighbors to become more important and more useful as an economic factor, and (4) what facts need to be emphasized in telling the Negro's story to the country at large.

The colored men who traveled with Mr. Washington represented organizations, professions, and business interests which must be seriously reckoned with today — and especially tomorrow — in the life of the Negro, in his progress, and in his gradual emancipation from ignorance, lack of skill, indifference, and superstition.

A list of Mr. Washington's party follows:

Emmett J. Scott, secretary of Tuskegee;

R. R. Moton, commandant of cadets at Hampton Institute and president of the Negro Organization Society of Virginia;

W. T. B. Williams, field agent Jeanes Fund and Slater Board;

M. W. Dogan, president Wiley University, Marshall, Texas, and president National Association of Teachers in Colored Schools;

R. E. Jones, editor of *Southwestern Christian Recorder,* New Orleans;

Walter L. Cohen, insurance broker, New Orleans;

The Rev. Alfred Lawless, Jr., superintendent of A.M.A. church work in Mississippi and Louisiana and field agent Straight University, New Orleans;

J. S. Clark, president Southern University, Baton Rouge;

O. L. Coleman, president Coleman College, Gibsland, La.;

J. S. Williams, Shreveport, president Louisiana State Negro Business League;

Clement Richardson, in charge of English department, Tuskegee;

Dr. J. A. Kenney, school physician, Tuskegee, and physician-in-charge at Andrew Memorial Hospital, Tuskegee;

Dr. N. J. Marmilian, Lake Charles, La.;

The Rev. H. H. Dunn, pastor colored Congregational Church, New Orleans;

H. W. Duncan, president Negro Business League, Shreveport;

Horace D. Slatter, newspaper correspondent, Birmingham, Ala.;

R. U. Clark, Jeanes Fund industrial teacher, Crowley, La.;

A. P. Bedou, photographer, New Orleans;

William Houston, druggist, Alexandria, La.;

A. R. Stewart, extension work, Tuskegee;
Nathan Hunt, secretary to Mr. Washington;
B. F. Easter, physician, New Iberia;
H. V. Baranco, Baton Rouge.

The Survey, 34 (June 19, 1915), 266–69.

To William Sidney Pittman

[Tuskegee, Ala.] June 20, 1915

Dear Mr. Pittman — Just as soon as the children reach home, or as soon thereafter as possible, I am quite sure that you ought to have their adenoids out. I do not believe that Booker and Sidney will be well until this is attended to. The longer it is put off the more danger they will be in.

Dr. Roman, I understand, is to be in Dallas in July, and I think he would be a good person to do this. Booker had considerable trouble with his nose for a number of years and was not cured until he was treated by Dr. Roman who did the work very well. I think you had better consider this whole matter very carefully. It ought not be delayed. Please write me what you decide. Yours very truly,

B. T. W.

TLpI   Con. 944   BTW Papers   DLC.

Emmett Jay Scott to Irvine Garland Penn

[Tuskegee, Ala.] June 21, 1915

My dear Dr. Penn: Dr. Washington had a very full, frank and free conference with me yesterday, Sunday, June 20th, at his home, at which time we discussed every possible angle of the suggestion which has come to me with reference to the Presidency of Clark University, Atlanta. You and Dr. Bowen made a profound impression on him and he was good enough to say to me that it would take a man of very great strength to resist accepting such a tentative offer as has been placed before me.[1]

He stated further that it would be a "calamity" from the Tuskegee Institute standpoint for me to leave the school and pointed out to me with particular insistence what he thinks is my duty and responsibility in the matter. He was careful to assure me that he would do nothing whatsoever to interfere with my promotion or with my acceptance of your offer, but he and his wife have taken pains to assure me that the interests of Tuskegee Institute would suffer in a way difficult to be understood by an outsider, if I should think of leaving the school just now.

He also went to the point of saying that he very much hopes that I may be disposed to await our Trustee meeting in New York City, June 30th, before reaching any decision. He is planning to talk the whole matter over with certain controlling members of the Board of Trustees. This means, of course, that such a date as that will be entirely too late for even a tentative decision on your part, so far as I am concerned.

I had quite fully made up my mind to enter the service of the Freedmens Aid Board, provided the opportunity were offered, until this conference with him, which as I have said, had in it all the elements of frankness and particular appreciation of the privileges and the opportunities which are to be and which would be offered under the plans being proposed for the new Clark University.

In obedience to his suggestion, I have agreed to put the matter over until next week and of course you know that I must agree at the same time to leave you free to do whatever in your judgment is wisest and best.

I am most grateful to you, to Dr. Bowen, to Dr. Jones, Bishop Scott and to all interested friends, who have been good enough to indicate their eagerness to have me enter the service of the Society. I can only hope that such friendship as I enjoyed at your hands and at the hands of these other brethren may continue and that opportunity to reciprocate their friendship and their confidence may be offered me from time to time.

With all good wishes, I am   Sincerely yours,

[Emmett J. Scott]

TLc Con. 13   BTW Papers   DLC.

[1] Two years earlier, Penn tentatively offered Scott the presidency of Walden University, including Meharry Medical College, and went to Tuskegee to urge Scott to accept. On that occasion Scott did not inform BTW of the offer until after he had rejected it. (Penn to Scott, June 13, 1913, Con. 15, Scott to Penn, Aug. 2, 1913, Con. 15, Scott to BTW, Sept. 25, 1913, Con. 634, BTW Papers, DLC.)

From Jacob Godfrey Schmidlapp

Cincinnati [Ohio]   June 24, 1915

My Dear Doctor Washington; Upon my return home I find your favor of the 18th, also a letter from our mutual friend, Mr. Rosenwald, under same date, requesting letter of introduction to my friend Mr. Ford.[1]

In this connection I wish to say that Mr. Ford cannot always be approached. I understand that when he is intensely engaged in his laboratory work, he does not allow anyone to see him. However, when I was there last he gave me practically a whole day, and seemed to have nothing whatever on his mind. A friend of mine here visits him almost every week on business, and if you will let me know a few days in advance I could arrange through him perhaps for a meeting.

I was sorry not to have seen you when you passed through Cincinnati, but am glad that some one took you to see our last proposition for the housing of colored people. I am very much interested in experimenting in the co-operative store, and shall give it a fair trial. My belief is that I can save for my tenants about ten percent on their purchases. Very truly yours,

J. G. Schmidlapp

TLS Con. 16 BTW Papers DLC.

[1] Schmidlapp enclosed a letter of introduction to the automobile manufacturer Henry Ford (1863–1947) of the same date, saying that BTW was anxious to meet Ford. He reported that a Cincinnati educator who had visited Tuskegee considered BTW "the greatest teacher in this country, white or black."

Nannie Helen Burroughs to Emmett Jay Scott

Lincoln Heights, Washington, D.C. June 29, 1915

Dear Mr. Scott: I am not going to write a criticism on the circular. The information on "Gains by the Race in Fifteen Years, and the Further Economic Progress" are valuable, but I want to say one or two things to you privately.

I have heard so much about Negro Progress during the past two years that I am inclined to sing, "My soul wants something that's new." I am beginning to think that we brag too much, and a lot of unscrupulous people are given a chance to exploit their wealth at the expense of the race.

The truth of the matter is that while we have made wonderful progress, that most of our enterprises compare poorly with similar enterprises conducted by other people. There is a great deal of inefficiency and slipshodness.

It seems to me that the Business League should depart a little from its usual custom, and instead of taking so much time bragging about what we have, let us set up a standard for the people and show them in this meeting how to come up to it. I think if the League would stress in this meeting the importance of making our stores and other enterprises ideal in their management and appointments, we would accomplish a great deal more.

The League ought to urge our people to have model stores and shops. We do not keep things up to the standard. Few of our business men are really progressive. Shops that are attractive and inviting, attendants that are courteous and business-like are not among our most valuable assets.

Most of our enterprises have written all around and about these words: "Negroes run this shop." Can't you get a few experts to talk to us on, How to Lift the Standard, How to Run Ideal Stores, How to Advertise? O, please let us strike a new note. I am tired of hearing Negro Millionaires tell of their wealth and influence.

Now to the question of economic progress. Please, please, please let us have some talks on "Keeping Up the Farm." I mean the physical appearance, the fences, the barns, the outhouses, the care of machinery, the care of animals and vehicles. I tell you, Mr. Scott, I am so tired of seeing dilapidated, broken-down wagons and neglected fences and barns, that I think it is time somebody should tell us just *what to buy* and *how to take care of it.* I have been thinking that it would be a good idea for the League to offer prizes for the best kept farm of ten acres, twenty acres, fifty acres, one hundred acres. This will have nothing to do with the soil and the growing of crops, but with the general physical surroundings. The Business League ought to be a "School of Methods for Managing Business."

I am trying to so arrange my engagements as to get to Boston to the meeting. I am praying for a successful meeting, and above all, a meeting that shall be most helpful along the lines that we need help most. With best wishes, I am   Yours truly,

Nannie H Burroughs

TLS   Con. 528   BTW Papers   DLC.

To J. D. Murray[1]

[Tuskegee, Ala.] June 29th, 1915

Dear Sir: Your letter of some days ago relating to the protest against exportation of munitions of war by this country received. I have read your letter with a great deal of interest and appreciation. I believe that, in every way, this nation should endeavor to preserve strict neutrality, and that every means that can be legitimately employed should be used to maintain this neutrality.

I am referring the petition of "The Organization of American Women for Strict Neutrality," to our Tuskegee Woman's Club. You should receive a communication from them in due course. Very truly yours,

Booker T. Washington

TLpSr   Con. 533   BTW Papers   DLC.

[1] J. D. Murray was a physician residing in Elkridge, Md. He sent BTW several publications on the question of U.S. neutrality, and wrote: "This country will surely be drawn into this war if this traffic in munitions of war be continued in." Murray said that his family could "claim to be a friend of the colored race in virtue of the act of Daniel Murray my grandfather, who freed his slaves in 1832, which impoverished him." (June 14, 1915, Con. 533, BTW Papers, DLC.)

To Florence E. Sewell Bond[1]

New York City, June 30, 1915

My dear Madam: Replying to yours of June 27th I would state that, we have no idea of permitting any pictures of Tuskegee to be exhibited in connection with The Birth of a Nation. We have been appealed to to make such an exhibit but have refused on the grounds that such an exhibit would be an indirect endorsement of The Birth of a Nation. We consider The Birth of a Nation a thoroughly harmful and vicious play, and want to do everything possible to prevent its being exhibited.

I feel quite sure that you have been misinformed regarding the attitude of Mr. William H. Lewis. He is thoroughly opposed to the play, as I know.

I thank you for writing me. Yours very truly,

[Booker T. Washington]

TLc Con. 75 BTW Papers DLC.

[1] Florence E. Sewell Bond was the cataloger in the Carnegie Library at Tuskegee Institute from 1905 to 1910. She later moved to Boston, where she married William P. Bond, a painter.

She wrote to BTW on June 27, 1915, with "a friendly warning," implying that William H. Lewis of Boston favored the showing of the film The Birth of a Nation. She also assumed as true the rumor that BTW was to allow scenes of Tuskegee Institute to be shown in conjunction with the film. (Con. 75, BTW Papers, DLC.)

To Jacob Godfrey Schmidlapp

New York City, July 1st, 1915

Dear Mr. Schmidlapp: I am very much obliged to you for your kind letter, and for the letter of introduction to Mr. Henry Ford of Detroit. I shall hope to have the privilege at some time of calling upon Mr. Ford, and I hope that we may be able to interest him in the work of Tuskegee Institute.

I am very much obliged to you for the information you have given me regarding Mr. Ford, and I hope that I may be able to meet him when "he may have nothing on his mind." Yours very truly,

[Booker T. Washington]

TLc Con. 536 BTW Papers DLC.

From Monroe Nathan Work

Tuskegee Ala July 1–15

(The lynching record for the first six months of 1915)

I find according to the records kept by the Department of Records and Research of the Tuskegee Institute that there have been during the first six months of the year 33 lynchings. This is 12 more than the number 21 for the same period last year. Of those lynched 23 were negroes and 10 were whites. This is three more negroes and nine more whites than were put to death by mobs in the first six months of 1914 when the record was 20 negroes and 1 white. Eight or one fourth of total lynchings occurred in the state of Georgia. Only 7, six negroes and one white of those put to death or 21 percent of the total were charged with rape. Other offenses and number lynched for were murder 8, three whites and five negroes. Killing officers of the law 4 two whites and two negroes. Clubbing an officer a family of four father son and two daughters. Stealing hogs 2 white. Disregarding warnings of night riders 2 white. Insulting a woman 1. Writing an insulting letter 1. Wounding a man 1. Stealing meat 1. Burglary 1. Charged with stealing a cow 1. In this instance it was later reported that the Negro had not been indicted that the woman to whom the cow belonged did not know that the accusation had been made. The cow which had simply strayed finally returned home.

Monroe N Work

TWSr Con. 664 BTW Papers DLC.

To James B. Washington

[Tuskegee, Ala.] July 6, 1915

Mr. J. B. Washington: I dislike very much to take up the following matter with you, but I am compelled to.

I have spoken to you and your wife several times concerning the conduct of your girls. I have also spoken to the girls individually and urged them to be careful of their actions. Very definite and strong promises were made to the effect that there would be no trouble in the future.

Some weeks ago I heard rumors to the effect that the girls were not keeping their promise and were going out at night with one of the chauffeurs in town. I did not want to do any one an injustice by acting upon rumors, so I took measures to find out for myself just what was going on.[1] I find that Norma, Bertha and Booker's wife go out frequently at night with one of the chauffeurs in town. Four to five times within the last two weeks they have left the grounds at night and remained out with this chauffeur until 10 and 11 o'clock at night. Just where they go or for what purpose I am not able to say, but there are all kinds of rumors regarding this. I do not say that each one of the three individuals mentioned has been in the car every night, but some of them have been at least from four to five times within the last two weeks.

Further, I find that when they do not go out in the car, some of them or all of them are out from your home at least until half past 10 and often until 11 o'clock at night either at Patterson's restaurant or somewhere else.

The young girl by the name of Missie who stays at your house has a bad reputation, and it is doing neither your family nor the community any good by keeping her in the community.

After getting hold of these definite facts I had made up my mind to take more drastic action than I am going to take at present, but I fear I am erring on the side of mercy. The action of these girls is very keenly and deeply felt by the teachers and other people in the community. They feel that they are not only disgracing your family but the whole teaching body.

I am writing to say that if I find at any time in the future any of these girls or all of them are guilty of loose conduct or of a repetition of their former mistakes I shall see at least that they sever their connection with directly and indirectly from all relationship with the school.

In regard to Missie, since she is not in any way, as I understand it, connected with your family and you are not obligated to her, I must ask that you take measures to see that she leaves the community as soon as possible. This is best for you, for her and for all of us.

I hope you will not mince matters. It is a matter you must look at frankly and squarely. You can do your children no good by trying to hide their faults. This is a case where you and Mrs. Washington need to stand up squarely and see that the right thing is done regardless of consequences. But, as I have said, I am willing to give the girls one more trial.

It is impossible for me to understand how parents could know that their children are staying out as late as 10 and 11 o'clock at night without something going wrong or their being criticised.

Booker T. Washington

TLpS Con. 665 BTW Papers DLC.

[1] See an unsigned report, dated July 5, 1915, concerning the use of the car by residents of J. B. Washington's house (Con. 82, BTW Papers, DLC.)

To James B. Washington

[Tuskegee, Ala.] July 13, 1915

Mr. J. B. Washington: I do not want to be misunderstood regarding the presence of that girl, Missie, in the community, and I am writing again to say that unless she gets out of the community I shall have to take very serious action regarding the matter, an action which I fear you will regret in the future.

I did not go into the matter hastily, but was sure of my ground before I wrote you in the first place, and I must insist that my request be carried out.

Booker T. Washington

TLpS Con. 665 BTW Papers DLC.

To Clark Howell

[Tuskegee, Ala.] July 16, 1915

Personal

My dear Sir: Please let me thank you again for your very fine and, I am quite sure, helpful editorial in today's Constitution on white people teaching Negro schools.[1]

Certainly, if we are to ever emerge from darkness into light, it is going to be very largely through the leadership and guidance of the white people, and we cannot make progress if the white people are prevented from teaching us.

The enclosed copy of a letter which I am sending you is written by one of the strongest white men in Alabama. He is a member of the present legislature. I am not permitted, however, to use his name without his permission. Yours very truly,

Booker T. Washington

TLpS Con. 528 BTW Papers DLC.

[1] The editorial, "An Unjust Measure," said that a bill before the legislature to forbid white persons teaching in black schools would repudiate every form of mission work and refuse to "the dependent race in the state the message of civilization for which the white man stands." (Atlanta *Constitution*, July 16, 1915, 6.)

To Benjamin Jefferson Davis

[Tuskegee, Ala.] July 16, 1915

Personal and Confidential

My dear Mr. Davis: You certainly ought to give our friend, Mr. Clark Howell, credit for the editorial which he has written in today's Constitution on white people teaching in colored schools. I think here is a chance for you to give him a lot of praise. Don't you think so? Yours very truly,

B. T. W.

TLpI Con. 529 BTW Papers DLC.

To William Phillips[1]

Tuskegee Institute, Alabama   July 16, 1915

Personal

My dear Mr. Phillips: I have no disposition or wish to meddle into political affairs, and I am writing with the hope that what I am going to suggest will not have the slightest political bearing.

I am deeply interested in Liberia. It was largely through my efforts that a commission was sent to Liberia by President Taft to make recommendations with a view to helping out the Liberians with reference to their debt. They still need guidance of a wise and sympathetic character, otherwise I fear the loan which was brought about through this government will not, in the last analysis, help the people very much.

What I am getting to is this: I very much hope you and the Secretary[2] might consider the wisdom of sending back to Liberia Mr. Ernest Lyon, who held the place of Minister for a number of years, and was there during the visit of the American Commission. Mr. Lyon really knows more about conditions there and is more able to help those people than anybody I know of.

I am suggesting this on the ground that the present Minister may not return. If he is to return and is rendering good service I have no suggestion to make. My only interest in the matter is to get somebody into the position who will be of permanent, helpful service to those people. The war has brought about very trying conditions in Liberia. Yours very truly,

Booker T. Washington

TLpS Con. 532   BTW Papers   DLC.

[1] William Phillips (1878–1968), Assistant U.S. Secretary of State.
[2] Robert Lansing (1864–1928), U.S. Secretary of State from 1915 to 1920.

From Annie Eichelburger

Boston, Mass., July 17 1915

Dear Sir Bro   I am going to have a space in Convention Hall to Sell my Cigars, & I would be more than delighted to have your cut on a Brand, if you will al[l]ow me the privilege of doing so. I will make them out of the best of Havana, & put them up in Boxes of Twenty Fives, & they will be very nice for the members to take back Home, if you will consent please send me one of your Photos so I can have a cut made, & I will return it. I was speaking to Dr Johnsen[1] about it & he thought it would be fine, as I am the only Colored Cigar manuf in the City. I will have the sole right, & if you will grant me that favor I will appreciate it very much. Trusting I will have the erilyest reply[2] possible I remain yours Fraternally

Mrs A. Eichelburger

ALS   Con. 530   BTW Papers   DLC.

[1] W. Alexander Johnson.
[2] E. J. Scott replied that BTW authorized the use of his name and his photograph on the cigars. (July 24, 1915, Con. 536, BTW Papers, DLC.)

To Samuel Edward Courtney

Tuskegee Institute, Alabama. July 31, 1915

Dear Dr. Courtney: I have just telegraphed you as follows:

"SERIOUSLY QUESTION WISDOM OF ENTERTAINING LEAGUE OFFICIALS AT YOUNG'S HOTEL[1] TUESDAY NIGHT IN VIEW OF OFFICERS OF LEAGUE MAKING HEADQUARTERS AT HOTEL MELBOURNE. FEAR WILL BE CRITICISED SEVERELY. HOPE YOU WILL CONSIDER FULLY. AM WRITING."

I learn from your telegram to Mr. Scott that you are planning to entertain the League Officers at Young's Hotel Tuesday Night, August 17th.

You can see how we are likely to provoke needless criticism by leaving Hotel Melbourne, which is a colored hotel, where most of the officers will be domiciled, to go to Young's Hotel.

I bring the matter to your attention with the hope that you will carefully consider this matter and with the further hope that you may decide to have the entertainment for the officers at Hotel Melbourne instead of at Young's Hotel. "Beggars must not be Choosers," still I think the suggestion I am making is entitled to consideration.

I am almost sure we would lay ourselves open to a lot of criticism which is not necessary to provoke if we follow out the plan of going to Young's Hotel. Yours very truly,

Booker T. Washington

TLpSr Con. 529 BTW Papers DLC.

¹ J. C. Napier, chairman of the executive committee of the NNBL, also wrote Courtney, arguing against the entertainment of the officers at Young's, a hotel owned by and generally used by whites, instead of at the headquarters hotel, owned by blacks. (July 31, 1915, Con. 529, BTW Papers, DLC.) Courtney arranged for the NNBL officers' banquet to be at the Hotel Melbourne. (Courtney to Scott, Aug. 2, 1915, Con. 529, BTW Papers, DLC.)

Alexander Robert Stewart to Julius Rosenwald

[Tuskegee, Ala.] 8/5/15

Dear Mr. Rosenwald: I want first to apologize to you for taking up even a few moments of your time. It is not for myself however, for I am a vigorous young man quite able to work for myself and family. It is for Dr. Booker T. Washington's sake that I write. I may even be wrong in doing this, I hesitate, I am sure, to speak to you or to any one of Mr. Washington's personal affairs, because he is a man who never thinks of himself and would never consent to have his friends do one thing for him, and yet it is his doing for other people all of the time that "keeps his nose at the grindstone."

Another reason for my writing you Mr. Rosenwald is that I happen to know that you and others are constantly giving here to have certain things done, certain ideas carried out and I know that Mr. Washington needs more physical strength, less personal worry over his own financial condition and thereby a longer lease on life to carry out his plans directed by yourself and others.

Mr. Washington is in debt to the amount of nearly twenty thousand dollars ($20,000), brought on by what he has tried to do for his family and others. Things he has done for himself and them, and much more that he has done in a financial way for others, which have brought no returns whatever. He has borrowed from the banks in Tuskegee, money which is due in Oct. and Jan. next, to the amount of nearly ten thousand dollars ($10,000). Mr. Washington is making more than human effort to pay these banks. He simply cannot do it. I worked for Mr. Washington for eleven years at a salary of $55. per month simply because I am [a] graduate of his and have felt that I ought to do what I could for him, and because Mrs. Washington has asked me again and again to work on. She knows their financial condition and is now letting me use every dollar she makes, in keeping the small bills, which they are obliged to make daily, paid up.

I can see plainly how both Mr. and Mrs. Washington are wearing under the strain of this heavy indebtedness.

In no sense do I wish to handle any man's money. You can take my word or write to Mr. W. W. Campbell, President Macon County Bank, or Mr. J. H. Drakeford, President the Bank of Tuskegee, both in Tuskegee, for further information.

I want to beg of you to treat this letter confidentially. I do not wish Mr. Washington to know that I have written you. It would be a great humiliation. You may not think it wise to do anything. I do not know, but I cannot be silent longer when a word might lift a heavy burden from the shoulders of a man who is carrying millions of people on his heart and mind.

I have been influenced too to write you especially instead of some one else, because of the fact that you and Mrs. Rosenwald so generously remembered the teachers here, who had served the school faithfully for fifteen years or more, and I realize that it was natural for you to regard Mr. Washington as not at all in need of this sort of help.

I thank you for the time that I have taken, Mr. Rosenwald, and sincerely hope that in some way, something will be done, in order that Mr. Washington's mind will be free to grasp and carry on his work, and perhaps this would mean added years to his life and service. Very sincerely yours,

A. R. Stewart

TLtSr Julius Rosenwald Papers ICU.

William G. Willcox to William Colfax Graves

[New York City] 8/13/15

Dear Mr. Graves: I have your letter of the 11th inst., with enclosed copy of a letter which Mr. Rosenwald received from Mr. A. R. Stewart, regarding Mr. Washington's personal affairs.

The information comes as a surprise to me, for, as you know, Mr. Carnegie's gift of $600,000 provided that $7,500 per annum of the income should be set aside for Mr. and Mrs. Washington's personal use. I can quite understand, however, that the many demands upon him may easily have overrun even this liberal provision.

I have shown the letter to Mr. Trumbull, and he agrees with me that the matter must be handled delicately and with much tact, and that it would probably be best for one, or both, of us to talk directly with Mr. Washington, rather than make any roundabout inquiries which might come to his ears and mortify or embarrass him. I think when he next comes to New York we can quite naturally ask him about his health, and follow with inquiries in regard to his personal affairs, on the ground that it is important to his health that he should avoid any unnecessary worry, and I believe in this way we might quite easily draw out a confidential statement from him.

As to what should be done if the facts prove to be what Mr. Stewart states, I have no definite suggestions as yet, but the first thing, obviously, is to get at the facts and to secure, if possible, Mr. Washington's confidence and frank statement regarding the situation.

In the meantime, it seems to me that Mr. Rosenwald can only reply to Mr. Stewart thanking him for his letter, and saying that he will confer, confidentially, with some of the other Trustees, and see whether it is possible to do anything to relieve the situation.

When Mr. Rosenwald is next in New York perhaps Mr. Trumbull and I can arrange to have a talk with him about it. Very sincerely

William G. Willcox

TLtSr   Julius Rosenwald Papers   ICU.

To Paul M. Gottlieb[1]

[Tuskegee, Ala.] August 16, 1915

Dear Sir: Replying to your letter of August 11th, I write to advise that I am in favor of Woman's Suffrage. Yours very truly,

Booker T. Washington

TLpSr   Con. 530   BTW Papers   DLC.

[1] Paul M. Gottlieb, born in Philadelphia in 1895, was a reporter on the Philadelphia *Inquirer*, political editor of the Philadelphia *North American*, and secretary to the treasurer and mayor of Philadelphia.

An Address before the National Negro Business League

Symphony Hall   Boston, Massachusetts,
Wednesday Night   August 18, 1915

At the beginning of my annual address as President, to this the sixteenth meeting of the National Negro Business League, let me emphasize, in so far as mere human words can, the deep depth of gratitude, which all of us owe to our Secretary, Mr. Emmett J. Scott, for the continued success of this organization. In a large measure, it is the hard work, the loyalty, unselfishness, and resourcefulness of Mr. Scott which make and keep this League the power for good that it is. Nor should I overlook the steadfastness and helpful interest and generosity of all the members of the Executive Committee, as well as the several officers.

In this catalogue there should not be omitted the name of our active and devoted National Organizer, Mr. Charles H. Moore, the loyalty and activity of many of the Local Leagues is a matter of constant surprise and gratification.

The difficult and practical work which has been done by the Boston Local League, together with the Cambridge League, and the citizens of Boston as a whole, to make this meeting a success, is also cause for congratulations and deep gratitude.

I wish now again, as in other years to thank the Colored Press throughout the country for its more than liberal and constant support of the work of this League. We of the Negro Race and of the White Race know little of the self-sacrificing and patriotic work that is constantly being done by the Negro Press.

This National Negro Business League was organized in the city of Boston fifteen years ago with a mere handful of men. The League during the fifteen years of its life has grown in power, in influence, and in usefulness, until, either, through its local leagues or individual members, it reaches practically every part of the country in which there are any considerable number of colored people. After fifteen years of testing useful service and growth, it is fitting that we should return to Boston, the place which gave us birth.

From the first, this National Negro Business League has clung strictly to the object for which it was founded. It was not founded to take the place of other organizations; nor was this league as a league, ever intended to go into business as an organization or to become a close, hide-bound concern, with grips and signs and pass words. We have such organizations and they are doing their work well, but the central purpose of this National Negro Business League has been, from the first to foster, to spread, and to create industrial, business and commercial enterprises among our people in every part of the country. How well we have succeeded, I shall let the facts tell the story later on.

The founders and promoters of the League fully recognize the fact that it cannot meet all the needs of the race, nor satisfy all its ambition. We fully and frankly recognize the fact that there is need for the particular and distinct work to be done by the religious, the educational, the political, the literary, the secret, and the fraternal bodies, as well as those that deal with the civil rights of our people.

All of these have their place and with none of them would we seek to interfere; but the history of civilization, throughout the world, shows that without economic and commercial success there can be no lasting or commanding success in other fields of endeavor. This League then has for one of its objects not the tearing down or weakening of other organizations, but rather to give them strength and stability.

Since our last annual meeting, there have been happenings that are of peculiar interest to our race. Among these has been the observance of a National Health Week which was promoted very largely by this Business League, acting in co-operation with the Virginia Organization Society. Health Week was perhaps more generally observed by all classes of our people in the South and in the North than has ever been true of any similar movement in the history of the race. Until ten years ago, the death-rate among our people was alarming, but the importance of good health and long life has been called to the attention of the race in so many ways during the last ten years that the death-rate has already been reduced by four per cent in certain parts of the country. It is the wish of many that the Health Week be observed again this year.

Since our last meeting the United States Supreme Court has rendered a decision in the Oklahoma case which is of far-reaching value and importance to our race. The main value of this decision, rendered by a Southern Supreme Court Justice and an ex-confederate soldier and ex-slave-holder, consists in the fact that it makes plain the idea, once and for all by the Supreme Court of the land, that neither color nor race can debar a man in this country from full citizenship.

I regret to note that the number of lynchings, during the first six months of the calendar year, has increased as compared with the same period a year ago. While the number of black people lynched is smaller; the number of white people lynched is larger. The increase in the total number lynched should not discourage but should make us renew our energies and double our determination to blot out the crime of lynching from our civilization, whether the man be a white man or a black man. And I here repeat that which I said in Louisiana a few weeks ago. We must have in this country, law administered by the court and not by the mob. Along with the blotting out of lynchings should go that other relic of barbarism. I refer to public hangings.

In all these matters I am pleading not in the interest of the Negro or the White man, but in the interest of a more strong and perfect civilization.

It is seldom that it is ever so true that, in the space of one generation, that so many evidences of real progress in the fundamental things of life can be seen. Perhaps the changes in Japan are the nearest akin to it.

Since the League met in Boston fifteen years ago, great changes have taken place among our people in property getting and in the promotion of industrial and business enterprises. These changes have taken place not solely because of the work of the League, but this and similar organizations have had much to do with bringing about this progress. Let me be more specific.

We have not the figures covering all the Negro's wealth, but the Federal Census Bureau has just released a document which gives the value of the Negro's farm property alone as $1,142,000,000. From 1900 to 1910, the Negro's farm property increased 128 per cent. In 1863 we had as a race 2000 small business enterprises of one kind and another. At the present time, the Negro owns and operates about 43,000 concerns, with an annual turn-over of about one billion dollars. Within fifty years we have made enough progress in business to warrant the operation of over 50 banks. With all that I have said, we are still a poor race as compared with many others; but I have given these figures to indicate the direction in which we are traveling. During the last 6 years we have experienced as a race not a few business failures, including the closing of several banks. We must not let these failures discourage us. We must remember that it is with a race, as it is with an individual, that it is only through seeming failure, as well as success, that we finally gain that experience and confidence which are necessary to permanent success. With all that I have said, we should remember that we have but scratched the surface of industrial and business success.

Our future is before us, not behind us. We are a new race in a comparatively new country. Let any who may be inclined toward pessimism or discord consider with me for a few moments the opportunities that are before us. It is always of more value to consider our advantages rather than disadvantages. In considering one's opportunities it is worth while not to overlook the size of our race.

There are only 14 nations in the world whose population exceeds the number of Negroes in the United States. Norway has a population of only 2,400,000; Denmark, 2,700,000; Bulgaria, 4,000,000; Chile, 4,000,000; Canada, 7,000,000; Argentina, 9,000,000. When we contemplate these figures, and then remember that we, in the United States alone are 10,000,000 Negroes, we can get some idea of the opportunities that are right about us. Let me be more specific in pointing the way to these opportunities. If you would ask where you are to begin, I would answer, begin where you are. As a rule the gold mine which we seek in a far-off country is right at our door.

Over a million of our people live in the Northern and Western States. In these States at the present time, our people operate about 4000 business enterprises. There are opportunities in the North and West for eight thousand business enterprises, or double the present number. In the Southern States, where the great bulk of our people live, we have about 40,000 business concerns. There should be within the next few years twenty thousand more business concerns. In all this, we should never forget that the ownership and cultivation of the soil constitute the foundation for great wealth and usefulness among our people. I have already indicated that we now operate about 800,000 farms. Within the next decade let us try to double the number. To realize a little more in directions of our opportunities: There are now 4000 truck farms operated by us, we ought to increase this number to 8000. We ought never to forget that in the ownership and cultivation of the soil in a very large measure we must lay the foundation for one's success.

A landless race is like a ship without a rudder. Emphasizing again our opportunities, especially as connected with the soil, we now have, for example, 122 poultry raisers. The number should be increased to 1500. We now have 200 dairymen. The number should be increased to 2000.

At present there are far too many of our people living in the cities in a hand-to-mouth way, dependent on someone else for an uncertain job. Aside from what the soil offers, there are other opportunities in business. For example, we now own and operate 75 bakeries. The number can be increased to 500. From 32 brickmakers the number can be increased to 3000. From 200 sawmills we can increase the number to 1000. From 50 furniture factories, the number can be increased to

300. Where we now have 9000 drygood stores and grocery merchants, we should have in the near future 15,000.

Where we now have 700 drug stores, we should have 3000. Where we now have 700 real estate dealers, we should have 3000. Where we now have 1000 millinery stores, we should have 5000. Where we now have 150 plumbers, we should have 600. Where we have 400 tailors we should have 2000. Where we now have 59 architects we should have 400. We now have 3000 contractors and builders, we should have 5000. Where we now have 51 banks, we should have 500.

Few people are aware of the fact that we now have in our race after only fifty years of freedom, 55 book stores, 18 department stores, 14 five-and-ten cent stores,[1] 20 jewelry stores, 790 junk dealers, 13 warehouses and cold storage plants, 152 wholesale merchants, 200 laundries, 350 livery stables, 953 undertakers, 400 photographers, 10 opticians, 75 hair goods manufacturers, 111 old-rag dealers, 12 buyers and shippers of live stock.

With our race as it has been and always will be with all races without economic and business foundation, it is hardly possible to have educational and religious growth or political freedom.

We can learn some mighty serious lessons just now from conditions in Liberia and Hayti. For years both in Liberia and Hayti, literary education and politics have been emphasized, but while doing this the people have failed to apply themselves to the development of the soil, mines and forests. The result is that, from an economic point of view, those two republics have become dependent upon other nations and races. In both republics the control of finances is in the hands of other nations, this being true not withstanding the fact that the two countries have natural resources greater than other countries similar in size. In the United States there is no hope for us, except in an increasing degree we teach our young people to apply their education to develop the natural resources and to promote human activities in the communities where we live. Mere abstract, unused education means little for a race or individual. An ounce of application is worth a ton of abstraction. We must not be afraid to pay the price for success in business — the price of sleepless nights, the price of toil when others rest, the price of planning today for tomorrow, this year for next year. If someone else endures the hardships, does the thinking, and pays the salaries, someone else will reap the harvest and enjoy the reward.

To accomplish what I have indicated, we must have a united race, men who are big enough and broad enough to forget and overlook personal and local differences and each willing to place upon the altar all that he holds for the benefit of the race and our country.

Sometimes it is suggested that some of us are over optimistic concerning the present conditions and future of our race. In part answer, it might be stated that one on the inside of a house looking out can often see more than the one on the outside looking in. No one enjoys riding in a pullman car so much as the one who has ridden in a freight car.

No matter how poor you are, how black you are, or how obscure your present work and position, I want each one to remember that there is a chance for him and the more difficulties he has to overcome, the greater will be his success.

Everywhere we should be proud of the Negro race and loyal to the great human family of whatever color. Whenever we consider what is now going on in Europe, where all the people are of one color, and then compare these conditions with present conditions and our task for our race, we ought to thank our Creator that conditions are so well with us and that we live beneath the Stars and Stripes.

Tuskegee Student, 27 (Sept. 4, 1915), 1–3.

¹ A typed version of the address in Con. 957, BTW Papers, DLC, included here: "81 hardware stores, 200 ice dealers, 100 insurance companies."

Emmett Jay Scott to Robert Russa Moton

[Tuskegee, Ala.] September 4, 1915

Personal

Dear Major Moton: Just as I was leaving New York City Wednesday, September 1st, Mr. Washington brought from his portfolio your letter with reference to the proposed trip to certain Northern Neck counties of Virginia.

On my return to the school I find here your letter in which you suggest the date, Sept. 13.

Mr. Washington asked me to write you and say that after the National Baptist Convention address that he would have to return direct to Tuskegee and remain here sometime in an effort to "get himself together," etc.

Quite confidentially, I want to say to you that Mr. Washington is, if anything, in worse condition than he was during the meeting of the Business League, and will be absolutely unable physically to undertake the trip with you if it is scheduled for September 13. In fact, I would not undertake to prophesy as to just when he could make such a trip. He has no business going out to Chicago, but he insisted on the trip and so we had to consent. Mr. Washington thinks he had better stick by the Petersburg engagement for the present.

You do not know, my dear friend, how much I appreciate your personal affection and regard. It has been worth a great deal to me to know that I have the good will of so splendid a man as yourself. Your tribute to me at the closing meeting of the Business League did not pass unnoticed by me or my wife; both of us feel very, very humble that persons like yourself can speak so cordially of my efforts to help Mr. Washington. I can only hope that I may continue to merit the respect of men like yourself. Yours very truly,

Emmett J. Scott

TLpS Con. 77 BTW Papers DLC.

From T. E. Taylor[1]

Independence, Ia   Sep 5 1915

Dear Brother; Mr Vardaman gave his lecture here on the "Race question" in which he asserted that the negroe's skull hardens at age of puberty & from that age on there is no mental development. I do not accept his theory. What facts can you give me on this point? Can you give me a list of *full blooded* negroes who have become eminent or students who have won honors in college & university? Please tell me what each has accomplished including yourself.

I would also be glad to get any material on the lynching question — statistics on the no. of whites & no. of negroes lynched say the last

10 yrs. I wish to prepare an answer to his arguments for our church paper. This Vardaman talk is having an effect on the attitude of our people toward freedmens aid work. Thanking you for your kindness I am Yours truly

T. E. Taylor

ALS Con. 537 BTW Papers DLC.

1 T. E. Taylor was a representative of the sixty-seventh district (Buchanan County) in the Iowa state legislature.

To Charlotte Everett Wise Hopkins

[Tuskegee, Ala.] September 9, 1915

My dear Mrs. Hopkins: I have your very kind letter of some days ago which I have given a very careful reading and which interests me very much.[1] The copy of the Architect's Journal containing your illustrated article is also received.

The effort to surround the poorer class of colored people of Washington with better living conditions, to replace the alley houses with modern and sanitary homes, is a most commendable undertaking. I am heartily in sympathy with the movement. It would be impossible for Washington or any other city to maintain the proper standard of health if one class of people allows a more unfortunate class to remain surrounded by the unwholesome and unsanitary conditions as is true of the residents of the alley sections of that city.

I hesitate, however, to ask Mr. Rosenwald's aid in the movement. I know that he is interested in any good cause, but he has done and is still doing so very much toward helping colored people to build Y.M.C.A. buildings and to improve their education facilities throughout the South that I feel I would be imposing upon his goodness to bring the movement in which you are so vitally interested to his attention at this time. In addition to the large amount of money he has given toward helping rural schools he gave $25,000 a few years ago toward the Colored Men's Branch, Y.M.C.A., of Washington. He has given a similar amount to several other cities.

I know of Mrs. Wilson's interest in this movement and am glad to know that Mr. Wilson heartily endorses the plan. Because of his endorsement I believe that much good will result.[2] I shall hope to be of service to you in some other way.

With kind regards from both Mrs. Washington and myself, I am Yours very truly,

Booker T. Washington

TLpS Con. 531 BTW Papers DLC.

[1] Hopkins advised BTW that she had raised over $5,000 toward her plan to improve the housing of blacks in the alleys of Washington, D.C., where 10,000 persons resided. She needed $25,000 to carry out the work, and urged BTW to solicit the aid of Julius Rosenwald. (Hopkins to BTW, Sept. 4, 1915, Con. 531, BTW Papers, DLC.)

[2] The alley reform movement reached a peak when Ellen Axson Wilson's deathbed request for abolishing the alley dwellings led to legislation to take effect in 1918. World War I intervened, however, and after several postponements the movement was killed by an adverse court decision. (Borchert, *Alley Life in Washington,* 47.)

From Marcus Mosiah Garvey

Kingston, Jamaica, September 11th 1915

My dear Dr: Washington, I take the opportunity of forwarding you under separate cover, copies of our local papers, containing Reports relative to the Universal Negro Improvement Association which I trust will interest you.

I shall be writing you by next mail relative to my coming visit to America.

As for Reports you will see that my Society has the support and recognition of the most influential men of this country.

I have up to the present been attacked in Jamaica by two correspondents, one under the nom de plume of "Progress" and an unknown dentist by the name of "Mr: Leo: Pink." These attacks have been rather personal, but as my integrity stands above the malice and envy of these persons in Jamaica I am in no way affected.

I shall be able to furnish you and the American public with the best proofs of my integrity.

No one can understand more quickly than you the sacrifices and heart aches that accompany men who endeavor from the purest motives to do something in the interest of the people.

My task at this end is a hard one in that we have firstly to dislodge the prejudice existing among the people themselves before we can achieve the success that efforts of this kind demand.

With very best wishes for yourself and those at Tuskegee. Your most humble and obedient Servant

Marcus Garvey

TLS Con. 530 BTW Papers DLC. On stationery of the Universal Negro Improvement Association.

To Richard Henry Boyd

[Tuskegee, Ala., Sept. 12, 1915]

I want to beg and urge that each convention remain in session till differences are composed. In the event that this can not be done, I hope that each convention will appoint a small committee or authorize some one to appoint committee that will have power to act regarding differences, so that next year there will be one convention. It is easier to bring about reconciliation now than it will be later. It will be a calamity to the Baptist Church, and to our race for the present split to continue. It will soon spread to all the churches and all the states. I urge that each side manifest a broad liberal spirit and be willing to sacrifice something for the good of the cause.

If I can be used at any time in any way my service is at your command.

Millions of our humble people throughout the country are depending upon leaders to settle this matter in a Christian spirit and the masses should not be disappointed.

Have sent a similar telegram to Dr. Morris.

Booker T. Washington

AWdS Con. 534 BTW Papers DLC. Dated from attached typed draft.

From Hollis Burke Frissell

Whitefield N.H. Sept 12th 15

Dear Dr Washington: From several sources I hear word that you need rest and need it very much. When I set you a good example you must follow it. I have been taking the whole summer to get up from my operation. Your life means altogether too much to the country and to your people to run any risks. It is a good thing for us to throw off our work on to other peoples shoulders. It helps them and it help[s] us. Nothing is quite so important at Tuskegee as that you keep your health so do be good.

Mrs Frissell joins me in affectionate regards to you and Mrs Washington. Sincerely Yours

H. B. Frissell

ALS Con. 76 BTW Papers DLC.

From Richard Henry Boyd

Chicago, Illinois, September 13th 1915

Accept appreciation for your interest in the denomination and race's future development. Only those who have large responsibilities and have been on the "firing line" as targets for numbers of years can appreciate what confronts the Baptists in this crisis. Differences can be adjusted. Awkward situation could have been avoided.

R. H. Boyd

TWSr Con. 534 BTW Papers DLC.

An Article in *The New Republic*

Tuskegee Institute, Alabama   September 13, 1915

MY VIEW OF SEGREGATION LAWS

In all of my experience I have never yet found a case where the masses of the people of any given city were interested in the matter of the segregation of white and colored people; that is, there has been no spontaneous demand for segregation ordinances. In certain cities politicians have taken the leadership in introducing such segregation ordinances into city councils, and after making an appeal to racial prejudices have succeeded in securing a backing for ordinances which would segregate the negro people from their white fellow citizens. After such ordinances have been introduced it is always difficult, in the present state of public opinion in the South, to have any considerable body of white people oppose them, because their attitude is likely to be misrepresented as favoring negroes against white people. They are, in the main, afraid of the stigma, "negro-lover."

It is probably useless to discuss the legality of segregation; that is a matter which the courts will finally pass upon. It is reasonably certain, however, that the courts in no section of the country would uphold a case where negroes sought to segregate white citizens. This is the most convincing argument that segregation is regarded as illegal, when viewed on its merits by the whole body of our white citizens.

Personally I have little faith in the doctrine that it is necessary to segregate the whites from the blacks to prevent race mixture. The whites are the dominant race in the South, they control the courts, the industries and the government in all of the cities, counties and states except in those few communities where the negroes, seeking some form of self-government, have established a number of experimental towns or communities.

I have never viewed except with amusement the sentiment that white people who live next to negro populations suffer physically, mentally and morally because of their proximity to colored people. Southern white people who have been brought up in this proximity are not inferior to other white people. The President of the United States was born and reared in the South in close contact with black people. Five members of the present Cabinet were born in the South;[1]

and many of them, I am sure, had black "mammies." The Speaker of the House of Representatives[2] is a Southern man, the chairmen of leading committees in both the United States Senate and the Lower House of Congress are Southern men. Throughout the country to-day, people occupying the highest positions not only in the government but in education, industry and science, are persons born in the South in close contact with the negro.

Attempts at legal segregation are unnecessary for the reason that the matter of residence is one which naturally settles itself. Both colored and whites are likely to select a section of the city where they will be surrounded by congenial neighbors. It is unusual to hear of a colored man attempting to live where he is surrounded by white people or where he is not welcome. Where attempts are being made to segregate the races legally, it should be noted that in the matter of business no attempt is made to keep the white man from placing his grocery store, his dry goods store, or other enterprise right in the heart of a negro district. This is another searching test which challenges the good faith of segregationists.

It is true that the negro opposes these attempts to restrain him from residing in certain sections of a city or community. He does this not because he wants to mix with the white man socially, but because he feels that such laws are unnecessary. The negro objects to being segregated because it usually means that he will receive inferior accommodations in return for the taxes he pays. If the negro is segregated, it will probably mean that the sewerage in his part of the city will be inferior; that the streets and sidewalks will be neglected, that the street lighting will be poor; that his section of the city will not be kept in order by the police and other authorities, and that the "undesirables" of other races will be placed near him, thereby making it difficult for him to rear his family in decency. It should always be kept in mind that while the negro may not be directly a large taxpayer, he does pay large taxes indirectly. In the last analysis, all will agree that the man who pays house rent pays large taxes, for the price paid for the rent includes payment of the taxes on the property.

Right here in Alabama nobody is thinking or talking about land and home segregation. It is rather remarkable that in the very heart of the Black Belt where the black man is most ignorant the white people should not find him so repulsive as to set him away off to himself. If living side by side is such a menace as some people think, it does seem as if the people who have had the bulk of the race question to handle during the past fifty years would have discovered the danger and adjusted to it long ago.

A segregated negro community is a terrible temptation to many white people. Such a community invariably provides certain types of white men with hiding-places — hiding-places from the law, from decent people of their own race, from their churches and their wives and daughters. In a negro district in a certain city in the South a house of ill-repute for white men was next door to a negro denominational school. In another town a similar kind of house is just across the street from the negro grammar school. In New Orleans the legalized vice section is set in the midst of the negro section, and near the spot where stood a negro school and a negro church, and near the place where the negro orphanage now operates. Now when a negro seeks to buy a house in a reputable street he does it not only to get police protection, lights and accommodations, but to remove his children to a locality in which vice is not paraded.

In New Orleans, Atlanta, Birmingham, Memphis — indeed in nearly every large city in the South — I have been in the homes of negroes who live in white neighborhoods, and I have yet to find any race friction; the negro goes about his business, the white man about his. Neither the wives nor the children have the slightest trouble.

White people who argue for the segregation of the masses of black people forget the tremendous power of objective teaching. To hedge any set of people off in a corner and sally among them now and then with a lecture or a sermon is merely to add misery to degradation. But put the black man where day by day he sees how the white man keeps his lawns, his windows; how he treats his wife and children, and you will do more real helpful teaching than a whole library of lectures and sermons. Moreover, this will help the white man. If he knows that his life is to be taken as a model, that his hours, dress, manners, are all to be patterns for someone less fortunate, he will deport himself better than he would otherwise. Practically all the real moral uplift the black people have got from the whites — and this has been great indeed — has come from this observation of the white man's conduct. The South to-day is still full of the type of negro with gentle manners. Where did he get them? From some master or mistress of the same type.

359

Summarizing the matter in the large, segregation is ill-advised because

1. It is unjust.
2. It invites other unjust measures.
3. It will not be productive of good, because practically every thoughtful negro resents its injustice and doubts its sincerity. Any race adjustment based on injustice finally defeats itself. The Civil War is the best illustration of what results where it is attempted to make wrong right or seem to be right.
4. It is unnecessary.
5. It is inconsistent. The negro is segregated from his white neighbor, but white business men are not prevented from doing business in negro neighborhoods.
6. There has been no case of segregation of negroes in the United States that has not widened the breach between the two races. Wherever a form of segregation exists it will be found that it has been administered in such a way as to embitter the negro and harm more or less the moral fibre of the white man. That the negro does not express this constant sense of wrong is no proof that he does not feel it.

It seems to me that the reasons given above, if carefully considered, should serve to prevent further passage of such segregation ordinances as have been adopted in Norfolk, Richmond, Louisville, Baltimore, and one or two cities in South Carolina.

Finally, as I have said in another place, as white and black learn daily to adjust, in a spirit of justice and fair play, those interests which are individual and racial, and to see and feel the importance of those fundamental interests which are common, so will both races grow and prosper. In the long run no individual and no race can succeed which sets itself at war against the common good; for "in the gain or loss of one race, all the rest have equal claim."

Booker T. Washington

New Republic, 5 (Dec. 4, 1915), 113–14.

[1] These were William Gibbs McAdoo, Secretary of the Treasury; Thomas Watt Gregory, Attorney General; Albert Sidney Burleson, Postmaster General; Josephus Daniels, Secretary of the Navy; and David Franklin Houston, Secretary of Agriculture.

[2] Champ Clark of Missouri.

To T. E. Taylor

[Tuskegee, Ala.] September 14th, 1915

Personal:

Dear Sir: I have read with much interest your letter of recent date concerning the visit of Senator Vardaman to your city and his lecture on the race problem. I am pleased to know that you did not agree with all that Mr. Vardaman said and that you are preparing a reply to be delivered in your city in the near future.

I take pleasure in sending you material for this address. As to the assertion that The Skull of a Negro Hardens at an Early Age and that his mental development is arrested I know that a great deal has been said. In my opinion the strongest argument against this view is that in every part of the South since schools for Negroes have been established, no account has ever been taken of this alleged deficiency. The courses of study in Negro public schools, normal schools and colleges throughout the South are about the same as the courses given in white schools and colleges of the South. In fact in the public schools the studies are identical and the period[s] allowed for completing courses are the same. The Negro children with inferior buildings and other facilities manage to complete the studies of a particular grade in about the same time as white children. In fact, as I generally point out in speaking to white audiences in the South the assumption appears to be that the Negro child has mental abilities superior to the white child for, with much less number of actual school days he is expected to do as well as the white child. As for example a white child in the public schools of Mississippi has annually $8.50 spent on it and the Negro child in the public schools of the same state has only $1.50 spent annually on its education. Another striking fact in this connection is that, although in the Negro schools there are all sorts of children from those who cannot be distinguished from white children to Negroes of pure descent, no difference is made in the public schools, the normal schools or colleges, in the studies or the length of time allowed to complete courses. I also understand that when graduates of Negro colleges in the South enter northern schools or universities, no distinction is made as to whether the applicant is a mulatto or a full-blooded Negro. Some of the best records that have been made in northern colleges and universities were made by full-blooded Negroes.

Mr. William Pickens, a pure Negro, who is now dean of Morgan College, Baltimore, Maryland, for his excellency in scholarship, was made a Phi Beta Kappa while taking the college course at Yale University. Altogether some twenty Negroes for their excellency in scholarship, have received the Phi Beta Kappa honor from Harvard, Yale, Oberlin and other leading white Institutions of learning in the north.

A number of Negroes have also received the degree of Doctor of Philosophy from northern universities. For a list of these see page 231 of the Negro Year Book which I am sending you under another cover. The facts contained in the section of the Negro Year Book on Education pages 198–265 will be of great assistance to you in the preparation of your address. The great progress which the Negroes of the South have made since their emancipation is in my opinion a further disapproval of the claim that the Negroes mental development is arrested at puberty.

For discussion of what the best scientists have to say concerning this question I refer you to the recent volume of the Macmillan Company entitled "The Mind of Primitive Man" by Professor Franz Boas of Columbia University, who is, I understand, the leading authority on the question of the mental ability of races. Another interesting discussion of this same subject is by Professor W. I. Thomas of the University of Chicago, in his book on "Sex and Society" in the chapter on "Mind of Woman and the Lower Races." If your public library has the back numbers of the American Journal of Sociology, you will find this same article by Professor Thomas published therein sometime during the period 1906–1908. Professor Boas sums up his view of the relative mental capacity of races as follows: "The whole anatomical and physiological comparison of the Negro and of the white race may be summed up in the statement that certain differences between the two races are so fundamental that they seem to form two quite distinct groups of the human species, the characteristics of which, notwithstanding the great variability of each race, do not overlap; while, in regard to other characteristics, the differences are so slight that the difference between the two races is insignificant, as compared to the range of variability exhibited in each race by itself; and that there are hardly any anatomical or physiological traits developed in such manner that we are justified in calling one race anatomically or physiologically higher than the other. The existing differences are differences in kind, not in value. This implies that the biological evidence also does not sustain the view, which is so often proposed, that the mental power of the one race is higher than that of the other, although their mental qualities show, presumably, differences analogous to the existing anatomical and physiological differences."

In the Negro Year Book pages 1–26 is a considerable amount of matter that will be useful to you, particularly pages 25–26, where an account is given of Negroes who, during the year of 1913, gained scholastic distinctions in the schools of the North. In fact I invite, for your careful reading, all of the matter contained in the Negro Year Book. I am also sending you some other literature which I trust will be of service to you.

In closing permit me to say that pure-blooded Africans directly from that continent have no difficulty in taking the courses as given in the leading universities of this country and of Europe. In fact, so far as I know, the customs in Africa with regard to education is [are] about the same as in this country. That is, the natives are taught the same studies as the white students with, however, emphasis on some phases of education which meet their needs. Likewise here in the South much of the emphasis with respect to Negro education has been placed on the industrial feature because the recently emancipated Negro needed to be taught to labor as a free man and made to understand that there is dignity in labor which heretofore, he had associated with slavery and degradation. Very sincerely yours,

Booker T. Washington

TLpSr Con. 537 BTW Papers DLC. Signature in E. J. Scott's hand.

From Elias Camp Morris

Helena, Ark., Sept. 15th. 1915

Dear Dr. Washington: Words will not express the deep gratitude I have for you, for your kindness in coming to the National Baptist Convention at such a perilous time, and with such a powerful and yet soothing address help to cement together the Baptist forces in this country.

I beg also to acknowledge in this same connection the receipt of your telegram asking that the two Conventions remain in session until committees could be appointed from each to arbitrate the differences which brought a division.

The telegram did not reach Chicago until after the Boyd faction had adjourned. (so I am informed)

Permit me to say, that any suggestion from you has full weight with me, and I am always glad to have; and follow any advice you may give, but in this case we are up against a stone wall, and our friend seems bent on self destruction. There was a time when I would have been only too glad to have done anything in my power to have kept Dr. Boyd in the place he has held for nineteen years, but not now. There will not be five per cent of the Baptists who will follow him. Should Boyd come back to the Convention, I shall do what I can to have him restored. My arrest at his instance will not stand in the way of peace, if it can be had without the sacrifice of principle. Very truly yours,

E. C. Morris

TLS Con. 534 BTW Papers DLC.

Emmett Jay Scott to Hightower T. Kealing

[Tuskegee, Ala.] September 15, 1915

My dear Friend: Your daughter, Frances,[1] has handed me your letter of September 12th. She has reached here and has already begun her work with very great enthusiasm. We are all very glad to have her here at the school and I hope she is going to enjoy teaching at Tuskegee.

I make note of what you say with reference to an early conference. Quite confidentially, I write to say that Dr. Washington is not as well as he should be. We are saving him every possible worry and annoyance, in fact, I am practically running the office, even though he is on the grounds. I know of no reason, however, why I could not meet you at Birmingham or Montgomery at sometime in the near future so as to go over the various matters you have in mind. Of course you know that any letter you may care to write me confidentially will be so regarded.

Please give my love to all of the family. Yours very truly,

Emmett J. Scott

Please write promptly — I am to leave here very soon!

TLpS Con. 11 BTW Papers DLC.

1 Frances F. Kealing taught mathematics at Tuskegee Institute.

A Statement Written for the Woman's Peace Party[1]

Tuskegee, Alabama, Sept. 15, 1915

War has never yet been able to balance the pages of its ledger. Over against the empires it has builded, the heroes it has created and the history it has made, there is an unpaid balance of suspicion and hate it has implanted in men and nations, written in the blood of human beings, which it can never settle with Christianity and civilization, and which centuries will not efface.

Booker T. Washington

TDS Con. 536 BTW Papers DLC.

1 Eva Marshall Shoutz, writing on stationery of the Woman's Peace Party in Chicago, asked BTW for a statement to be used on a "Peace Calendar." (Aug. 10, 1915, Con. 536, BTW Papers, DLC.)

To Fritz George Schmidt[1]

[Tuskegee, Ala.] September 17, 1915

My dear Sir: The glasses have arrived, and for distance seeing they are very very fine and a great relief. I am not quite sure, though, whether I can adjust myself to them so far as reading is concerned. The field of vision seems to be narrow, but perhaps it is all my fault in not having learned to adjust myself to the condition of the glasses. I am trying to do this.

I am very grateful for your interest in the matter. Yours very truly,

Booker T. Washington

TLpS Con. 536 BTW Papers DLC.

¹ Fritz George Schmidt (1864–1937) was an optician in New York City.

To Hollis Burke Frissell

Coden, Alabama, September 19, 1915

Dear Mr. Frissell: I have received your letter, and thank you very much for your thought of me. I am glad to say that I am a great deal better than I was in August, in fact many per cent better. I had a good rest in New York and got the very best medical advice. I am now off on the Mobile Bay fishing and having a good restful time. I intend to remain here for some days.

I am very glad to hear that your health is improving, and that you are planning to be back in Hampton in October. Yours very truly,

[Booker T. Washington]

TLc Con. 76 BTW Papers DLC.

To Warren Logan

Coden, Alabama, Sept. 19, 1915

Personal

Dear Mr. Logan: I have just had a long talk with Dr. Kenney concerning Mrs. Logan's condition, and I was glad to have him state that there was no organic trouble but her trouble is mainly nervous.

My earnest advice to you is to drop everything and take Mrs. Logan to Battle Creek. I have studied conditions and hospitals pretty well throughout the country, and I am convinced that there is no hospital in the country that has such fine arrangements for patients with nervous troubles as they have at Battle Creek, and I believe she would be speedily helped there, if not cured. They have physical appliances for taking care of nervous patients that no other institution in the country has.

I hope certainly you will consider this matter very carefully and seriously. Yours very truly,

[Booker T. Washington]

TLc   Con. 658   BTW Papers   DLC.

To Carter Godwin Woodson[1]

[Tuskegee, Ala., ca. Sept. 20, 1915]

Dear Sir: I have received a copy of your book, *The Education of the Negro Prior to 1861,* and have examined it with a great deal of interest and appreciation.

I was, of course, especially interested in the chapter dealing with vocational training and the facts you have brought out concerning the efforts to establish schools for industrial training in the period before the Civil War. In writing the life of Frederick Douglass, I came to know of his efforts along this line. I did not know, however, of the many other efforts in this direction which from time to time had been made.

Another thing that interested me was what you have brought out concerning the favorable attitude of many white people in the South toward Negro education before the Civil War. To me, however, the most important fact of all brought out in this valuable work is the persistent efforts that the colored people of this country, from Revolutionary times down to the present, have made to provide education for themselves.

I again extend to you an invitation to visit Tuskegee Institute during your contemplated trip to the South the coming year, and deliver one or more lectures before our faculty. Yours very truly,

Booker T. Washington

TLpS   Con. 538   BTW Papers   DLC.

[1] Carter Godwin Woodson (1875–1950) was the chief early promoter of black history as a field of scholarship. Born in Buckingham County, Va., he moved to

Huntington, W.Va., in 1892 in order to attend high school, working in the Fayette County coal mines during part of the year to pay the expenses of his education. He studied for two years at Berea College, then integrated, and began to teach school, returning to Berea every summer until his graduation in 1903. Meanwhile he became principal of the high school he had once attended. He later earned a B.A. and M.A. at the University of Chicago, and in 1912 became a Harvard Ph.D. in history, writing his dissertation on "The Disruption of Virginia."

In 1915 Woodson founded the Association for the Study of Negro Life and History and was its executive director for life. In 1916 he began the association's quarterly, the *Journal of Negro History,* serving as its editor. Meanwhile, he taught and administered at a number of schools, including both of the District of Columbia's black high schools, Howard University, and West Virginia State University. From 1922 until his death he devoted himself exclusively to the association, the *Journal of Negro History,* and more than a dozen books in black history, including *The Negro in Our History,* the standard textbook for twenty-five years after its first publication in 1922.

Woodson's work was noteworthy not only for its pioneer character but because he kept a balance between professional scholarship, missionary zeal for his subject, and promotion of black solidarity through the study of history. (Toppin, *Biographical History of Blacks in America,* 472–75.)

While Woodson was an intellectual of the Talented Tenth and a member of the American Negro Academy, he was not actively anti-Bookerite. In 1909 he asked BTW to recommend him for a vacancy in the presidency of West Virginia Colored Institute, but BTW had already recommended someone else. (Woodson to BTW, Oct. 1, 1909, E. J. Scott to Woodson, Oct. 11, 15, 1909, Woodson to Scott, Oct. 13, 1909, Con. 901, BTW Papers, DLC.)

Charles H. Fearing to
Nettie Blair Hancock Washington

[Tuskegee, Ala.] September 22, 1915

I am sending a package of letters to which please sign Mr. Washington's name writing as boldly as you can: that is, please make the signature look as much like a man's as possible. Do not try to imitate Mr. Washington's signature. He does not desire that this be done. On Mr. Washington's return to the school, he will decide the rate the school will pay for such work. As soon as you return each batch of letters I will send another.

Charles H. Fearing
Acting Secretary

TLS   Con. 657   BTW Papers   DLC.

An Article for the
Jewish Immigration Bulletin

[Tuskegee, Ala., ca. Sept. 22, 1915][1]

What Has the Immigrant Contributed to American Life

Unlike the Nations of Europe, the United States is essentially an immigrant country. The immigrants and their descendants of the first, second, third and fourth generations have to a large extent made it. In many instances the people who have come to this country in recent years are spoken of as though they constituted the only special body of immigrants which this nation has had. The Puritan immigrants of New England are forgotten, likewise the Dutch of New Amsterdam, the Quakers of Pennsylvania, the Catholics of Maryland, the Cavaliers of Virginia and the Huguenots of the Carolinas, who as immigrants laid the foundations for the Nation and established those ideals of Justice and equity which found expression in the Declaration of Independence and the Constitution.

As I understand it the second group of immigrants were those who came during the first and middle parts of the past century. They were mainly North European people; English, Irish, Germans and Scandinavians: a large proportion settled in the middle west. They helped to reduce the wilderness to civilization. They contributed a great deal, not only in brawn and muscle to clear the forests and till the soil; but also in intellectual life and ideals as to what a democracy should be. This I understand was especially true of those Germans who came in the forties and fifties, the most conspicuous representative of whom was Carl Schurz.

In gathering material for my book "The Man Farthest Down" I had occasion both through literature and first hand to study the European peasants living in those regions from which the greatest number of immigrants to this country now come. In my book I pointed out that the problems of the European peasant and the problem of the Negro in the South are very similar. Both are more or less disadvantageously situated; both are struggling to rise. As I understand it the immigration of the European peasant to this country is a part of his effort to rise to better his condition. Here, where there is a great demand for labor, he has in recent years come in ever increasing numbers. A large part of the demand for labor in this country has been in the cities. Not only has this demand drawn millions of immigrants from Europe but also from the rural districts of this country. In the twenty years from 1890 to 1910 the increase in the number of Negroes in the cities of the country was over 1,200,000. One result of the phenomenal growth of cities has been the creation of problems which to a considerable degree cities in the nineteenth century did not have. The immigrant and the Negro thrown into the midst of these city problems are so intimately bound up with them as to appear in many instances to be the problems themselves. It is a question in my mind, however, whether practically every problem which cities have to deal with would not have arisen if there had been no additions to their population of either immigrants or Negroes.

While I do not claim to be a special student of this subject it appears to me that the immigrants of today as well as those of yesterday are contributing much to American life. While I write there comes to my mind the great work which Jacob Riis did, the splendid lessons which Mary Antin[2] is teaching us. The European peasant and the Negro, however, I believe are at present contributing most to American life by teaching the lessons of helpfulness, patience, tolerance, forbearance, brotherliness, in fact all those things which are comprehended under what is characterized as the broader humanity.

[Booker T. Washington]

TMd Con. 534 BTW Papers DLC.

[1] BTW enclosed the typescript of this article in a letter to the editor, Samuel Joseph of New York City, Sept. 22, 1915. (Con. 534, BTW Papers, DLC.) The article had been solicited for a forthcoming special edition in 1916. BTW's article was not published.

[2] Mary Antin (Grabau) (1881–1949) came to the United States from Poland in 1894. She wrote several books on the immigrant experience, including *The Promised Land* (1912).

From James A. R. Kinney[1]

Halifax, N.S. Sep. 24, 1915

Dear Dr. Washington: I thank you for your letter of the 18th inst., and much appreciate your kindness in returning my pamphlets, and your recent publications which will be read with intense interest.

I do not wish to bore you with details of my life, but let me say this much: My father died when I was 2½ years old, and at my most impressionistic age, between 15 and 18, I began to read of you, and I treasure these pamphlets because they taught me the rules of the game of success in life —

> 1st. That it made no difference what color you were, if you could deliver the goods when opportunity arrived.
>
> 2nd. Dip down your bucket among the white men you know, and who know you.

Now Dr. I am yet striving to live by these rules, never allowing, if possible, a white man to surpass me in knowledge of my business, and while I have not achieved greatness, I am travelling on the upward way.

I am anxious that you should full realize how you have touched my life, and while I have not been Tuskegee trained, I feel I am one of her products. Yours very respectfully,

Jas. A. R. Kinney

TLS Con. 532 BTW Papers DLC.

[1] James A. R. Kinney (1878–1940) was the black minister of the Cornwallis Street Baptist Church of Halifax, Nova Scotia. He was the leading spokesman in Nova Scotia for BTW's doctrines of black pride, self-help, and separate development. In 1921 he withdrew from his pastorate to become superintendent of the Nova Scotia Home for Colored Children. (Winks, *Blacks in Canada,* 348–49.)

Emmett Jay Scott to Willard W. Hadnott[1]

Coden, Alabama, Sept. 25, 1915

Personal

My dear Mr. Hadnott: I have had opportunity to frame a letter to be sent to Mr. Parsons, and have gone over it with both Dr. Washington and Mr. Tulane. It goes forward today. I have made out the best case possible and they have endorsed what I have written and also the suggestions of the letter which we are forwarding to Mr. Parsons.

Please tell Dr. Mason that in addition to this, Dr. Washington has telegraphed to Mr. Parsons to enquire if he is coming South at any time soon, and if so as to where he may meet him. In addition to this matters are going to be taken up with Mr. Willcox as soon as we reach Tuskegee. In other words, we are on the job, and it is incumbent that our Birmingham friends do everything possible to make the directors realize their responsibility.

Why would it not be a good idea to institute suits against the heaviest debtors and thus get the fear of the Lord into their souls. There is no reason on earth why you and Dr. Mason and those of us here should be working to extract the bank from its difficulties while these other people are supinely sitting down doing nothing. It seems to me it is up to them to come across with something very definite in the way of renewals of subscriptions to the capital stock or a very substantial reduction in their loans. Dr. Washington is most anxious of not having the responsibility of carrying this matter put on his shoulders without the Birmingham directors sharing to the fullest extent their own personal responsibilities.

Will you and Dr. Mason not go over this matter and write to me at Tuskegee Institute, where I will be Wednesday night. Please mark your letter to me there "Personal." Yours very truly,

E J S

TLIc Con. 11 BTW Papers DLC.

[1] Willard W. Hadnott was vice-president of the Alabama Penny-Prudential Savings Bank in Birmingham.

From Marcus Mosiah Garvey

Kingston, Jamaica, September 27th 1915

Dear Dr: Washington, I send you under separate cover copies of local daily papers. I have been outrageously criticized in one of the local papers by an inspired Class of our coloured men numbering in all about four; although only two of the number had the courage to sign their names.

These persons have attacked me from Parochial, political and other personal reasons. They were (with one exception) unknown to the public and to the people until this attack.

I held a Public Meeting at the Collegiate Hall at which over four hundred of our Members, friends and sympathizers assembled and these persons were composed of the most intelligent and cultured of the black people. The Meeting was presided over by Mr: R. W. Bryant, an Englishman, Vice-Chairman of the Mayor and Council of this city and an Ex-Mayor. The Meeting was most enthusiastic and after I had spoken the Meeting was thrown open for free opinion. One Gentleman from the audience spoke in high favour of my attitude and the Society. The Meeting afterwards endorsed my attitude and supported me right through.

The Newspapers here are manned by a narrow minded lot of Journalists who sacrifice general interest at any time so as to air personal views which are generally mingled with like or dislike of the individual criticized.

The News Editor of the paper that has attacked me through inspired correspondence has allowed this because I happen to pass his paper over when giving advertisements out to the Press. He is also among the coloured few who object to the name "Negro" in connection with my Association. As I have explained to you already the difficulties in the development of the race rests with our own people as some do not like to call themselves "Negroes" which will eventually lead them into an awkward position later on if they be allowed to continue in their blind ignorance.

I am about to tour the country delivering addresses and I will write you later.

With very best wishes   Your most humble and obedient Servant

Marcus Garvey

TLS Con. 530 BTW Papers DLC.

Harry Centennial Oppenheimer[1]
to Emmett Jay Scott

New York   Oct., 1st, 1915

My dear Mr. Scott; Your letter from Como to hand and am happy to see that you are working out the scenarios which no doubt will come in handy, as this letter will presently show you.

Mr. McMahon told me that he had written you in reference to Mr. Ince's decision, but do not think we should feel this disappointment very keenly as our original proposition together with some of the subsequent ones will in all likelihood be put through.

On Tuesday I called on the Universal Film Co., having an appointment with Mr. Stern the manager. I spent some time with him, and then went over to their offices at #1600 Broadway, where I had a conference with their manager Mr. Brandt and their educational film man, Mr. Shipowich.

It seems that the Elaine Sterne Film has been accepted in a more or less indefinite manner, and is now undergoing certain changes before being produced.

The main plot of this scenario (as I understood it) shows that the Negro was in a good measure responsible for the freedom which the North gained for the Negro Race. I told Mr. Brandt that which we wanted to answer in the "Birth of a Nation" more than anything else was the reconstruction period either by showing in some subtle manner that the White man was as much responsible for the "Scally Wag" legislation that, took place after peace was declared as the Colored man was; or by a more direct manner, showing the activities at the present time, of some of the Colored Race.

I tried to get a proposition from them relative to taking some of this film at Tuskegee, i.e. fixing the scenes so as to interpolate some of the activities of the Institute, and thought Tuskegee was entitled to some consideration. They however, would not hear of this (that is the consideration part), saying that they thought if they went to Tuskegee and showed the pictures of the Institute, as the pictures will be shown all around the country, they were entitled to some recompence.

After about one hour of pros and cons, we reached a tentative agreement subject to your approval which is as follows; That the scenario is to be submitted to you and Dr. Washington before production, and if you both approve of same, their man will come to Tuskegee and endeavor to bring in some pictures of Tuskegee Institute, during the course of the film, i.e. they will remodel their scenario so as to be able to insert these scenes. In return for this, you are to lend them whatever help you can in taking these pictures. No monetary consideration on either side.

I tried very hard to get the rights of this picture after it had been shown in their exchanges, so that we could use same in the Negro Churches, Lyceum Theatres etc., through the South. They would not hear of this, but said that if we cared to buy them, why they would be pleased to make arrangements with us.

Just one thing more which we may be able to work out, and that is, I told Mr. Brandt in view of all the publicity which his firm would get, and the added prominence that the influence of Tuskegee would give to this picture, that we were at least entitled to have them take some film for us to be used as educational films for these Colored Theatres, etc. He did not agree to anything definite regarding this, but said that after they got to Tuskegee and had seen what you had to offer them, and felt that it was something worth while in their picture, he would, as he expressed it (out of goodness of heart) take a couple of thousand feet of educational film of this kind for you.

As the Sterne picture had not been started in production, I did not think it out of place in telling him that we had a very big picture in mind to which you held the rights (Up From Slavery). I spoke to him about this wonderful book which he had not read, therefore promptly sent it to him, and perhaps something will develop out of this.

Taking it all in all, I think the Universal proposition is a fair one, in as much as the original offer made by them called for quite a substantial sum of money to be given over by Tuskegee and its friends, in return for the publicity that this film would bring them.

Please let me hear from you as soon as possible with regard to this, so that I can take this matter up further with Mr. Brandt, and assuring you again that anything I can do for you in New York I shall be more than pleased to give whatever time I can to fulfill.

I am with kindest regards, Sincerely yours,

Harry C. Oppenheimer

375

When their camera men get to Tuskegee it will be possible to arrange taking the educational pictures at a consideration. (if no goodness of heart appears)

TLS Con. 13 BTW Papers DLC.

¹ Harry Centennial Oppenheimer (1889–1962) was a New York City textile manufacturer who founded and was president of Brand and Oppenheimer, Inc. A philanthropist and champion of black rights, he was outraged by the film *The Birth of a Nation,* and traveled to Tuskegee to consult BTW about it.

To Marcus Mosiah Garvey

[Tuskegee, Ala.] October 2nd 1915

My dear Sir: I am writing to acknowledge receipt of your letter of recent date relative to the organization of the Universal Negro Improvement association and to say that I hope you may be wholly successful in putting the plans suggested in your letter into active operation.

This is the age of "getting together" and everywhere we look, we see evidences of that constructive accomplishment which are the result of friendly cooperation and mutual helpfulness. Such, I am sure, is the object of your Association and I am only too sorry that I cannot afford the time just now to give careful study to your plans as outlined.

Thanking you for your letter advising me of your plans and wishing you much success in your efforts, I am   Yours very truly,

Booker T. Washington

TLpSr Con. 530 BTW Papers DLC. Signature in E. J. Scott's hand.

To John Harvey Kellogg

[Tuskegee, Ala.] October 4th, 1915

Personal and Confidential
Dear Dr. Kellogg: Mr. Warren Logan, our Treasurer, is planning and hoping to send his wife to Battle Creek for treatment. Mrs. Logan,

as you will perhaps remember, is one of our oldest and most capable workers. She became a teacher at the school in the early years of its history, and has been connected with it in one way or another from that time until this. She has recently become a good deal run down nervously, and I have advised Mr. Logan to send her to Battle Creek.

In considering the matter of admitting Mrs. Logan to the Sanitarium, I want to be perfectly frank. I understand that naturally there might be some objection to colored people entering the Sanitarium on the part of certain classes. I am sure that Mr. and Mrs. Logan would be the very last persons to sail under false colors, but at the same time I thought I might say to you if no one chooses to call attention to the fact, no one would know from her appearance that Mrs. Logan is colored. The same is true of her daughter, Miss Ruth Logan,[1] who is planning to accompany her to the Sanitarium. Miss Logan is a graduate of Dr. Sargent's school for physical training at Harvard University, and is at present instructor in physical training at this institution.

It will be a great relief and a great favor if you can see your way clear to admit Mrs. Logan and to accord her every opportunity and do everything possible to see that she regains her health.

We think of you constantly, and hope we may see you at Tuskegee again some time soon.

We are constantly getting lessons from you that are helping our whole work. Yours very truly,

Booker T. Washington

TLpS Con. 532 BTW Papers DLC.

[1] Ruth Mackie Logan (b. 1891), a Tuskegee graduate in 1907, graduated from the Sargent School for Physical Training at Harvard University and became in 1913 head of physical training at Tuskegee Institute. She later married the prominent Harlem physician Eugene P. Roberts.

From George Washington Albert Johnston

Birmingham, Ala. Oct. 4th, '15

Dear Uncle Booker: I trust that you are back from Coden in fine physical shape, but I am certain that those few days spent there are not enough to give you back all the vitality you have lost during this last year when you have worked so very hard and suffered so very much, therefore I hope and trust that you will, as you have always forced others to do in whom you have been deeply interested, go off somewhere with Aunt Jacobum and take at least a months rest and the proper treatment. You have arrived at that age now where if you do not take the proper care of yourself, you cannot hope to enjoy the years of usefulness which is needed to carry out the work you have done so much for, and I am sure that you will agree that it is worth more to add a few years to your life by taking a month or so off than it is for you to stick hard at it, unfit, and shorten the years that might still be yours.

Why not take Battle Creek or some of the many good places you must know of. Certainly all of those whom you have trained up for so many years can run things along and let you off for this length of time. It will be too late after you have completely broken down, and I must be truthful and say that you have shown many signs of giving out during the past year.

I realize the cost will be great and you may not see your way clear, but even this should not stand in your way and I hope you will consider this and act on it favorably without delay.

I have been far from well recently but am up and around again and at work. Hope to pull through the winter somehow. Baby and Edythe are in good health and send remembrance.

Things are running pretty smooth here and business is improving daily. Most sincerely,

Albert

TLS Con. 532 BTW Papers DLC.

To Sarah Newlin

[Tuskegee, Ala.] October 6, 1915

My dear Miss Newlin: The question you raise in your letter of September 19th is one which has given me considerable concern. I do not know how many of the schools in the South come under the head that you refer to,[1] but at Tuskegee the students are charged $18.00 per month for board, room, light, fuel, laundry, etc., and this amount covers such expenses.

I do not believe that we could bring our children to wear wooden shoes.[2] The European civilization is not sufficiently transplanted in this country to make them feel that they belong to the peasant class, which wears wooden shoes in Europe.

The question which you raise concerning wooden shoes reminds me of my own boyhood days. I cannot recall how old I was, but I was certainly not very old. During the days of the Civil War, conditions in the South became so desperate that many of the slave owners found it necessary to have their slaves wear wooden shoes. I can remember as a child that a pair of wooden shoes was given to me and I wore them for some time. Of course it was a common thing in those days where I lived in Virginia, for the older people to wear wooden shoes, but custom and fashion has such a strong hold on people that I very much fear it would be impossible to introduce the use of wooden shoes among our people anywhere in this country today. Yours very truly,

Booker T. Washington

TLpS   Con. 534   BTW Papers   DLC.

[1] Sarah Newlin wrote that she had been shocked to find at least three of the "children" schools of Hampton and Tuskegee, "which are so well brought up in many ways, not having their pupils 'pay their board & lodging' with anything like fullness, and that the contributions are constantly drawn upon for these expenses." She was particularly concerned about economizing because of the calls upon the charitable for aid to war victims. (Sept. 19, 1915, Con. 539, BTW Papers, DLC.)

[2] This was another economy measure Sarah Newlin suggested.

To Charles Banks

[Tuskegee, Ala.] October 7, 1915

Dear Mr. Banks: On my return to Tuskegee from Coden-on-the-Bay, near Mobile, I find your letter of September 30th.

I congratulate you most heartily upon the final accomplishment of your purpose looking to the re-opening of your bank. I know you have had a long road to travel.

I agree with you that it will be a good thing for Mr. Scott to be present at the time that you have your formal opening; if you will let me know just about what time this is likely to be I will try to plan accordingly.

It is going to mean a great deal to have two Negro banks in Mississippi, operating under the Guaranteed Department of the banking laws of the State of Mississippi.

With all good wishes, I am   Yours very truly,

Booker T. Washington

TLpS Con. 75 BTW Papers DLC.

To George Washington Albert Johnston

[Tuskegee, Ala.] October 7, 1915

Dear Albert: I have received your kind letter and thank you for writing me. I shall keep in mind what you say.

I am getting on pretty well. I am not working very hard.

I am glad to hear that matters at the bank are improving, and that your family is well. Your uncle,

B. T. W.

TLpI Con. 532 BTW Papers DLC.

To Henry A. Rucker

[Tuskegee, Ala.] October 7th, 1915

My dear Mr. Rucker: Mr. Scott has shown me an extract from your letter regarding the growth of mob spirit in Atlanta.[1]

I am wondering if it will not be a good plan for a half dozen of the leading and strongest colored people in Atlanta to call together an equal number of the strongest and best white people in Atlanta and put the situation squarely before them. Now is the time to act, it seems to me. Yours very truly,

Booker T. Washington

TLpS   Con. 535   BTW Papers   DLC.

¹ There was indeed a revival of the mob spirit in Atlanta. On Aug. 16, 1915, twenty-five armed men took Leo Frank from the state penitentiary and hanged him. On Thanksgiving night in 1915 the Ku Klux Klan was reborn at a cross-burning on Stone Mountain, near Atlanta. (Dittmer, *Black Georgia*, 184–85.)

Emmett Jay Scott to Harry Centennial Oppenheimer

[Tuskegee, Ala.] October 7, 1915

Dear Mr. Oppenheimer: I am enclosing herewith the first page of The Washington Bee, published at Washington, D.C. The statement here referred to is in the main essentials true. I saw this Mr. Griswold in Birmingham last week and he told me that he had received letters and telegrams from all portions of the country asking for rental of Mr. Fisher's film; and said to me that he is planning to devote all of his time and education to the matter of providing films of Negro life because he knows that he can make a big drive on them. The thing that interested me particularly is that this man did not seem to be very well educated, and in addition to that he has not even been able to incorporate his company in Alabama, and he has been making his living only off of this one film.

I did not tell him anything about the discussion you and I had had along this same line, but I declined to enter upon an arrangement with him. He wishes me to give him the benefit of the Tuskegee influence in return for a royalty or partnership agreement.

I am mentioning all of this to you simply to indicate that here is a man who is actually trying out the very scheme which you, Mr. Mac-Mahon and I talked over, and by the letters and telegrams he showed me there is a bona fide demand for films of this character.

I have heard nothing from Mr. MacMahon since our interview, although, of course you have seen by the clipping I sent you that they have published in the newspaper the matter of my interview with him.

I do not know whether there is any way to find out what Mr. Ince has decided, but you will know how to proceed in the matter.

I would appreciate it very much if, when you write again, you would send me your house address. Yours very truly,

[Emmett J. Scott]

TLc Con. 13 BTW Papers DLC.

To John Henry Washington

[Tuskegee, Ala.] October 8, 1915

Dear Brother: Through you I wish to make known to the Faculty the deep gratitude which I feel to them for their thoughtful and unexpected kindness in presenting me with the two very useful presents in the form of a chair and a shotgun. I am sure I can use both of these to the very best advantage and I cannot find words with which to sufficiently express to the Faculty how deeply their thought of me has touched me. I shall hope, however, to make these two presents the means of being additionally useful to the school and to our race.

Booker T. Washington

TLpS Con. 658 BTW Papers DLC.

To Robert Russa Moton

[Tuskegee, Ala.] Oct. 10, 1915

Find myself confronted with serious obligation to be in North Dakota on important matter November fifth. Have not been able to secure release as had hoped. Am anxious to be with you at Petersburg and will very much appreciate it if you will arrange to change date of meeting so as to let me speak Sunday night October thirty first or Monday night November first. Will be willing to bear any expense necessary in connection with change and advertising of new date. Please telegraph answer. Would not bother you except for serious condition mentioned.

Booker T. Washington

TWpSr   Con. 845   BTW Papers   DLC.

From Robert Russa Moton

Hampton, Virginia, October 11th 1915

Am not sure we can change date of meeting. Not sure either that we can secure Academy of Music. Am very sorry to disappoint our people again. Have never been as much embarrassed as on the Northern Neck trip few weeks ago. People white and colored felt we had deliberately deceived them. More than one white person reminded me you were in Chicago week before this date. You remember we set this date a year ago coming over from Norfolk. I wrote you later concerning it and have tried to keep it before you and Mr. Scott ever since. Will put me in awkward position before people not to have you with us in Petersburg. In justice to the people and myself personally you ought to come to this meeting as originally planned. Cannot deceive people two times in a month. In the last analysis you must decide which is the more important meeting; one in Dakota among Northern white people or meeting in Petersburg among Southern white people and Negroes.[1]

R. R. Moton

TWSr   Con. 845   BTW Papers   DLC.

[1] BTW replied that he would plan to be in Petersburg on Nov. 5, and added: "Sorry to put you to so much trouble." (Oct. 14, 1915, Con. 845, BTW Papers, DLC.)

To George Edgar Vincent[1]

[Tuskegee, Ala.] October 11, 1915

My dear President Vincent: It is probable that I shall want to go to Rochester sometime within the next few weeks for a physical examination on the part of Doctors Mayo and I am wondering if you will give me a personal letter of introduction to the Mayo brothers that I may use, in case I go there.[2]

I hope sometime that we may see you here at Tuskegee. Yours very truly,

Booker T. Washington

TLpS   Con. 538   BTW Papers   DLC.

[1] George Edgar Vincent (1864–1941) was president of the University of Minnesota (1911–17) and president of the Chautauqua Institution (1907–15), founded by his father. From 1917 to 1929 he was president of the Rockefeller Foundation.

[2] Vincent sent BTW the letter of introduction. (George E. Vincent to William J. Mayo, Oct. 15, 1915, Con. 538, BTW Papers, DLC.) BTW died, however, before he could carry out his plan to go to the Mayo Clinic.

To Booker Taliaferro Washington, Jr.

[Tuskegee, Ala.] October 11, 1915

My dear Booker: I have not forgotten or overlooked the matter of a barn at your house, but the fact is I am compelled to get rid of some of my pressing debts before I can assume any further obligations. I think it wise for you to go over these plans again very carefully and when you do, I am quite sure you will find that you can get along with a much smaller barn and one that will cost about half the amount you name. Later, if you need, you can add to the barn.

I am very glad to see how nicely you are fixing up your front yard.

Papa
B T W

TLpI   Con. 655   BTW Papers   DLC.

To Richard Henry Boyd

[Tuskegee, Ala.] October 14, 1915

Personal and Confidential.

My dear Dr. Boyd: I have been hoping that I might make it possible to run up to Nashville and have a talk with you and your son, but several matters have occurred recently which make it impossible for me to get away from here at an early date.

Would it be possible for you and your son to come down here some day before the 23d and be my guests for a day or two?

What I have in mind is to talk matters over with you and your son and see if we cannot reach some basis upon which to begin a movement to bring about harmony. I confess that as to the merits of the controversy I am ignorant. I do not know who is right and I do not know who is wrong, but I do know that it is possible, if people will act with bigness instead of littleness to compose difficulties and I believe that if we can get together for some hours we can lay down a plan by which all parties can begin working toward harmony. I know it cannot be done quickly, but I have in mind a plan which I believe you and Dr. Morris and his friends will agree to. I am not, however, taking the matter up with Dr. Morris as I am doing with you, as yet.

If the difficulties are not composed at once, or soon, you will find that your whole life work is going to be largely thrown away and in your old age you will find yourself burdened with difficulties which you ought to be free from.

More and more you will find that many of the people, if you take the advice of lawyers and others to any large extent, have but one object in view and that is to get hold of your pocketbook and you will find further that many people who pretend to be your friends and are urging you to stand out, have but one goal in view and that goal is Dr. Boyd's pocketbook.

You will find that keeping up a separate Convention is going to prove extremely expensive, financially, physically, morally and spiritually. You are getting to the point now where you ought to take things easy and get a lot of comfort and satisfaction out of the magnificent and unusual piece of work which you have done in behalf of the race. I beg of you to think of these matters. Yours very truly,

Booker T. Washington

TLpS Con. 534 BTW Papers DLC.

To Julius Rosenwald

Tuskegee Institute, Alabama, October 15, 1915

My dear Mr. Rosenwald: In acknowledging receipt of your check for Thirteen Thousand Dollars ($13,000.00) you do not know how grateful we are for the privilege of having some part in the expenditure of this money which is accomplishing so much good. In fact, when we realize how thoroughly you are trusting us in the expenditure of this money, it makes us feel very humble and at the same time increases our sense of responsibility in a genuine way.

I often wish that you could have time to hear and see for yourself some of the little incidents that occur in connection with this work. I wish you could hear the expressions of approval that now come from white people — white people who a few years ago would not think of anything bearing upon Negro education. I wish you could hear the expressions of gratitude uttered over and over again by the most humble classes of colored people.

Let me repeat, that we count it a great privilege to have some little share in this glorious work.

Of course we shall be very glad to send you all the information you desire for the album including photographs, etc. We have already taken measures to get the photographs and the other information which you have suggested.

I am planning to see you in Chicago sometime during the first week in November and go over matters a little more in detail. Yours very truly,

Booker T. Washington

TLS Julius Rosenwald Papers ICU. A press copy is in Con. 78, BTW Papers, DLC.

To Laura Murray Washington

[Tuskegee, Ala.] October 15, 1915

My dear Laura: I know you think I am pretty tardy in writing. The fact is, I have been pretty busy since you left here. I have thought of you constantly, as all of us have. I hope very much that you are well and enjoying your studies and life at Spelman. We are all well.

I sent you a little book the other day, which I hope you will read and enjoy. Please let me know if you need any pictures or anything like that for your room.

I do not know when I can see you, but sometime in the near future I am hoping to stop by to see you.

I hope you have some good agreeable roommates.

We think of you constantly.

Papa
B. T. W.

TLpI   Con. 538   BTW Papers   DLC.

To George Cleveland Hall

[Tuskegee, Ala.] October 16, 1915

Dear Dr. Hall: In the rough, I may be able to carry out the following program.

I am to speak for Major Moton at Petersburg, Virginia, on November 5th. It is my present plan to go to Chicago from Petersburg, reaching there perhaps on the 7th or 8th. I have an engagement to see Mr. Rosenwald about that time.

Would it be possible and practicable for you to go up to Rochester with me for a few days at my expense? This meets with the approval of Dr. Kenney and Mrs. Washington.

I am glad to say that I am feeling fifty per cent better than I was when I was at Coden. The experience there did me a lot of good.

You will be glad to know that since the storm diamond back turtles have been reduced to $40 a dozen. Of course we shall have the dinner while I am in Chicago. Yours very truly,

Booker T. Washington

P.S. — While I am in the vicinity of Chicago, would it be possible to have a meeting at your house or elsewhere, say of twelve or fifteen of the strongest business men and women in Chicago for the purpose of reviving and re-establishing the Local Negro Business League. It seems too bad that in a city of so large a population as there is in Chicago that there should not be some central organization for promoting commercial and business welfare.

B. T. W.

TLpS Con. 532 BTW Papers DLC.

To John Christopher Schwab[1]

[Tuskegee, Ala.] October 16, 1915

My dear Professor Schwab: I have just received a note from Mr. Harry R. Miles,[2] Chairman of Entertainment Committee, saying I am to be your guest while in New Haven. I remember with the greatest satisfaction and happiness my delightful stay at your house at the time of the Yale bicentennial, and I shall be very glad to meet you and your family again.

In order that I may inconvenience you just as little as possible, I am writing to say that I shall not reach New Haven until about the middle of the afternoon of the 25th. I have an engagement sometime in the afternoon with Mr. Anson Phelps Stokes, Jr., of Yale University, and after speaking at Woolsey Hall I think I am to speak at a colored church and am planning to take the boat from New Haven to New York that night. Perhaps I will go straight from the colored church to the boat. I have an early engagement in New York the following morning which I must meet. Yours very truly,

Booker T. Washington

TLpS Con. 536 BTW Papers DLC.

[1] John Christopher Schwab (1865–1916) was the librarian of Yale University.
[2] Harry Roberts Miles (1865–1951) was the minister of the Dwight Place Congregational Church, New Haven, Conn., from 1913 to 1924.

From Theodore Roosevelt

Sagamore Hill. [N.Y.] Oct 17th 1915

My dear Dr. Washington, The bearer, Mohammed Yohari,[1] was known to me, favorably, in Africa as one of Mr. Cherry Kearton's[2] attendants. He suddenly turned up in New York, as a sequel to wanderings of which he will tell you, and came out to me. I have been boarding him. I offered to ship him back to Mozambique, but he begged so hard to be given a chance to go to school here, paying his way by any work to which he is set, that I send him to you. He speaks English and in Africa I found him hardworking, respectful and self-respectful, and intelligent. Will you try him, and see whether he can earn his keep while studying so as to fit himself for work here? He evidently hates to go back to Africa where he might sink to the beehive-hut stage of existence again! Sincerely yours

Theodore Roosevelt

ALS   Con. 7   BTW Papers   DLC.

[1] Actually it was Mohammed Jama, son of the gun bearer Juma Yohari of the Roosevelt safari in East Africa in 1909. Jama arrived at Tuskegee on Oct. 24, 1915, to enroll as a student. He could neither read nor write English on his arrival, and he quit after a disappointing year and a half at the institute. (King, *Pan-Africanism and Education,* 1–2.)
[2] Cherry Kearton (1871–1940), born in Thwaite, Yorkshire, England, was a pioneer naturalist-photographer, the first to illustrate natural history books entirely with photographs. He traveled all over the world to photograph wildlife.

A Sunday Evening Talk

[Tuskegee, Ala.] October 17, 1915

ON TEAM WORK

Every large and successful business, or other organization, has been built up by what has been called "team-work," not by one individual, but by a number of individuals working together. In what I shall attempt to say tonight, I want to emphasize the importance of team-work in an institution like this — people working together with a common end in view.

We have an illustration in the business or industrial world of what can be accomplished by team-work in the Panama canal, which has been completed at so large an expense. Perhaps there has never been in history an illustration which represents so perfectly how it is possible for a number of individuals to accomplish what seemed to have been an impossible task a few years ago simply by working together. They learned how to do team-work.

We have another illustration of it in the case of the great Standard Oil Company. A great many people think that it has been built up by one man, Mr. Rockefeller. That is far from true. It has been built up through the co-operation, through sacrifices, through the unselfishness of a number of individuals working together as one man. * * * * * Then, though I do not wish to speak too much in praise of this institution, Tuskegee Institute has been built up, and been sustained largely through the co-operation of a number of individuals who have been willing to stand by it, who have been willing to sacrifice their all, nearly; who have pinned their faith to it, who have worked in season and out of season in order that it might succeed. Thus far, I think there are few institutions in the history of the country that can present a more perfect example in the form of team-work than is true of this institution. But it is most important that this team-work continue, if we are to continue to hold our own, if we are to continue to grow — so far as the future is concerned.

Let me illustrate by a few hasty and rude sketches what we can accomplish through team-work — what I mean by team-work: I very much wish that there might exist throughout the institution a spirit that would make it impossible for any person not to be on time in keeping an engagement — on time at his class, on time at the drill, on time at any stated appointment.

At West Point, where I was a few weeks ago, the Adjutant told me the thing they strove most for was to bring about team-work in the matter of promptness, to let it be felt when a student enters that institution until he graduates that it is most disgraceful for him to be late or to be tardy. You will find that spirit running all through that institution and you can find illustrations of the same thing in every large and successful institution and enterprise. I wish we might have it exhibited here more and more each year — the matter of team-work — in our sports. If we are going to play some other institution in football, or basketball, let us have team-work and let the whole institution stand back of the Tuskegee team. Let us stand by it with our prayers, with our yells, and with everything else, and in that way you learn to do team-work and you will take that spirit with you and when you go out into the world and organize a school of your own, or a Young Men's Christian Association of your own, you will find that having learned how to do team-work here, you will take that same spirit with you into other enterprises.

I hope, too, we may have team-work more and more each year in the matter of keeping down expenses. You can realize when there is a large number of people gathered together, all consuming something and few producing anything, what it means in the matter of keeping down expenses for each individual to do his part. I hope throughout this institution we shall have the spirit that shall say from morning until night:

"I am not going to be responsible for any expense that might be cut off."

"I am going to put my thought and conscience into it and I am not going to be the cause of any extra expense being placed upon this institution, even though it be to the amount of a half-cent."

Remember if all of us can save through some effort of our own even half a cent each day for the institution it will mean a great deal at the end of the year.

We want to have team-work in the direction of keeping down waste. That is the same thing as useless expense. If each one will make up his mind that he is going to help the general spirit of economy in the dining room, in the kitchen, in the class room, economy everywhere, it will tell immensely in running the institution in so far as finances are concerned. Above all, it will help you lay the foundation for something that will be useful for you all through life.

Then we want to have the spirit that shall bring about team-work in the matter of cleanliness. Let us have a clean institution. Let us have no department of the institution that we would be ashamed at any time, night or day, to throw open to the public. Let us not have to clean up when some visitors are coming, when the Trustees, or somebody else, are coming, but let us have the institution clean in every corner from morning until night, from the beginning of one season to the end of that season.

Then, as I intimated a few nights ago, we not only want the institution to be clean, but we want to go further than that. We want to have the grounds beautiful; we want to have the yards beautiful; we want to have the class rooms beautiful. We want to have everything beautiful that the students touch here, for in beauty there is always great inspiration.

We want to have such a team-work as shall make it impossible for a student to remain here and be comfortable if he is not doing honest work. We shall want to make it so uncomfortable for every student here who is not doing honest work that he will say: "I had better get out of this place. This is not the place for me." And when I say honest work, I mean honest work on the farm, in the shop, in the class room. Make it impossible for any student to learn here who goes to his classes day by day pretending to know something that he does not know, pretending to have studied a lesson that he has not studied. Make it impossible for a student to slip by in his examinations, who will pretend to have done that which he has not done.

Happily the world has at last reached the point where it no longer feels that in order for a person to be a great scholar, he has got to master a number of text books, that he has got to read a certain number of foreign languages, but the world has come to the conclusion that the person who has learned to use his mind — whether it has come about through the use of a tool or through the use of any other implement — that the person who has mastered something, who understands what he is doing, who is master of himself in the class room, out in the world, master of himself everywhere, that person is a scholar.

We want to have such team-work here that shall make it impossible for any student to remain connected with the institution who is dishonest in the matter of the use of other people's property. In plain language, every year we have too many students here who steal, who have not learned that other people's property cannot be used by them without their permission, without their consent. We have too many students who slide in here, who slip in here in one way and another, and begin by taking little things at first, a postage stamp, then a pencil perhaps, a book, then ten cents, and so on. Let us make it impossible for a student to stay here who is guilty of stealing and that means that you must consider more and more that this institution is your home and all of us part of one great big family. Every student who disgraces this family by stealing, by dishonesty, by weaknesses in any of these directions, is just as much disgracing you as if he were a part of your own blood and kin.

Let us have, then, running throughout the institution team-work in the direction of seeing that no dishonest student is permitted to stay here. In the same direction we want to have such team-work that shall make it absolutely impossible for an unclean character to be here, unclean in his morals, unclean in his living, unclean in his actions, in any direction — and going along with that we want to have such team-work here that it shall be impossible for a student to stay here who habitually tells untruths, falsehoods; who deceives. Let us have such team-work as shall put a premium upon truth and shall make it so disagreeable for every student who utters an untruth, who utters a lie, that he cannot stay at Tuskegee in peace. As I said a minute ago, in proportion as we have the reputation for truth-telling, we shall have an institution that shall make every one of you proud to be a member of it.

Then we want to have team-work, not only in the directions to which I have referred, but most of all, highest of all, we want to have team-work in our spiritual life, in our religious life, everywhere, in the prayer meetings, in the preaching services, in every devotional exercise, in the Young Men's Christian Association, in the Young Women's Christian Association, in the Bible School, everywhere, we want to have team-work, all working together in the direction which shall bring about the highest spiritual usefulness in this institution.

We can get it by each one forgetting his own personal ambitions, forgetting selfishness, forgetting all that stands in the way of perfect team-work.

Tuskegee Student, 27 (Nov. 13, 1915), 1–2. Stenographically reported. A pamphlet version with minor editorial differences is in Con. 977, BTW Papers, DLC. This was BTW's last Sunday Evening Talk.

An Article in the New York *Age*

Tuskegee Institute, Ala., October 18, 1915

DR. BOOKER T. WASHINGTON ON AMERICAN OCCUPATION OF HAITI

TUSKEGEE EDUCATOR SOUNDS NOTE OF WARNING, URGING UNITED STATES TO BE PATIENT WITH BLACK REPUBLIC

UPHOLDING THE MONROE DOCTRINE A NECESSITY

HAITI'S INDEBTEDNESS TO EUROPEAN COUNTRIES, WHO WERE DEMANDING PAYMENT, IMPELLED THIS COUNTRY TO TAKE STEPS TO AVOID EUROPEAN INTERFERENCE AND OCCUPATION — THE COUNTRY TEEMS WITH NATURAL WEALTH AND GREAT POSSIBILITIES

HAITI'S PRIDE UNSCATHED AND CONFIDENCE UNSHAKEN

LACK OF PRACTICAL EDUCATION PREVENTS MASS OF THE PEOPLE FROM PRODUCING THEIR OWN WEALTH IN THEIR OWN COUNTRY, SO THE COUNTRY HAS HAD TO SEND AWAY FOR NECESSITIES WHICH COULD BE PRODUCED MORE CHEAPLY AT HOME — ONLY BIG-BRAINED MEN AND MEN FREE FROM PREJUDICE SHOULD BE SENT BY THE ADMINISTRATION TO HAITI

Haiti is only a few hours ride from the American shore on an island midway between Cuba and Porto Rico. It is about the size of South Carolina and has a population of about two and one-half million people. Notwithstanding this, I venture the assertion that comparatively few people in the United States know as much about Haiti as they do about the far off Balkans.

The northern part of the island is occupied by the Republic of Santo Domingo and the southern portion by Haiti. The Dominicans speak the Spanish language. On the other hand, the Haitians speak the French language and cling to French customs and traditions. The Haitians, for the most part, are pure black, and are a very proud, mercurial people, with Latin characteristics.

"Humility," it is stated, "except when assumed for ulterior purposes, is no part of the Haitian character. With all of his faults, which he will ordinarily admit, his pride remains unscathed and his confidence in the ultimate success of his race in all the avenues of human endeavor continues unshaken. * * * He has the resistant qualities — lacking in the Dominican — which go to make up the obstructionist and fighter who never surrenders, and he has these qualities in a pre-eminent degree."

The Haitians won their independence over a hundred years ago from France under the leadership of Toussaint L'Ouverture, "one of the grandest characters produced by any race in the 18th century, though an ordinary black man, a slave and the son of slaves," at the price of hard fighting and much sacrifice. From that time until the present, the Haitians through many ups and downs have maintained their independence and have preserved some semblance of a republican form of government.

The Monroe Doctrine and United States Occupation

A few months ago the Government of the United States found it necessary to take a hand in the affairs of Haiti. It was absolutely necessary for the United States to do this or permit others to do so. This was unthinkable. Haiti unfortunately has suffered itself to get largely in debt to European countries. The European countries had been demanding their money.

The United States had said that "under the Monroe Doctrine we cannot permit you to come in and take control of Haiti and collect your money."

The European countries, of course, at once replied, "If you will not permit us to do it, you must do it."

This, as I understand it, is the justification asserted by the United States for landing marines on Haitian soil and assuming control of the custom houses, etc.

Haiti has been brought to its present unhappy condition not because of any great fault of the masses of the people. Everyone who has visited Haiti and studied its physical resources has been surprised to learn of the vast resources of the country. It is a country teeming with natural wealth and great possibilities. Sugar cane, for example, once planted, it is said will grow for twenty years without again being replanted.

The great mass of the people are, in a very primitive way, farmers. They are an unlettered people but, in their way, are an industrious, law abiding, sober people, seeking only to be let alone to earn their living. The masses of the people are of the peasant class who, as I have said, constitute the masses of the people. They are teachable and easily led and guided.

HAITIAN LEADERS ADOPT FRENCH IDEAS

The great difficulty is that Haiti, for many years, has been exploited by (1) selfish politicians who have used the government merely to enrich themselves without seeking to help the masses of the people; and (2) by promoters from the United States and several of the European countries, chiefly Germany and France, and in lesser degree, Great Britain and Belgium. I mean white men. These adventurers, or promoters, or by whatever name called, are largely responsible for stirring up the numerous revolutions that have disgraced and upset Haiti. The masses of the people have little interest in these revolutions, know little about them and care little about them.

And yet the Haitians themselves are largely at fault for their present unhappy conditions. They have been content to merely ape French civilization, content to get the veneer of French civilization without its substance and reality. The result is that while the bulk of the people — some 95 per cent., it is said — are ignorant, many of the leaders have been educated in France and other countries. Their education, however, has been unsuited for Haitian conditions. It has been an education that has fitted them to live and work anywhere except in Haiti.

The bulk of the people must depend upon agriculture, in some form, for their existence. Despite this, practically nothing has been done in Haiti during all the years of its independence to give the masses of the people practical education in agriculture, mechanics and the domestic arts. The leaders have devoted themselves to politics, little knowing, it seems, that political independence disappears without economic independence, that economic independence is the foundation of political independence.

Because of the neglect of practical education in Haiti, the country has been spending more than it has been earning. It has sent out of the country to get the necessities of life which might be produced at less cost in Haiti. While it is true that a large part of the revenues of the country have been stolen by white and black intriguers, these revenue receipts, even if honestly administered, have not been large enough to finance governmental expenditures. Because of the lack of encouraging the development of the natural resources of the country, it has not produced even a small proportion of what these physical resources may be made to produce. Haiti has been compelled to borrow money from foreigners simply because the people have not been taught to produce their own wealth, in their own country.

THE UNITED STATES AND ITS RELATIONS TO HAITI

This is preliminary to my making the following observations upon the United States and its relations to Haiti.

Associated Press dispatches a few days ago stated that forty or fifty Haitians had been killed on Haytian soil in one day by American marines and a number of marines wounded. To every black man in the United States this dispatch brought a feeling of disappointment and sorrow. While, as I have stated, the United States, under the circumstances, was compelled to take notice of conditions in Haiti and is being compelled to control matters, largely because of the fault of the Haitians, I had hoped that the United States would be patient in dealing with the Haitian Government and people. The United States has been patient with Germany. It has been patient in the Philippines. It has been exceedingly patient in dealing with Mexico. I hope this country will be equally patient and more than patient in dealing with Haiti — a weaker and more unfortunate country!

I very much wish that it might have been possible for the United States to have taken a little more time in making known to the Haitians the purposes we have in mind in taking over the control of their custom houses and their governmental affairs. While everything that we intend to do, and have in mind to do, is perfectly plain to the officials of the United States, we must remember that all this is not perfectly plain to the Haitians. It would have been worth while, in my opinion, before attempting arbitrarily to force Haiti to sign the treaty put before its officials, to have spent a little time and a little patience in informing the Haitian people of the unselfish benevolence of our intentions. They, in time, would have understood why it is necessary to intervene in their affairs.

Another reason, in my opinion, why patience may be manifested in this matter is that the treaty, even at the best, cannot be ratified by the United States Senate until it meets in regular session in December, unless the President calls it in special session earlier.

THE TREATY SEEMS HARSH AND PRECIPITATE

I confess that while I am unschooled in such matters, since reading the treaty the Haitians have been told they must ratify, it seems to me rather harsh and precipitate; one cannot be surprised that the Haitians have hesitated to agree to all the conditions provided for in this treaty. No wonder they have hesitated when they have had so little time in which to understand it, when the masses of the Haitian people know little or nothing of what the treaty contemplates.

The way matters are now going, there is likely to be bitterness and war. The United States, in the end, will conquer, will control, will have its way, but it is one thing to conquer a people through love, through unselfish interest in their welfare, and another thing to conquer them through the bullet, through the shotgun. Shooting civilization into the Haitians on their own soil will be an amazing spectacle. Sending marines as diplomats and Mauser bullets as messengers of destruction breed riot and anarchy, and are likely to leave a legacy of age-long hatreds and regrets.

I also hope the United States will not pursue a mere negative policy in Haiti, that is, a policy of controlling the customs and what not, without going further in progressive, constructive directions. In a word, the United States now has an opportunity to do a big piece of fine work for Haiti in the way of education, something the island has never had. I hope some way will be provided by which a portion of the revenues will be used in giving the people a thorough up-to-date system of common school, agricultural and industrial education. Here is an excellent opportunity for some of the young colored men and women of the United States who have been educated in the best methods of education in this country to go to Haiti and help their fellows. Here is an opportunity for some of the most promising Haitian boys and girls to be sent to schools in the United States. Here is an opportunity for us to use our influence and power in giving the Haitians something they have never had, and that is education, real education. At least 95 per cent. of the people, as I have said, are unlettered and ignorant so far as books are concerned.

THE UNITED STATES MUST BE VERY PATIENT WITH HAITI

In carrying all these suggestions into practice, let me repeat again and again that we will have to be patient with Haiti. We ought to be patient. We are big enough and strong enough to be patient, not arbitrary and force-compelling in our relations with her.

Also, we ought to be careful in the class of white men sent to Haiti as officials. Here is the first experience American white people have had to live and work in a black man's country, with black men and women. This is quite a different thing from living in what is called a "white man's country." Every Haitian would rather be swept from the face of the earth than give up his independence or his country. He does not wish the dominance of the white man. They are a proud people, albeit an ignorant people, often mistaken in their ideals and methods, but nevertheless a proud people determined to preserve the independence won by their ancestors in the face of great odds. The average American white man is not fitted to work with these Haitians. The average army officer, or naval officer, is not fitted to work with these Haitians. The average white soldier or white marine is not fitted to live and work among these Haitians. The racial lines which are drawn in this and other countries will not be tolerated in Haiti and American white men who go there should understand this. They must fit themselves to be white men in a black man's country if they want to live there and work there and have any influence there.

An American who, in an official capacity, had opportunity to observe Haitian affairs, writes:

"Degeneracy has been charged against the Haitian, but it is a charge in error. *The Haitians are by far the most virile people of the West Indies.* . . . Americans have never understood why any Latin-American country should be distrustful of the intentions of the United States when it appears in the role of the Big Brother offering assistance in the deepest sincerity, yet Latin-Americans conscientiously feel that there is good and sufficient ground for their distrust and will cite you many occurrences of history which they insist are proof that the United States has maintained a continuous policy of territorial expansion under the cloak of benevolent aid."

DIFFICULT FOR WHITE MEN TO UNDERSTAND BLACK MEN

It is very necessary then for us to recognize two things. First, the virility of the Haitian people, and, second, their distrust of American intentions. They should be won over and their distrust should not be accentuated by any action which may seem to suggest the dominance of an alien government as a permanent factor in their affairs. In other words, it should be made perfectly plain to the Haitians and to all others that the United States has but one object in view in going into Haiti and that is to help the Haitians govern their own country.

It is very difficult for any white man to understand, to put himself in a black man's place, to understand black people, to understand their motives, their methods, their ideals. There are only a few white men in the United States who understand, or even undertake to understand, the American Negro, and there are still fewer white men in this country who can go into Haiti and get the sympathy, the co-operation and the confidence of the Haitians, simply and mainly because it is not possible for many white people to even try to understand and work with black people.

We should remember that the United States is at a great disadvantage in dealing with Haiti as compared with Germany and France, for example, both of which countries have interests in Haiti, because the Haitians have a deep-seated prejudice against white Americans. Year after year they have read about lynchings and manifestations of prejudice against members of their race in the United States. The Haitians, in consequence, have thoroughly made up their minds that the dominant people of the United States are prejudiced against black people and do not mean to trust them with fairness or justice.

The intervention of the United States in the affairs of Haiti should enable this country to change, if we are wise, the idea which the Haitians entertain regarding white Americans. We have the opportunity of proving to these people on the little island in the Caribbean Sea who are striving, despite their many falls from grace, to establish a republican form of government on the basic principles of liberty, fraternity and equality, that in spite of the many wrongs inflicted upon their fellows in the United States that in all the real things of civilization these ten millions of black people in the United States are further ahead of any similar number of black people anywhere in the world.

My whole object, then, my only object, in writing this article is to urge that now is the time to exercise a little patience with Haiti; now is the time to put in a constructive, progressive policy in education and civilization for the Haitians which will gradually win them. It will make them feel that we are not their enemies, but their permanent helpers and benefactors. The ten million black people in the United States are watching this government prayerfully, watching to see if it will exercise the same patience with Haiti that it has exercised with larger and more important countries that have been as disorderly as Haiti.

I feel that we should embrace the opportunity for a constructive policy that will remake Haiti, that will make the Haitians a new people, and from an economic point of view and every other point of view will make Haiti of increasing value not alone to the Haitians but to our own country and civilization as well.

New York *Age,* Oct. 21, 1915, 1, 5.

Emmett Jay Scott to Edwin L. Barker[1]

[Tuskegee, Ala.] October 18, 1915

Personal.

My dear Sir: I am sending you under separate cover today a copy of Dr. Washington's autobiography, "Up From Slavery." This book has been translated probably into more languages than any book written in America, with the possible exception of "Uncle Tom's Cabin."

With your permission I should like to put before you copies of a number of comments from the most influential men in America in commendation of this book. Recently, I secured from Doubleday, Page & Company, the publishers, the rights to the film reproduction of the book.

It has occurred to me that the Barker-Swan Service might be disposed to consider filming the story of "Up From Slavery." I am quite sure than an interesting picture can be made which should include not only Dr. Washington's personal strivings, but also the strivings of the race climbing up from the tragic period represented by slavery in America.

I write to inquire if the matter in any way interests you. Yours very truly,

Emmett J Scott

TLpS Con. 15   BTW Papers   DLC.

¹ Edwin L. Barker was general manager of the Advance Motion Picture Co., in Chicago.

To Paul Dwight Moody[1]

Tuskegee Institute, Alabama   October 19, 1915

Dear Sir: This letter will be handed you by my younger son, E. Davidson Washington, who is in Vermont at my request for the purpose of getting aid for our institution. Any service that you can render him will be very much appreciated. He will explain to you further in detail what he has in mind, if you will give him the opportunity. Yours very truly,

Booker T. Washington

TLS   James Weldon Johnson Collection   CtY.

¹ Paul Dwight Moody (1879–1947), son of the famous evangelist Dwight L. Moody, was pastor of the South Congregational Church in St. Johnsbury, Vt., from 1912 to 1917. He was an army chaplain in World War I and in 1921 became president of Middlebury College in Vermont.

To the Editor of the Montgomery *Advertiser*

[Tuskegee, Ala., Oct. 20, 1915][1]

In no other Southern state, in fact in no state in the Union where there are so many colored people living in proportion to the white people, do more friendly and sympathetic relations exist between the colored people and white people than is true of the State of Alabama. This fine relationship between the two races has been brought about very largely by reason of the fact that we have been fortunate in having in Alabama for the most part, a liberal and courageous press that has urged racial cooperation and racial peace, and above all, justice to the colored people.

The result of this encouragement on the part of the press and the white people in Alabama generally is shown by the fact that in Alabama the colored people have made remarkable progress, owning and paying taxes upon about 18,000 farms. The total farm property of all kinds upon which colored people pay taxes in Alabama is worth about $22,500,000. Besides this, they own and operate about 2,000 grocery stores, drug stores, dry goods stores and other business concerns. Some of the most successful insurance companies conducted by our people anywhere in the country are located in Alabama. In the matter of educational institutions and churches, Alabama is certainly equal to other Southern states if not ahead of them.

I repeat, this progress could not have been made by us except as we have had help from the best white people in Alabama.

The Montgomery Advertiser, which has been the leader in the directions to which I have referred, is proposing to publish soon a state wide special edition in which a special section will be given to showing the progress of the colored people in Alabama.

I want to urge that every individual and every business concern, every organization of any character, educational, religious or secular among us, take advantage of this opportunity to show what we are doing in the way of taking advantage of our opportunities in this great state. We should be well represented in this special edition.

It will help our race, not only in Alabama but throughout the country. The Tuskegee Normal and Industrial Institute will attempt to put before the people of Alabama, and of the country, a story of the work we are doing here in the heart of the Black Belt of the South. We have found in the past that such advertising has been of the greatest value to us, and I am sure it will prove of equal value to all of our people who may cooperate with the Advertiser in making this edition what the owners and editors of the Advertiser plan that it shall be.

Booker T. Washington

TMpS Con. 534 BTW Papers DLC.

¹ BTW forwarded the letter to W. T. Sheehan of the Montgomery *Advertiser* on Oct. 20, 1915. Sheehan replied: "It was all and more than we could ask for." (BTW to Sheehan, Oct. 20, 1915, and Sheehan to BTW, Oct. 27, 1915, Con. 534, BTW Papers, DLC.)

To John Andrew Kenney

[Tuskegee, Ala.] October 21, 1915

Dr. Kenney: I find that there is a good deal of feeling in the town of Tuskegee and vicinity to the effect that our hospital is too restricted in the number of physicians permitted to practice there and to send their patients there. Under present conditions, a good many colored people complain that they cannot be taken into the hospital unless they are the patients of certain doctors.

Of course when the hospital was first erected and organized, conditions were different and I am wondering if the time has not come when we should change the rules to a certain extent so as to allow a larger latitude in the number of physicians who are permitted to use the hospital; for example, I learned that the City Physician under present regulations is not permitted to have free use of the hospital on the same basis as other physicians. You can see that this kind of arrangement would easily place the school in an awkward position.

I believe it would be best for all concerned for you to take the whole matter up with the hospital staff and consider it from a broad, generous point of view and see if the rules cannot be so amended so as to give greater satisfaction.

I am very anxious that the hospital be used in a way to serve the largest number of people and we are also anxious that our nurses get into as many families as possible in the town and county. Under present conditions, I cannot feel that the patronage is as large from the county as it should be and I also fear that our nurses are being kept out of many families where they might otherwise be of service.

Of course I do not wish in any way to dictate to the Staff as to the individuals who shall practice there and restrict the Staff in detailed decisions. I think the Staff would be justified in guarding pretty carefully the number and character of the doctors who operate surgically in the hospital. More liberality might be shown in the matter of people who do not need surgical attention.

Booker T. Washington

TLpS   Con. 662   BTW Papers   DLC.

From John Andrew Kenney

[Tuskegee, Ala.] Oct. 21, 1915

Mr. Washington   With reference to the suggestion for enlarging our hospital staff I wish you to bear in mind, as is well known there are few men nearer than Montgomery who do good surgery, that there are many men who want to learn, and many who will take any kind of chances on our people. Once in, they do anything they wish. How can we get them out? With me that is and always has been a very serious consideration and also one of the chief reasons why our staff was made and restricted as it was in the beginning.

I must confess it is a very delicate question with me about enlarging our *surgical* staff. It would be a simpler matter to enlarge the *medical* staff. I feel it my duty to throw this out as a hint and warning while we are in process of considering this matter. We are jealous of our surgical reputation here. To have persons with no special interest except what they can get out of it come in and increase our mortality will do us a great deal more harm than they can possibly counteract with the good they can render.

I would make this suggestion: Any addition to the Staff should be for one (1) year only, service to cease automatically at the expiration of the year unless formally reelected. Yours very truly

John A. Kenney

TLS   Con. 662   BTW Papers   DLC.

To George Cleveland Hall

[Tuskegee, Ala.] October 22, 1915

Confidential

My dear Dr. Hall: Since writing you a little while ago, regarding my Rochester trip, something has occurred which may delay my going to Rochester for a few days. This is confidential.

Mr. Rosenwald has just notified us that he is likely to be here about the 10th of November and in case he carries out that plan, I should like to be here when he comes. He is not planning, however, to remain more than one or two days and it would be my plan to leave here as soon as Mr. Rosenwald leaves.

Thank you very much for the pictures which have just come and for your good letter which Mrs. Washington and I appreciate very much.

We are so glad that you had such a good and restful time at Coden. Do not forget the Diamond Backs. Yours very truly,

Booker T. Washington

TLpS   Con. 532   BTW Papers   DLC.

To Whitefield McKinlay

[Tuskegee, Ala.] October 22, 1915

My dear Mr. McKinlay: I know you think I am acting very shabbily in regard to the Douglass Home matter, but I am simply trying to find a time and season to take up the matter in a large comprehensive way and finish it up.

The way that I see matters now, I fear an effort in this direction would fail because of the scarcity of money throughout the country. This is not only true among colored people, but among white people everywhere and I do not want to make another failure. You have no idea how many people who have the reputation of being rich have little or no money to give away for anything at present.

If you have any further suggestions to make, please let me have them and I shall consider them very carefully. I realize thoroughly the position in which you and the other Trustees are placed.

You have no idea how hard conditions are in the South. People who a year ago made fifty bales of cotton have now made only about 15 or 20 bales. True the price is higher, but they have no cotton to sell.

I hope you and your family are well. Yours very truly,

Booker T. Washington

TLpS   Con. 826   BTW Papers   DLC.

Emmett Jay Scott to Frederick Randolph Moore

[Tuskegee, Ala.] October 23, 1915

My dear Mr. Moore: I do not know how the rumor could have originated to the effect that Dr. Washington is seriously ill. It is certainly far from the truth. In fact, he is in better health now than he has been for several weeks or months.[1] He is leaving today for New York City, and you will probably be meeting him within the next day or two.

I am waiting every day to hear from you as to the position which has been promised by Governor Whitman. I want to congratulate you in advance.

We are looking for the 200 papers containing the article on Haiti, and we are planning to mark them and send them out to an important class of people.

I wish you great success in the trip through North Carolina. I wish I could make the trip with you.

With all good wishes, I am   Sincerely yours,

Emmett J. Scott

TLpS Con. 77 BTW Papers DLC.

[1] BTW mentioned in a letter to trustee Charles E. Mason that he had been a patient at the Tuskegee Institute hospital for a day in mid-October. (Oct. 22, 1915, Con. 77, BTW Papers, DLC.)

Emmett Jay Scott to Harry Centennial Oppenheimer

[Tuskegee, Ala.] October 23, 1915

Personal:

Dear Mr. Oppenheimer: I have this week written Miss Vorhaus in some detail regarding Miss Sterne's photo-play. She may go over the matter with you.

Now, with reference to the Griswold Photo-Play Company about which you have written:

Mr. Griswold, in my opinion, has not the dramatic instinct nor the financial backing to pull off anything very satisfactory. His commercial instinct, however, is well developed, and I believe what he has in mind is to cash in as quickly as possible upon the proper desire of the Negro people to see films which show something of their life and general activities. If I should happen to be going to Birmingham again soon, I will talk with him and write you again.

Referring again to Miss Sterne's Photo-Play: You will learn from my letter to Miss Vorhaus my attitude with reference to the Lincoln Dream picture. It may be after hearing from you or Miss Vorhaus that we can again take up the matter of having the Tuskegee Institute included in the Lincoln Dream scenario.

I wish you would turn over in your mind the thought of the organization of a group to be known as the "Famous Negro Players Company" including such persons as Bert Williams and a group of actors who are in a way quite superior. There are many such whom you would be very much pleased to meet, I am sure. I can easily get together a most satisfactory organization of such individuals representing the highest artistic possibilities of the race, and it might be that the L'Ouverture film and the Up From Slavery film might be developed without very great outlay and to the mutual profit of all concerned.

Please remember me kindly to Mr. Brandt, whom I have had the pleasure of meeting once. Yours very truly,

Emmett J. Scott

P.S. Will you kindly let me have your home address so that the Tuskegee Student may be sent there instead of to your office.

TLpS Con. 13 BTW Papers DLC.

George Cleveland Hall to Julius Rosenwald

Chi[cago]. 10/25/15

My Dear Mr. Rosenwald: I am writing you confidentially relative to Dr. B. T. Washington's health. I hope you will pardon my presuming that you will want to take up the matter further — but as a friend and trustee of Dr. Washington and Tuskegee, I hope that you will consider the condition of his health, and also some arrangement by which he can be relieved for at least a period of six months or a year.

As you know I was with Dr. Washington 15 days last month, and during that time he had three severe attacks of kidney trouble — he also is suffering from high blood pressure — extremely high — and is taking a chance every time he exerts himself mentally as well as physically. In a confidential talk with me he indicated it would be a great relief to him if he could stay at home quietly and not have to worry about the running expenses of the school — and that he would be on the train and in the hotels ⅔ of his time; — in other words he needs mental and physical rest and quiet at home — Anything that could be done to relieve this condition would in my opinion and best professional judgment, go a long ways in prolonging his life and usefulness.

I have written to you very plainly as well as I could put the case and trust the graveness of it will justify my taking it up with you.

With high personal regards, I am, Sincerely yours

Geo. C. Hall

TLtSr Julius Rosenwald Papers ICU.

An Address before
the American Missionary Association and
National Council of Congregational Churches

New Haven, Connecticut, October 25, 1915

Mr. Chairman, Ladies and Gentlemen:

A few days ago I visited a little colony of black people near Mobile, Alabama, several of whom were born in Africa and came here on the last slave ship to reach America. Several of the older people still survive and tell interesting stories about their early and varied experiences. A little way from the colony may be seen the hulk of the slave ship on which they were brought to this country.

This has occurred practically within a single generation. What a transformation has been wrought to my race since the landing of the first slaves at Jamestown and the landing of the last slaves at Mobile! This transformation involves growth in number, mental awakening, self-support, securing of property, moral and religious development, and adjustment of relations between the races. To what in a single generation are we more indebted for this transformation in the direction of a higher civilization than the American Missionary Association?

I have said we have grown in numbers. Do you realize that today there are as many Negroes in the United States as there are persons in the whole of Minnesota, Iowa, Missouri, North Dakota, South Dakota, Nebraska, and Kansas? And do you know, as of course you do, that the American Missionary Association was the pioneer factor in the educational work of Negroes? Your association established on September 16, 1861, at Fortress Monroe, Virginia, the first school for freedmen. In this school the first experiment among the freedmen in industrial education was made. Out of this school the Hampton Institute grew. I am, therefore, in a way the product of your association.

No one of the religious organizations which have engaged in the work of educating the Negro has done a more useful work than your association. You are maintaining more schools for the higher and secondary education of the Negro than any other board or association. I have had opportunity to visit practically every Negro institution in the country. In so doing I have been very favorably impressed with the good work which the educational institutions under the auspices of your association are doing. I have in mind not only the larger and more prominent schools, such as Fisk and Talladega, but also the smaller and less well known institutions.

Fifty years ago the education of the Negro in the South had just begun. There were less than 100 schools devoted to this purpose. In 1867 there were only 1,938 schools for the freedmen, with 2,087 teachers, of whom 699 were colored. There were 111,442 pupils. Of these, 18,758 pupils were studying the alphabet, 55,163 were in the spelling and easy reading classes, 42,879 were learning to write, 40,454 were studying arithmetic, 4,611 were studying the higher branches. Thirty-five industrial schools were reported, in which there were 2,624 students who were taught sewing, knitting, straw-braiding, repairing and making garments. In 1915 there are almost 2,000,000 Negro children enrolled in the public schools of the South, and over 100,000 in the normal schools and colleges. The 699 colored teachers have increased to over 34,000, of whom 3,000 are teachers in colleges and normal and industrial schools.

When the American Missionary Association began its work among the freedmen there were in the South no institutions for higher and secondary education of the Negro. There were only 4 in the entire United States. In 1915 there are in the South 50 colleges devoted to their training. There are 13 institutions for the education of Negro women. There are 26 theological schools and departments. There are 3 schools of law, 4 of medicine, 2 of dentistry, 3 of pharmacy, 17 state agricultural and mechanical colleges, and over 200 normal and industrial schools.

Fifty years ago the value of the school property used in the education of the freedmen was small. The value of the property now owned by institutions for their secondary and higher training is over $17,000,000.

Fifty years ago only a few thousand dollars was being expended for the education of the Negroes. In 1914 over $4,100,000 was expended for their higher and industrial training, and $9,700,000 in their public schools.

Although there has been great progress in Negro education during the past fifty years, the equipments and facilities in Negro schools are, on the whole, far below those in white schools. The majority of the rural schools in the South are still without school buildings, and the average length of their terms is from three to five months. The Negroes constitute about 11 per cent of the total population of the country. A little less than 2 per cent of the expenditures of over $700,000,000 expended annually for education is spent upon them. Of the $600,000,000 spent on public schools the Negroes receive about 1½ per cent. More money is spent on special schools for Indians, about $4,800,000 annually, than is expended for higher and industrial training for the Negro, a little more than $4,100,000.

I find that in some instances there is a belief that Negro education has advanced far enough for the various philanthropic and religious associations to gradually withdraw their support and use their resources in other directions. The truth of the matter, however, is that after fifty years there is still as great a need for the work of the American Missionary Association and similar organizations to assist in Negro education as there was immediately following Emancipation.

There are about 1,800,000 Negro children in the South enrolled in the public schools. This is a large number but not as large, however, as the number not in school. According to the United States census reports, 52 per cent of the Negro children in the South of school age are not attending school. There are yet in the South over 2,000,000 Negroes who are unable to read or write. Almost 1,000,000 of these are of school age.

Although there are perhaps 100,000 Negro students enrolled in normal schools and colleges, statistics show that only about one fourth of these are doing work above the elementary grades, and only about one third are receiving industrial education. In the fifty colleges devoted to Negro education there are, according to statistics, less than 3,000 students who are doing work of the collegiate grade.

In the North the Jew, the Slav, the Italian, many of whom are such recent arrivals that they have not yet become citizens and voters, even under the easy terms granted them by the federal naturalization laws, have all the advantages of education that are granted to every other portion of the population. In several states an effort is now being made to give immigrant people special opportunities for education over and above those given to the average citizen. In some instances night schools are started for their special benefit. Frequently schools which run nine months in the winter are continued throughout the summer, whenever a sufficient number of people can be induced to attend them. Sometimes, for example, as in New York state, where a large number of men were employed in digging the Erie Canal and in excavating the Croton Aqueduct, camp schools were started where the men employed on these public works in the day might have an opportunity to learn the English language at night. In some cases a special kind of textbook, written in two or three different languages, was prepared for use in these immigrant schools, and frequently teachers were specially employed who could teach in the native languages if necessary.

While in the North all this effort is being made to provide education for these foreign peoples, many of whom are sojourners in this country and will return in a few months to their homes in Europe, the Negro in the South has, as is often true in the country districts, no school at all, or one with a term of no more than four or five months, taught in the wreck of a log cabin and by a teacher who is paid about half the price received for the hire of a first-class convict.

There is sometimes much talk about the inferiority of the Negro. In practice, however, the idea appears to be that he is a sort of superman. He is expected, with about one fifth of what the whites receive for their education, to make as much progress as they are making. Taking the Southern states as a whole, about $10.23 per capita is spent in educating the average white boy or girl, and the sum of $2.82 per capita in educating the average black child.

In order to furnish the Negro with educational facilities so that the two million children of school age now out of school and the one million who are unable to read or write can have the proper chance in life, it will be necessary to increase the nine million dollars now being expended annually for Negro public school education in the South to about twenty-five or fifty million dollars.

I find that the total value of all the property owned by institutions devoted to the industrial, secondary, and higher training of Negroes amounts to about twenty million dollars, which is less than the combined values of the property owned by two institutions alone — the

University of Chicago and Columbia University. The total value of the property owned by institutions for whites in the United States for secondary, higher, and industrial training amounts to almost one billion dollars. The value of the manual training and industrial schools for whites is almost fifty million dollars. If the amount of property devoted to Negro higher education were at all proportionate to the number of Negroes in the population of the country, they would have for their higher training about one hundred million dollars invested in property instead of the twenty million dollars which they now have.

In order to give the Negro youth in the South adequate facilities for obtaining thorough training in normal and college courses, it will be necessary to increase the little more than four million dollars now being expended annually for Negro higher and secondary education to ten million dollars or more. In other words Negro higher and secondary education needs about six million dollars more annually than it is now receiving.

At the present rate it is taking, not a few days or a few years, but a century or more to get Negro education on a plane at all similar to that on which the education of the whites is. To bring Negro education up where it ought to be, it will take the combined and increased efforts of all the agencies now engaged in this work. The North, the South, the religious associations, the educational boards, white people and black people, all will have to coöperate in a great effort to this common end.

Ernest Davidson Washington, ed., *Selected Speeches of Booker T. Washington* (Garden City, N.Y.: Doubleday, Doran and Co., 1932), 277–83.

To Margaret James Murray Washington

[New York City] Oct. 26, 1915

Spoke at two large meetings at Yale last night and felt no bad effects. Am getting on very well.

B. T. W.

TWcIr Con. 542 BTW Papers DLC.

From George Cleveland Hall

Chicago   Oct 27–15

Dear Dr Washington, I am very much pleased with the improvement of your health and also of your determination to go to the Mayos and have them give you a thorough examination. I shall be very glad at any time it suits you to be present while you stay there.

I had a long talk with Mr Rosenwald the other day and talked very plainly to him concerning the method of financing Tuskegee, and of your having to be away so much on the train & in hotels and have asked that he try to arrange the matter so as to give you the needed relief. I am writing to you so that you will know when the matter comes up that they know your health condition and that the complaint is not coming from you but from me as a friend and medical observer of your condition. I have suggested that you be relieved for at least 6 mo or a year of the chief burden of the financial support etc. Now Mr. Rosenwald is in perfect sympathy with the whole scheme as I put it to him, and suggested that I write him a letter so that he would have something to show the other members with whom he expects to take it up. *He does* not know *that you know any thing about my seeing him* so while you may seem surprised I hope you will not in any way attempt to minimize what I have said about your needing a rest and your desire for it and also the globe trotting. They claim that they want to help you and you won't let them; now for once I hope you will be perfectly frank and disabuse their minds of the idea that they can't help you.

You need rest mental & physical. You must slow up. You deserve it *now*, while it will benefit you, not after it is too late to seek it. I have thrown the fear into them and you must not be so modest as to attempt to appear able to continue to throw off these terrific attacks with out help. You owe this to yourself your family your friends and the entire country to guard your health *now*. Yours Sincerely

Geo C Hall

PS   be sure and let me know about the time you are coming so that I can have the diamond backs at $40 per dozen.

I nearly left out the most mainest thing as Tulane says. Mrs Hall is planning to have Hortense christened at the house during your next visit to Chicago. She complains that she has never had an answer from you to her request that you act as God Father. Of course to her Hortense is the greatest thing in the world and the most distinguished man & citizen thereof is none to[o] big to act as her sponsor. I dont think she would hesitate to ask President Wilson if she had any confidence in his character. Will you set her mind at ease on this point. It is not a public affair private at the house. Sincerely

G C Hall

ALS   Con. 531   BTW Papers   DLC.

From Margaret James Murray Washington

Tuskegee Ala   Oct 27 1915

LETTER SENT YOU TODAY BILTMORE HOTEL   CALL FOR IT   BE VERY CAREFUL WHAT YOU EAT

M

TWIr   Con. 951   BTW Papers   DLC.   Addressed to the Herald Square Hotel, New York City.

From Emmett Jay Scott

Tuskegee Institute, Alabama   October 28, 1915

Dear Mr. Washington: I attach herewith clipping from The Atlanta Constitution last Sunday with reference to "The Birth of the Nation."[1] This play has already been shown in Houston, Texas, and the result of it was that at the first showing a large number of white people sprang to their feet in the scene where a colored man is shown pursuing a young white girl to yell: "Lynch him. Lynch him."

You can thus see how matters are going, especially in view of the statement in the Constitution to the effect that the play is to be shown throughout the South.

The last two lines of this clipping show just exactly where the appeal of the picture lies. Yours very truly,

E J Scott

TLS Con. 657 BTW Papers DLC.

¹ The Atlanta *Constitution* reported that the "great triumph of scenic art" would soon appear in Atlanta and assured the reader that the mayor would probably reject the petition of a committee of three citizens to suppress the spectacle. It implied that there was nothing to justify the fear that the picture "might stir up race prejudice," and stressed instead its healing effect upon sectionalism, quoting the Americus (Ga.) *Times-Recorder:* "Sons of the south and sons of the north can join hands in the righteous feeling of love and good fellowship as they see it." The last two lines of the clipping read: "Hundreds of Atlantans have seen and enjoyed the picture. They have told their countless friends of its wonders and its great attractiveness." (Atlanta *Constitution,* Oct. 24, 1915, 3F.)

From Margaret James Murray Washington

Tuskegee Ala Oct 28 1915

DOCTOR KENNEY AND I BOTH FEEL THAT YOU MAKE A GREAT MISTAKE TO MAKE THIS EXTRA TRIP TO TUSKEGEE TAKE THE TIME TO REST UNTIL YOU GO TO VIRGINIA

M

TWIr Con. 542 BTW Papers DLC.

Emmett Jay Scott to Charles Clinton Spaulding

[Tuskegee, Ala.] October 30, 1915

My dear Friend: I sincerely appreciate your telegram of inquiry regarding Dr. Washington. There is, however, nothing in the rumor to the effect that he is seriously ill.

He left here a week ago to speak at New Haven, Connecticut, at the annual meeting of the American Missionary Association, and is spending this week in New York City in the interest of the Institute.

417

Next week he will speak at Petersburg, before the Virginia Organization Society, and will then attend the Inaugural Exercises at Fisk University.

As you know, he was not altogether well at the Boston meeting of the Business League, but he has been steadily improving in health since then. Yours very truly,

Emmett J. Scott

It is most kind of you to send this inquiry. We keenly appreciate it.

TLpS Con. 536 BTW Papers DLC. Postscript in Scott's hand.

To Margaret James Murray Washington

[New York City] Oct. 30, 1915

Have decided not to come home before going to Petersburg. I may not go to Fisk. Am getting on well. Tell Mr. Scott.

B. T. W.

TWIr Con. 542 BTW Papers DLC.

William G. Willcox to Julius Rosenwald

New York 10/30/15

Dear Mr. Rosenwald: Mr. Low and I had a conference with Dr. Washington a few days ago in regard to his health and in regard to his finances. We do not find that he is seriously worried about his financial affairs. He says that Mrs. Washington has charge of them almost entirely, and while what money he has saved has been invested in unproductive real estate, which is a considerable drain in the way of interest and taxes, we could get from him nothing which would justify the opinion expressed by Mr. Stewart that worry over his financial affairs is having a serious effect upon his health. He said he would ask Mrs. Washington to send us a full statement of his present finances, and we shall probably hear from her in the near future, but neither

Mr. Low nor I felt that there was any occasion apparent for taking any steps to relieve him in this direction.

As regards his physical condition, I found that he had been relying upon Dr. Kenney and young Dr. Janvrin[1] here in New York, both of whom feel that his condition is better than it was some time ago. I called up Dr. W. A. Bastedo,[2] a specialist in abdominal diseases, whom I happen to know quite well, and asked him about Dr. Janvrin. I found that he is a recent graduate, and, in fact, a pupil of Dr. Bastedo's, and while Dr. Bastedo speaks very well of him as a promising young man, it seemed to me wise to have some further advice, and I was, therefore, glad to accept Dr. Bastedo's suggestion that he should go over Dr. Washington's case himself. Dr. Washington has been there yesterday and again today, and I have been just talking to Dr. Bastedo over the telephone, and he tells me that Dr. Washington has pretty serious kidney trouble and blood pressure of 215. He is making some further tests, and I shall have a more detailed report next week.

At the suggestion of Dr. Flexner[3] and Dr. Frissell, Dr. Washington is also going to the Rockefeller Institute to see Dr. Cole[4] there, today, and Dr. Bastedo is going to give Dr. Cole a statement of his findings.

I am afraid that his condition is more serious than any of us had suspected, and I think we must at least look forward to an almost complete cessation of his trips about the country and of public addresses.

I am sending Mr. Low and Mr. Trumbull a copy of this letter, merely as a preliminary report, for I think we must all give serious consideration to the matter, not only in its bearing on Mr. Washington himself, but in its bearing upon the future of the Institute.

I regret to say that I see no prospect of being able to go with you to Nashville and Tuskegee, and I think I must definitely decide against this attractive suggestion.

With kind regards, I am, Sincerely,

William G. Willcox

TLtSr   Julius Rosenwald Papers   ICU.

[1] Edmund R. P. Janvrin, born in 1884.

[2] Walter A. Bastedo (1873–1952), a Canadian with an M.D. degree from Columbia University, was associated with St. Luke's Hospital on 113th Street in New York City from 1904 to 1927 as an associate and attending physician. He taught pharmacology at Columbia Medical School (1903–21), wrote several med-

ical texts, and was president of the American Pharmacopoeial Convention (1930–40).

³ Simon Flexner.

⁴ Rufus Cole (1872–1966) was director of the hospital of the Rockefeller Institute in New York from 1909 to 1937. An M.D. of Johns Hopkins University (1899), he was connected with Johns Hopkins as a resident physician and instructor in medicine from 1899 to 1907. He contributed a chapter on gonococcus infections in Osler's *System of Medicine,* and wrote many articles in medical journals.

A Draft of an Article on Fishing in Mobile Bay[1]

[ca. October 1915]

A PARADISE OF FISH & SEA FOOD

Aside from hunting and horseback-riding, nothing rests me more and delights my soul more than to get on some stream near an old-fashioned swimming pool, with the root of a tree close by and to spend as many hours as I can in fishing with the old-time pole and line. The new fangled fishing apparatus I have never had any use for or any success with.

In recent years, however, I confess I have become almost discouraged in fishing for the reason that I have found it almost impossible to find a spot where any fish "actually exist" and "bite." I have had glowing pictures painted for me, but in nearly every case when I went to the spot something had just happened: the fish had disappeared; the water was too muddy, or it was too cold, or bait could not be secured, or the season for that special kind of fish had just run out, or the fish and game law was in force; usually the excuse has been that fish were biting last week or last month but for some inexplainable reason, they seem to have quit biting at the special time I would make my visit.

In fact, I have been disappointed so systematically and constantly in recent years in really finding fish that I was almost ready to agree with one who made the statement a short time ago to the effect that he believed, that after all there was only one true fisherman and that was Peter who said, "We have toiled all night long and have caught nothing." My fortune, or luck, however, changed in September. My readers I suppose would think that the very southernmost point in Alabama, thirty miles south of Mobile, would not be a very pleasant place to spend a short vacation in fishing, but this is the spot I chose and shall seek to describe.

I selected for my headquarters during my brief stay Coden. It is located on Mobile Bay. I expected before going there to encounter heat, gnats, mosquitoes and every pest conceivable, but to my great surprise and delight there were practically no mosquitoes or other bothersome insects and the weather was so cool and pleasant that on several occasions it was necessary at night to use a blanket. There is something in the atmosphere that makes one go to sleep as soon as he strikes the bed and he sleeps soundly until the next morning.

At this point Mobile Bay has numerous inlets, rivers, bayous, etc., reaching into the surrounding country and this makes an extremely attractive place for fishing; fishing is not only good in the open deep water, but especially good in these numerous inlets. The whole atmosphere is one of sea-food. I have never been in any section of the country where I came into contact so constantly with the richest variety of practically every kind of sea-food including nearly every kind of fish existing in salt water, the largest oysters I have ever seen; shrimps, crabs of every variety and every variety of other sea-food products.

To see a diamond terrapin farm is worth a trip to Mobile Bay; Messrs. Clark Brothers, near Coden, has in one pen about 700 fine diamond-back terrapins which he is preparing for the New York market. I had never witnessed such a sight before, but Clark Brothers have learned the trick of growing them and are doing it most successfully.

The region around about Coden is much varied and unspoiled; there is nothing of the atmosphere of the professional tourist in the community and little or nothing of commercialism. Everybody, white and black, wants to make one's stay pleasant and is constantly offering to do something that will add to one's pleasure and comfort. If one's neighbor has fresh rolls for breakfast, she wants to be sure that her neighbor and her company get some of these rolls. One is not likely to be in the community long before some neighbor will send some of the finest soft-shell crabs for his meal that can be found anywhere in the country. When one has a big catch of fish, he is glad to share them with his neighbors.

One does not grow tired of the scenery in this section of Mobile Bay. There is an ever-changing panorama; one can go to a new fishing place every day and can catch a different kind of fish. I should be ashamed to tell just how many fish I caught within a single hour; sufficient to say that I caught more fish in the few days I was in the region of Coden than I have ever caught in all of my experience in fishing in all parts of the country combined. I caught so many that even the truth would be taken for the usual fish story.

Coden is a difficult place to get away from; the longer one stays, the more he hears from neighbors about other inviting, and enchanting fishing grounds; the longer one stays, the longer one wants to stay; the more he gets acquainted with the people, the better he likes them and the more enchanting the whole atmosphere becomes. The only kind of embarrassment that one experiences, I say again, is that which grows out of being overshad[ow]ed by kindness.

TMd Con. 658 BTW Papers DLC.

[1] BTW was at Coden, Ala., at the summer home of Mr. and Mrs. Clarence W. Allen from Sept. 18 to Sept. 30, 1915. The article, containing editorial corrections in the handwriting of both BTW and E. J. Scott, may have been prepared for publication in the *Tuskegee Student*.

From William H. Jackson[1]

New Haven Ct Nov 1st 1915

Dear sir, Perhaps you will remember that just a week ago to-day you was in New Haven and in the vicinity Yale Univ about 3 p.m. talking with ex president Taft and after you had finished talking with Mr. Taft a humble colored man addressed you saying; Mr. Washington please permit me to satisfy my ambition to shake the hand of the man whom he had been reading so much of and trying to follow the examples and teaching of him and remember also how readily you extended your hand and gave him that sincere grip which he will long remember and honor.

Well I am that boy or man I should say. You advised me to write you and you would send me another one of your books the latest written. I am now writing for that book and any other message that you may have which you care to send. I am sure that anything you send will be heartily appreciated both by me and members of my family my wife in particular. I want to say that I had the pleasure of hearing your address in Woosley [Woolsey] Hall Nov [Oct.] 25 past and I also heard you speak in the A.M.E.Z. church the same night and enjoyed them both immensely. Eloquent as your address was at Woosley Hall I enjoyed your heart to heart talk at Zion church more. Why? Because you were among your own people and you could appeal direct to them in a confidential manner even better than you could in a great meeting such as Woosley Hall and Carnegie Hall in New York. In this little place you could and did point out their fault and short comings in a manner in which they appreciated. You also prescribed a remedy which remedy I am sure will be followed even until the last drop of the medicine has been taken.

I am sincere when I say that by your speech in Zion church you have arouse an awakening in New Haven such as the colored people in this vicinity has ever had before. And it was these words largely that did it, you say that you are criticised for preaching *industrial Education* and right here in New Haven the centre of intelligence where there is higher education in front of one higher education in back of one, on the side etc. In fact it is almost impossible to escape learning here where school and colleges both day and night are continually open and yet a city where there are more than five thousand colored people in it only two natives are attending Yale University. Yes sir those remark of yours struck deep and I think fell on good soil and the results will be forthcoming. The colored folk of New Haven are sadly ashamed of their showing in the higher branches of learning. Those remarks won more people over to your method than perhap[s] many great flights of oratory and volumes of books. You pressed home the results of your many years work in those few words. Sir, it was the home run stroke which won the game when the score was a tie.

For fear of fatiguing you by farther discourse I close hoping to hear from you soon. Sincerely yours

Wm H Jackson

ALS Con. 532 BTW Papers DLC.

1 William H. Jackson was listed in the New Haven, Conn., city directory as a bartender.

Julius Rosenwald to William G. Willcox

[Chicago] Nov. 1, 1915

Dear Mr. Willcox: Your letter of Oct. 30 in regard to Dr. Washington is rather a little discouraging. I shall be anxious to hear what Dr. Cole reports, although I am rather fearful that Dr. Bastedo is correct, as his report corroborates what Dr. Hall told me.

I am expecting to be in New York a week from next Saturday, coming direct from Tuskegee, which would bring me there in the afternoon. If you, Mr. Trumbull and Mr. Low consider it of sufficient importance to call a meeting of the Trustees for Friday afternoon, November 12, I will cut my visit short one day and arrange to be in New York on Friday instead of Saturday as I had planned. I have asked Mr. Low to join me on the trip south; but doubt very much if he will make the sacrifice which acceptance would entail. It seems to me rather important that the trustees talk over the situation if conditions prove to be such as Dr. Bastedo reports. This merely occurs to me on first thought and I offer it as a suggestion.

With kindest regards, I am   Very truly yours,

[Julius Rosenwald]

TLt   Julius Rosenwald Papers   ICU.

To Robert Russa Moton

[New York City] Nov. 4, 1915

It is perfectly exasperating and heartbreaking for me not to be with you tomorrow night as I had fully counted on being there and had made all my plans but when I explain to you I am sure you will agree that I am acting wisely. Treat this as confidential. Shall be here for about ten days longer care Herald Square Hotel.

Booker T. Washington

TWcSr   Con. 542   BTW Papers   DLC.

To Emmett Jay Scott

[New York City] Nov. 4, 1915

Tell Dr. Kenney doctors and trustees here want me to begin on a new course of treatment. In order that he may understand how to carry it out they think important that he come here and stay three or four days. If he starts next Monday will be satisfactory. Tell him see Dr. Roberts[1] when he gets here. He understands matters. They all think it important that both Dr. Kenney and Mrs. Washington understand course of treatment at first hand. Treat this confidential. Have telegraphed Mrs. Washington. Answer.

Booker T. Washington

TWcSr Con. 542 BTW Papers DLC. A typed copy of the telegram, incorrectly dated Oct. 5, 1915, is in Con. 952, BTW Papers, DLC.

[1] Eugene P. Roberts.

To Margaret James Murray Washington

[New York City] Nov. 5, 1915

You ought to come at once. Doctors are giving me certain new treatment which they and trustees want you and Dr. Kenney thoroughly understand. They expect you not later than Sunday. Mr. Scott or someone ought to represent school at Fisk inauguration.

B. T. W.

TWcIr Con. 542 BTW Papers DLC.

To Clinton Joseph Calloway

[New York City] Nov. 8, 1915

Be sure Mr. Rosenwald sees Chehaw schoolhouse. Perhaps he can see it when he takes train Thursday night. Have people there.

Booker T. Washington

TWcSr Con. 542 BTW Papers DLC.

To Fayette Avery McKenzie

[New York City] Nov. 8, 1915

It is matter of deep regret that Mrs. Washington and I cannot be present at your inauguration. Both of us had fully planned to be there, but circumstances forbid. We are so glad Mr. Rosenwald and other loyal friends can be present. We wish for you a great day and useful administration.

Booker T. Washington

TWcSr Con. 542 BTW Papers DLC.

To Julius Rosenwald

[New York City] Nov. 8 1915

Greatly regret Mrs. Washington and I cannot be at inauguration at Fisk and cannot be present to welcome you at Tuskegee. Everyone at Tuskegee will do everything possible to make your visit enjoyable and interesting. Mr. Wil[l]cox, Mr. Low and other trustees here insist I must take a few days complete rest. Everyone is most kind here.

Booker T. Washington

HWSr Con. 78 BTW Papers DLC.

426

John Henry Washington
to Margaret James Murray Washington

Tuscogee [Tuskegee] Ala   Nov 9 1915

Please let me know condition of my brother   many rumors here about his condition

J H Washington

HWSr   Con. 542   BTW Papers   DLC.

To Albon Lewis Holsey[1]

[New York City] Nov. 10, 1915

Send notice to Greenwood families as to hour Mr. Rosenwald speaks in chapel.

Booker T. Washington

TWcSr   Con. 542   BTW Papers   DLC.

[1] Albon Lewis Holsey, born in Athens, Ga., in 1883, was educated at Atlanta University. He was assistant to BTW's secretary, E. J. Scott, beginning in 1914, and also served as associate editor of the *Tuskegee Student* and secretary of the NNBL.

To Ezra C. Roberts

[New York City] Nov. 10, 1915

Remember Mr. Rosenwald likes to see how fully we coordinate the work.

Booker T. Washington

TWcSr   Con. 542   BTW Papers   DLC.

427

To Alexander Robert Stewart

[New York City] Nov. 10, 1915

Be sure my yard is well cleaned.

B. T. W.

TWcIr   Con. 542   BTW Papers   DLC.

From Alexander Robert Stewart

Tuskegee Ala   Nov 10 1915

MACON COUNTY BANK EIGHT THOUSAND TWO HUNDRED THIRTY TWO
SECURITIES THIRTY FOUR HUNDRED PROPERTY VALUE FORTY THOU-
SAND

A R STEWART

TWSr   Con. 953   BTW Papers   DLC.

A News Item in the New York *Tribune*

[New York City] Nov. 10, 1915

DR. WASHINGTON
IN HOSPITAL HERE
———
NEGRO EDUCATOR, ILL FROM
NERVOUS BREAKDOWN,
PATIENT AT ST. LUKE'S

Suffering from a nervous breakdown, Dr. Booker T. Washington, principal of Tuskegee Institute, is confined in a private room in St. Luke's Hospital, at Amsterdam Avenue and 113th Street. Only his wife, his secretary[1] and William G. Willcox, a trustee of the institute, have been allowed to see him. Dr. Washington was taken to the hospital last Friday after an examination by Dr. W. A. Bastedo, of 57

428

West Fifty-eighth Street, who is now in charge of the case. The examination was made by advice of Seth Low, who is also a trustee.

"Dr. Washington has been suffering from severe headaches for more than a month," said Dr. Bastedo last night. "His condition became serious enough to alarm the trustees, who, I understand, have no successor in mind for the position of principal.

"At the request of Mr. Low and Mr. Willcox I made an examination of Dr. Washington a few days ago and found him completely worn out. He had been overworking and was in no condition to resume his work at Tuskegee. Mr. Low insisted that he be removed to St. Luke's for further observation. We have thoroughly overhauled him and find that he is ageing rapidly.

"There is a noticeable hardening of the arteries and he is extremely nervous.

"Racial characteristics are, I think, in part responsible for Dr. Washington's breakdown. He is prone to worry under the strain of work, and while there is nothing to indicate that he is mentally unbalanced he is in no shape to go back to Tuskegee."

At St. Luke's it was said that Dr. Washington had been there in the past for treatment.

When admitted to the hospital, four days ago, Dr. Washington requested that no information be given out to the effect that he was ill. Dr. Bastedo refused to let reporters see the patient yesterday. He said, however, that Dr. Washington had received many gifts of flowers from Mr. Low, Mr. Willcox and other acquaintances in New York.

Asked how soon Dr. Washington would leave the hospital, Dr. Bastedo said:

"I don't know. I hope it will not be long. We want him to have a complete rest, however, and he is getting it now."

Mr. Low said last night that the trustees of Tuskegee were not considering the retirement of Dr. Washington.

"If he were well he would not be in a hospital," said Mr. Low, "but I hope that he will soon be able to resume his duties as principal. We have not contemplated choosing a successor.

"I have not called on Dr. Washington yet, but I hope to do so next week."

New York *Tribune*, Nov. 10, 1915, 14.

1 Nathan Hunt.

George Cleveland Hall to Emmett Jay Scott

Chicago, Illinois, November 10th 1915

Sorry Dr. Washington is ill. Keep me informed condition. If his Doctor is quoted correctly, his future interviews should be censored. Headline Tribune Dr. Bastedo says he suffers from Racial characteristics which interpreted means specific nature. Show this to Mr. Rosenwald. Express our sympathy to family.

(Dr) George C. Hall

TWpSr Copy   Con. 952   BTW Papers   DLC.

Emmett Jay Scott to George Cleveland Hall

[Tuskegee, Ala.] November 10, 1915

Dear Dr. Hall: Your telegram came to hand this morning and I have shown it to Mr. Rosenwald and am sending it forward today, also, to Mrs. Washington. Thank you very much!

I agree with you that Dr. Bastedo's statements needed to be censored. However, in The Birmingham Age Herald, the paragraph with reference to racial characteristics is so stated as to indicate that Dr. Washington is worrying under the strain of work, the implication being that this means that Negroes generally worry under the strain of work. Still I do not understand why he should be giving out interviews to the public press of this particular character. Yours very truly,

Emmett J. Scott

TLpS   Con. 952   BTW Papers   DLC.

Ernest Davidson Washington
to Margaret James Murray Washington

Rutland Vt Nov 10–1915

HAVE JUST LEARNED THROUGH PAPER OF FATHERS ILLNESS   PLEASE
WIRE ME BARDWELL HOTEL RUTLAND IF NECESSARY TO COME

DAVE

TWSr   Con. 952   BTW Papers   DLC.

A News Item in the Boston *Herald*

[Boston, Mass.] Nov. 10, 1915

DR. WASHINGTON
SERIOUSLY ILL

NEGRO EDUCATOR IS UNDER EXAM-
INATION IN ST. LUKE'S HOS-
PITAL, NEW YORK

NEW YORK, Nov. 9 — Booker T. Washington, the noted educator
and head of the Tuskegee Institute for Negroes, is a patient in a private
room in St. Luke's Hospital. He entered the hospital very quietly five
days ago at the request of some of the trustees of Tuskegee, who
thought that it would be better that Dr. Washington should receive a
thorough medical examination and observation before going South to
take up his work there again.

"Played out" is the way Mr. Gardner, superintendent of the hospital, speaks of Dr. Washington's condition, but it has been more
than that, so much more that it was thought his going to St. Luke's
was imperative. No attempt has been made yet to definitely diagnose
his case, and this will not be done until he is rested, and will not be
considered complete until Dr. Washington has been under observation
for some time.

Dr. Washington came to St. Luke's accompanied by Dr. Walter A.
Bastedo of 57 West Fifty-eighth street and William G. Willcox, presi-

dent of the board of education, and a trustee of Tuskegee Institute. For many months Dr. Washington has been bending every effort in the carrying on of his work, and for several weeks business kept him in this city. His health has not been of the best, it is said, and for some time his friends and the trustees of Tuskegee have been urging him to take a rest and undergo a thorough medical examination.

President Wilson and Seth Low were among those who urged him to care for his health. They felt that he could ill be spared from his work as head of the great educational institution, but they also felt that the time had come to call a halt until he could at least find out what was wrong. He was reluctant to do this, but of late severe sick headaches made the step imperative, and he consented to go to the hospital.

Boston *Herald,* Nov. 10, 1915, 9. Clipping in Con. 528, BTW Papers, DLC.

Charles William Anderson to Emmett Jay Scott

New York, November 11, 1915

Personal

My dear Emmett, The daily newspapers of yesterday carried a very disturbing paragraph regarding the Doctor's condition. I note from them that he is now in St. Luke's Hospital, although I was not aware of his presence in the City until yesterday. Please let me know all about his condition. I sincerely hope and pray that it is not serious. He is one of the men of whom the world is not yet worthy, and we cannot afford to lose him. Kindly write me all details about his case in strictest confidence. I am greatly perturbed and apprehensive.

Did you come upon the enclosed clipping from the New York Sun of the day before yesterday? It refers to a ruling made by me as Collector of Internal Revenue. It was opposed by nearly all the corporation lawyers of this city at the time, and has since been attacked by a number of corporation suits. The corporation mentioned in the clipping won its suit in the U.S. District Court and in the U.S. Circuit Court of Appeals, which looked a little bad for my interpretation of the law, but happily the United States Supreme Court reversed them both and sustained my ruling. I am not exactly sprouting pin feathers over it, but I am not at all displeased to find my law sustained by the highest tribunal of the country.

With warmest regards to friends and family, I remain Faithfully yours,

Charles

William Colfax Graves to Julius Rosenwald

Chicago, 11/11/15

Mr. Rosenwald: Dr. George C. Hall is much put out because of the "racial characteristics" statement as applied to the case mentioned and credited to Dr. Bastedo in attached clippings. That expression, Dr. Hall says, means a "syphilitic history" when referring to Colored people and he declares a doctor making such a diagnosis in this case isn't the right kind to treat this patient. I think Dr. Hall sent a night letter to Mr. Scott at Tuskegee last night to bring his opinion to your notice. I gave him your New York address and you may hear from him direct. Respectfully

W. C. G.

William Colfax Graves to Julius Rosenwald

[Chicago, Ill.] 11/11/15

Mr. Rosenwald: It occurred to me after I had sent you the bulletin about Dr. Hall that you might want to show same to Mr. Willcox and other Trustees in New York. Therefore, I am writing a substitute to be shown to them if you see fit. The original is a little too rough, although it accurately expresses Dr. Hall's feelings. In fact, for your private information, he was indignant about it and spoke of the publicity as an "outrage" and said that at least 50 people, Colored and

433

White, had seen that notice in the Tribune and had expressed to him their indignation. Dr. Hall felt that if Dr. Bastedo did give out that statement, he is not a fit man to have charge of our friend's case. Respectfully

W. C. G.

TLtIr   Julius Rosenwald Papers   ICU.

William Colfax Graves to Julius Rosenwald

[Chicago, Ill.] 11/11/15

Mr. Rosenwald: Dr. Geo. C. Hall was surprised at the "racial characteristics" statement attributed to Dr. Bastedo in two of the attached clippings. That expression, Dr. Hall said, was understood to mean, when a Colored man is the patient, "a syphilitic history." He was quite emphatic in voicing his distress of mind on account of this publication and expressed the opinion that, if correctly quoted, Dr. Bastedo had violated the code of medical ethics in talking for publication about a patient's private matters. Dr. Hall said so far as he was aware this patient had not had a Wasserman test (to detect whether syphilis was present) and did not need one and that his condition was due to other causes. I think Dr. Hall sent a night letter to Mr. Scott at Tuskegee last night to bring his opinion to your notice. I gave him your New York address and you may hear from him direct. Respectfully

W. C. G.

TLtIr   Julius Rosenwald Papers   ICU.

From Julius Rosenwald

[Tuskegee, Ala., ca. Nov. 11, 1915]

I earnestly hope you are convalescing rapidly. My visit here has been thoroughly enjoyable & interesting my comforts have been perfectly looked after.[1] Thank you & Mrs. Washington for all attentions. The

Chrysanthemum exhibit was most creditable. I shall be at St Regis Hotel Saturday morning Please notify me there if I can see you Kindest regards to you & Mrs Washington

Julius Rosenwald

AWS Con. 78 BTW Papers DLC.

¹ There is a photograph album illustrating Rosenwald's visit to Tuskegee Institute in the Julius Rosenwald Papers, ICU.

Margaret James Murray Washington to Julius Rosenwald

St. Luke's Hospital [New York City] 11–12 [1915]

Dear Mr. Rosenwald. Washington is very weak — very ill. The doctors all agree that I should go South at once. We wanted to see you but think we must go on — every day he is weaker and weaker. I am so glad that you were at Tuskegee. It is so hard for him to be away but he simply could not stand up another moment. It is terrible Mr. Rosenwald to see him so broken all at once it seems and yet he has not been well for a long time. Remember me to Mrs. Rosenwald and the rest of the family. We leave at 4:35 today.

Margaret J. Washington

Thank you again and again for what you are to us all.

TLtSr Julius Rosenwald Papers ICU.

Margaret James Murray Washington
to Emmett Jay Scott

New York City, November 12th 1915

We are leaving for home this afternoon. Will reach Chehaw on train due at nine o'clock Saturday Night. Please have two good autos meet train and wait if it is late. Also notify Booker and Portia.

Mrs. Washington

TWSr Con. 542 BTW Papers DLC.

Emmett Jay Scott to Charles Banks

[Tuskegee, Ala.] November 13, 1915

Confidential.

My dear Mr. Banks: It is absolutely out of the question for me to think of leaving Tuskegee just now. I am sending you herewith a clipping which explains itself, and which is a very guarded statement of the true facts. I am just this morning in receipt of a most distressful letter from Mrs. Washington. She tells me that she is planning to reach here tonight. Of course it would never do for me to be away from Tuskegee at a time like this. There is much that I can say about Mr. Washington's condition in person, that I must not write, but if I say to you that he is quite seriously ill, I think you will understand. Please return this clipping to me, as I want to take it up with Mr. Low, the Chairman of the Board, in protest against a statement like this being given out, and in further protest against one of the statements referring to "racial characteristics." I do not know what the man can be talking about, or referring to.

I appreciate the situation quite seriously with reference to the disappointment which may be occasioned you, and yet it is more personal than otherwise. I was looking forward to another season of delightful personal converse with you, and that we shall have a bit later.

436

I came South from Nashville with Mr. Rosenwald. We had berths in the same Pullman car. The next morning he came back and sat with me, and we talked for two hours or more on the train, and in an automobile coming up from Montgomery, regarding those matters of mutual interest and concern. You can appreciate the fact how an opportunity like this offered me the privilege of getting at him on your matters without seeming to drag them in. I told him in great detail of Harvey's perfidy, and of how hard you have had to work to keep them from confiscating the Oil Mill. I also spoke to him in great detail of Mr. Owens' courageous attitude and of his valiant services. I made some remarks to the effect that I hoped he would not permit his confidence in you and the proposition there to lag. He very warmly replied to this by saying that he hoped I did not entertain any such thought of lack of confidence, etc., etc. The thought he had, he said, was that probably the Oil Mill was too large a proposition for a little town and a section like that, and that the financial depression had probably put you on the blink as it had many other institutions throughout the country, both North and South. He told me that he said to Mr. Adler, his attorney, that he wanted his interests protected. What he meant by this, particularly, to use his own words, is that "if they were going to confiscate the mill he did not wish his $25,000.00 confiscated along with the rest."

To make a long story short, I am sure I was able to render you a real service, and I am also relatively sure that there will be no disposition on his part to be unduly exacting or oppressive.

I have made this a rather long letter, but I wanted you to understand matters from the standpoint of my being with you at the opening of the Bank, Wednesday, and with further reference to the service I have tried to render you in connection with Mr. Rosenwald. If you are satisfied you simply need to write, "Well done, faithful friend."

I wish, in return, you would make some effort to relieve me of the Montgomery and Birmingham embarrassments. They are making it more or less uncomfortable for me by calling attention to the failure to have the Certificates of Deposit properly protected. They both say that the matter has gone over for more than two years now, and that it is up to me to see that something is done — but what can I do.
Yours very sincerely,

Emmett J. Scott

Please explain fully to my *father* why I cannot be there next week. I am greatly disappointed.

TLpS Con. 75 BTW Papers DLC. Postscript in Scott's hand.

Emmett Jay Scott to Joseph Oswalt Thompson

[Tuskegee, Ala.] November 13, 1915

Confidential

My dear Mr. Thompson: All of us have been very much distressed by Dr. Washington's breakdown. As you say, however, it was certainly to be expected, considering the fact that he has refused to heed the advice of those who most cared for him. He has gone on from year to year, burning up his vitality.

We are hoping, however, that he will be able to come to Tuskegee early next week.

We are planning to relieve him, absolutely, of every duty and responsibility, and to carry on the work as best we can.

In case he should not come home early next week, and should be in New York when you go there, he can be found at St. Luke's Hospital, Amsterdam Avenue and 113th Street.

There is really nothing that you can do, Mr. Thompson, to help him. In fact, there is nothing that any one can do except to ask him to take the rest he so greatly needs.

I hope you received a letter I recently sent you at your Birmingham office. Yours very truly,

Emmett J. Scott

TLpS Con. 538 BTW Papers DLC.

Margaret James Murray Washington
to Emmett Jay Scott

Charlotte, North Carolina   November 13th 1915

Send ambulance to Chehaw tonight nine oclock train with plenty blankets and sheets. Also send two automobiles. Wish you, Booker and J. H. Washington meet train.

Mrs. Washington

TWSr   Con. 542   BTW Papers   DLC.

Emmett Jay Scott to Seth Low

[Tuskegee, Ala., Nov. 14, 1915]

Dr. Washington accompanied by Mrs. Washington reached institute grounds from New York twelve o'clock last night. It becomes my solemn duty to inform you that he passed away this morning at four forty five oclock. Funeral services to be held Tuesday morning.

Emmett J. Scott

TWpSr   Con. 542   BTW Papers   DLC.

Emmett Jay Scott to Ernest Davidson Washington

[Tuskegee, Ala.] Nov. 14, 1915

Your father passed away four forty five this Sunday morning. Come immediately. Answer soon as you receive this telegram when may expect you.

Emmett J. Scott

TWpSr   Con. 542   BTW Papers   DLC.   Addressed to E. D. Washington at Rutland, Vt.

Charles Banks to Emmett Jay Scott

Mound Bayou Miss   Nov 14–1915

WITH THE ENTIRE RACE I AM BOWED IN MOURNING THE LOSS OF THE
GREATEST MAN THE RACE HAS PRODUCED IN ANY EPOCH   ONE OF
AMERICA'S FOREMOST CITIZENS REGARDLESS OF RACE   THE PEER OF
ANY EDUCATOR IN ANY CLIME   CONVEY TO MRS WASHINGTON AND THE
BEREAVED FAMILY MY DEEPEST SYMPATHY   WILL ARRIVE TUESDAY.

CHAS BANKS

TWSr Con. 951 BTW Papers DLC.

George Horton to Seth Low

N.Y. [City] Nov. 14/15

My Dear Sir, Pardon me for writing you, but because of your devotion
to my race and your interest in the great educational work of our
lamented citizen, B. T. Washington, I ask you to use your influence
to perpetuate, one of the best epitaphs that can be written for him. It
is a quotation from one of his many great speeches or writings, —
"Judge me not from the heights attained but from the depths from
whence I came.["]

I am an humble letter carrier at College Stn P.O. N. Y. City, W.
140 St.

With the greatest respect for your work towards the elevation of
the negro race — I am   Very Respectfully Yours

George Horton

ALS Con. 532 BTW Papers DLC.

Seth Low to Margaret James Murray Washington

Katonah, N.Y. Nov 14–1915

MRS. LOW AND I SEND TO YOU AND YOUR CHILDREN OUR HEARTFELT SYMPATHY   I AM GLAD THAT DOCTOR WASHINGTON BREATHED HIS LIFE AWAY IN THE SCENE OF HIS LABORS SURROUNDED BY THE SYMBOLS OF HIS GREAT ACHIEVEMENTS AND IN THE MIDST OF THOSE WHO LOOKED UP TO HIM AND LOVED HIM AS A LEADER SENT FROM GOD   LET ME REMIND YOU IN YOUR GREAT SORROW THAT OUR GOD IS NOT THE GOD OF THE DEAD BUT OF THE LIVING.

SETH LOW

TWSr   Con. 952   BTW Papers   DLC.

Theodore Roosevelt
to Margaret James Murray Washington

Oyster Bay N Y   Nov 14–1915

PRAY ACCEPT MY DEEPEST SYMPATHY IN THIS DEATH OF YOUR DISTINGUISHED HUSBAND   NO MAN RENDERED GREATER SERVICE TO HIS RACE AND HIS LOSS CANNOT BE SUPPLIED   HE WAS ONE OF THE CITIZENS OF WHOM THIS ENTIRE COUNTRY SHOULD BE PROUD.

THEODORE ROOSEVELT

TWSr   Con. 952   BTW Papers   DLC.

Julius Rosenwald to
Margaret James Murray Washington

New York   Nov 14th 1915

Dear Mrs Washington, My heart is too sad to attempt words of consolation for you in your and our country's great loss. One of our noblest and foremost citizens has passed to his reward. The service he has rendered his fellowmen will live forever. Mrs Rosenwald joins me in the hope that you bear up under this terrible affliction.

Julius Rosenwald

TWSr Con. 952 BTW Papers DLC.

A News Item in the Montgomery *Advertiser*

Tuskegee Institute, Ala., Nov. 14 [1915]

WASHINGTON
DIES AT HOME
IN TUSKEGEE

NEGRO EDUCATOR SUCCUMBS TO
HARDENING OF ARTERIES AND
NERVOUS BREAKDOWN

HAD REACHED HOME
FOUR HOURS BEFORE

BORN IN SLAVERY, WASHINGTON
BECAME FAMOUS AS WRITER
AND EDUCATOR

Booker T. Washington, educator, writer and the universally recognized leader of the negro race, lies dead here at his home, "The Oaks," in the midst of the great institution which he built out of his belief in the future of his race and to see which, pilgrims have come from all parts of the earth.

Dr. Washington's passing was as simple as the life which he had lived. Realizing that the end was near, he asked that he be brought from New York to the South — the South in which he had been born, in and for which he had labored, and where he had always declared his intention to die and be buried. And, so, with his wife, Dr. J. A. Kenney of the Tuskegee Institute, and his stenographer, Nathan Hunt, the long trip was begun.

When Chehaw, Alabama, was reached, where passengers change for Tuskegee, he was aroused by his wife, who said: "Father, this is Chehaw." He answered and roused himself with great effort; and when Booker Washington, Jr., appeared, asked: "How is Booker?" meaning young Booker's infant son.

Then began the slow but careful auto trip to the institute; but earth for Booker Washington was receding fast and soon unconsciousness came. At 4:45 o'clock this morning, surrounded by the members of his family who were present, the families of one son and daughter being absent, the distinguished negro leader breathed his last.

FUNERAL PROGRAM

The funeral exercises will be held on the institute grounds, Wednesday morning at 10 o'clock, and the body will be buried on the grounds of the school to build which his life has been given. The remains will lie in state in the institute chapel from 12 o'clock midday, Tuesday until Wednesday, November 17.

Telegrams of condolence from all parts of the world are pouring into the school.

Through the years, it has been the ideal of organization and efficiency here that nothing shall disturb the orderly working of all parts of the institution. So far as the letter of this ideal is concerned, nothing is out of gear at Tuskegee; but the spirit broke down — broke down completely when the man who founded Tuskegee passed away this morning. Mechanically, bells, calling the school to its duties, have been rung and routine work taken up, but the heart is out of things. From the humblest pupil up through the faculty and the bereaved family at the institute, to the white and colored citizens of the town of Tuskegee, there is the feeling of personal loss. Nobody is hiding his tears. Nobody is free from gloom. Nobody can talk about the great loss which the school, the race and the country have sustained.

Silently, the student lines formed for Sunday morning inspection for chapel service; but there was no band music for the parade grounds; and yet in the quiet and calm of the Sabbath day, the band played a sacred march to the chapel, because the principal would have had it so.

The Sunday morning sermon by Chaplain Whittaker was in behalf of "Bleeding Armenia," because it was what the late Dr. Washington had wanted done. But the sweetness was gone from the songs of the students today; and when the choir sang: "Still, Still With Thee," hearts broke.

BELIEVED IN THE SOUTH

Booker Washington's life was dedicated to the education and uplift of his race and the promotion of better relations between negroes and whites throughout the country.

In season and out, he carried the message of economic fitness for the negro and of peace between the races. In particular, he hoped, he believed that in the South the negro would, at last, find his greatest opportunity; and he was, to the end, a friend of the South. With his passing, this section and the whole country has lost a great friend.

The Tuskegee educator's life was replete with many unselfish activities in behalf of his race. Possessing rare executive and constructive ability, he devoted himself with much of self-sacrifice to the upbuilding and regeneration of his race along moral, material and educational lines. The National Negro Business League, composed of negro business men and women, is the product of his creative genius and has come to a place of commanding influence in the life of the negro people.

He is survived by his wife; a brother, John H. Washington, superintendent of industries; three children and four grand-children.

The negro leader had been in failing health for several months prior to his death; but he would not relax his activities. During the month of September, he spent a week on Mobile bay fishing and resting and appeared to be greatly strengthened by the outing. His reserve strength, however, was not equal to the increasing burdens in the interest of the Tuskegee Institute and of his race.

On the 23rd of October, he left here to attend the annual meeting of the American Missionary Association which was held in conjunction with the National Conference of Congregational Churches, and on the evening of October 25th, spoke before this meeting. This was his last public appearance.

TRIBUTES TO HIS LIFE

William G. Willcox, treasurer of the Investment Committee of the Board of Trustees, sent the following telegram to Secretary Emmett J. Scott:

"Please express my deepest sympathy to all the teachers and pupils of the Institute in their great loss. Dr. Washington's death is a national calamity, but his spirit will still live to inspire and carry forward his great work; and those left behind must bravely and loyally take up the great trust which now falls upon their shoulders."

Emmett J. Scott, the confidential secretary of the deceased for eighteen years, said, speaking of him:

"The glory of the life which came to an end here this morning, was its dedication to the service of both races, North and South. He will be remembered as an educational enthusiast whose sympathies and activities were broad enough to include all races and all movements looking to the betterment of mankind."

Isaac Fisher, president of the Tuskegee Alumni Association, said:

"With the death of Dr. Washington, closes one complete chapter of negro history. The whole world is poorer today because he has gone."

Treasurer Warren Logan, with Dr. Washington almost since the founding of the school, is acting principal.

BORN IN SLAVERY

Washington was born in slavery near Hale's Ford, Va., in 1857, or 1858. After the emancipation of his race he moved with his family to West Virginia. He was an ambitious boy and saved his money for an education. When he was able to scrape together sufficient funds to pay his stage coach fare to Hampton, Va., he entered General Armstrong's School for Negroes there and worked his way through an academic course, graduating in 1875.

Later he became a teacher in the Hampton Institute, where he remained until 1881, when he organized an industrial school for negroes at Tuskegee. He remained principal of this school up to the time of his death.

The Institute started in a rented shanty church and today it owns 3,500 acres of land in Alabama and has nearly 100 buildings valued at half a million dollars.

Washington won the sympathy and support of leading Southerners by a speech in behalf of his race at the Cotton States Exposition in Atlanta in 1895. Of undoubted ability and breadth of vision, his sane leadership enabled him to accomplish more for and among the negroes of the United States than any negro of his time.

ROOSEVELT INCIDENT

In addition to his prominence as an educator, Washington gained considerable fame as an author. He received an honorary degree of master of arts from Harvard University in 1896, and was given an honorary degree of doctor of laws by Dartmouth College in 1901.

An incident of Washington's career made him a figure of national prominence during the administration of President Roosevelt. He sat down to lunch with the President at the white house either by formal or informal invitation. There was a storm of protest, particularly from the South, but in spite of the resulting hostility shown toward him by many white persons, Washington continued to exert a wide-spread influence toward the betterment of his people.

Montgomery *Advertiser,* Nov. 15, 1915, 1, 2.

Melvin Jack Chisum to Emmett Jay Scott

Oklahoma City, Oklahoma   Nov 15th 1915

My dear Mr Scott: None more than your goodself feels the awful blow which struck our race before sun rise yesterday. I bow my head with you all in sorrow. He was my friend too. My good friend.

Peace to his ashes and I am hurt — shocked — overwhelmed with sorrow. The King is dead and it seems to me that you must take his place. Long live the King.

I wired a message to several of the Press Gang today.

I am yours to command,

Chisum

ALS   Con. 950   BTW Papers   DLC.

An Elegy by Capp Jefferson[1]

Oklahoma City Oklahoma   Nov. 15, 1915

To Mrs. Booker T. Washington and family, together with the Good People of Tuskegee Greetings: If it is not an imposition on your elaborate program, I am thanking you in advance, and asking in the same breath, that the following verse constitute a part of your euligies on the death of the GREATEST NEGRO that America has produced. Pardon me if you please, for my vain attempt to do him honor, and yet I feel safe to say that the English Language is inadequate for words to do him justice. It follows then.

> Comes now the question, no dispute
> Where can we find a substitute
> To carry out unfinished plans
> And fill the stead of this "Great Man"?
>
> No poet-laureate of earth
> Can e'er in words express his worth
> To all the colored sons of toil
> Who earn their living from the soil.
>
> He dignified the human hands
> And paralleled them with the brains,
> Then said to those who never shirk
> There is a "PREMIUM" sirs on work.
>
> And ere death angel closed his mouth
> He proved unto the "SOLID SOUTH"
> That any Negro will advance
> If he or she gets half a chance.
>
> The North, the South, the East, the West
> Admits he stood the crucial test
> Of every living odd perhaps
> While putting Negroes on the map.
>
> He was the FOUNDER of the school
> Of forty acres and a mule;
> I simply mean by that to say
> He proved, "BACK TO THE SOIL" will pay.

He taught the teachers not to snurl
At washer-women, farmers girls;
It also seemed to be his plan
To dignify the working man.
Now while this was his occupation
He was a friend to education,
In every lecture as a rule
He'd point our girls and boys to school.
And now to all the Negro race
Who, who on earth will fill the place
Of Virginia's NOBLE SON
In person of BOOKER T. WASHINGTON.

By Capp Jefferson

on behalf of the Negroes of Oklahoma

TDS   Con. 953   BTW Papers   DLC.

[1] Capp Jefferson, of Oklahoma City, Okla., was listed in the 1915 city directory as being in the real estate business.

Ulysses Grant Mason
to Margaret James Murray Washington
and Family

Birmingham, Ala. [Nov.] 15th, 1915

WAS OUT OF THE CITY WHEN YOUR TELEGRAM CAME SUNDAY. I WANT TO EXTEND TO YOU THE DEEPEST SYMPATHY OF WHICH MAN IS CAPABLE IN YOUR HOUR OF DISTRESS OVER THE DEATH OF YOUR DISTINGUISHED HUSBAND AND FATHER AND MY FRIEND. HE SPENT HIS LIFE IN HELPING HUMANITY PARTICULARLY THE NEGRO RACE AND HIS LIFE WAS ONE OF CONSECRATION AND SACRIFICE THAT THE NEGRO MIGHT BE EMANCIPATED FROM IGNORANCE AND INDOLENCE TO THE HIGHER IDEALS OF CIVILIZATION THROUGH LITERARY AND INDUSTRIAL EFFICIENCY. HE WAS IN MY OPINION THE GREATEST LIVING AMERICAN: THE NOBLEST MAN AND THE GREATEST CHARACTER. ALWAYS

WILLING TO HELP THE MAN FARTHEST DOWN. ALL WHO KNEW HIM LOVED AND HONORED HIM. THOSE WHO DIFFERED FROM HIS POLICIES DID SO ONLY IN NON ESSENTIALS. I AM GLAD TO HAVE BEEN NUMBERED AMONG HIS BEST FRIENDS. THE RACE HAS LOST ITS GREATEST ASSET.

U. G. MASON

TWSr Copy   Con. 533   BTW Papers   DLC.

Madame C. J. Walker to Margaret James Murray Washington

Garrison Mont   Nov 15-15

ACCEPT MY MOST SINCERE REGRETS OF THE UNTIMELY PASSING AWAY OF DR BOOKER T. WASHINGTON. THE GREATEST MAN AMERICA EVER KNEW. WE AS A RACE FEEL THAT IN HIM WE HAVE LOST THE TRUEST FRIEND THE RACE EVER HAD   I MOURN WITH YOU YOUR GREAT LOSS   YOURS IN DEEPEST SORROW.

MADAM C. J. WALKER

TWSr   Con. 952   BTW Papers   DLC.

Charles William Anderson to Emmett Jay Scott

New York City   November 16, 1915

My dear Emmett: I am not sufficiently rich in the resources of the language to be able to adequately tell you of my own and the nation's loss in the death of Dr. Washington. I can hardly trust myself to write about it. This is partly due to the suddenness of the blow, and partly to the precarious condition of my own health, which sometimes inclines me to believe that I am rapidly approaching physical bankruptcy. I cannot tell why it is, but somehow or other, I have been troubled with what ought to be styled "Mental Atrophy," since the Doctor's death. I think I can best describe my condition by saying that I have become what steel becomes when it is de-magnetized.

449

You, perhaps of all people in the world, know best how dearly I loved him, and how long he honored me with his warm and constant friendship. It is therefore especially difficult for me to realize that I shall never see him again. At the same time, it was a high privilege to have been so intimately associated with him and to have rendered some trifling service in holding up his hands.

I do not think we have ever had precisely the same kind of a man in the Public life of this country. He was so thoroughly genuine that he remained simple, unaffected and sympathetic, after he had achieved a distinction which would have turned the heads of most of the sanest men the world has produced. He had the rare gift of keeping his eyes fixed on the goal and not the prize, and of steadily urging his way onward, while the hounds of Acteon were in full cry and baying at his heels. When I recall the last few months of his life, and remember how uncomplainingly he toiled on, under the prolonged tortures of a most painful malady, while clinging to hopes which vanished almost as soon as they were formed, I am made to think better of mankind and to fully comprehend the real meaning of those lines of Emerson's which say:

"So nigh is grandeur to our dust
So near is God to man;
When duty whispers, lo thou must
The youth replies, I can."

If, in this great cosmic scheme of things which we call life, any loss could be permanently irreparable, his certainly would be such a loss. But I have faith to believe that his work will not be allowed to drag but will be carried forward along the lines which he adopted.

Already there is much speculation here about his successor. The Contributing Editor of the New York Age, in a conversation with Ralph Langston and myself on Sunday, stated that Major Moton, in his judgment, was the best fitted man for the place. I think I expressed the sentiment of most of the thinking people here, when I said that the man to take up the Doctor's work was the man who knew most about it and who was most familiar with the Doctor's high purposes and aims, and the man who has practically conducted the school for the past ten years. I leave you to guess the name of the man whom I mentioned. The New York Sun's Editorial of yesterday ended with an interrogation point. The question asked by the Sun was whether or not Doctor Washington had trained up anyone to take his place. It pathetically happens that the work of really great men often dies with them and is buried in their graves. Napoleon was a great man, but the Empire he founded is buried, never again to be resurrected. Cromwell was great, but the Commonwealth for which he fought and prayed and hoped has given place to a Monarchy. John Bright was truly great, but the peace of the country for which he toiled all his life is now broken, and that country is engaged in the greatest war of all time. But one great man has lived whose work will endure, for he had the foresight to train a younger man to whom the torch could be passed on as in the torch bearing days of the ancient world. But I must close. I did not mean to preach when I commenced this letter. In closing, I want you to permit me to say that it is my earnest wish that the Doctor's great work may be carried forward under the ample leadership of his ablest lieutenant and most loyal associate, Emmett J. Scott.

Please assure Mrs. Washington, the family, and all the friends, of my deep sympathy in this hour of sadness and bereavement. In the days that are to come all of us who followed him, and believed in him, and supported him, will never cease to long for the

> "touch of a vanished hand
> And the sound of a voice that is still."

Yours faithfully,

Charles W. Anderson

TLS Con. 75 BTW Papers DLC.

Roscoe Conkling Bruce to Emmett Jay Scott

Washington D C Nov 16 1915

BY ORDER BOARD OF EDUCATION SCHOOL FLAGS ARE AT HALF MAST IN HONOR OF BOOKER T WASHINGTON DURING FUNERAL EVERY TEACHER WILL TELL CLASS OF WASHINGTONS GREAT AND MEMORIAL CAREER

ROSCOE C BRUCE

TWSr Con. 951 BTW Papers DLC.

Charles Waddell Chesnutt to
Margaret James Murray Washington

Cleveland O Nov 16 1915

MRS CHESNUTT AND OUR ENTIRE FAMILY JOIN ME IN DEEP REGRET FOR THE LOSS OF MR WASHINGTON AND IN PROFOUND SYMPATHY FOR YOU AND YOUR FAMILY IN YOUR BEREAVEMENT WE WERE ALL VERY FOND OF HIM BECAUSE WE KNEW HIM AND TO KNOW HIM WAS TO LOVE AND ADMIRE HIM

CHARLES W CHESNUTT

TWSr Con. 951 BTW Papers DLC.

W. P. Watts to Margaret James Murray Washington

Waverly Hall Ga 11-16-1915

Dear Madam: I sympathise with you in the loss of your great & brilliant Husband. Respectfully

W. P. Watts Ex Confederate & Ex Slaveholder born & raised in Henry Co Ala.

ALS Con. 950 BTW Papers DLC.

A Press Release

Tuskegee, Alabama, November 16, 1915

Final arrangements for the funeral of Dr. Booker T. Washington were completed this afternoon.

The noted educator will be buried from the Chapel where his body was placed in state this noon, at ten o'clock tomorrow morning. Funeral services will be conducted by the Rev. John Whittaker, Chaplain of the Institute. The interment will be by the side of the Chapel in a tomb built by students of the Institute.

As now arranged the services will be most simple consisting only of scripture reading and songs without any eulogy.

Mrs. Washington, who is bearing up well, is in receipt of hundreds of telegrams of condolence from people of all walks of life. Among those telegraphing today being John D. Rockefeller, Miss Caroline Hazard,[1] Rev. Anson Phelps Stokes, Secretary of Yale University.

Leaders in education and Negro uplift from all over the South have begun to arrive with the indications that tomorrow's crowd will be the largest ever seen at the Institute.

This afternoon's train brought in a car load of flowers.

Emmett J. Scott, Correspondent

TDSr Con. 953 BTW Papers DLC. Addressed to the Associated Press in Atlanta, Ga., and Washington, D.C.

[1] Caroline Hazard (1856–1945) was president of Wellesley College (1889–1910) and the author of several volumes of verse and works on women's education. She had arranged for Portia Washington to attend Wellesley in 1901–2, and after Portia's termination Hazard issued a public statement defending the school against charges of racial discrimination. (See her letter to the editor in the Boston *Transcript,* Nov. 10, 1902, 8.)

An Account of Washington's Funeral
by Isaac Fisher

[Tuskegee, Ala., Nov. 18, 1915]

FUNERAL OF BOOKER T. WASHINGTON

Dr. Booker T. Washington, most famous negro in the world, the man who climbed "Up from Slavery," until he stood before kings and nobles in Europe and had received more distinguished honors in America than have ever been accorded any other negro was buried here Wednesday with the same simplicity and lack of studied pomp and ceremony with which God's own hand buried Moses in the land of Moab.

453

No labored eulogies; no boastings of his great work; no gorgeous trappings of horses; no streaming banners; no mysterious ceremonies of lodges — just the usual line of teachers, trustees, graduates, students and visitors which so often marched to the chapel just as it did Wednesday, and the simple and impressive — impressive because simple — service for the dead, said for the humblest, said so often for those who die, in all walks of life.

If there was aught out of the ordinary, it was the great crowd of negro leaders from all parts of the continent, the hosts of whites, the multitudes of the simple country folk whom Dr. Washington loved so well, the garden of flowers and plants sent in offering to the dead, a casket before which student guards changed watch every few minutes during the entire service and the tears which fell from all faces — fell like rain.

But any other kind of service less simple would have mocked the kind of life that Dr. Washington had lived.

PROGRAM OF SERVICES

At high noon Wednesday [Tuesday] the remains of the distinguished negro leader were placed into a hearse driven by students and escorted from "The Oaks" by vice principal Warren Logan and Secretary Emmett J. Scott, and a guard of forty-four officers of the student battalions to the Institute Chapel where it lay in state until Wednesday. Thousands gazed into the casket where the dead chieftain lay.

At twenty minutes after ten Wednesday morning, a procession line composed of trustees, faculty, alumni, visitors, honorary and active pall bearers, and students began to move slowly from "The Oaks" toward the chapel. The line was long and moved to muffled drums; but the procession ended at last.

Inside, the building was packed to suffocation. Chaplain John W. Whittaker and Dean G. L. Imes of the Phelps Hall Bible School, conducted the exercises.

Softly the choir began singing a negro melody: "We Shall Walk Through the Valley and Shadow of Death in Peace." No songs were so sweet to Dr. Washington as these melodies of his race. Before the sweetness of the song had dissolved, the chaplain was intoning the simple words of the most simple burial service. A pause, and the school was singing "How Firm a Foundation." More reading of the burial

service and the choir rendered Cardinal Newman's deathless classic —
"Lead Kindly Light Amid the Encircling Gloom."

Here prayer was made by Dr. H. B. Frissell, president of Hampton
Institute and one of Dr. Washington's former teachers. Once more the
choir sung a melody, this time two in number, "Tell all my Father's
Children Don't You Grieve For Me," and "Swing Low, Sweet Chariot" and the tears were falling fast.

"Taps" Are Sounded

At this point, Secretary Scott read a telegram of consolation from
President Seth Low of New York, of the board of trustees, in which
the support of that body was unqualified[ly] promised to the school and
its friends. Trustee Wm. G. Willcox of New York next brought a strong
message of encouragement.

"Still, still with Thee" was next rendered, the benediction pronounced and the casket and audience moved to a vault, just outside of
the chapel and specially constructed for the sad purpose of today.

Briefly, the last words of the burial service were said, the institute
bandmaster stood at the head of the vault and sounded "taps" and a
heavy-hearted crowd turned slowly and sadly away from the tomb
of their prophet.

An unusual honor was accorded this leader of his people by Mayor
E. W. Thompson of the town of Tuskegee. Mayor Thompson personally carried a petition to all of the business houses of the town and
asked them to agree to close their stores during the funeral services. All
were glad to do so.

Throughout the town there was general sadness and there were none
who had aught but the kindest words about Dr. Washington's life.

A Pathetic Incident

But most pathetic of all was the sight of the humble and unlettered
colored people of the cotton fields who literally packed the school
grounds. They had sustained a loss which they did not know how to
voice. You could see them looking into every face near them for encouragement to say how much they were hurt and would miss their
devoted friend.

Unless the visitors Wednesday had been with Dr. Washington
through a quarter of a century and observed how much he loved these

455

simple poor of his race, how anxiously he worked to help them, he could not understand how broken-hearted these older colored people were. In the past, when they have come to Tuskegee, Dr. Washington has treated them as if they were princes. They were thinking of this when they gazed for the last time upon his silent form.

One old couple, themselves near the sunset of life, walked a long, long distance to be here. Piteously, the man approached one of the instructors and with trembling lips and eyes that overflowed asked: "Do you reckon they will let us see Booker?" and he hurried to explain: "We have come so fur jes' to see him de las' time. Do you reckon they will mind us looking at him?" They were especially escorted to the casket and given their heart's desire; for Dr. Washington's love for them when he was here can not be described.

COUNTRY PAYS RESPECTS

The country paused to pay honor to Dr. Washington. From thousands of telegrams the following are selected:

Governor, State of Alabama — "[I] learn with great regret of the death of Dr. Washington. — Charles Henderson."[1]

Theodore Roosevelt — "Pray accept my deepest sympathy in this death of your distinguished husband. No man rendered greater service to his race, and his loss cannot be supplied. He was one of the citizens of whom this country should be proud."

Charles W. Fairbanks, former vice-president of the United States — "Washington was a man of great power and of wide and wholesome influence, not only among his own race but other races. His death is distinctly a public loss."

Julius Rosenwald — "My heart is too sad to attempt words of consolation for you in your and our country's great loss. One of our noblest and foremost citizens has passed to his reward. The service he has rendered his fellowmen will live forever. . . ."

Andrew Carnegie — "I mourn with you today as one who shares your sorrow. America has lost one of her best and greatest citizens. History is to tell of two Washingtons: One the father of his country, the other the leader of his race. Mrs. Carnegie joins me in deep sympathy."

John D. Rockefeller — "I learn with sorrow of the death of Dr. Washington. Be assured of my sympathy for you in this sudden and sad bereavement. He rendered invaluable services to his race in a life devoted to their uplift and he was most highly appreciated by multitudes of the best people in the land. He will be greatly missed and his memory will be cherished with grateful affection for generations to come."

TAFT'S HIGH TRIBUTE

William H. Taft, Ex-President of the United States, to Emmett J. Scott: "Please convey to the family of Booker T. Washington my deep sympathy in their sorrow. His death is in what ought to be his prime, an irretrievable loss to the nation. He was one of the most powerful forces for the proper settlement of the race question that has appeared in his generation. His loving candor to his fellow negroes, his inspiring encouragement to make themselves individually valuable to the community, his urging upon the homely virtues, on industry, thrift and persistent use of their opportunities, with a promise of higher achievements as a reward, have done more for the negro race than any other one factor in their progress.

"I knew Booker T. Washington well and valued him highly as a friend and a patriot. He united with a signal power of eloquence and great intellectual force and practical executive faculty a saving commonsense which made him the great man he was."

Carolyn B. Hazard, former president Wellesley College — "Deep sympathy in your loss. A loss to the whole country."

Seth Low, chairman board of trustees — "Warren Logan Vice Principal Tuskegee Institute: On behalf of the board of trustees I send to you, and through you to the officers, teachers and students of the Tuskegee Institute our warmest sympathy in the death of the school's great founder, Booker T. Washington. In his death the country has lost a great patriot and the negro race an inspiring leader. It is now the hour to show, without his majestic presence, by your loyalty to the school and to his high ideals how truly you have caught the inspiration of his spirit and of his devoted life of service.

"The trustees will not fail you in your hour of need, and we count confidently on your loyal co-operation in keeping Tuskegee a worthy memorial of the great man with whom you have worked so long and so well. Please see that this telegram is read at the funeral service."

Practically every prominent negro in the country sent a telegram paying his respects; and it is certain that no other funeral has ever brought together so large a number of the most distinguished and well-known negroes as assembled here Wednesday.

So great was the list of notable persons present that if it were published it would beggar the newspaper space of any great daily.

DEVOTION TO THE WORK

The keynote of all being said here Wednesday was those who have worked with Dr. Washington will loyally carry forward the work which he founded here.

Among other things, Mr. Wm. A. Willcox spoke at the funeral; for the board he said:

"Let us take heart and press forward, therefore, with fresh courage and enthusiasm and with a high resolve to prove worthy of the great trust which now falls upon our shoulders. In the work before us, the cause is everything, the individual is nothing. There is no room for personal ambition, jealousy or fractional difference.

"The crisis demands as never before unselfish, disinterested and loyal co-operation. The trustees will not fail you, and they know you will not fail them; and together we shall carry forward the great work for the Institute and for the entire colored race. This new bond of sympathy will draw the races together more closely than ever before and friends of both races will redouble their interest and support."

Montgomery *Advertiser,* Nov. 21, 1915, 16.

[1] Charles Henderson (1860–1937) was governor of Alabama from 1915 to 1919.

Emmett Jay Scott to Charles William Anderson

[Tuskegee, Ala.] November 19, 1915

My dear Friend: How good it is of you to write me as you have under date of November 16th: As you say, I did know how much you loved him and I knew how much the Doctor loved and cared for you. It was with him, I think, one of his precious virtues that he loved and admired strong men and he gave you, as you have said, his esteem and constant friendship.

I am not unappreciative of your kindly references to myself, but as an old friend you are entitled to absolute frankness from me. I have not the slightest desire or ambition to succeed Dr. Washington as the Principal of Tuskegee Institute; and there will not be the slightest disposition on the part of the Trustees of Tuskegee Institute to have me accept this place and so, of course, I rest under no delusions.

I shall call your letter to Mrs. Washington's attention, as I shall of course, also, to Mrs. Scott's attention. Both of them will want to read what you have written. I shall treasure for many and many a year your beautiful sentiments of esteem and regard. Yours very truly,

Emmett J. Scott

TLpS Con. 75 BTW Papers DLC.

William G. Willcox to Julius Rosenwald

[New York City] Nov. 19, 1915

My dear Mr. Rosenwald: Dr. Schieffelin and I have just returned from Tuskegee. We had a wonderful time which I should like to tell you about but I cannot write fully today. It was very fortunate that we went as I was able to say a few words of encouragement which were very much needed and had a very good effect. I am sending you a rather mutilated copy. It was really touching to see how much all the teachers appreciated and the confidence and support of the Trustees.

We found a very strong sentiment for Major Moton as a successor. We were relieved to find that Mr. Logan does not consider that he is fitted for the position and is not aspiring to it. He thinks that Major Moton is the only man to take Mr. Washington's place. Mrs. Washington is very strongly of the same opinion, in fact, she said that to appoint either Mr. Logan or Mr. Scott "would split the Institution wide open." Mr. Taylor is also of the opinion that there is no one at the Institute fitted to take Mr. Washington's place and that Major Moton is the only man in sight.

Dr. Thomas Jesse Jones of the United States Bureau of Education, Washington, Mr. Davis of the General Education Board and Mr. Sibley, are all very strongly of the same opinion which is also endorsed by

459

Dr. Elbert of Wilmington and Dr. Courtney of Boston, two fine negro physicians who are members of the Executive Committee of the National Negro Business League, are also strongly of the opinion that Major Moton is the one man for the appointment.

I have just had a talk with Mr. Low who says that he has felt all along that Major Moton was the man and that Mr. Trumbull with whom he has just been talking agrees with him that Mr. Scott would not carry sufficient weight either at the school or throughout the country.

Mr. Mason is also in favor of Major Moton and Dr. Frissell who was at Tuskegee told me that while he preferred not to be quoted, since he might be considered biased, yet he could not help feeling that Major Moton is the man to fill the position and while he will be a great loss to Hampton yet Hampton would of course, give him up if Tuskegee wants him.

We are to have a conference of the Trustees Monday noon instead of Tuesday and Mr. Low asked me to suggest that you should telegraph your views Monday forenoon, if possible. Of course, we shall not take any formal action without calling a regular meeting of the Board but we would like to know that you concur in our judgment, before even discussing the matter of Major Moton.

It is quite generally suggested that a memorial to Mr. Washington should take the form of a nation wide subscription to a memorial fund to add to the endowment fund. With the five hundred negro business leagues, two hundred negro Y.M.C.A.'s and innumerable colored churches, it is believed that it might be possible to raise a Million Dollars from the colored people, that is, if a general campaign was organized now while the sentiment is at its height. This would be a wonderful tribute from the colored people and Dr. Schieffelin and I feel that we should attempt it and that it would also be a great help in securing publicity and interest among the white people. It is suggested that a Nation wide committee of one hundred should be formed with a subcommittee for each State to organize the campaign.

I know you are not much in favor of endowment funds but I believe you will agree with me that in this case such a memorial fund would be the most appropriate memorial for Mr. Washington. The Tuskegee Institute is his great monument and the idea of a fund to continue and propitiate [propagate?] its work, will appeal to a great many friends of both races.[1]

I wish you could have been with us at Tuskegee. While it was very sad, it was most inspiring. I suppose over five thousand people were present and I understand that at least two thousand telegrams were received from men and women in all ranks and stations in life and from all parts of the country. It was a wonderful tribute to a great life. Sincerely yours,

William G. Willcox

I have just been talking with Dr. Flexner. He thinks Maj. Moton by all odds the best man and his only question is whether Hampton could spare him.[2]

TLtSr   Julius Rosenwald Papers   ICU.

[1] In the original this word was typed "graces." The person who subsequently transcribed the letter rendered it "graces" followed by "sic."
[2] The transcriber noted that this postscript was "added in script."

An Editorial in *The New Republic*

November 20, 1915

A LEADER OF HUMANITY

The death of Booker T. Washington closes a career in many respects the most remarkable in his generation. No man in our time has obtained a greatness under heavier handicaps. He was the son of a slave mother and of a white father, of whom nothing is known beyond what can be inferred from his unacknowledged parenthood. Politically emancipated as a child, he still had resting upon him the colossal burdens of a race despised and oppressed, of an illiterate tradition, of extreme poverty. Yet by his fortieth year he had attained national distinction, and at the time of his death he was respected and admired not only throughout his own country, but wherever men are sincerely attempting to elevate the common man and correct the wrongs of the ages. We used to describe Booker T. Washington, somewhat patronizingly, as a leader of the negro race. So he was indeed, and one of the best racial leaders in history. He displayed a nearly unique capacity for exciting in his people a healthy pride of race without employing the means of invidious disparagement of other races. He elevated the

American negroes in their own eyes and in the eyes of the whites — a vastly significant achievement. But what is still more significant, he strengthened the bonds of affection subsisting between the two races.

Booker T. Washington's work as an educator has scarcely a parallel even in this country of extraordinary educational organizers. Thirty-five years ago all there was of Tuskegee was a shanty housing some thirty raw negro pupils and a single teacher with potentialities recognized only by himself. It was a bad time for negro education. The old abolitionist doctrine of racial equality had about run its course. The North was beginning to yield to the Southerner's doubts as to the expediency of trying to educate the colored race. There was apparently no satisfactory place in the scheme of the world for the educated negro. Since it was to be the destiny of the race to remain servile and dependent, why awaken aspirations that could never be realized, that could only lead to unrest and disorder? What the negro really needed, so it was asserted, was a docile and contented existence under the benevolent control of the whites. It was the formidable obstacle of this attitude that Booker T. Washington's little school at Tuskegee had to overcome. And it has been overcome entirely. Negro education as organized in Tuskegee has few detractors. The thousands of graduates of the Institute have no difficulty in finding their place in the world. To-day they are scattered throughout the South, and they are pushing themselves forward in farming, handicrafts and business, or are engaged in teaching others of their race how to advance. The reports of the Negro Business Men's League — an association founded by Booker T. Washington — indicate an astonishing progress of the race toward economic independence.

There are, it is true, representatives of the older school of negro leadership who have viewed askance the tendencies implicit in Booker T. Washington's work. It is natural that a negro of intelligence and refinement should chafe under the political and social disabilities that have been imposed upon his race, and should regard their removal as the one thing in life worth fighting for. Booker T. Washington's counsel to hold the political and social claims of the negro in abeyance and concentrate effort upon his economic advancement, has appeared to negro leaders of the old school as an abject surrender to the racial arrogance of the whites. And the universal approval, on the part of the whites, of Booker T. Washington's methods and aims has enhanced the suspicion and bitterness of the intransigeants. Why did the whites approve of the industrial education of the negro? Because a negro trained industrially makes a better hand. Why did they approve of the efforts to cultivate thrift in the negroes and the ambition for land-ownership? Because the thrifty, land-hungry negro raises the price of land and makes a good customer for the white business man. Booker T. Washington was approved by the whites, it has often been insinuated, because he played into the hands of the whites. Not merely that he made the negro more useful to the whites; what was more ominous, he diverted the energies of the negroes and of their white friends from the struggle for political and social equality.

Such a view of Booker T. Washington and his work has merely a subjective validity. It can be explained; it arises naturally out of the conditions in which its exponents find themselves. But no one who has studied the history of oppressed races can question the correctness of Booker T. Washington's tactics or the soundness of his philosophy. For he had a philosophy, coherent enough even if its exposition is scattered through his hastily composed and voluminous writings. In this philosophy there is no postulate of the racial inferiority of the negro. In America the negro is "the man farthest down," in a position strictly analogous to that of the Slovenes in Hungary or the Ukrainians in Galicia or South Russia. All the degrading characteristics imputed to the negro by the ruling whites are imputed to the Slovenes and Ukrainians by the ruling Magyars, Poles and Russians. As in our own South the whites own most of the land, monopolize the civil service and the professions, so in those parts of Europe where an oppressed race is held under by its historical conquerors, land ownership, the civil service and the professions are the domain of the ruling race. For hundreds of years the oppressed races of Europe have struggled to raise themselves through political agitation and social striving — in vain. These are not solvents sufficiently powerful to relax the cohesion of the ruling caste. But where the Slovene or Ukrainian has succeeded in gaining economic power the weight of oppression begins to lift. If the goal of an oppressed race is political equality, economic progress is usually the only feasible road to its attainment.

The conflict between races established on the same soil is an insuperable barrier to the progress of democracy. A ruling race will never relax its grip upon the political power in response to the moral and intellectual striving of a subject race. But a ruling race will countenance attempts on the part of the oppressed to increase their economic efficiency, partly because the members of the ruling race hope to profit thereby and partly because a ruling race affects to despise the purely economic field and whatever goes on in it. The subject race can elevate itself, through industry and thrift, without encountering any serious opposition. To develop these qualities by education, precept, organized propaganda, is the first duty of the leader of a race which finds itself in a condition of political subjection. Booker T. Washington saw more clearly than any other American the fundamental conditions upon which the progress of his race must depend, and he created an effective technique accordingly. Thereby he made himself not only the foremost leader of his own race, but also gave a fruitful example to other oppressed races of whatever color; and since the problem of the oppressed races and classes is universal, Booker T. Washington is entitled to rank as a leader of humanity.

The New Republic, 5 (Nov. 20, 1915), 60–61.

Emmett Jay Scott to Alexander E. Manning

[Tuskegee, Ala.] November 24, 1915

Dear Mr. Manning: I wrote you just a day or two ago thanking you for coming to Tuskegee at the last sad hour.

I am now writing to express my sincere regret that you should have been a victim of pick-pockets. It certainly marred a very sad occasion to feel that thugs and criminals should seek to take advantage of a time like that to prey upon people. Three of the criminals have been apprehended and are in jail here at Tuskegee — their trials to be held very soon. I have no doubt but that they will get all that is coming to them. Yours very truly,

Emmett J. Scott

TLpS Con. 533 BTW Papers DLC.

Emmett Jay Scott to Frederick Randolph Moore

[Tuskegee, Ala.] November 24, 1915

Dear Fred: Nothing would be more harmful than for you to urge and for you to follow the suggestions contained in Mr. Albert Johnson's letter. I appreciate most fully his very kind feeling and his disposition to be of help to me, but I cannot permit any of my friends to take the leadership in any organized movement of the character here mentioned. As I explained to you most fully, I am not either an active, passive or receptive candidate for the Principalship of Tuskegee Institute. I am quite sure that nothing ought to be done to embarrass the Trustees so that they may do the wisest and best thing when they come to decide about the matter of keeping Tuskegee alive.

It was certainly good to have you at Tuskegee for a few days last week. I enjoyed each and every moment of your stay here. Sincerely yours,

Emmett

TLpS Con. 77 BTW Papers DLC.

An Obituary in *Outlook*

Nov. 24, 1915

BOOKER WASHINGTON AND HIS RACE

Booker Washington's death is a National calamity.

To very few men is it given to serve the Nation so fruitfully as it was given to this great man. Besides the gifts of discernment and abounding common sense, he had great gifts of character — in particular, that noble kind of humility that is the very highest mark of self-respect. And all his gifts, with all his strength, he devoted unceasingly to his race and his country. It is quite impossible to say whether he rendered the larger service to the blacks or to the whites.

It was because he spent himself without stint that death came to him when he was but fifty-six or fifty-seven years old. As one of his associates, the cook at Tuskegee Institute, is reported to have said, his

465

death brings him "the first rest he's had these thirty-five years." After many months of ill health, which did not prevent him from doing a great deal of work, he suffered a nervous breakdown early in November. A few days later he was taken to Tuskegee, Alabama, for, as he had said, he had been born in the South, he had lived in the South, and he wished to die in the South, and on November 14, within five hours of his arrival home, he died.

From the time of his young boyhood he had been inured to hard work. He was somewhere between twelve and fourteen years old (he never knew even the year of his birth) when, after several years of labor — including long hours in the salt furnaces and coal mines of West Virginia — he decided to go to Hampton Institute. His admission examination consisted in cleaning a room, and he passed it triumphantly. It was there, under General Armstrong, that he received his impulse to serve his people and to establish a school for Negroes. From that day to the day of his death he was almost incessantly at work. His labors were widely various — attending to the administrative details of Tuskegee Institute, lecturing, writing, raising money by personal solicitation, organizing meetings of Negroes, studying the problems of his race, and on every occasion between whiles giving individual counsel and assistance to the struggling black man wherever he found him. His most famous book is his autobiography, "Up from Slavery." This he wrote on scraps of paper wherever he happened to be — mainly while traveling. It is one of the most notable autobiographies written in our times.

To the staff of The Outlook Dr. Washington's death brings a special sense of personal loss, for he was a frequent contributor to The Outlook and an adviser whose wisdom we often sought. "Up from Slavery" was planned in the office of The Outlook, and was first published in its pages; and probably the last thing that he wrote for publication was the letter from him that appeared in The Outlook a week ago.

But it was not merely by his words that he exercised his leadership. He did not merely tell people what to do, but he practiced what he preached. He proved his doctrines as he went along. Tuskegee Institute is the living, growing evidence of the faith that was in him.

Booker Washington was a practical idealist. He never troubled himself about what the people who brought slaves to Virginia in 1619 ought to have done; he set out to show what could be done in the nineteenth and twentieth centuries. For that reason he encountered the hostility of some demagogues and dreamers who have no use for an ideal unless it is irrational and unattainable. Such people, black and white, did much to impede his work, but they never seemed to embitter him or turn him aside from construction to altercation. As he wrote in his account of slave insurrections in his "Story of the Negro" — which is a history of the race: "It requires no real courage for a man to stand up before a sympathetic audience and denounce wrongs that had been committed by people thousands of miles away."

His ideals were of the sort that the ordinary man, if he wishes, can bring appreciably nearer. "I think," he wrote in "Up from Slavery," "that the whole future of my race hinges on the question as to whether or not it can make itself of such indispensable value that the people in the town and the State where we reside will feel that our presence is necessary to the happiness and well-being of the community." The Negro who said that about his race could not have been other than an idealist. To transform a seemingly insoluble problem into an indispensable blessing to the community requires idealism; but it is the sort of idealism that any member of the race can begin at once to practice. And Booker Washington patiently showed by word and deed, again and again, how the ordinary Negro could begin to put that idealism into practice. "One farm bought, one house built, one home neatly kept, one man the largest taxpayer and depositor in the local bank, one school or church maintained, one factory running successfully, one truck garden profitably cultivated, one patient cured by a Negro doctor, one sermon well preached, one office well filled, one life cleanly lived — these," wrote Dr. Washington in his book on "Working with the Hands," "will tell more in our favor than all the abstract eloquence that can be summoned to plead our cause."

It was not only or chiefly that Booker Washington wanted for his people the blessings of material prosperity that he preached his practical idealism in terms of hogs and corn, of land-owning, house-building, banks, and factories; it was because it was by means of such things as these that the Negroes could make themselves indispensable. His idea of Negro success was to be of use. It is a good idea of success for any one.

This is why he laid stress on industrial education. It was not because he would deny the value of other forms of training; but because the great majority of Negroes can be of most use by practicing some forms of productive industry. And this is true of others than Negroes. He once illustrated this by the following anecdote:

"Not long ago a missionary who was going into a foreign field very kindly asked of me advice as to how he should proceed to convert the people to Christianity. I asked him, first, upon what the people depended mostly for a living in the country where he was to labor; he replied that for the most part they were engaged in sheep-raising. I said to him at once that if I were going into that country as a missionary, I should begin my efforts by teaching the people to raise more sheep and better sheep. If he could convince them that Christianity could raise more sheep and better sheep than paganism, he would at once get a hold on their sympathy and confidence in a way he could not do by following more abstract methods of converting them." And Dr. Washington added: "The average man can discern more quickly the difference between good sheep and bad sheep than he can the difference between Unitarianism and Trinitarianism."

It was not labor for its own sake that Booker Washington sought to exalt in his emphasis on industrial education, but labor as a means of building character through willing service of others. To those of his race who objected to his teaching on the ground that the Negro for two hundred and fifty years had been worked as a slave and had now become free he replied again and again that there was a vast difference between being worked and working — "that being worked meant degradation, that working meant civilization" — and he quoted the old Negro farmer who, holding up some stalks of cotton which he had raised and which showed a progressive improvement from one or two bolls to six or twelve bolls a stalk, remarked to his audience at a farmers' institute, "I'se had no chance to study science, but I'se making some science myself."

If any one knew the hardships of the Negroes, their wrongs, the inequities from which they suffer, the barriers which have been raised in the path of their progress, Booker Washington knew them; but he never made use of them as a subject of complaint. He left it to others to talk about grievances while he talked about opportunities; he left it to others to talk about rights while he talked about duties.

The remark of an old Union officer, long resident in Virginia, that "the Negroes must be pioneers in an old country," expressed Booker

Washington's attitude. "To me," he wrote as he concluded "The Story of the Negro," "the history of the Negro people in America seems like the story of a great adventure, in which, for my own part, I am glad to have had a share."

And one incentive to him in this adventure was his pride in his race. He liked to show how much more successfully the Negro had survived in America than the Indian, and declared that "the Negro seems to be about the only race that has been able to look the white man in the face and live," and he acknowledged his preference for Negro music over the music of the greatest of European composers. In little ways as well as large ways Dr. Washington was solicitous for the honor of his race. Formerly The Outlook did not use a capital letter in spelling Negro any more than it does in spelling white man; it was Dr. Washington's advocacy of the use of a capital letter for Negro as a capital letter is used in Indian that led us to make the change — a small matter, but a sign of Booker Washington's loyalty to his race.

It was just because he was loyal to his race that he refused to make his race an issue in every problem. Indeed, he saw that the so-called Negro Problem was only a group of common social problems — problems of housing, of health, of self-support, of education, and so on — knotted together by a race complication. What he sought to do was to remove the race complication so that the constituent problems could be attacked separately. The social intimacy (or so-called social equality) that some disloyal Negroes have craved and the sort of politics that created the evils of the reconstruction era have been the two main causes of the race complication. Booker Washington steadily refused to inject these matters into questions of education and housing, and land-ownership, and business, and moral progress, and true religion. He firmly believed that political privileges would come when they were earned, and that the only social intimacy the Negro required was that open to him among his own people. As he said in his great speech at Atlanta, which did more than anything else to bring him as a leader of race adjustment before the whites as well as the colored people of the South: "In all things purely social we can be as separate as the fingers" — and he held his open hand up, then, clenching his fist — "yet one as the hand in all things essential to mutual progress."

It is by Booker Washington's way that progress is to be found for the Negro in America and for America with the Negro. His death is a calamity to his own race; but it is a greater calamity to the whites.

There will not soon be likely to arise a Negro leader whom the white people of the South and of the North will so readily heed. It is not probable that such a man will appear twice in a generation. The Negroes' chief spokesman before their white fellow-men is gone. And this is the white people's loss. It is a greater injury to misunderstand than to be misunderstood, and without this spokesman the white people will be more in danger of misunderstanding their black fellow-countrymen. To this degree at least, the burden which this one black man has been bearing will now fall largely on white shoulders.

Outlook, 111 (Nov. 24, 1915), 701–3.

Seth Low to Emmett Jay Scott

New York, N.Y. Nov. 30–1915

PLEASE CALL SPECIAL MEETING OF THE TRUSTEES TO BE HELD AT THE INSTITUTE ON MONDAY MORNING DECEMBER THIRTEENTH AT NINE THIRTY FOR THE PURPOSE OF ELECTING A SUCCESSOR TO DOCTOR WASHINGTON AND FOR THE TRANSACTION OF ANY OTHER BUSINESS THAT MAY BE BROUGHT BEFORE THE BOARD AN ANNOUNCEMENT WILL APPEAR IN THE PAPERS TOMORROW MORNING CONCERNING THE MEMORIAL FUND I AM ASKED BY THE INVESTMENT COMMITTEE TO REQUEST YOU TO TAKE CHARGE OF THE COLLECTION OF THE FUND SO FAR AS IT APPEALS TO NEGROES.

SETH LOW

TWSr   Con. 657   BTW Papers   DLC.

Margaret James Murray Washington
to Augusta Nusbaum Rosenwald

[Tuskegee, Ala.] Nov. 30, 1915

My Dear Mrs. Rosenwald: I have tried to write you several time[s] lately but I could not. I simply cannot. Your family has been so near and dear to *us* both that I did not trust myself to come to you even in writing. It was so terrible. When the trustees come down in December, I do hope you will come even tho Mr. Low says they are not going to bring their families surely you come [can?] and will come. We need you. I want the question of the principal settled just as soon as possible. It is better that it be done as early as possible. We are depending absolutely on the trustees. We know that they *know*. We are all of one mind. Mr. Washington's work must go on and the best that can be found to carry it on, will have our support. These newspaper reports are simply the work of one or two people. I do wish you would come Mrs. Rosenwald. Try. We would like to see you. My best love to Mr. Rosenwald. Yours sincerely

Margaret J. Washington

TLtSr Julius Rosenwald Papers ICU.

James Carroll Napier to Julius Rosenwald

Nashville, Tennessee November Thirty Fifteen

COPY

Dear sir: Like legions of others in all parts of the country I feel the deepest interest in hoping that the right man will be selected by the Board of Trustees as Mr. Washington's successor at Tuskegee. Therefore, I trust you will not think what I shall say here indelicate or out of place.

For a great many years, to my own knowledge, those most deeply interested in the success of Tuskegee and the promulgation of Mr. Washington's ideals have regarded Mr. Emmett J. Scott as his logical successor. His thorough insight to all the interests of Tuskegee as well as his deep, unselfish and loyal devotion to Mr. Washington's methods and ideals more peculiarly fit him for the duties of this position than will be found in any other man in the country.

With Mr. Scott at the head of affairs at Tuskegee I believe that things will move on and that the school will prosper and grow just as if Mr. Washington himself were on the ground.

I hope, therefore, that you may see fit to do whatever may lie in your power to induce the Board of Trustees to make this selection.

Again apologizing for this intrusion upon your time, I remain, Very truly yours,

[J. C. Napier]

TL Copy   Con. 534   BTW Papers   DLC.

An Editorial in *Christian Endeavor World*

December 2, 1915

BOOKER T. WASHINGTON

AN APPRECIATION BY A SOUTHERNER

"Thou shalt be missed, because thy seat will be empty."

Officially there will be a successor; personally there can be none. Generous as is Providence in other beneficence, He gives sparingly of really great men. One or two for a single race, and the limit of His favor for a generation has been reached.

Booker T. Washington was God's supreme gift to the negroes of this generation, and, on behalf of the negroes, to the world. Others as great, possibly even greater, may emerge; but he was the greatest that ever came, or that ever can come, "up from slavery." Nor is there anything invidious in this. Opportunities, while they do not make men great, do disclose true greatness. Booker T. Washington had unexampled opportunities, and he made the most of them.

His theory was an inspiration. Race-betterment as he conceived it lay not in the direction of a vain clamor for social recognition — all men claim the right to choose their companions from the ranks of the consenting; it lay toward self-respect, self-support, and resulting racial pride. "Own, order, elevate, and protect your own home," was the core of his creed, and for any race, that, in the spirit of Christ, is a saving faith, the plan of salvation. More than any other man, living or dead, he was responsible for the fact that thousands of negroes could sing, with the joy of proprietorship, the closing lines of Frank L. Stanton's inimitable poem,

"Jes er li'l' cabin whah de blue smoke rise an' curl
Kin hol' ernough ob happiness ter re'ch eroun' dis worl';
Dey tells me dat I poah, but de woman's in de doah.
An' de chillun's on de floah,
Er singin' an' er singin' in de mo'nin'."

Booker T. Washington did not escape the penalties of all greatness. He was misunderstood by many, misrepresented by multitudes, and maliciously maligned by some. While he was the idol of thousands of his race, perhaps his own people supplied his severest critics, if not his cruelest foes. Indeed, it is just possible that among the intelligent white Christian people of the South his sincerity and the sanity of his theories were more nearly universally acknowledged and applauded than they were by the religious and educational leaders of his own race, many of whom, though gifted and powerful, are honest in their bitter opposition to the Tuskegee sage's philosophy.

But the shadows lengthen and loom larger as the sun sets, and this man's greatness is secure. His teachings — the cardinal ones — will come to be esteemed by the negroes at the South as worthy of all acceptation. The false philosophies of many generations are seldom destroyed by the blows of a single man in one generation.

Over any mistakes made by this prophet of his people — and he made mistakes — and over any weaknesses he had — and of his inheritance and early environment who dare demand perfection? — let there be drawn the kindly curtain of the Golden Rule. It is enough to remember that a gifted and cultured man labored for forty years in the midst of ignorance that he did not selfishly commercialize, and surrounded by weakness that he did not exploit for his own gratification. It is achievement monumental enough to enrich all the generations that shall supply the channel for his onflowing blood that, having the confidence of American philanthropy, he made his drafts payable to an up-struggling race's industrial, moral, and intellectual weal. Such men cannot die, because they live in deeds, and the deeds of such men are immortal.

But if Booker T. Washington, being physically dead, shall yet speak as persuasively and eloquently as living he could do so incomparably well, the large benefactors of the negro race must bestow their bounty, not alone upon one school, but upon many schools, for the industrial, mental, and religious training of those for whom this pioneer, this Afro-

American John the Baptist, lived and died. Not less money for Tuskegee should flow Southward and up from the South, but more for a hundred other centres; more for intelligent missionary work and religious education and true evangelism among the children and grandchildren of a slavery which, hateful as it may have been and deserving of death as it certainly was, still paid a heed to character-building from which modern methods may learn this single supreme truth:

The welfare of every Southern community where white and black people must dwell in neighborhood can be created and safeguarded alone by merited mutual good will and confidence. These, in turn, can be secured not alone, not even mainly, by long-range philanthropy. The intelligent and liberal Northern friend of the negro, eager to improve Southern conditions, together with the unselfish and equally benevolent Southern white man, who knows those conditions, must sit down with the trained Christian negro himself; and these three must counsel and work and give as they are severally able toward what will then be the certain solution of whatever troublesome remnants of the race problem are left — a problem which we inherited in almost equal measure from the monstrous legalized blunder of the slave-traffic and the sudden and terrible manner and political sequences of its destruction, both of them natural and regrettable and generally conceded mistakes of another and more heroic generation than our own, mistakes which we shall do well if we condemn but little the while that we try in brotherhood to correct them in entirety.

If every great reformation claims at least one martyrdom, this pending reformation has had its human sacrifice. He died from over-service and too soon. Let the friends of Booker T. Washington — and their name in both races is legion — now get together and stay together for the good of both races and for the glory of the God of both.

IRA LANDRITH[1]

Christian Endeavor World, 30 (Dec. 2, 1915), proof, Con. 950, BTW Papers, DLC.

[1] Ira Landrith (1865–1941), a Presbyterian clergyman, was president of Belmont College in Nashville, Tenn., from 1904 to 1912. For many years he was superintendent of the International Society of Christian Endeavor, and in 1916 he was the Prohibition party candidate for President of the United States.

Charles William Anderson to Emmett Jay Scott

New York City   December 4, 1915

Personal

My dear Emmett: In writing you on yesterday I forgot to say that a Memorial meeting for Dr. Washington, will be held at St. Marks Church on Thursday evening, December Ninth, at which several speakers, including myself, are to make addresses. Undoubtedly Rev. W. H. Brooks has communicated with you concerning this meeting. If so I wish you would in your answer to him, note the fact that you were pleased to note my name among the speakers and make mention of my long and constant friendship for the Doctor, and my interest in the great work at Tuskegee as evidenced by my turning over to the School, the money subscribed by merchants for a present for me, and my good offices in securing a contribution from Mr. Belmont. The reason why I would like to have these facts developed, is that the speakers who are clamoring for the front places on all of the programs now, are those who opposed the Doctor during his entire lifetime. They are so fulsome in their praise of him now that he is dead, that the uninformed masses hereabouts, look upon these speakers as having been the Doctor's lifelong friends and followers.

A case in point, is the Memorial meeting held by John M. Royall in Harlem, sometime ago. During the last campaign, when Royall was running for Alderman, he criticised and abused the Doctor almost nightly in his public speeches, and now he is weeping over his death because it is *popular to do so.* One or two of this same kidney will speak at the St. Marks meeting, and I am anxious to differentiate myself from them, without having to do so by any statement of mine that would seem to be an attempt to exalt myself by depreciating the other fellows. I think you see my point.

I did not speak at the Bethel Church meeting two Sundays ago, for the reason that those in charge of it sent letters to Messrs. Schiff, Wanamaker, Clews and other friends of the Doctor's, inviting them to be present at the Memorial meeting and soliciting contributions for the expense of the meeting. This attempt to commercialize the Doctor's death was so disgusting to me that I declined to be one of the speakers, on the ground that it would be impossible for me to make a speech which would be even remotely worthy of [the] subject, on a single days notice.

Hoping you are very well, and with warmest regards to the family and friends, I remain   Yours very truly,

Charles

TLS   Con. 9   BTW Papers   DLC.

A News Item in the St. Louis *Post-Dispatch*

Tuskegee, Ala., Dec. 4. 1915

3 MEN DISCUSSED
FOR PLACE BOOKER
WASHINGTON HELD

Two Aids Talked of as Logical
Candidates for Presidency of
Tuskegee Institute

MAJ. MOTON MENTIONED

Warren Logan and Emmett J.
Scott Lieutenants of Negro
Educator for Years

The question of a probable successor to Booker T. Washington as head of the Tuskegee Institute has been frequently discussed here since the funeral of Washington two weeks ago. While there is a desire among the supporters of the school to have a new president named soon, in order that there may be as little interruption as possible in the work of the institute, it is realized that the Board of Trustees having the matter in charge will wait a reasonable time before naming their selection, out of respect to the great negro educator.

It is generally known that trustees are considering the matter informally with leading negroes and with whites identified with educational problems.

The desire to have the various points of view before making a decision is commented upon as showing that the board realizes the importance of the question, and does not intend to select a successor until it

476

has given the whole field a careful study. A definite decision is expected here, however, some time before the annual meeting of the Board of Trustees next February.

DISCUSSION OF CANDIDATES

In the meantime there is a great deal of unofficial discussion of the question by interested groups. It is generally agreed that the logical candidates are Warren Logan and Emmett J. Scott, who have for years been Dr. Washington's chief lieutenants, or that some outside man should be selected for his national reputation as a leader, educator and administrator, rather than for his intimate association with Tuskegee and its work. Maj. R. R. Moton, commandant at Hampton Institute, and Dr. Frissell's right-hand man there, is the only man spoken of [as] a candidate from this national field.

Logan came to Tuskegee in 1883, two years after its foundation, as vice principal and treasurer, and has given a very good account of himself. His work has kept him almost exclusively at the institute, and he is therefore not well known outside of the circle of people who are actively interested in Tuskegee.

Scott came to the institute nearly 20 years ago as private secretary to Dr. Washington, later being made secretary of the institute. No one who has followed his work there has anything but praise for the way in which it has been done. He has a wider acquaintance throughout the country than Logan, having been appointed by President Taft as special envoy to Liberia and having served as secretary of the National Negro Business League, a strong and growing organization started by Dr. Washington 15 years ago.

Both men have considerable followings within the institute, and either would be perfectly acceptable to the white population in the town of Tuskegee and throughout that part of the county.

ARGUMENTS FOR MOTON

As to the arguments given by those who would like to see Maj. Moton selected, in the first place, they say, the following question must be answered before there is any discussion of candidates:

Will Tuskegee Institute be content to become merely the largest and most complete industrial institution for the negro in the far South, or

477

does it wish to continue the identification which Dr. Washington gave it with the leadership of the race?

Those who would like to see the trustees select Maj. Moton answer the first part of the question negatively and the second part with an emphatic yes. They feel that, if Tuskegee is to be a going institution, it must be kept to the fore through the recognized leadership of its head.

Moton, they say, has a national reputation, as well as the confidence of both the whites and the negroes. He was one of the closest friends that Dr. Washington had, spoke from the same platform with him on many a trip through both the North and the South, and knows as well as or better than any other negro Dr. Washington's attitude towards the strong and weak points in his race, and his aspirations for Tuskegee and for his people.

SEEN AS FOREMOST FIGURE

Now that Washington is dead, Moton naturally becomes the foremost figure of the race, his supporters say, and he should therefore succeed to the position of head of the greatest institution ever developed by a negro. This identification of the leader with the greatest constructive force in the race is believed by them to be of the utmost importance, unless the country wishes to see the negro's struggle for full recognition as a citizen shift its emphasis from that of trying to make himself capable and worthy of citizenship to that of protesting that he is not treated as a citizen.

Whatever the decision of the trustees, they can feel sure that they have the confidence of all the groups, if the many opinions expressed here are an index. This is especially true of the negroes, who show almost a touching gratitude towards those who are helping the race to solve its problems. As for the Southern whites, they have several able representatives on the board. The feeling generally here is that although the individual candidates have their personal followings, all three are such strong men that any one of them would make an able head of the institute.

St. Louis *Post-Dispatch,* Dec. 5, 1915, 17.

Margaret James Murray Washington
to Julius Rosenwald

Tuskegee Institute, Alabama   December Tenth, Nineteen-fifteen

My dear Mr. Rosenwald: With all the cares, so far as Tuskegee is concerned, which you have, I am venturing to ask you to at least consider another.

For years, in a way, the school has borne the financial burden of the Business League, at least it did this year. I think the debt is still here to be paid and probably will be paid. When Mr. Washington came home this fall, we all knew that he was so worn out that we did not urge him to do one solitary thing — not even to pick up a pen to write his name when he could help it and so the bills for the meeting in Boston were not signed by him.

However, Mr. Scott tells me that he thinks things are going to come out alright. I am very anxious about the meeting for this coming summer. All of the interests which Mr. Washington carried some how or other seems to me ought to be carried on. I am not sure how it can all be done, but the Business League is a thing which kept the men of the race together, I mean the fine, strong, men and made them see the importance of holding the others in check.

While you are here I wish you would take up the matter with Mr. Scott and in some way arrange it so, that the financial part of the work can be carried on here at Tuskegee as it has been done before, at least for this year, until we can pull ourselves together.

I am writing Mr. Mason also because I know how thoroughly Mr. Washington depended upon his friends for help and advice in this particular. Yours sincerely,

Margaret J Washington

TLS   Julius Rosenwald Papers   ICU.

Theodore Roosevelt to Julius Rosenwald

New York   December 15, 1915

My dear Mr. Rosenwald: Mr. Low showed me both your telegrams; and we were all a good deal concerned over them, for my dear sir, you do not need to be told that the others are already your warm admirers and supporters and that now I too have become among the foremost of that number! We all of us ardently wished you had been with us on the train when we saw Major Moton. I will of course have nothing to say in the action of the Committee of Five. Nevertheless, I wish to write you my impressions.

As you know, I went down to Tuskegee, believing that Mr. Scott should be given the place. I studied him carefully while there and studied the whole situation. I retain undiminished my regard and respect for him; but I have come positively to the conclusion that he is not able to meet the very onerous demands of the situation. I feel this so strongly that in case the Committee of Five do not agree on Major Moton, I shall very earnestly advise their extending their enquiries and looking throughout the Union to find the best man for the position. But in my judgment, after seeing and having a thoroughly satisfactory talk with Major Moton, there is no need for them to go farther. I am more impressed than I can well express with Major Moton. It is the greatest relief to me to say that I believe that if he is appointed we ensure for ourselves every reasonable probability of success in carrying on the great work of Booker Washington. I believe that he can run the institution. I believe that he will get on with the southern people as well as any negro now living — I bar Booker Washington because he was a genius such as does not arise in a generation. I believe that he will get on with the northern white men and be able to help us in getting the necessary funds. Finally, I believe that there is a good chance of his becoming what the President of Tuskegee should be — the leader of his race in this country. He has a very powerful and at the same time an engaging and attractive personality. He has great strength, and yet he is absolutely free from the bumptiousness or self-assertiveness which would at once ensure failure in his position. I cannot speak too strongly about the favorable impression he has made upon me.

Now, my dear Mr. Rosenwald, remember two things. Winter is on now and neither Perkins's Palisades Park nor my own place at Sagamore Hill is particularly attractive. But in the spring I very earnestly wish you to make a tour of Perkins's Palisades Park for the reasons I gave you, and moreover if you are in New York at that time I want Mrs. Rosenwald and you to come out and take lunch with us at Sagamore Hill.

With regard, Faithfully yours,

Theodore Roosevelt

TLtSr   Julius Rosenwald Papers   ICU.

Emmett Jay Scott to Wright W. Campbell

Tuskegee Institute, Alabama   December 15, 1915

Dear Sir: The sub-committee, which has been empowered by the Board of Trustees to select a Principal for the Tuskegee Normal and Industrial Institute, of which you are a member, will soon meet. I feel moved to write you as follows:

Dr. Washington, in the organization of the Tuskegee Board of Trustees, sought to bring together Southern white men, Northern white men, and colored men. That was his idea of the solution of the so-called Negro question. He believed if Southern white men, and Northern white men, and colored men could come together for conference and interchange of views, that they would better understand each other, and in that way, adjust whatever misunderstandings that might exist between them.

In my opinion, it would be most unfortunate if the impression should obtain in any quarter that there are radical differences of opinion between our Southern and our Northern Trustees in reference to this matter. You have doubtless seen The Montgomery Advertiser of this morning and will appreciate to what I am referring.

Without regard to any personal considerations whatsoever, I sincerely beg that you will use your influence to bring about an early settlement of the question of the Principalship of Tuskegee Institute,

to the end that there may not continue to exist in the South or elsewhere any feeling over this matter.

I have come to the conclusion that, for the good of the cause, which
is the paramount thing, my name should not be further considered by
the Board of Trustees. As you know, I have not been either an active,
passive or receptive candidate for the vacant Principalship. I have in
no way sought to have my name considered by members of the Board
of Trustees. Therefore, there are no disappointments, or unsatisfied
ambitions involved. I shall continue my best service, and through you,
I pledge my earnest and sincere support of the work of Tuskegee Institute with the same unfaltering loyalty and devotion as in the past.
As I said in my remarks at the Memorial Exercises, held in Dr. Washington's memory, Sunday night, December 12th, the CAUSE is the
thing, and everything must be subordinated to that.

I trust I may have your approval of my thought in this matter and
of the action I have decided to take. Most willingly would I seek to
relieve the situation of all considerations involving myself. Yours very
truly,

Emmett J. Scott

TLS   Seth Low Papers   NNC.

Julius Rosenwald to Seth Low

[Chicago, Ill.] Dec. 16, 1915

My Dear Mr. Low. — Upon my return this morning I find your wire
from Charlotte in reply to my telegram from Evansville (en route).
I agree that we can safely await the conclusions of the Committee of
Five, and whatever they are I shall consider myself bound by them,
but having had an opportunity to think the matter over calmly and
deliberately in all its phases, deemed it best to give the members of
your party the result of my thought.

I look upon Mr. Attwell as one of the most level-headed and reliable
men at the Institute, and at my request he accompanied me to Montgomery. Mr. Sibley had suggested my talking to him about the rural
schools, and he had no intimation that I would speak to him on the

matter of the selection of a principal. I asked him to tell me just exactly what course he would pursue if it were put up to him to select a successor to Booker T. Washington, not only as Principal of Tuskegee Institute but as a leader for the colored people. He unhesitatingly outlined to me all the reasons why he thought that Scott would unquestionably be the better man. The gist of his conversation is contained in my telegram sent to you to Salisbury — not literally, but using my own language in some cases.

Attwell says Mr. Scott, in addition to being an intelligent, highly-cultured man himself, has taken advantage of the opportunity he had to imbibe Mr. Washington's spirit, and knows thoroughly all of the various activities in which he was interested and why he was interested in them — in fact he knew his innermost thoughts.

In speaking of Major Moton, he said that although the Major had been at Tuskegee a number of times, he had never heard him make an address, but whenever he appeared there it was either to crack a joke or in connection with the singing, and also that his jokes, while not in any sense vulgar, were often cheap and undignified for a man of his position. I was especially interested in this, as you will remember that he impresses me as being rather flippant.

Now please bear in mind, my dear Mr. Low, that Mr. Attwell spoke to me in a way he would not have spoken to any one else, and in particular emphasized the fact that he had no personal feeling against Moton whatsoever, but felt it his duty to be perfectly frank, as I had requested he should be. In his opinion Moton would not compare with Scott in education, nor does he think he is looked upon as a leader by the Southern white and black people in any sense as Mr. Scott is.

Attwell tells me Dr. Schieffelin called him aside in the chapel and told him that Moton had been decided upon, and that both Dr. Hall and Dr. Schieffelin had given that impression generally to quite a number of the important people at Tuskegee. They were given to understand that the Trustees wanted Moton and were made to feel it was the desire of the Trustees that they look favorably upon Moton's coming, and in Mr. Attwell's opinion this had much to do with the shaping of their and of Mrs. Washington's views. I am sure that you will agree that it is not unnatural or unusual for people to want to get into the "band wagon." I was greatly impressed with Mr. Attwell's sincerity and earnestness.

Upon questioning Mr. Richardson, the head of the English Department, who was also with us but whom we were careful should not overhear our conversation, he expressed himself practically in the same way Mr. Attwell did, and both feel convinced that this would be the feeling almost universally throughout the Institute had there been no previous intimation as to the attitude of the trustees.

I am under the impression that none of the trustees who were present at the meeting ever heard Moton deliver an address, and it would seem to me to be of vital importance that some of them should hear him — and more than once — before he is selected. If any of his addresses have been printed, or if he has written anything by which we might have an opportunity of judging him, I think it would be well that the trustees be sent as much of such printed matter as possible. If I am not mistaken, Mr. Scott has a book which he expects to have published in the near future.

In spite of the fact that I advocated our coming to a decision at the meeting, I am most grateful to Colonel Roosevelt for insisting upon delaying, since I am now convinced that had it been settled then we might have made a grave mistake.

It does seem to me that the only justification for our seeking a leader from the outside would be that we could secure one who is *preeminently* better fitted than any one connected with the Institute. I say this in spite of the fact that I was willing to join the other trustees if in their wisdom such a course seemed the proper one, but I confess that I should have regretted having done so.

Nevertheless, as stated at the beginning of this letter, I shall back up whatever decision is arrived at by the Committee of Five. Very respectfully yours,

[Julius Rosenwald]

TLt Julius Rosenwald Papers ICU.

Pinckney Benton Stewart Pinchback
to Emmett Jay Scott

Wash: Dec 17/15

My dear Friend: Your favors of the 1st, 7th Dec. came to hand by due course of mail. They found me in my usual state of health but still depressed. It seems impossible to get from under the shadow of our great loss. Note difficulty in writing.

I am very glad to learn that Mrs. Washington and the friends at Tuskegee, especially your good self were pleased at my coming to Tuskegee to attend Dr. Washingtons funeral. As soon as I learned of his death I decided to attend the funeral. I felt it was the least I could do to pay the dear man this last mark of respect.

And after all, my dear Emmett, I am not certain that the sudden departure of the Doctor is not the best way for him to have gone. He died with the harness on and at the full tide of his glorious career. The whole civilized world mourns his departure. In contemplating its world-wide effect and remembering my own decadence, I fear, my stay has been too long.

I see by the press, the Trustees are carefully considering Dr. Washingtons successor. I sincerely trust they may see thier way to offer you the place. In my judgement that would be the wisest and best thing for them to do. If you do not desire the place you can decline it.

Please remember me very kindly to Mrs. Washington and the members of your family. Sincerely your friend

Pinchback

ALS Con. 13 BTW Papers DLC.

Seth Low to Emmett Jay Scott

New York City, December 20, 1915

The committee after a most anxious canvass of all the elements of its problem, selected Major Moton as Principal of the Institute to

485

succeed Dr. Washington. They wish me to express to you their great appreciation of your high-mindedness and the confident belief that you will give to Major Moton and the Institute under its new head your whole-hearted support. It is their purpose to recognize your efficient and devoted service and your unselfishness in some wholly appropriate way.

Seth Low

TWSr Copy   Con. 164   BTW Papers   DLC.

John E. Bush to Emmett Jay Scott

Little Rock, Ark, Dec. 22–1915

My Dear Friend; Replying to yours under date of Dec. 20, 1915, I have to say,

That I have all along noted what the New York Age had to say upon the matter of Dr. Washington's successor and in no instance have I noticed one line in your favor. Fred seems to have gone astray or I misunderstand him.

Early this morning in reading the newspaper, I saw a dispatch in it, from New York, in which it said that Major R. R. Moton had been elected as the successor of our late friend Dr. Washington as head of the Tuskegee Institute. I was disgusted, chagrined and made to feel that merit does not always go to him that justly deserves it. Of course I do not understand any of the inside workings of the selection, but I certainly know how the people in this part of the country feel about it and I so wrote Mr. Lowe.

Major R. R. Moton is a splendid man, a fine gentleman and in a great many ways one of the "Boys" but why he should succeed Dr. Washington over and above you and Mr. Logan, that have trodden the wine press lo these many years, in making Tuskegee what it is, I am unable to say.

After arriving at my office I rec'd your letter, and in it I note you say, "For reasons which are entirely satisfactory to me," those words gave me some relief, remember friend that good things come to those who learn to labor and to wait.

My very best regards to your wife and family, I am yours,

J E Bush

TLS   Con. 528   BTW Papers   DLC.

Emmett Jay Scott to John E. Bush

[Tuskegee, Ala.] December 29, 1915

Dear Mr. Bush: You must not feel badly about Major Moton's selection. Everything is going to come out all right: in fact, I am sure that my friends will be pleased with the way matters are shaping themselves up, even now. The worse thing that could have happened to your old friend would have been for him to have been selected as Dr. Washington's successor.

My wife is a rather sane woman, and it seems to me that she has stated it quite right when she said — the question for me to decide was whether or not I was willing to die for fifteen hundred children or live for five children.

You must not be unduly disturbed either about our friend, Mr. Moore, of the New York Age. He is not the kind of fellow whom one would trust his entire fortunes to. At least I have not thought so. I am sure, however, that even he will come around all right.

I am in a forgiving mood today, you will notice.

Please remember me to all the family. Yours very truly,

Emmett J. Scott

Love to *you* always.

TLpS   Con. 528   BTW Papers   DLC.

Emmett Jay Scott to Richard W. Thompson

[Tuskegee, Ala.] December 30, 1915

Dear Thompson: I do not want you or any of my friends to feel badly about Major Moton's selection. He is going to make a splendid successor to our beloved friend, Dr. Washington. I know it is difficult for my friends to believe me when I say that I nurse no disappointed hopes or unsatisfied ambitions, but that expresses my attitude absolutely and precisely. Everything is going to come out all right and the Trustees have been most generous in their attitude toward me. I am sure you will be pleased when I have opportunity to talk with you about the matter.

I have been doing all I could to prevent any unauthorized movement in this matter of securing funds for a monument for Dr. Washington. I think the matter is now in pretty good shape.

Mr. Banks, Mr. Napier and I are all agreed that Mr. Napier shall stand for the Presidency of the Business League. We will give him the same kind of support we gave the "wizard." I am quite determined that the League and all the interests to which Dr. Washington devoted himself with such unremitting industry shall be kept alive. Sincerely yours,

Emmett J. Scott

TLpS Con. 79 BTW Papers DLC.

A Reminiscence by Frank P. Chisholm

[New York City, ca. December 1915]

PERSONAL REMINISCENCES OF THE LATE DR. WASHINGTON

I am a graduate of Tuskegee Institute, and for the past ten years have been officially identified with the work of this institution. It does not become me, therefore, to attempt an estimate of the services of my lamented Chief, to our race and to the nation. My purpose here is merely to narrate some of my own personal reminiscences of our dead hero.

I first heard of my late Chieftain in 1896 when I was almost ready to graduate from the grammar school at my home, Savannah, Georgia. While trying to decide the question as to what I would do after graduating, I read the famous Atlanta speech of Dr. Washington which had attracted the eyes of the country toward him. One of the passages of that speech was this: "No race will ever get up on its feet until it learns that there is as much dignity in tilling the soil as in writing a poem." About this time I also came across a quotation of his printed in an Almanack which ran: "A fool in Africa is no better off than a fool in America." This utterance doubtless grew out of the question of the expatriation of the Negro to Africa, which was being agitated at the time as a solution of the Negro problem. Both of these thoughts made a profound impression upon my youthful mind. I coupled them together and gleaned from them that his two-fold idea was: (1) That training for farm work was just as important and as necessary as book education; and (2) that no matter whether the Negro was sent to Africa or remained in America he had to be educated. These common sense ideas of his had much to do with my deciding to go to Tuskegee Institute to pursue further training for my life's work.

During my student days at Tuskegee, I had seen Mr. Washington on many a real cold, bitter morning, come down to the students' dining room with no top shirt on, his overcoat snugly buttoned up, and go from table to table inquiring into the comfort of the students. He would ask: "Are you getting enough to eat? If not come to the office and report it. The food here is simple but we mean to have it well cooked and we want you to get a plenty of what we have." At night in the Chapel, when the students marched out, he would be standing at a point where the students would have to pass him. His keen, piercing eyes were sure to detect any grease-spots that were on the students' clothes or any buttons that by chance were conspicuous by their abscence from the students' clothing. Any offender in this respect was sure to be pulled out of line and spoken to by Mr. Washington and cautioned against letting this thing happen a second time, in which case the student would be properly disciplined.

These glimpses show another side of the character of this great man. Although he was Principal of the school and had a number of assistants whose duty it was to look after these apparently small matters, he was absolutely unselfish and constantly exhibited the deepest interest in the bodily and personal comfort and happiness of his students. I question whether there are many heads of big schools in America who exercise a similar degree of interest in the personal side of their students.

One of the iron clad rules of Tuskegee Institute is that no student must ever be released from his trade contract. After I had served two years of my apprenticeship at my printer's trade I desired to be released from my third year in order to enter the day school a year earlier than my contract would have permitted. When I discussed the matter with Mr. Washington he asked me why it was that I wished to be released from my contract. I said to him frankly that my ambition was to be a lawyer, that I had come to Tuskegee to spend only four years and that after graduating from Tuskegee was going to attend Howard University for the purpose of studying law. Dr. Washington did not take so well to the idea. He not only refused to authorize my being released from my contract but earnestly advised me against studying law and urged me to stick to my printer's trade and some day conduct a successful print shop in the South.

He had me understand, however, that he was not opposed to the study of law by Negroes. Rather, he raised the question whether I would render the race in its present condition the greatest service as a lawyer; whether legal advice was the greatest need of an ignorant, backward, struggling people. At the time I thought he was wrong and I was right. From experience and careful study into the real needs and conditions of the masses of our people, I have learned that he was right and I was wrong.

Mr. Washington was a most patient patient. I remember one night he had a bad cold and a sick headache. Mrs. Washington sent for me and invited me to stay all night with him so as to give him every two hours the medicine the doctor had prescribed. I had to wake him from his slumber every two hours to give him his medicine, but not a single time did he seem to exhibit any impatience or disgust with me because of the frequency of my visits.

Throughout my senior year when any Northern visitors were expected at Tuskegee, Mr. Washington would invariably send for me and instruct me to practice the students with the school yells and the Chautauqua salutes. I always felt that I must have satisfied him in this matter of the school yells, otherwise he would not have repeatedly asked me to lead the students in giving them.

During the past ten years, it has been my privilege to arrange for Mr. Washington many meetings in the North where he would speak in the interest of the School. He would frequently send me a telegram to meet him at the Parker House in Boston or at the Biltmore Hotel in New York City, then he would give me instructions in regard to the arranging of meetings in Boston or New York or Brooklyn or some other point. Time and again on these trips in the North he would be carrying some parcel or his travelling bags. When I would volunteer to carry these things for him, he would always decline my invitation. He seemed never to want other people to serve him; rather he wanted to save others any seeming inconvenience.

I recall but one exception to this general rule of his. This was during what proved to be his last visit to Chicago, in September. The officers of Tuskegee realized that he was in a weakened physical condition, and so the word was given to do everything to save him as long as possible. I carried his travelling bags, sent his telegrams, answered his phone calls, ordered his carriages, bought his newspapers, and even carried for him his light fall overcoat. At first, he exhibited a good deal of anxiety at my seeming over-politeness, but finally gave in, as I firmly insisted that he must be spared the slightest inconvenience. After his speech before the National Negro Baptist Convention in Chicago, together with a half dozen policemen, I found a lane for him to pass through to his waiting carriage. We had to do this in order to protect him from the hundreds of his friends and admirers who surged around him to shake his hand. His strength was not equal to the physical effort involved. His death shortly after he delivered this speech in Chicago suggests that at the time of its delivery he seemed to realize that he was closing up his life's work and was making his last speech before this great national body of Negro Baptists. This doubtless accounted for the very earnest, whole-souled and vigorous manner in which he spoke on that occasion.

I shook his hand and bade him good-bye Saturday afternoon September 11th as he was leaving Chicago for Montgomery, Alabama. I seemed to realize that he was making his last long trip South from the Windy City. He has gone now and I shall greatly miss him and his many instructions which he was wont to give to me in short, crisp sentences, but I shall always derive consolation from the fact that I shared his confidence and labored with him in his great work of uplift and betterment of all the people. I shall always cherish his memory as my great teacher and inspirer.

TMc Con. 75 BTW Papers DLC. Published with minor changes in the New York *Age,* Dec. 30, 1915. Clipping in Con. 954, BTW Papers, DLC.

An Editorial in *The Crisis*
by William Edward Burghardt Du Bois[1]

[December 1915]

BOOKER T. WASHINGTON

The death of Mr. Washington marks an epoch in the history of America. He was the greatest Negro leader since Frederick Douglass, and the most distinguished man, white or black, who has come out of the South since the Civil War. His fame was international and his influence far-reaching. Of the good that he accomplished there can be no doubt: he directed the attention of the Negro race in America to the pressing necessity of economic development; he emphasized technical education and he did much to pave the way for an understanding between the white and darker races.

On the other hand there can be no doubt of Mr. Washington's mistakes and short comings: he never adequately grasped the growing bond of politics and industry; he did not understand the deeper foundations of human training and his basis of better understanding between white and black was founded on caste.

We may then generously and with deep earnestness lay on the grave of Booker T. Washington testimony of our thankfulness for his undoubted help in the accumulation of Negro land and property, his establishment of Tuskegee and spreading of industrial education and his compelling of the white south to at least think of the Negro as a possible man.

On the other hand, in stern justice, we must lay on the soul of this man, a heavy responsibility for the consummation of Negro disfranchisement, the decline of the Negro college and public school and the firmer establishment of color caste in this land.

492

What is done is done. This is no fit time for recrimination or complaint. Gravely and with bowed head let us receive what this great figure gave of good, silently rejecting all else. Firmly and unfalteringly let the Negro race in America, in bleeding Hayti and throughout the world close ranks and march steadily on, determined as never before to work and save and endure, but never to swerve from their great goal: the right to vote, the right to know, and the right to stand as men among men throughout the world.

It is rumored that Mr. Washington's successor at Tuskegee will be Robert Russa Moton, Commandant of Cadets at Hampton. If this proves true Major Moton will enter on his new duties with the sympathy and good will of his many friends both black and white.

The Crisis, 11 (Dec. 1915), 82.

[1] Du Bois acknowledged authorship in his autobiography *Dusk of Dawn,* 242–43.

Addenda

Extracts from an Address
at the Unitarian Club of New York

[New York City, ca. January 1899]

OUR DUTY IN THE SOUTH

In the present condition of affairs in the South it is easier to find errors than remedies; yet I am tempted to say that any one who can so far lift himself above party, race, and geographical divisions as to make a calm, philosophical study of the past and the present condition of the negro in the South must conclude that at the beginning of our freedom there were three errors committed.

These errors I mention only that we may draw a lesson from them for our future guidance. It was unfortunate that those of the white race, with few exceptions, from the North, who got the political control of the South in the beginning of our freedom, were not men of such high and unselfish natures as to lead them to do something that fundamentally and permanently would help the negro rather than yield to the temptation to use him as a means to lift themselves into political power and eminence. This mistake had the effect of making the negro and the Southern white men political enemies.

It was unfortunate, at the beginning of the negro's freedom, when we were without education, without property, without experience in government, that the burden of the government in the South was so largely thrown upon our shoulders in the way that I have mentioned. This was done when our strength should have been concentrated in the direction of securing property, education, and character as a basis for our citizenship. Any race or nationality, I fear, under similar conditions would have made the same kind of blunders that are now charged to the account of my race. Put the government of Cuba to-day completely into the hands of the inexperienced natives, even of the white race, and I think you will see a repetition of what took place in the South, from the Anglo-Saxon standpoint of government.

It was unfortunate that the negro got the idea that every Southern white man was opposed by nature to his higher interest and advancement, and that he could only find a friend in the white man who was removed from him by a distance of thousands of miles. And just here, though I stand in New York, I cannot forbear adding that I should be false to the highest interests of my race, false to the South, and false to my whole country, if I did not assert, notwithstanding the inexcusable wrong which you and I unite in condemning, which has been perpetrated against my race in the South during the last three months, that there are native Southern white men whose hearts beat in just as earnest sympathy for all that concerns the highest and permanent interest of the negro as is true of any found in any section of our country. Their way may not be the negro's way, their way may not be your way or my way; but since the end they seek is the same end that you and I seek, and that the negro seeks for himself, we should lend those of the Southern whites, whose hearts are right, our aid and sympathy in every honest, manly way, where no sacrifice of principle is involved. This assertion I make after an experience of seventeen years in the heart of the South.

In the third place it was unfortunate that the wisest and best element of the Southern white people did not at the beginning of our freedom take the negro by the hand, and enter heartily into his preparation for citizenship, and thus convince the negro by indisputable evidence, before his political affections were alienated, that his interest was identical with that of the Southern white man and that he could find no better friend in any State than he was. It has been equally unfortunate that the negro has long retained the idea that any member of his own race who sought in a manly, independent, and unselfish manner to thus encourage the Southerner to enter into active sympathy with the negro must necessarily be a trimmer or traitor to the highest interest of his race.

Friends of humanity, raise yourselves above yourselves, above race, above party, above everything, if you can save the highest welfare of ten millions of my people, whose interests are permanently interwoven by decree of God with those of sixty millions of yours, and seek with me a way out of this great race-problem, which hangs over our country, like a shadow of death, by night and by day; find any method of escape save that of patiently, wisely, bravely, manfully bringing the Southern white man and the negro into closer sympathetic and friendly relations through education, industrial, and business development and that touch of high Christian sympathy which makes all the world akin, find any way out of our present condition save this, and I am ready to lay down all my plans and will follow where you lead.

But the task is not hopeless: it is in no degree discouraging. Already in the seeming darkness the sunlight begins to appear. Only a few weeks ago in Washington, in a national convention of black people, whose spirit was controlled by such members of the race as Mr. T. Thomas Fortune, Mrs. Ida Wells Barnett, and Mr. Judson W. Lyons, we find a resolution passed to the effect that, whenever it would serve the highest welfare of the negro race in a given situation in the future the negro vote shall be divided among all political parties. This is the most advanced position taken by any responsible negro representative body since our freedom. There is further encouragement in the fact that almost without exception, North and South, between both races, there is an agreement that what the negro most needs is education. As to the form of education in the South, we of both races have grown to the point where practically all are united in the opinion that just now industrial education, coupled with thorough religious and academic training, without circumscribing the ambition and inclination of those who have the means to secure what is regarded as the higher education, is now most needed. This industrial training will teach the negro thrift, economy, the dignity of labor, and will soonest enable him to become an intelligent producer in the highest sphere of life, a property holder, a larger tax-payer, a greater commercial factor, will enable him to knit himself into the business life of the South.

It seems to me that the highest duty which the generous and patriotic people of this country owe to themselves and their country is to give willingly the means for the support of such institutions as Tuskegee, which are, without doubt, solving this serious and perplexing problem. If we had the means at Tuskegee, we could make our work tell in a hundred-fold larger degree in the settlement of this great question. You of the North have in a large measure the money for education which is to settle this vital problem.

Christian Register, 78 (Feb. 2, 1899), 121–22.

To Ellen Collins

Tuskegee, Ala., Jan. 9, 1901

My dear Miss Collins: I read with pleasure the article in "The Spectator" to which you call my attention. Two things struck me as I read this article. One is the seeming, unconscious egotism of the average Anglo-Saxon.

I remember last May that I sat for two days listening to the addresses being delivered at the Montgomery Conference and I do not think that a single individual spoke who did not lay special stress upon the superiority of his own race and the weaknesses of other races as compared with his. Now I cannot see why it is not in just as bad taste as it would be for an individual to be continually praising himself to the disadvantage of some other individual. Superiority, it seems to me, consists of possessing a spirit of humility and humbleness and not of arrogance and self-consciousness. I cannot agree with the writer that any race ever goes backward. I think that races, like individuals, for a time may drift the wrong way but take them on the average, and I believe that all races go forward instead of backward. I think we have gotten to the point in the case of my own race where it is not a debatable question as to whether or not the race is going forward or backward.

No person who keeps his eyes and ears open can fail to be convinced that the race is continually making great progress.

I am planning to be in New York for a few hours on the 20th and shall hope to see you that day or the day after. Mrs. Washington desires to be remembered to you.

I shall remember what you say about William Edwards. He had a very excellent meeting in Trinity Church Chapel where Dr. Donald, Mr. Edwards and myself spoke. Yours truly,

[Booker T. Washington]

TLd Con. 170 BTW Papers DLC. Several minor editorial changes in E. J. Scott's hand.

An Article in *The Sunday School Times*

November 2, 1901

LYNCH LAW AND ANARCHY

The average citizen may not appreciate the fact that a lynching has taken place within the last twenty years within every one of our states except five, and this unfortunate disposition to disregard the law, and inflict violent and summary punishment, has grown to an extent that is difficult to check. In order that the whole country may get back upon sure and safe ground, it will require the wisest and bravest efforts of our Christian men and women. The habit of lynching was begun in some of our states a few years ago as a punishment for one crime; but so true is it that lawlessness breeds lawlessness that it has now grown until statistics show that more people have been lynched for other crimes, such as murder, stealing, etc., than for the single crime of assault. It is proper that I state in the beginning that I have no kind of sympathy with any race or with any individual who is guilty of committing any kind of an assault, and the united effort of our best people in every community should be in the direction of getting rid of worthless and idle people from whose ranks most of the criminals come. But crime of some nature has been committed since the foundation of the world, even in the most highly civilized communities; and the facts show that, wherever the law is most fully observed in the punishment of crime, there crime is less likely to be committed. In my judgment, there is but one way for us in this country to get rid of the habit of lynching, and that is for all to unite in a strong and earnest effort to see that the law is complied with.

During the exciting days following the shooting of the late President McKinley, it was my privilege to mingle a good deal with the people in one of our Western states, and almost every other man who referred to the crime expressed himself as being in favor of burning or the execution without trial of Czolgosz. As I listened to these expressions day after day, it convinced me, as never before, that a spirit of lawlessness had gotten a hold upon the whole country that few of us realize.

I fear we have not yet realized that every open and flagrant defiance of law is anarchy. It is easy enough to decry the avowed anarchist who belongs to organizations that are anarchistic in their character, but it is not easy to put in the same class the people who set at defiance law by an illegal hanging or burning.

Perhaps the most demoralizing and hurtful result of mob violence is the hardening effect which it has upon our youth. I think it is safe to say that on an average fifty persons witnessed the execution by lynching of every man or woman that has taken place in this country. According to this, it is safe to say that, within the last sixteen years, one hundred and twenty-five thousand persons have been present when lynchings took place. In each case a large proportion of those who had been drawn to witness the unlawful execution have been children, or those of tender age. One of the saddest remarks that I ever heard come from the lips of a child was when he said, in my presence, that he wished he could see a man burned. I do not think the impression made upon a youth by reason of the fact that he has witnessed the unlawful execution of an individual ever wholly disappears. In some instances, the executions by mobs have not only been witnessed by boys of tender age, but by women.

It is also a notable fact, that in the communities where every crime, no matter how heinous, is taken hold of by the strong arm of the law, the crimes which provoke lynching very seldom occur.

The time would seem to have come when the subject of the majesty of the law should be taken up by the ministers in our pulpits through-out the country, and by our Sunday-school teachers, in a way that has never been done before. If Christianity is to mean anything in shaping the lives of our people, it must not only deal with matters pertaining to the future world, but must most effectually deal with matters grow-ing out of the relation of man to man in this world. In too many com-munities I very much fear the pulpit and the Sunday-school teacher have been silent on this subject.

I am not, in this article, pleading for the man who has been guilty of crime, but I am pleading most for those who are so unfortunate as to be led into the temptation of degrading themselves and disregarding the law, disrespecting the authority of governors, judges, and sheriffs. It is impossible for a youth to be so influenced that he can be made to feel that he can break the law in one case and keep it in other cases without being permanently harmed.

A great many citizens who have thought seriously upon the subject feel that perhaps the shooting of our late President was an outgrowth of the spirit of lawlessness which has been so prevalent in our country of late years. If this is true, how great a price have we paid for our error! I am glad to note that, since the President's death, a new spirit seems to have taken possession of the people, and that very few lynchings have occurred in any part of the country. It is also a praiseworthy fact that the daily and religious press, especially in the South, is speaking out fearlessly and strongly against lynching. It is also equally encouraging to note the brave words, and, what is more than brave words, equally brave acts, on the part of many of our Southern governors. Now if the words and acts of these officers can be re-enforced in the pulpit and in the Sunday-school, I feel that the time is not far when lynchings will be a thing of the past.

And since the greater proportions of these lynchings involve members of my own race, I think it my duty to say that the negro minister and teacher has an equal and special responsibility. The negro leader should see to it that his people are constantly reminded about the importance of keeping the law, and that our idle and unworthy classes should be made to deport themselves in such a manner that they will not bring disgrace upon the race. For a number of years I have advocated industrial education largely with the idea that, in proportion as our people learn to love labor for its own sake, they would not yield to the temptation to grow up in idleness. The members of my race who are charged, in most cases, with committing crimes, are not those who have received careful mental, religious, and industrial education, but those who have been permitted, as a rule, to grow up in idleness and ignorance. Every effort put forth on the part of the white ministers, daily press, and state officials, to reduce crime, should be heartily re-enforced by the members of my own race.

Perhaps this country needed the lesson which has been brought home to it in such a sad manner by the death of our President to wake it up to the tremendous responsibility which is resting upon it in relation to bringing about a different and higher spirit in favor of respect for law and order.

I have referred to the responsibility of the pulpit in regard to this matter. And right here I think I cannot do better than to quote from a sermon recently preached by the Rev. Quincy Ewing, of St. James Episcopal Church, Greenville, Mississippi. Mr. Ewing is a native of Mississippi, and no finer or braver words have been spoken anywhere in the country on the subject of lynching than Mr. Ewing has uttered:

"It is no pleasure to me to speak upon this subject to-day. It is very decidedly painful to me, a Southern white man, sired and grandsired, mothered and grandmothered, by Southern people, born and reared farther South than the latitude of this town, — it is very decidedly painful to me to have to deal with this subject, and, in dealing with it, to say what the time demands shall be said. It could give me no pleasure to need to speak out in denunciation of crime, lawlessness, brutality, anywhere on the earth; but perhaps it is a pardonable infirmity of human nature for one to feel more pain in acknowledging and denouncing the sins of one's own land, one's own people, than in holding up the standard of moral protest against the crimes of people separated from one by an ocean, or a Mason and Dixon's line. I confess to such an infirmity.

"But I should be unfit to stand in this place if I allowed that infirmity to blind my eyes to one of the dismalest crimes of the ages because it is being perpetrated in this Southern land by Southern men, or to seal my lips from denunciation of that crime, and the moral tone of the South, and especially of this state, to-day, — the moral tone which permits it, and in certain quarters makes a virtue of it.

"If some one were to declare in Boston that there were more Massachusetts murderers in Massachusetts outside than inside the state penitentiary, or that the great majority of Massachusetts murderers were not hanged, or imprisoned, or brought to trial, or arrested, who would doubt but that a very untrue and foolish thing had been said; that an absurd slander had been uttered against the fair name of Massachusetts? But if some one were to stand up in Greenville to-day, and declare that there are more Mississippi murderers outside than inside the state prison; that the great majority of the Mississippi murderers are never hanged, or imprisoned, or brought to trial, or indicted, or arrested, or forced to flee from one county to another, or seriously bothered in any way, — if some one were to stand up in Greenville and say that, who could be sure that he said an untrue thing? Who could truthfully declare that an absurd slander had been uttered against the state? Who could fairly deny but that the simple truth had been spoken? Who could be so blind and so dull as to contend that the men of all colors and races who have been hanged, or imprisoned, or tried, or arrested, or fined, or bothered, for murder, have not been outnumbered during the past ten years by the men of one race, and that race the race to which we belong, — by the men of one race who have met together in bands and crowds, and deliberately slain their fellowmen, setting aside all the forms of law, and making of themselves murderers as clearly as he who lies in ambush and sends a bullet through the heart of his foe?"

Within the last ten days it has been my privilege to be in Greenville, Mississippi, and meet Mr. Ewing, and it was most interesting to note the strong influence of this Christian gentleman upon that whole section of Mississippi. I was informed by the colored people that the influence of this sermon, as well as other words often spoken by Mr. Ewing in the same direction, have proved most beneficial in keeping kindly relations existing between the races, and in educating the public sentiment to the point where every man felt that, if he were charged with crime, he would receive a fair, patient, and legal trial.

Of course, mere condemnation of this kind will not constitute the whole remedy. We must go deeper. Crime will not disappear in any large degree from the section where it is most prevalent until all the people are more generally educated. In this respect there is an opportunity for the rich of our country to use their money in a way that will make every section of the United States their debtor.

The Sunday School Times, 43 (Nov. 2, 1901), 713–14.

To Samuel McCune Lindsay

[Tuskegee, Ala.] May 20, 1902

Dear Sir: I beg to acknowledge receipt of your favor asking for detailed information regarding the fifteen Porto Rican students sent to this institution under the provisions of an act of the Porto Rican Legislature. I am glad that the Legislature has decided to continue the appropriation. Having consulted the different teachers who come in immediate contact with these students in the class room, the work shop and other places, I give you the benefit of the opinions expressed by them, as well as my own individual opinion.

In the first place, we are willing to take fifteen boys and girls for next year and all agree that it is better to keep these we have rather than have others sent over to take their places. Our school year, 1902–1903, begins Tuesday, September 9th, and closes May 28th. The two hundred and fifty dollars allowed for each one will be sufficient to cover all expenses during the school year as well as during the vacation. By compelling them to exercise the most rigid economy we have been able to come to the close of the present year with a credit balance to each account, save one, as the financial statement sent herewith will show. The second year ought not to be quite so hard for them especially since the monthly allowance is increased slightly.

The questions asked under paragraph number 2 in your letter are rather more difficult to answer explicitly and with positiveness. The opinion of the instructors is in effect that almost all of them show at least sufficient earnestness to indicate that they are worthy of additional help for another year. My opinion concurs with theirs. This earnestness is much more apparent in connection with their academic studies than with those in the industrial departments. Generally speaking they do not like to work and it is a hard matter to get them to see the advantage of learning a trade. Perhaps they have not been here quite long enough for us to judge them fairly. Our experience with some *Cuban* students is that they have to remain here about two years or longer before they really acquire the American spirit. And too, the conditions of life under which they have been reared in Porto Rico doubtless, in a certain measure, are responsible for the characteristics they exhibit. Here as there they like to dress gaudily and extravagantly, to spend much time in powdering their faces and in congregating for idle gossip. Of the boys, Saturnio Sierra[1] and Felix Reina[2] are worse than the others, being less earnest both at study and at work and less inclined to respect authority. Of the girls, Lina Gonzales Nieves[3] and Catalina Rojas[4] give considerable trouble, the former being decidedly the worst one of the entire fifteen. With these four exceptions they do reasonably well, and as I have already said, no one of them seems too bad to give another year's trial. The habits, customs and standards of requirements in the two countries, Porto Rico and the United States, differing so greatly, the comparatively short time these girls and boys have been with us, as well as the youthful ages at which some of them come to us, cause some hesitation in answering the questions: "Of what sort of stuff are they made?" and "Will the results pay for the outlay?" As we judge boys and girls in this country, they do not seem to have the "stuff" in them, but considering all things, such judgment at this time is manifestly unfair to them. So let me simply repeat that the results and indications are such as to warrant that they be helped a while longer. The boys and the girls also are assigned to some useful trade at which they work certain hours during the day in connection with their academic studies.

I think the summer vacation should be spent partly in study and partly in work here at the institution. We are arranging to have them work half a day and study the other half under one of the instructors who will remain here during the summer. This arrangement is satisfactory to them.

I regret to say that we have no means at our disposal from which we could aid other Porto Rican students. There is only one other boy from there here and he comes on the same terms as do the American boys. Of course the same opportunities would be given to other young Porto Ricans as are given to students from the states. This young Porto Rican not supported by the Government provision is named Antonio Guill[5] and is well known to Dr. Barbosa,[6] of San Juan, as a worthy young man.

He has made a good record here in every way and is deserving of help if only some means of assisting him could be found.

I enclose herewith a Circular of Information regarding the admission of students to Tuskegee.

Trusting that I have answered all questions satisfactorily and have given you such information as will be helpful, I am, Yours very truly,

Booker T. Washington

TLpS Con. 282A BTW Papers DLC.

[1] Saturnino Sierra of San Juan, P.R., was a Tuskegee student from 1901 to 1906, progressing from the A preparatory to the B middle class.

[2] Felix Reina of Aguadilla, P.R., was a Tuskegee student from 1901 until his graduation in 1906.

[3] Lina Gonzales Nieves of San Juan, P.R., was in the C preparatory class in 1902–3.

[4] Catalina Hernandez Rojas of Humacao, P.R., was in the B preparatory class in 1902–3.

[5] Antonio Trujillo Guil of San Juan, P.R., was a student at Tuskegee from 1900, when he was in the B preparatory class, until his graduation in 1905.

[6] Probably J. C. Barbosa, of San Juan.

From the Anagarika H. Dharmapala[1]

$$\frac{2447}{}$$

Chicago, Ill. 20 June. 1903

Dear Mr Washington, I am in receipt of your letter and learn therefrom that you will be at Tuskegee till the 4th July.

I start for Tuskegee tomorrow afternoon by the Chicago & East. Ill. and hope to reach Tuskegee in due time.[2] I shall stay two days with you studying the methods and on the 25th I shall start for Washington. I have also a desire to see the Fiske University.

India has an illiterate population of 250 millions: 100 millions are in a state of starvation; and over 50 millions of children have no schools of any kind. The terrible poverty that is to be found in India is not found elsewhere. I love children and for their welfare I am working. The missionaries that go to teach Christianity preach a post mortem salvation; but neglect the greater opportunity of making man happy in this world where he is to live, at any rate expected to live at least for a generation.

I am going to have my first experience with your people. I hope it will be pleasant. I see Prof Du Bois in his Souls of the Black People takes a different view from yours. On the whole it is healthy that two parties are at work on two different lines; and there is no energy lost. The moral, political and industrial development are the three sides of a triangle.

Hoping to meet you at the Ry Depot. I am   Yours affectionately

The Anagarika H. Dharmapala

ALS BTW Papers ATT. Written on stationery of the American Maha-Bodhi Society, of which the Anagarika H. Dharmapala was "general secretary Maha-Bodhi Society of India and official representative of the Buddhists of Asia."

[1] The Anagarika H. Dharmapala (1864–1933), born David Hewartivarne, played three important roles: as a Sinhalese patriot and modernizer, as a revivalist and modernizer of Buddhism in Sri Lanka and in its original homeland, India, and as a propagandist for Buddhism, as the only flawless religion, not only in the West but throughout Asia. The son of a furniture manufacturer in Colombo, he attended Catholic and Anglican schools and took a civil service position, but through the Theosophical Society he found his way back to Buddhism and Sinhalese patriotism. He became the leader in Ceylon of a pristine Buddhism free of the astrology and demonology that folk religion still clung to. He sought to make this reformed religion an effective counterforce to the Christian missionary movements and Western

culture that accompanied colonialism. His most important institutional achievement was the founding of the Maha-Bodhi Society to restore the old shrines and to propagandize for Buddhism.

The Anagarika's counsels often paralleled those of BTW, emphasizing group solidarity, material advancement, self-help, and education. According to one scholar, he sought the "fusion of modern technology and economic methods with traditional Buddhist values" and held up to the Sinhalese the example of contemporary Japan. (Gokhale, "Anagarika Dharmapala," 30–39.)

The Anagarika made an extensive tour of the United States in 1903–4, met BTW in San Jose, Calif., and heard him speak in San Francisco. He visited Tuskegee Institute and the Carlisle Indian School as well as other industrial schools while on his tour.

[2] A marginal note indicated the time as 5:29 P.M.

From the Anagarika H. Dharmapala

$\frac{2447}{}$
N.Y. [City] 26 December 1903

Dear Mr Washington, I invite you in the name of 50 millions of neglected children of illiterate, destitute and starving parents to visit India, if possible next year and bring to them the joyful message that there is hope through a life of education and training in the arts and crafts.[1]

I have gained from my visit to Tuskegee an experience that I shall never forget and when I saw the Tuskegee Institute with its manifold branches under enlightened teachers I rejoiced that you have made all this glorious work a consummation within a generation; and I thought of the Viceroy in India who with the millions of children starving for education and bread that he should waste in sky rockets and tomfoolery and vain show to please a few loafing lords who came from England last January six million dollars in thirteen days! He is not worth to loose the latchet of your shoe. Yours Sincerely

The Anagarika Dharmapala

ALS Con. 255 BTW Papers DLC.

[1] BTW replied that "such a visit as you mention is quite out of the question for anything like early consideration." He said he could not "spare the time from my exacting duties here." (Dec. 31, 1903, Con. 255, BTW Papers, DLC.)

To Timothy Thomas Fortune

Tuskegee, Alabama.   June 9, 1904

My dear Mr. Fortune: Enclosed I send you my check for $200 according to promise, as the first payment for the work on "The Negro in Business." I have also given Mr. Logan my check for $100 and asked him to credit it on your note.

As I stated in my former letter, the first thing will be for you to make a careful analysis of the book so that we can go over it together before anything is done. The publishers are anxious to have the matter in hand at the very earliest possible date.

The suggestions made in your letter of June 6th are admirable. I think, however, it is well for you to send me the full names and addresses of all the parties to whom you wish me to write. I have already written to those mentioned in your letter and shall write to others as fast as I hear from you.

I want to include in the book the Outlook article on the Negro colony in Michigan.[1] I send it by this mail.

I do not want to write to people for matter and then not use it after it has been received; this will give them a bad feeling. To avoid this, a thorough analysis of what we want is all the more necessary. I think the first thing is for you to make a thorough analysis of the contents of the book so that we can go over it together before you begin writing. Certainly we should know what we are going to do before the work is begun.

I think I ought also to add that I am very anxious that men who have been successful in the fundamental affairs of life be given the most prominence, I mean large and successful planters, contractors, etc., rather than men who have succeeded in lines of business not so fundamental.

I should think the check ought to reach you within a week or ten days. I had to send to Chicago for it.

Since writing the above it occurs to me to say this: As soon as you have made the analysis of what the book is to contain and give me the names as far as you can of the individuals about whom you want to write, I will send a personal letter to each one asking him to write a history of his life, and as soon as the information has been received

I will turn it over to you for editing. This, it seems to me, will very much simplify and lighten your work. This is the way I got the information concerning Groves.[2]

Now replying to yours of May 30th I will say that the publishers are on their heads to get the manuscript by at least September 1st.

As soon as I reach New York I think I can help in your coming to an understanding with Mr. Moore regarding your work on the Colored American Magazine as well as other matters. Yours very truly,

Booker T. Washington

TLS Con. 50 (new series) BTW Papers DLC.

[1] See An Article in *Outlook*, Feb. 7, 1903, above, 7:40–54.
[2] Junius G. Groves. See An Article in *Outlook*, May 14, 1904, above, 7:499–505.

To Emmett Jay Scott

South Weymouth, Mass. July 28, 1904

Dear Mr. Scott: I note what you say about Mr. Adams.[1] I am receiving on an average about four letters a day from him. They reach me here, in New York and everywhere I go. Sometimes they are by special delivery and sometimes common letters. They all say about the same thing. Several of them I have not taken the pains as yet to open.

If I were you, I would hold on to the Voice of the Negro for the present in spite of Barber's foolish letter.[2] Just as soon as I get opportunity for a conference with Mr. Hertel I shall ask him to dismiss Barber from the magazine. I am quite sure Hertel will do practically anything I ask of him. When I see Hertel I should like to show him a copy of this letter. Yours truly,

Booker T. Washington

TLS Con. 24 BTW Papers DLC.

[1] Cyrus Field Adams was in charge of transportation arrangements for the NNBL meeting to be held the following month. He also hoped to have charge of the Republican western headquarters in Chicago for campaigning among black voters, but BTW explained to him that in 1904 there would probably be no Chicago

headquarters. (Adams to BTW, July 28, 1904, BTW Papers, ATT; BTW to Adams, July 28, 1904, Con. 18, BTW Papers, DLC.)

² Barber's letter to Scott has not been located. It was probably the letter in which Barber alleged that Scott had a conflict of interest between the *Voice of the Negro* and another journal owned by BTW, the *Colored American Magazine*. See Scott to Hertel, Jenkins and Company, Aug. 4, 1904, and Austin N. Jenkins to Scott, Aug. 5, 1904, above, 8:38–40.

From Clifford H. Plummer

Boston Highlands Mass. Oct 1 1904

They¹ hired oddfellows hall   have circulars printed   I have two thirds of them in my possession   will go over tomorrow morning and collect three that will [be] placed at Churches.

C. H. P.

TWIr   Con. 19   BTW Papers   DLC.

¹ William Monroe Trotter and other anti-Bookerites planned an indignation meeting on the same night BTW was to speak in Cambridge, Mass. This telegram is in reply to BTW to Plummer, Sept. 29, 1904, above, 8:75.

From Bradley Gilman

Boston Mass   Dec 31/1904

My dear Mr Washington, I hope that if Dr. Courtney saw you, at the train, in Boston, en route for New York, that he gave a good account of my effort at the meeting of the "Boston Literary Society." I tried to be discreet, and I fancy that I was, because our friend Trotter was not drawn from his lair in a ferocious mood; he spoke, after me, but not excitedly, and did not mention you by name.

Both Villard and I said our say about you, firmly and warmly, but not defiantly.

It seems a pity that so ably edited a paper as the Guardian should be on the wrong side of your work. I wish it could be bought up and steered in the right direction. When Trotter referred indirectly to you, in his speech, I thought I saw that most persons present took his words "with a grain of salt," smiles went around, and an air of easy toleration seemed to be general. I have not presented all the letters of introduction which you gave me. Courtney is a very charming, sensible man.

The editor of the "Citizen"[1] has just written, asking me to have a talk with him. His paper is not as good as the Guardian. I wonder if it could be developed, and thus crowd the Guardian out, or make it more sensible.

My best wishes to you, my dear friend, for your work in the New Year. Yours

Bradley Gilman

ALS   Con. 302   BTW Papers   DLC.

[1] Charles Alexander, editor of the Boston *Colored Citizen*.

To Charles William Eliot

Tuskegee Institute, Alabama. March 7, 1906

My dear President Eliot: Yours of recent date relating to the subjects to be covered by your address at Tuskegee has been received.[1] I think that the idea of your advocating the subsidizing of one at least of such institutions as Tuskegee and Hampton in each of the Southern states is a good one and will bear good fruit. Also that of placing emphasis upon the fact that there is a difference between social intermingling and political intermingling will prove helpful.

Now as to the other point. I confess I always have a fear of anything that one who may not live in the South says in regard to separating the races, mainly for the reason that it is almost impossible for a stranger to understand the line of separation or to appreciate the occasions upon which separation is supposed to take place. For example, in some of the Southern cities it is perfectly proper for members of the two races to sit side by side in the same street car; a few miles away it is considered practicing social equality for them to ride in the same manner. In Montgomery, Alabama, the two races go into the same waiting room at the same depot and buy railroad tickets from the same agents, that is considered right and proper; in Atlanta the two races are not permitted to enter the depot by the same door, if a colored man attempts to enter the same door through which the white people enter, it is considered that he is trying to practice social equality. It is almost the universal custom in the South for colored and white people to shave in different barber shops; on the other hand, one will find right in the same block where the people are separated in the barber shops a dentist who puts the same tools into the mouths of his colored patients that he uses for his white patients and nothing is thought of it. In Nashville, Tenn., there is a colored dentist, seventy per cent of whose patients are among the best white people in that city. There are a number of depots in the South where colored people can stand up right by the side of white people and eat their dinner, but if they were to go two yards away and sit down at the table together there would be trouble. These are but a few of the instances. In Montgomery, Ala., nine-tenths of the mail carriers are colored, and I think I run no risk in saying that if any one were to substitute white mail carriers in their places that the white people along their routes, especially the women, would make a loud protest, but in many parts of the South the white people would object seriously to colored people handing them a letter through the post office window, but would make no objection to a colored mail carrier handing them a letter at their door.

There is a class of white people in the South and in the North who are always ready to insist on unreasonable and unjust separations to the extent that I very much fear that anything that you might say in this direction would be twisted into an endorsement of unjust and unreasonable separation.

Another element that enters into the consideration of the subject is the fact that wherever separation is insisted upon in the case of public carriers especially, the colored people, with few exceptions, receive inferior accommodations for the same pay. There is almost no railroad in the South that furnishes first class accommodations for colored people, but they are made to pay first class fare. Where they are separated in restaurants and in waiting rooms the same difference in accommodations is apparent.

In certain directions where the reasons for separation are well defined and acquiesced in by the members of both races, such as in the education of the colored people in the South, I believe that it is proper and wise to insist upon taking hold of the system and making it stand for the very highest and best things for both races. I do not believe, for example, that it would be desirable or practicable on the part of either race to attempt to bring about coeducation in the South.

In regard to the point that you suggest advocating separation in the North in the public schools where the colored population is large, I am wondering whether or not the result might not be that the colored people would receive inferior opportunities for education rather than equal opportunities?

What I have said is merely suggestive, and whatever you say at Tuskegee will receive a respectful and serious attention. We shall, of course, be very glad to have your paper as far in advance as possible.

In all things that are purely social, the colored people do not object to separation, as I have often stated, but the difficulty is in the South that in many cases civil privileges are confounded with social intercourse. Yours very truly,

Booker T. Washington

TLS   Charles William Eliot Papers   MH-Ar.

¹ Eliot was one of the principal speakers at the twenty-fifth anniversary celebration of Tuskegee Institute.

To Charles William Anderson

[Tuskegee, Ala.] Oct. 4, 1906

Personal

My dear Mr. Anderson: I spent some time in Atlanta last week looking into conditions there and trying to help matters out as far as I could, and I now feel satisfied that there is going to be no more trouble and that there is a general spirit of repentance and sorrow among the white people. They are now working to cooperate with the colored people and give them justice in a way that I have never seen white people do in any other Southern city.

My special point, however, is to urge you to use your influence in connection with the coming meeting of the Afro-American Council to have conservative utterance and action both in resolution and in speech. Fiery, hysteric, incendiary speeches just now will not help us among our friends at the North, and certainly will not help the race at the South. I hear that Milholland is going to hold a meeting at Cooper Union. He and his kind can accomplish little good for the South just now. Yours very truly,

Booker T. Washington

TLpS Con. 32 BTW Papers DLC.

Emmett Jay Scott to Samuel Laing Williams

[Tuskegee, Ala.] October 19, 1906

My dear Mr. Williams: I am answering your letter of some days ago to the Doctor.

I beg to say that the Doctor's speech was prepared, typewritten, and the copies carried from here to Atlanta and distributed among the various newspapers before the Doctor had opportunity to meet the various editors of the several newspapers. It would seem that a man of the type represented by Barbour[1] would understand that Dr. Washington in calling upon these newspaper editors could have nothing in view except the lessening of the acute tension then existing. The distortion and misrepresentation to which they have resorted is a tribute to their ingenuity as scoundrels entitled to little or no respect.

My candid opinion is that there was no reason whatever for Barbour to get scared and leave Atlanta as he did. Bowen, Crogman and others were persecuted but yet they stood their ground. It would seem that a man who claimed to partake of the spirit of John Brown would face the enemy instead of flying at the first rumor of danger.

I send you herewith a copy of the Atlanta address as requested.

With kindest regards to Mrs. Williams and all friends, I am Faithfully yours

Emmett J. Scott

TLpS Con. 34 BTW Papers DLC.

[1] Jesse Max Barber.

515

To Whitefield McKinlay

Tuskegee Institute, Alabama. November 7, 1906

Personal & Confidential:

Dear Mr. McKinlay: Enclosed I send you copy of a letter from the President which explains itself. I did my utmost to prevent his taking the action that he did. I feel that I did my full duty in the matter which the enclosed copy of a letter from him will show.

When I found that I could not prevent the action, I tried to get him to postpone it until he came back from Panama. Of course this is for your own information only. Yours truly,

Booker T. Washington

TLS Con. 4 Carter G. Woodson Collection DLC. Enclosed was a copy of Theodore Roosevelt to BTW, Nov. 5, 1906, above, 9:118.

From Nicholas Chiles

Topeka, Kansas. Nov. 12, 1906

Dear Sir: Your letter of Oct. 23d received and you must excuse my delay, which has been due to extreme pressure of business, but in answer to your suggestions will say that we all cannot fight along the same lines of advancement of manhood, intelligence and wealth in this country. Your line of procedure may be alright for the South, but ours is decidedly right for the entire world. We believe in manhood, as well as courage, everywhere and also in demanding the same everywhere from everyone.

The article to which you refer, signed by myself, was sent broadcast over the Southland before you had seen it. So your statement that had it been republished or the parties gotten hold of it, there would have been, probable bloodshed and loss of life, is untrue, and useless, now. But, instead of destroying lives and property of the colored people, they at Seneca, S.C. avenged the wrongs perpetrated upon them by those poor and insignificant whites, who blew up the college, destroying $150,000 worth of property. Up to this time, we have failed to hear of a single arrest or any great loss of life.

We have also seen an account of a happening in Mississippi, where the Negroes with arms, energy and courage broke up a mob and also a Ku Klux Klan. We have, too, received a few subscriptions from Seneca people with encouraging letters, saying "Keep up the good work." We think you will finally come to realize that it is not only wealth and education that are needed by the Negro in this country, but a little manhood and courage to go along with it.

We have no objection to your fighting along your line of thought, and hope you will not take any exception to ours, for we think we are making it better for you and the entire race by continually keeping before the people of this country that we are not going to stand these outrages, always without resenting them. The sooner these Southern whites learn this, the better it will be for all concerned.

We are looking forward to great success for the Business League in 1907. Truly,

Nick Chiles

TLS   Con. 317   BTW Papers   DLC.

To Nicholas Chiles

[Tuskegee, Ala.] Nov. 17, 1906

Personal

My dear Mr. Chiles: I thank you for your frank letter of November 12. I always enjoy writing you because I find you are a man with whom one can discuss matters, and even disagree, without personalities and abuse entering in.

In the first place, there is no disagreement between us as to the end to be accomplished. Perhaps our only disagreement is as to the method, and I know that in all you write and do you are seeking the larger good of our race throughout the country, and I did feel when I wrote you that if any of the Southern white radical papers had gotten hold of your utterance at the time that it would have used what you say in a way to hurt. You speak of your paper having been circulated in the

South at the time, but it did not reach the columns of the class of white papers to which I am referring. I might have been over-cautious in the matter in my strong desire to protect the interests of the race as best I can at all times.

I realize fully, and have always said so on every proper occasion, that there are two lines of work to [be] accomplished. One is in the direction of agitation, calling attention to wrongs and the condemnation of these wrongs. Along with this there should go efforts in the direction of education, moral and religious teaching and helping of the race to strengthen itself in material and financial directions. There is a wide field in all this for every man of the race who wants to give service.

One other subject. I very much hope that you will begin now and keep it up until the summer, the stirring up of our people in that section of the country in regard to the League meeting. I find that we have taken a great burden upon our shoulders in carrying the League so far away from the center of its most active membership. Several people have already criticised me for this. Can you not keep the matter of [the] League constantly before the people of the Indian Territory, Arkansas, Kansas and Missouri in a way to give us the largest and most successful meeting that we have ever had.

Also remember that if you have any more fireworks to put off, please be sure to light them all and let them explode thoroughly before we get out into that territory.

I see that the fire which you lighted over the head of our friend, Governor Hoch,[1] was pretty hard to put out. You came very nearly starting in to extinguish it too late.

By this mail I send you a little book called "Putting the Most Into Life," which I thought you might like to have in your home. Yours truly,

Booker T. Washington

TLpS Con. 317 BTW Papers DLC.

[1] Edward Wallis Hoch (1849–1925) was governor of Kansas from 1905 to 1909.

From Charles William Anderson

New York, N.Y. December 11, 1906

(Confidential)

My dear Doctor: Only a line to say that I saw Mr. Wetmore on yesterday, who gave me in detail some of the circumstances of Mrs. Mary Church Terrell's recent visit to this city. It appears she remained here from Thursday until the following Monday, in order to have a conference with Milholland. It also appears that in her lecture at Mount Olivet Church, she devoted considerable time to drastic criticisms of that sort of race leadership, which holds up the seamy-side of the race, tells dialect stories at the expense of the race, advises the race not to retaliate, but to seek the approval of those who approve of negroes, only as subordinates and inferiors, and counsels the race to acquire only an inferior sort of education. This was meant for you, he said. This evidently pleased my informer, for he invited her the next evening to occupy a box at one of the theaters, and after the performance to dine with him at one of the restaurants. This is for your private information. Yours truly,

Charles W. Anderson

P.S. Wetmore said: "why, she did everything but call his name. She told me she was going to unshirt him, and she did."

C. W. A.

TLS Con. 32 BTW Papers DLC. Postscript in Anderson's hand.

To Daniel Hale Williams

[Tuskegee, Ala.] October 30, 1907

Personal

My dear Dr. Williams: I hear that our friend Fortune has gone to Chicago, is perhaps there now. I hope that you and Mrs. Williams will keep an eye on him. I want to say to you in a very confidential way that for several months he has been in bad shape, physically and mentally, as you perhaps have observed if you have been in contact with him. He has not been able to do any work for several months on his paper for the reason that he seems to have lost his mental balance, going off on a religious craze. I understand that Mr. Moore has paid him a good sum for his paper, and I presume for this reason he has some cash. It would be a great pity for him to squander this cash, especially as it is the only thing he will have to live on the rest of his life, in a fruitless effort to start another paper. In his present condition it is impossible for him to do this. The danger is some unscrupulous people will get hold of him and use him in a way to stir up trouble.

I have instructed Mr. Scott to write you that I have not only endorsed no one from Chicago, but no one has even mentioned a single individual living in Chicago for the place. Yours very truly,

Booker T. Washington

TLpS Con. 363 BTW Papers DLC.

To Samuel Laing Williams

New York   March 16, 1908

Personal

My dear Mr. Williams: I have your kind letter of recent date. If not causing too much trouble, I should like to look over the proposed plans before they are sent to Miss Emery.

Poor Barber. He seems to have the idea that I control the universe. What passed between him and Mr. Trice concerning the publication of our Conference matter I do not know. Mr. Trice, when I saw him in Chicago, suggested that whatever I wanted to get in the Conservator should be sent to him. I followed his advice. It is pitiful to find a man of Barber's education who seems to succeed so well in being a failure, but the number of such men I fear is increasing.

I shall hope to see you when I go to Chicago for the meeting in April. Yours truly,

[Booker T. Washington]

TLc Con. 42 BTW Papers DLC.

To Theodore Roosevelt

[Tuskegee, Ala.] March 30, 1908

My dear Mr. President: You do not know how grateful I am to you for what you have done regarding Mr. S. Laing Williams. I am not only personally deeply grateful to you for this action, but am quite sure that it will help very much in a large racial sense. I am taking means to see that it is given wide circulation in racial papers.

I wonder if you recall that the Williams appointment takes care of every colored man whom we discussed for office when you first went into the Presidency. Besides you have appointed more men than was decided upon for appointment.

I have just written you that I would see you at an early date regarding the Liberian matter. Yours truly,

Booker T. Washington

TLpS   Con. 7   BTW Papers   DLC.

From Theodore Roosevelt

[Washington, D.C.] April 2, 1908

My dear Mr. Washington: Pending our correspondence the Commission forwarded to me a statement that the Nashville and Chattanooga Railway had declined to comply with its order of June 27th last. Accordingly it seemed best not to write to the Commission, but to write to the Attorney General requesting that immediate steps be taken by the Department of Justice for the purpose of enforcing the order. I enclose a copy of my communication to the Attorney General. I have adopted substantially the changes you suggested, except that I did not add the paragraph about freight and human beings, because I thought it would look a little bit ad captandum; and there was also one sentence where I think you confused my allusion to the Federal law with your allusion to the State law.

I was delighted that we were able to appoint Williams. Yes, I recall that we now have got in office all the men whom you and I discuss when I first came into the Presidency; and I wish to thank you now, not so much on my own account as on behalf of the people of this country, and especially the colored people, for the high character of the men whom you have suggested.

I look forward to seeing you on April 7th or 8th, as you indicate in your letter to Mr. Loeb. Sincerely yours,

Theodore Roosevelt

TLpS Theodore Roosevelt Papers DLC.

From Allen Allensworth[1]

Los Angeles, Calif., June 27, 1908

Dear Sir: I have just read with a great degree of satisfaction a mention of your condolence to Mrs. Cleveland in our behalf. This action I appreciate very much, and I think the great mass of our people will do the same.

I take great pleasure in informing you that I have just completed an organization to be known as the California Colony and Home Promoting Association. The object of this Association is to unite with you in creating favorable sentiment for the race.

One of the chief purposes of this association will be to mold public opinion, favorable to intellectual and industrial liberty. To this end I have secured over nine thousand acres of the richest land in central California, where the Colony will be located, on the main line of the Santa Fe railroad. A town will be established upon the most scientific basis and improved methods of city building.

As it is just as cheap to begin right as wrong, we will commence with the ownership of public utilities. We intend to demonstrate to the world that we can *be* and *do,* thus meeting the expectation of our friends, and to encourage our people to develop the best there is in them under the most favorable conditions of mind and body. This we have in California, as you are aware.

It is my desire to have our streets given names of historical and educational value. In the midst of this city we will have a lake, surrounded by a park, to be named — if you have no objection — "Washington" Park, in honor of the greatest negro sentiment maker in the world. Have you any objection?[2] Respectfully yours,

Allen Allensworth,
Lieut-Colonel U.S.A.
Retired

TLS Con. 364 BTW Papers DLC.

[1] Allen Allensworth (1843–1914) spent only the last decade of his varied life in California. Born a slave in Louisville, Ky., he obtained his freedom in 1863 and entered the U.S. Navy for the remaining two years of the Civil War. He then gained some education, became a Freedmen's Bureau teacher, a jockey, and a Baptist minister in Kentucky. While he was pastor of the Union Baptist Church in Cincinnati, Grover Cleveland appointed him chaplain of the 24th U.S. Infantry regiment. He rose to the rank of lieutenant-colonel before retiring in 1906. Moving to California, he tried to form a self-sufficient all-black town in Tulare County, Calif. In 1910 the first of several hundred settlers arrived. A water shortage and lack of rail connections were crucial elements in the town's failure to survive. Another difficulty was that many blacks, particularly in Los Angeles, opposed the voluntary segregation feature of the town. The colonel also proposed establishment of an industrial school modeled on Tuskegee, but Los Angeles blacks identified with the Niagara Movement and the NAACP succeeded in preventing its establishment. After Allensworth's death the population dwindled until it became a ghost town. In the 1970s it became a state historical site and restoration efforts began. (Lapp, *Afro-Americans in California*, 34–35.)

[2] BTW replied that he had no objection to naming the park after him, and thanked Allensworth for thinking of him. (July 7, 1908, Con. 364, BTW Papers, DLC.)

To William Hayes Ward

[Tuskegee, Ala.] January 18, 1911

Personal.

My dear Sir: I send you herewith, in compliance with your request of January 13th, a short article covering the decision in the Alonzo Bailey case.[1] I hope that this statement may prove satisfactory to you.[2] Yours very truly,

Booker T. Washington

[*Enclosure*]

In April, 1908, Alonzo Bailey, a Negro of Montgomery, Alabama, was arrested and indicted before the grand jury for failure to complete a labor contract. Previous to this Bailey had formed a contract with the Riverside Company, a farming company, and upon this contract had secured the sum of $15 which he was to repay out of his wages at the rate of $2.25 a month. After working a month and a few days, Bailey quit the company without repaying the remainder due on his loan.

Now the laws of Alabama are very severe against an offense of this kind. For more than a decade it has been a state regulation that if a laborer formed a contract with another person with the intent to defraud and quit before the money secured on the basis of the contract had been repaid or without refunding he should be guilty of a misdemeanor, and the quitting per se made "prima facie evidence of his intent to defraud his employer." Moreover, the "defendant cannot testify in his own behalf as to his unexpressed intent." The penalty for this offence was that the offender "must on conviction be punished by a fine in double the damage suffered by the injured party, but not more than $300, one-half of said fine to go to the county and one-half to the party injured.["]

Under this law Alonzo Bailey was therefore guilty of a misdemeanor and subject to the penalty just mentioned. As soon as Bailey was indicted his counsels instituted proceedings for habeas corpus, arguing that the labor contract law was contrary to both the federal constitution and to the constitution of the state, the latter of which reads that "The right of trial by jury shall remain inviolate." The lower court and the Alabama supreme court, however, refused the writ of habeas corpus and sustained the contract law. Whereupon the case was appealed to the Supreme Court of the United States. The Supreme Court refusing upon a writ of error at first, the case was returned to Montgomery, Bailey duly tried and convicted and the case once more returned to the Supreme Court.

The decision of this court was rendered Tuesday, January 3d. The court declared, one dissenting, with Justice Hughes as spokesman, that such a law reduced hundreds of Negroes to a state closely akin to that of peonage and that a state could not reduce men to involuntary servitude by classing a debt as a crime. Justice Hughes, however, dismissed the question of Bailey's race or color by saying that there was nothing in the statutes to indicate discrimination against color but that the law would operate just the same in New York or Idaho. On the other hand, he characterized this law as "an instrument of compulsion peculiarly effective as against the poor and ignorant, its most likely victims."

One is inclined to clap his hands at this decision. Too long have both white and black men of the South been tangled in meshes of this sort with the state, and this is the saddest part of it all, aiding in the entanglement. It is needless to think that the white man as the oppressor does not suffer. He as well as the black man has been the victim of this unfortunate labor system throughout the South.

In spite of the courtesy of the Supreme Court, on the other hand none will be fooled with the intention and working of this law. If the offender could refund or repay, his misdemeanor then and there ceased to be a crime, that is the offense it seems was not in itself a crime. Upon the same reasoning a shoplifter could return the goods when overtaken and thereupon cease to be a criminal.

The decision strikes a hard blow at labor contract all over the country. It especially unties the hands of employer and employee in the Southern states. Georgia, Florida and the Gulf states generally, following the example of North and South Carolina, will have to reshape their labor contract laws to avoid conflict with the ruling of the Supreme Court. South Carolina it will be remembered threw off this yoke some months ago declaring, to use the words of one of its judges in reply to an argument that such a contract was necessary to the prosperity of the state, that "Liberty is better than prosperity."

Perhaps the brightest side of the whole situation is, after all, not so much that the case was thus settled by the Supreme Court, but that throughout the fight there prevailed in two particular instances a disinterested love for justice. In the Supreme Court there were several justices whose sympathies undoubtedly would have dictated another ruling, being both Democrats and Southerners, while from Alabama's point of view the case was fought out from beginning to end by Southern men. As far as can be learned no Negro or Northern man took a hand in the fight, but Southern lawyers backed by some unknown Southern private citizens fought the battle through to the end. When the South can get more disinterested lawyers like Ed S. White, Fred S. Ball, and W. H. Harr, Bailey's counsels, we shall not only see the last traces of peonage rubbed away but lynching and many other cruel practices in the South will also disappear.

TLpS and enclosure   Con. 445   BTW Papers   DLC.

[1] Washington had suggested to Ward that *The Independent* give attention to the Bailey case as the beginning of the end of peonage. Hayes encouraged BTW to send him some facts on which to base an editorial. (Ward to BTW, Jan. 13, 1911, Con. 445, BTW Papers, DLC.)

[2] BTW's draft article appeared almost verbatim as an unsigned editorial in *The Independent,* 70 (Jan. 26, 1911), 213–14. The only changes were a few punctuation marks.

BIBLIOGRAPHY

T HIS BIBLIOGRAPHY gives fuller information on works cited in the annotations and endnotes. It is not intended to be comprehensive of works on the subjects dealt with in the volume or of works consulted in the process of annotation.

Borchert, James. *Alley Life in Washington: Family, Community, Religion, and Folklife in the City, 1850–1970.* Urbana: University of Illinois Press, 1980.

Cripps, Thomas. *Slow Fade to Black: The Negro in American Film, 1900–1942.* New York: Oxford University Press, 1977.

Cronon, E. David. *Black Moses: The Story of Marcus Garvey and the Universal Negro Improvement Association.* Madison: University of Wisconsin Press, 1955.

Dabney, Charles W. *Universal Education in the South.* 2 vols. Chapel Hill: University of North Carolina Press, 1936.

Dittmer, John. *Black Georgia in the Progressive Era, 1900–1920.* Urbana: University of Illinois Press, 1977.

Du Bois, W. E. B. *Dusk of Dawn: An Essay toward an Autobiography of a Race Concept.* New York: Harcourt, Brace & World, Inc., 1940; reprint: New York: Schocken Books, 1968.

Evans, Maurice Smethurst. *Black and White in South East Africa.* London: Longmans, Green and Co., 1911.

Gokhale, Balkrishna Govind. "Anagarika Dharmapala: Toward Modernity through Tradition in Ceylon," in Bardwell L. Smith, ed., *Tradition and Change in Theravada Buddhism: Essays on Ceylon and Thailand in the 19th and 20th Centuries.* Leiden: E. J. Brill, 1973, pp. 30–39.

Harlan, Louis R. *Separate and Unequal: Public School Campaigns and Racism in the Southern Seaboard States, 1901–1915.* New York: Atheneum, 1969.

Hughes, William Hardin, and Frederick D. Patterson, eds. *Robert Russa Moton of Hampton and Tuskegee.* Chapel Hill: University of North Carolina Press, 1956.

King, Kenneth J. *Pan-Africanism and Education: A Study of Race, Philanthropy and Education in the Southern States of America and East Africa.* Oxford: Clarendon Press, 1971.

Lamon, Lester C. *Black Tennesseans, 1900–1930.* Knoxville: University of Tennessee Press, 1977.

Lapp, Rudolph M. *Afro-Americans in California.* San Francisco: Boyd and Fraser Publishing Co., 1979.

McCulloch, James Edward, ed. *Battling for Social Betterment: Southern Sociological Congress, Memphis, Tennessee, May 6–10, 1914.* [Nashville?]: Southern Sociological Congress, 1914.

Martin, Tony. *Race First: The Ideological and Organizational Struggles of Marcus Garvey and the Universal Negro Improvement Association.* Westport, Conn.: Greenwood Press, 1976.

Redkey, Edwin S. *Black Exodus: Black Nationalist and Back-to-Africa Movements, 1890–1910.* New Haven, Conn.: Yale University Press, 1969.

Toppin, Edgar A. *A Biographical History of Blacks in America since 1528.* New York: David McKay Company, Inc., 1971.

Vincent, Charles. "Booker T. Washington's Tour of Louisiana, April, 1915." *Louisiana History,* 22 (Spring, 1981), 189–98.

Vincent, Theodore G. *Black Power and the Garvey Movement.* Berkeley, Calif.: Ramparts Press, 1971.

Washington, Ernest Davidson, ed. *Selected Speeches of Booker T. Washington.* Garden City, N.Y.: Doubleday, Doran and Co., 1932.

Weiss, Nancy J. *The National Urban League, 1900–1940.* New York: Oxford University Press, 1974.

Winks, Robin W. *The Blacks in Canada: A History.* New Haven, Conn.: Yale University Press, 1971.

Wolters, Raymond. *The New Negro on Campus: Black College Rebellions of the 1920s.* Princeton, N.J.: Princeton University Press, 1975.

INDEX

390; conduct criticized by BTW, 337; letter from C. H. Fearing, 368; signs BTW's name to letters, 368

Washington, Norma: conduct criticized by BTW, 337

Washington, Portia Marshall. *See* Pittman, Portia Marshall Washington

Washington *Bee,* 381; subsidized by R. C. Bruce, 43

Washington *Sun,* 146, 157; subsidized by NAACP supporters, 43

Watterson, Henry, *10:354; 61

Watts, W. P.: letter to M. J. M. Washington, 452

Wayland Seminary (D.C.), 212

Wehle, Louis Brandeis, *320

Wellesley College (Mass.), 453

Wells-Barnett, Ida B., *3:108-9; 498

West Side Colored Protective Association (Chicago), 217

West Virginia Colored Institute, 290-91, 368

West Virginia State University, 368

Western Railway of Alabama, 64, 309, 310

Western Reserve University (Ohio), 30

The Western Torch Light, 135

Western Union Telegraph Co., 56

Westinghouse Air Brake Co., 306, 314

Wetmore, J. Douglas, *8:189; pleased by attack on BTW, 519

Wheat, Virginia Mitchell: letter to, *82

White, Alfred Tredway: letter to, 314-*16

White, Ed S., 525

White, Francis Shelley (Frank), *6:55; 90, 244

White House dinner, 446

Whitman, Charles Seymour, *11:32; 256, 407; BTW congratulates on election, 164; letter to, 164

Whittaker, John W., *2:396; 443, 452; conducts BTW's funeral service, 454

Wickersham, Charles Allmond, *8:453; 70; letter to, 185-86

Wiley University (Tex.), 329

Willcox, William G., *5:481; 280, 372, 431-32, 433; aids failing black bank, 235; approves pension for S. H. Por-

ter, 116; approves plans for Baldwin Farms, 70; attends trustees' meeting at Tuskegee Institute, 301; BTW advises on Association of Negro and Industrial Schools, 27, 28; concerned about BTW's finances, 344-45, 418-19; concerned about BTW's health, 418-19; discusses successor to BTW, 459-61; donation to Baldwin Farms, 198, 309; donation to power plant at Tuskegee Institute, 253; insists BTW take a rest, 426; letter from J. Rosenwald, 424; letters to, 32-33, 46-47, 162, 189, 234-35; letter to E. J. Scott, 444-45; letter to W. C. Graves, 344-45; letters to J. Rosenwald, 418-19, 459-61; sends condolences on BTW's death, 444-45; speaks at BTW's funeral, 455, 458; visits Baldwin Farms, 242; visits BTW in hospital, 428, 429

William and Mary College (Va.), 181; BTW speaks at, 173, 174

Williams, Bert. *See* Williams, Egbert Austin

Williams, Daniel Hale, *4:274-75; letter to, 519-20

Williams, Egbert Austin (Bert), *10:334; 408

Williams, J. S., 329

Williams, Samuel Laing, *3:518-19; appointed to federal office by T. Roosevelt, 521-22; letter from E. J. Scott, 515; letter to, 520

Williams, William Taylor Burwell, *10:148-49; 29, 329

Williamson, H. R.: letter to, *224

Wilson, Clarence Rich, 57, *58, 62, 108

Wilson, Ellen Axson: interest in Washington, D.C., alley dwellings, 354

Wilson, Woodrow, *4:98; 52, 205, 206, 220, 316, 357, 360, 416; attitude towards blacks praised, 181; BTW seeks to influence, 3; concerned about Howard University appropriation, 243-44; considers Tuskegee Institute post office, 55; grants BTW's requests, 114; letter from, 55; letter from Tuskegee Institute trustees, 243; letter to, 51-52; peace position

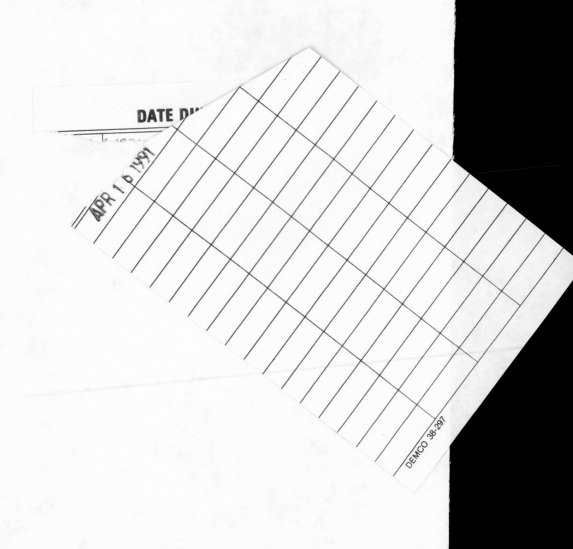